'. . . forged in the white heat of this revolution'
Sir Harold Wilson speaking on technology, October 1963

WHITE HEAT
The New Warfare 1914–18
John Terraine

Sidgwick & Jackson
London

First published in Great Britain in 1982
by Sidgwick and Jackson Limited

Edited, designed, and produced by Guild Publishing,
the Original Publications Department of
Book Club Associates

Designed by Graham Keen
Picture Research by Jonathan Moore

ISBN 0–283–98828–2

Set in 11 on 12pt Plantin
Printed in Great Britain by Mackays of Chatham Ltd
for Sidgwick and Jackson Limited
1 Tavistock Chambers, Bloomsbury Way
London WC1A 2SG

Endpapers: *An aircraft emerging from a low-level bombing attack*

Contents

Foreword

THIS IS MY TENTH BOOK on the subject of the First World War. The number reflects my firm belief that that war was a major watershed in history, akin to, say, the Fall of Rome, or the French Revolution. War is, of course, always a compound of many factors: military, political, economic, psychological, ideological, technological. When I began writing about the First World War I was content to confine myself to the military aspect. And, indeed, there are periods when the military aspect is, to all intents and purposes, the entire war. So when I wrote about that very first, highly significant campaign in the West which the French would call the Battles of the Frontiers and the retreat to the Marne, and the British always associate with the single name of Mons, I think the approach was fair enough. The war was simply not old enough for the other factors to play any considerable part; the whole thing was embraced in what was happening to the soldiers, and the effect that this was having on the minds of their generals.

Almost immediately after the Battle of the Marne, however, that ceased to be the case. This is not surprising, because war reflects the societies which conduct it, and the elements which shape those societies will shape their wars. For the British, for very clear reasons closely connected with the nature of British democracy, the political element soon became very important, and remained so until the end. The interplay of political and military affairs interested me more and more, and has been a large theme in several of my books. At the same time, economic and technological factors also claimed attention as I perceived more clearly that the event belongs, historically, to a span encompassed by the First Industrial Revolution. And this book is, I think, unlike all the rest because that is the aspect with which it is almost exclusively concerned. On the pages that follow there is very little strategy, scarcely any politics, no ideology and—I confess—almost no psychology. This is a book about the sinews of the greatest *First* Industrial Revolution war. In other words, it is about the very inner nature of the war, and may thus, I hope, illuminate its other aspects too.

Introduction

THE MIDDLE DECADES of the nineteenth century witnessed the accelerating spread of a change in the mode of human life more profound than anything since the domestication of the horse some time during the third millennium BC. There is no precise date for that event, and cannot be. Nor is it possible to fix a precise date for the beginning of the First Industrial Revolution, but it is convenient to associate that beginning with the young James Watt watching the rise and fall of a kettle lid under the pressure of steam, and drawing certain conclusions. Steam was the power-source of the First Industrial Revolution, the first stage in the transition from horses to horse-power, and Watt produced his first large steam-engine in 1781. Britain was undoubtedly the birthplace of this revolution in technology and virtually monopolised its benefits (and drawbacks) for some fifty years. By the 1830s, however, the new influence was perceptible in most European countries and in North America. The great technological mutation was on the march across the world; every aspect of human affairs would be touched by it, for better or worse. War would be transformed by it.

The transformation of war has two aspects, which we may call 'qualitative' and 'quantitative'. The qualitative aspect embraces that continuing stream—or flood—of inventions and developments of techniques which characterises the entire period. The quantitative aspect goes far beyond the matter of productive capacities, though these are impressive and important; it has a profound social significance also. Everywhere (with one conspicuous and curious exception) we find rising levels of industrialization accompanied by unprecedented increases in population. In the fifty years 1821–1871 the population of Britain nearly doubled (from 14 million to 26 million); the population of Germany (a late-starter in the industrial race) rose from 26 million to 41 million, that of the United States (assisted, of course, by large immigration) from $9\frac{1}{2}$ million to 39 million. Later on the process became even more dramatic. Between 1880–1913 Britain's population rose by 12 millions and Germany's by 22 millions (in the period 1900–1913 Germans were increasing at the rate of one million a year). In the thirty years 1881–1911, America's population rose from 53 to 94 millions. The conspicuous and puzzling exception to what would otherwise be a general rule is France, where a population of just over 30 millions in 1821 had risen by only 9 millions a century later.

These large population increases are central to the great wars of the First Industrial Revolution; the mass populations supplied the mass armies which are the particular feature of those wars. Mass armies—nations in arms—are the modern version of the warfare of primitive armed hordes and the later Asiatic invasions, whose savage style briefly receded from the military history of Europe during the eighteenth century but reappeared with the French *levée en masse* in 1793. That year heard what has been called 'the birth cry of total war'[1] — the explicit attempt to mobilize a whole large nation for a life-and-death struggle. But there is a substantial difference between an infant's birth cry and the *fortissimo* of a mature singer. Lazare Carnot's brilliant organization of the *levée en masse* increased the French Army from 300,000 in 1793 to over three quarters of a million in 1794; Napoleon I — always a believer in big battalions — inherited Carnot's system and put larger armies into the field than any that Europe had yet seen. What strikes one, however, about both the wars of the French Revolution and of Napoleon is, on the one hand, the skill involved in creating and fielding such big armies and, on the other, the extent to which they were invariably whittled down at the point of impact.

In the Russian campaign of 1812, Napoleon's initial strength was about 530,000, an amazing figure. Eight weeks later, however, we find him approaching Smolensk with no more than 175,000 available for battle. This was, indeed, still a very large force, but at the Moskva (Borodino) just over a fortnight later it was already reduced to 127,000; for the entry into Moscow a week after that the Grand Army was down to 95,000. For the 1813 campaign conscription gave Napoleon some 430,000 men despite the losses in Russia, but for his first battle, Lützen, he had only 85,000 under his hand. At Leipzig, the 'Battle of the Nations', according to one authority[2] he had 177,500 men and 700 guns. This was the highest numerical peak in battle of his career and the defeat of this army meant that he would be forced on to the defensive with no such numbers available ever again. At Waterloo, in 1815, his army numbered 72,000 and Wellington's 68,000. Clearly, during the early decades of the nineteenth century, there remained a substantial gap between the raising of mass armies, and maintaining them effectively in the field; this would be steadily narrowed by the techniques of the Industrial Revolution.

Every war conducted by the industrial nations displayed some facet of the great mutation. The Crimean War (1854–55) is generally thought of as a series of old-fashioned blunders committed by old-fashioned people, and a quick glance at the British Army as it stormed the Alma heights in a manner reminiscent of Waterloo readily confirms that impression. Yet this interpretation misses some cardinal points. The Crimean War has been called 'a turning point in naval history', and with reason — not merely because of the uneasy marriage of sail and steam, nor because of such largely ineffective devices as the Russian floating mines (later to become a very serious matter), but because the absolute destruction (as opposed to capture or damage) of the Turkish squadron at Sinope taught all the Admiralties that wooden warships had reached the end of their day. And an equally significant maritime revolution is contained in the fact that a ship from England 'could reach the Crimea in a quarter of the time a waggon would take on the overland journey from Moscow.'[3] The vessel, of course, would be a steamship, and Mrs Woodham-Smith makes a similarly strong point when she says that steamers

'Artillery war': the Russians mounted some 3,000 guns in the fortress of Sebastopol. 1854–55. This photograph shows the sophistication of the defences and the destructiveness of the bombardment.

'reached the East in from ten to twelve days while sailing ships took as much as sixty or seventy.'[4] This was an entirely new version of mobility; linked to the electric telegraph, it made possible new dimensions of manoeuvre.

On land as well as at sea, the Crimean War was a 'transition war' whose innovations cast long shadows over the future. In Britain the name of Miss Florence Nightingale is revered for her reorganization of the hospital services in the field; less well remembered is the creation of an Ambulance Corps and a Sanitary Corps. These were beginnings; another sixty years would be required to give reality to the idea of a continuously healthy army. Looking equally directly towards the future was the new element of land transport. The departure of the Scots Fusilier Guards on 27 February 1854 illustrates the point. The regiment paraded in Wellington Barracks at 3am; at 7am it marched across to Buckingham Palace to be reviewed by the Queen and the Royal Family. It then marched off, via Pall Mall, Trafalgar Square and the Strand and then 'across Waterloo Bridge to the terminus of the South Western Railway, in which the whole force was soon lodged.'[5] At 1pm it passed through the dock gates at Portsmouth and embarked that same afternoon. So railways had arrived as arteries of war; five years later the French Army made substantial use of them in the war against Austria, and very shortly after that, as we shall see, they were fully established as part of the apparatus of First Industrial Revolution war. In the Crimea, 1855 saw a further development which would come to fruition some sixty years later: a railway line was constructed to carry supplies from the British base at Balaklava Harbour right up to the trenches.

Because the central event of the Crimean War was an attack upon a great fortress (not a siege, because Sebastopol was never surrounded by the Anglo-French forces, never cut off from supply or reinforcement or escape) the chief weapon of the Industrial Revolution wars quickly put its brand upon the scene: it was an artillery war. The guns used were still almost all smooth-bores firing spherical shot and shell to ranges of less than 3,000 yards; ten years later that picture would be changed drastically, but meanwhile the novelty lay in the numbers used. In Sebastopol itself, the Russians had some 3,000 pieces of heavy artillery—far more than they could mount or man, but guaranteeing constant replacement of losses. By the time of the fourth bombardment (17 June 1855) they had 10,697 artillerymen in the fortress (compared with 43,000 infantry). The Allies deployed 588 siege guns for this occasion; for the final bombardment (5–8 September) this number had risen to over 800 of which 183, including the heaviest and most powerful, were British—57 supplied by the Royal Navy. These batteries produced the greatest bombardments that the world had yet seen, a total of $1\frac{1}{4}$ million projectiles fired by the Allies into Sebastopol, producing a sound and fury of destruction which were true precursors of the great artillery battles of the Western Front between 1914–18.

All the wars of this period contained their portents. In 1859 the French made a great impression in Italy with the accuracy of their new rifled field artillery, though these were still bronze muzzle-loaders. Herr Krupp's steel breech-loaders made a slow start (because of bursts due to the difficulty of casting flawless steel) but by 1870 they carried full conviction and the days of bronze guns were numbered. In 1854 one British infantry division went to war armed with the smooth-bore muzzle-loading Tower Musket ('Brown Bess') which had made its first appearance in the reign of William III, and could not be depended on to hit a man-sized target beyond about 80 yards. Such an anachronism only served to point up the progress that had been made with firearms. The fulminate of mercury percussion cap had given them a new all-weather reliability, and two able Frenchmen had improved range and accuracy beyond measure. It was Captain Delvigne in 1841 who worked out a way of overcoming the great difficulty of the muzzle-loading rifle—forcing the bullet down the grooves of the rifling, a slow, laborious process. Captain Minié took Delvigne's idea and made it practical with a conical bullet which slipped easily down the barrel but had a hollow base which expanded on firing to grip the grooves. In 1850–51 both French and British Armies adopted Minié's rifle, though the British quickly switched to an improved and lighter Enfield model using the Minié 'ball'. The Enfield rifle had a very useful future before it, as we shall see; yet both Minié and Enfield versions were already out of date. As early as 1842 the Prussian Army had adopted Herr Johann Dreyse's breech-loading 'needle-gun', the true precursor of the modern rifle. They tried it out to their satisfaction in their war with Denmark in 1848–49, surprisingly without attracting any particular foreign attention. Denmark received a second dose of the medicine in 1864, and in 1866 the Prussians stunned the world by defeating the Austrian Empire and its allies in ten weeks, largely thanks to the efficiency of this weapon. In that same year, however, the French Army adopted M. Chassepot's admirable breech-loader, sighted up to 1,600 yards.

So the qualitative change in war was vigorously active during these middle decades. But none of these wars was a life-and-death struggle between great industrial nations; they were limited wars for limited objectives, a very different matter. And this was even true of the Franco-Prussian War of 1870–71, despite the passions engendered, the ferocity of some of its scenes and the apparent utter overthrow of France notwithstanding an attempt to turn this into a 'national war'. It was however, precisely during this period that unlimited, 'total' war with an industrial base did make its début—in America. The Civil War of 1861–65 was fought on one side for the very existence of the Confederacy, and on the other for the survival of the Union as hitherto known and understood. The institution of slavery created the unbridgeable divide between the two societies:

'It provided the symbol of North-South differentiation, and it provided the element of moral passion, prejudice and idealism in the sectional argument which led to the ultimate refusal to compromise.'[6]

Slavery was the unreconcilable factor, what made this a war *à outrance*, to the destruction of one side or the other, and thus the first Great War of the Industrial Revolution. It accordingly provides essential clues to the understanding of its only two successors, the First and Second World Wars.

The similarities of 1861–65 and 1914–18 are very striking; as General J. F. C. Fuller says,

'The war fought by Grant and Lee, Sherman and Johnston and others closely resembled the first of the World Wars. No other war, not even the Russo-Japanese War of 1904–1905, offers so exact a parallel.'[7]

Fuller offers an impressive list of technical resemblances to support his case: magazine rifles, trenches and wire entanglements, even machine-guns; rifled cannon, mortars, explosive bullets, a flame projector, a request for gas ('stink-shells', to cause 'suffocating effect'); balloons, armoured trains, land mines, lamp and flag signalling and the field telegraph; armoured ships, revolving turrets, torpedoes, even submarines. But though all this is indeed important, I would suggest that there are other resemblances which are more so.

To begin with, both contestants in this war leaned heavily upon the products of industry, and one of them, the North, was a major industrial state in its own right. Michael Glover tells us that the North, in 1861, had 110,000 factories employing 1,131,000 workers; these, and the raw materials provided by unceasing westward expansion, made the North practically self-sufficient. At the outbreak of war there were some 30,000 miles of railway in the United States, the product of an unmatched construction boom; over two-thirds of this mileage lay in what now became the North, rather less than a third in the South. Economically and strategically, it is impossible to exaggerate the importance of these statistics; as one American historian says,

'The railroad tied the North and West into one massive free economy.'[8]

And it was the steam locomotives drawing their long trains along these iron roads, linked to the steam-boats plying the coasts and rivers, that made it possible for the North to mobilize and move its vastly superior manpower.

The population of the United States in 1861 was some $31\frac{1}{2}$ million (thanks to an extraordinary leap of over 14 millions in the preceding twenty years). Of this total, approximately 9 million inhabited what became the Southern Confederacy; but of that number, about $3\frac{1}{2}$ million were Negro slaves. In the North itself there were some 19 million people, and in the border states (with divided loyalties) over $3\frac{1}{2}$ million. The Northern preponderance was

'Steam locomotives . . . made it possible for the North to mobilize and move its vastly superior manpower.' Union troops about to entrain, Virginia, 1864.

clearly massive, and the more so when we realise that, because of immigration, the North had 4,010,000 white males between the ages of 15 and 40, compared with only 1,140,000 in the South. For the North, the persisting problem of the war was how to make this preponderance effective.

When we examine the translation of populations into armies in the American Civil War, certain facts stand out at once. The first is that nowhere shall we see armies of the size of those which fought the greatest Napoleonic battles (*see table below*). In only nine occasions in America between 1861–65 do we find armies of 100,000 or more on either side; on one (only) of those occasions did the Confederates have the advantage (Seven Days, June–July 1862); on *no* occasion did *both* sides have 100,000 or more present. The reason for the contrast is simple: despite the dramatic recent leap in America's population, it was still less than that of France, and not much larger than France's 25 millions in 1793. In that year the combined populations of Austria, Prussia and England roughly equalled the French, giving these four European powers alone some 20 millions more than America in 1861.

Within that limitation, the American mobilization figures are nevertheless striking. Reliable estimates suggest that from first to last the Confederacy put some 850–900,000 men into the field, that is to say, over 15 per cent of the total white population. This compares very directly with 1914–18 proportions: France, 20 per cent; Germany, 18 per cent; Italy, 15 per cent; Austria-Hungary, 14 per cent; Great Britain, 13 per cent. But expressed as a proportion of the white males of military age, the Confederate total becomes a staggering 74.5 per cent, a true reflection of war *à outrance*, war for survival. The North, from first to last, is reliably said to have put 1,556,678 men in the field; this figure represents just under 8 per cent of the total population (compared with about 11 per cent in the Second World War) but over 21 per

WAGRAM (1809)
French 170,500
Austrians 146,000

BORODINO (1812)
French 127,000
Russians 120,000

BAUTZEN (1813)
French 200,000
Allies 96,000

DRESDEN (1813)
French 120,000
Allies 170,000

LEIPZIG
French 195,000
Allies 365,000

cent of the white males of military age. At its peak, the Northern army rose to 622,000 men present for duty in seventeen separate commands. To achieve these totals both the Union and the Confederacy had to adopt conscription, as France had done in 1793; the South being, not surprisingly, the first to do so, in April 1862, about a year before the North. All told, some $2\frac{1}{2}$ million Americans bore arms in the four years of the war; the pointer towards the future was clear.

It is not enough, however, to collect two and a half million men together in groups and call them soldiers; for that they must be armed and clothed, fed and moved. In all these matters the industrial North enjoyed great advantages. The South, with its cotton-based economy, had only 20,000 factories, employing only as many workers as there were factories in the North. This meant, obviously, that the South depended far more on imports than the North, and preventing those imports by blockade was an essential element of Northern strategy. In 1861 the United States Navy had 90 vessels on its books (more than half of them sailing ships, no ironclads) but only 42 in commission, of which only 13 were in home waters. To declare blockade of the great Southern littoral with a fleet of that size seemed ridiculous, yet as Peter Parish says, 'The blockade was the central fact of the war at sea.' The increase of the Union Navy to 670 vessels in 1865 is a significant tribute to the North's shipbuilding capacity. Meanwhile the war had witnessed the first conflict of ironclads and naval warfare would never be the same again.

The weakness of her industrial base and the increasing effectiveness of the blockade meant that the South was in a more or less permanent position of penury throughout the war. Blockade-running had some spectacular successes—some 600,000 small arms, nearly 2 million pounds of saltpetre, $1\frac{1}{2}$ million pounds of lead, 600,000 pairs of boots were among the items brought in through the blockade during the war—but nothing could alter the fundamental vulnerability of the South due to lack of industry. Even the North had to shop abroad for certain essentials; no less than 726,000 small arms were purchased in Europe by November 1862, but from then onwards, significantly, American production became sufficient to meet all needs. It may be noted that no less than 428,292 Enfields were among the foreign rifles imported, and were highly thought of. But the basic weapon of the Northern Army was increasingly the home-produced Springfield (one of whose attractions was that its ammunition was interchangeable with that of the Enfield—both using Minié bullets). Springfield supplied 1,472,614 rifles, with an annual production rate of 200,000 a year—ten times pre-war output.

With artillery the picture was similar: Northern foundries cast 7,892 cannon during the course of the war, many of them of very heavy calibre. This growth in the proportion of heavy calibre guns and mortars was another characteristic in common with the First World War. Field artillery, on the other hand, found itself at a technological hiatus. Both sides used field guns in substantial numbers (at Fredericksburg, December 1862, the Confederates had 306, the Union army 374) though often the terrain was unsuitable. By the following year about half the Union's field artillery was rifled, but

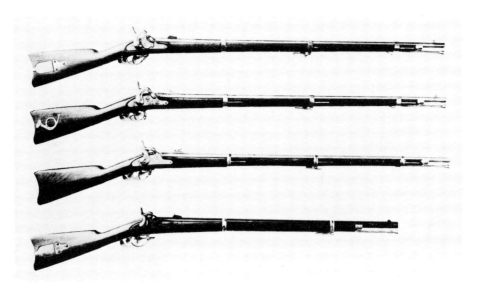

Types of Enfield rifle imported by the Union and Confederate Governments. The Union imported 428,292; their ammunition was interchangeable with that of the home-produced Springfield.

then the proportion dropped away somewhat; in close, wooded country range was not important, and it was found that while smooth-bores lacked range, rifled guns lacked killing power. On the other hand, improvements in musketry (including the introduction of the repeating rifle) would clearly bring an imperative need to extend the range of cannon. In all these matters the North's advantage was formidable and one can only admire the gift for improvisation and imitation which enabled the South to keep its armies equipped to take the field.

In the case of clothing and shelter—vital needs which are too often overlooked—the same applied, perhaps even more seriously than with weapons. Southern soldiers were lucky if they possessed grey uniforms (or any at all) after 1862, lucky at all times to possess a greatcoat and a blanket, incredulous at the good fortune of having a pair of actual boots (unless taken from a dead Yankee). Northern factories made nothing of supplying such commodities; their armies were the best equipped that the world had yet seen, their camps the wonder of foreign observers. Their soldiers grumbled ceaselessly about the food, but to European eyes it was if anything too plentiful, even if not particularly appetising. Weapons, uniforms, blankets, boots, tents, huts, waggons—the factories of the North produced them all in unheard-of abundance, as the factories of Europe would do sixty years later, and Quartermaster-General Montgomery Meigs's Bureau offered a preview of the great administrative staffs which would be such a feature of the First World War. In 1861 the Quartermaster-General's office employed 13 clerks; at the end of the war it had nearly 600 civilian employees. A typical triumph (of which Meigs was justly proud) was seen in 1864, when General W. T.

Sherman's army arrived at Savannah at the end of its long march through Georgia—and found a complete new clothing outfit for all its 70,000 men awaiting it.

Great armies and great mountains of supplies are equally useless if they cannot be moved. Water transport was still a prime factor, and command of the sea was invaluable to the North; command of the sea made possible an attack on the Confederate capital, Richmond, via the Yorktown peninsula (though General George B. McClellan bungled the campaign); command of the sea made possible the capture of the South's largest city and port, New Orleans, with no bungling at all when the war was only a year old. The capture of New Orleans was the first stage towards command of the mighty Mississippi, the greatest artery of transport and communication in the North American continent. On the Mississippi, the Ohio, and their tributary waters some 2,000 steamers and other boats were in constant use to carry men, animals, raw materials, foodstuffs, and goods, with a similar fleet on the Great Lakes. The logistical effort implied in this waterway traffic provided one of the remorseless pressures by which the South was ultimately crushed. The other was provided by the railways.

'Railways in war,' wrote Colonel G. F. R. Henderson, 'are good servants but bad masters.'[9] The problem, of course, is to separate these rôles; in America during the Civil War, as in Europe during the First World War, they were servants and masters at the same time. America's vast distances and Europe's vast armies required the servant rôle of railways in order to conduct operations of war at all effectively. But the railways themselves then decided where and how those operations would be conducted—a mastery from which there would be no escape until the advent of a second industrial revolution. This was the technology of the internal combustion engine fuelled by oil which, in the Second World War, made it possible again to conduct campaigns independently of railways and to offset another serious limitation imposed by them during both the American Civil War and the First World War. An American historian writes:

'It was the railroad and the river steamboat which robbed the great battlefield victories of finality. It was these devices, managed by telegraphic communications, which made it possible promptly to repair the terrible casualties of the major battles, to re-supply and re-equip, to draw reinforcements from another theatre to plug the gaps which the enemy opened up, to manoeuver not only armies but groups of armies so as to prevent defeat from turning into destruction.'[10]

He might have been writing about 1914, or 1918.

So we see the lineaments of First Industrial Revolution warfare becoming clearly defined between 1861–65. The very landscape changed to match the new style; scenes hitherto associated with siege operations against particular localities now became normal on all the major battlefields. The new fire-power dictated new tactics; instinctively, as the lead-storms swept them with unprecedented accuracy, the soldiers of both sides sought cover. In country that was generally well-timbered they did what the Japanese did in jungles in the Second World War: they built up logs into parapets, covering them with earth from trenches, shelters, and bombproofs dug behind. Against riflemen thus entrenched, assault after assault withered away; the bayonet became useful chiefly as a cooking instrument or for opening tins or boxes, scarcely ever as a weapon of war. The arts of trench warfare were universally culti-vated; 'the armies went into the ground completely at the end.'[11]

Dig as they might, the Civil War armies could no more avoid heavy losses than their successors in the First World War. Political leaders, military theorists, and the general public of the world alike, in the last decades of the nineteenth century, continued to think in terms of 'great captains' and 'thunderclaps of war'. They dwelt upon such events as Jackson's Shenan-doah Valley campaign in 1862, or Lee's 'perfect battle' at Chancellorsville in 1863. They generally failed to notice what war was becoming in its industrial guise; above all they failed to notice what it was likely to cost. In the course of the Civil War 115 regiments (63 Union and 52 Confederate) sustained losses of more than 50 per cent in a single engagement. The highest *rate* of loss of the whole war was that of the 1st Texas Regiment at Antietam (1862): 82.3 per cent. This was very nearly matched by the 1st Minnesota at Gettysburg the following year: 82 per cent. These figures compare very precisely with, say, the 84 per cent losses (100 per cent of officers) of the 1/Newfoundland Regiment on 1 July 1916, on the Somme. It was also at Gettysburg that the 26th North Carolina Regiment reported 100 per cent losses in Company F, and only 2 alive and unharmed out of 82 officers and men in Company E. The regiment lost 549 out of about 800 men in that battle. Three Confederate divisions had over 50 per cent casualties in the three days of Gettysburg: Pickett's, 67 per cent; Pettigrew's, 60 per cent; Trimble's, 52 per cent. On the Union side, Gibbon's had 40 per cent. It has been pointed out that when American casualties amounted to 17 per cent at Tarawa Atoll in April 1944, this was regarded as something of a scandal. On the other hand, at Okinawa in 1945, according to the American Official History, 'there was only one kind of Japanese casualty—the dead', of whom there were not less than 100,000. The new technology favoured only those who possessed it with preponder-ance; American Civil War losses, like those of the First World War, simply reveal what can happen when a lethal balance of force is struck.

Some 200,000 Americans were killed in battle during the Civil War—and twice as many by what continued to be war's great destroyer, disease. Mortality, landscape, technology, all indicated that 'this was the first of the modern total wars'. But there was an even surer sign, posted up for all to see by the two great commanders of the North's victorious last year: Ulysses S. Grant and William T. Sherman. It was Grant, the Union's new General-in-Chief, who propounded the strategy of all-out attack and unrelenting pres-sure in all theatres. It was Sherman, his principal lieutenant, who advocated and executed a significant addendum:

'If the Southern people persisted in the folly of rebellion after three years, they must

take the consequences. As he swept across their land, he would seize or destroy their crops, their animals, their barns and mills and wagons, not as a wanton act of destruction for its own sake, nor as an act of vengeance, but as a means of destroying the Southern capacity, and above all the Southern will, to make war.'[12]

So what had started as the conventional conflict of armies and navies had now become 'deeply overlaid by the beginnings of the war of organisation and the machine, the war against civilians and resources as well as against the uniformed soldiery of the enemy, the war of conscripted peoples rather than of volunteer armies.'[13] In other words, total industrial war had arrived—war which would demand the 'unconditional surrender' not just of armies in the field (the sense in which Grant coined the phrase in 1862) but of nations. The twentieth century would merely underline the lesson.

NOTES
1   Major-General J. F. C. Fuller: *The Decisive Battles of the Western World*, Eyre & Spottiswoode, 1955; ii p. 348.
2   David G. Chandler: *The Campaigns of Napoleon*, Weidenfeld & Nicolson, 1967; p. 924.
3   Michael Glover: *Warfare From Waterloo to Mons*, Cassell, 1980; p. 80.
4   Cecil Woodham-Smith: *The Reason Why*, Constable, 1953; Chapter 8.
5   *Bell's Weekly Messenger*, 4 March 1854, quoted in *Crimean War Reader* by Kellow Chesney, Frederick Muller, 1960; pp. 26–9.
6   Peter J. Parish: *The American Civil War*, Eyre Methuen, 1975; p. 30.
7   Fuller, op. cit. iii p. 89.
8   William Miller: *A New History of the United States*, Paladin, 1970; p. 185.
9   Colonel G. F. R. Henderson: *The Science of War*, Longmans, Green & Co., 1908; p. 33.
10 Walter Millis: *Arms and Men: A Study of American Military History*, Mentor Books (New York), 1958; p. 111.
11 Ibid, p. 116.
12 Parish, op. cit. p. 455.
13 Millis, op. cit. p. 110.

Part One:

The Setting

CHAPTER I

New Dimensions

BY 1914 THE FIRST INDUSTRIAL REVOLUTION had reached its apogee, the Second was well into its stride, and the signs of a Third were visible. The First World War reflected the technologies of all three.

The most important characteristic of the war was its scale. The mass populations had arrived: by 1913 Russia had 161 million people, America 95.5, Germany nearly 67, Austria-Hungary over 51, Great Britain (including Ireland) 45.7, France 37.7, almost matched by Italy's 35.5. The mass populations bred the great armies: the proportions mobilized mentioned above (p. 13) translate into mass armies such as the world had never seen (but would see far surpassed in World War II).

In August 1914 some six million men marched off to war. Germany, with a peace-strength army of about 870,000, could call on 4,300,000 trained men for reserves and replacements, and ultimately mobilized some 11 million. France, with a peace strength of 673,000, had some 4 million trained men available and ultimately mobilized that staggering 20 per cent of her population—7,800,000. Russia's peace strength was approximately $1\frac{1}{4}$ million officers and men, but her terms of service gave her only just over 4 million trained men; her estimated 10 per cent mobilization comes to about 16 million. The British Regular Army numbered 247,432 in 1914; with all categories of reserves including the Territorial Army (268,777) added, Britain had 948,965 available. Wartime recruitment, including conscription, produced a full United Kingdom total of 5,704,416, and a British Empire total of 8,654,467. Both these totals were undreamed of in 1914; both would be surpassed between 1939–45. What cannot be doubted is that these statistics gave the war both its shape and its character. It was the presence of these masses that ensured that it would be a long war, a violent war, and a costly war.

To bring such masses of men to battle the belligerents of 1914 used basically the same technology as the Americans in 1861–65—steamships at sea and steam-powered locomotives pulling their railway trains. But of course the intervening years had seen great increases (Britain alone possessed 21 million tons of merchant shipping in 1914, compared with less than 6 million tons in 1866) and considerable technical improvements in both, to say nothing of the growth of the elaborate complex of railroad systems of western and central Europe now available to both sides. In all countries the war potential of railways had been carefully studied. In France, General Joseph Joffre (himself an Engineer) was appointed Director of the Services of the Rear in 1910; this post, he says,

'in particular concentrated my attention upon the importance of the railway *transport of troops during the course of operations, and I had already arrived at the conviction that in a modern war of masses the true strategic instrument of the Commander-in-Chief would be the railway.*[1]

In 1911 Joffre conducted two exercises involving the movement of large bodies of troops from one flank of an army to the other; they offer, he remarks, 'a considerable retrospective interest, because it seems to me that there can be found in them the characteristic elements of the manoeuvre of the Marne' three years later. For mobilization, all the railways of France at once came under military control; 4,278 trains had been earmarked for the transport of troops, but more had to be added. In the event between 2 August and 18 August, 7,000 trains, at some periods following each other at intervals of eight minutes, carried 3,781,000 men to their points of assembly.

In Britain, on mobilization, the railways came under national control, exercised through a Railway Executive Committee consisting of the managers of the leading companies. As ill luck would have it, the war crisis coincided with particular pressures on the railway system; not only was August the height of the holiday season, but 3 August, the very eve of war, was a Bank Holiday; this was also the period of Territorial Army annual camps, with men in movement to and from these all over the country. Nevertheless, thanks to careful prewar preparation, the mobilization arrangements went forward with complete efficiency.

A complication, often insufficiently taken into account, was the fact that some 60 per cent of the British Expeditionary Force consisted of Reservists, who had to be carried by rail to their depots, and then on to join their appropriate units. What this might mean can be judged from the case of the 1/Gordon Highlanders. This battalion, in August 1914, was stationed at Crowhill, Plymouth, 400 miles from its depot. It received its mobilization order at 5.20pm on 4 August. On 6 August it received 235 Reservists from Aberdeen, and on 7 August 296 more. On 14 August it reached Boulogne. The Official History fills in the general picture:

'*In the five days of greatest activity 1,800 special trains were run in Great Britain and Ireland; on the busiest day of all, eighty trains, containing the equivalent of a division, were run into Southampton Docks; the daily average of ships despatched was thirteen, with an average daily tonnage of about 52,000 tons gross.*'[2]

In Germany, thanks to her geographical position (entirely unlike Britain's), railways and strategy were always intimately linked. Being a central power, with strong potential enemies to East and West, her strategic nightmare had always been war on two fronts simultaneously. On the other hand, being in the middle did confer upon her that important advantage which soldiers call 'the interior lines'. The solution of the war-on-two-fronts problem—given an adequate railway system—would be to switch forces across the diameter in order to destroy enemies on opposite arcs in detail. Every main German railway line thus had a strategic rôle—but there was more than that. As her

'180,000 miles of railroad track': the main European railway lines in 1914.

'The British Expeditionary Force possessed 1,200 lorries': one is seen at the left, but more significant is the pile of petrol cans—a new munition of war.

ambitious war-plan (*see below*) developed, Germany began rapidly to construct a network of purely strategic railways. These were lines coming to their termini close to the frontiers of Luxemburg, Belgium, and Holland, for which there was no conceivable civilian need. A British officer passed through a section of this system in the empty Moselle region in June 1914:

'*Elaborate detraining stations were passed every few miles . . . On one stretch of perhaps half-a-dozen miles connecting two insignificant townships were to be seen eight lines running parallel to each other. Twopenny-halfpenny little trains doddered along, occasionally taking up or putting down a single passenger at some halting-place that was large enough to serve a Coventry or a Croydon.*'[3]

It was to these 'ghost' railheads that, only a few weeks later, Germany's thirteen main lines carried 1,500,000 men in ten days to launch the most massive offensive seen in history to that date.

By 1914 the First Industrial Revolution had conferred upon Europe 180,000 miles of railroad track. Needless to say, its density and its efficiency varied greatly. In the Austro-Hungarian Empire railways, like virtually every other facet of that strange institution, displayed contradictions which reflected those of the Empire itself. Both Austria and Hungary had well-developed systems—but Hungarian nationalism so fiercely impeded sensible connections between these that in order to reach Lemberg (Lvov) in Galicia from Vienna, you had to travel via Prague and Cracow, while to the end of the

Empire's days the route from Vienna to Zagreb, Sarajevo, or Split was via Budapest. Evidently, if we call Germany's network 'strategic', with all the advantages that that implies, we should call her chief partner's 'anti-strategic'—and the consequences will not surprise us.

In two significant areas railway development was backward or even non-existent. In the Balkans (large portions of which had only recently been freed from Turkish rule, and all still very poor) there were only two lines worth noting: the main Belgrade–Nish–Constantinople route and its strategically important branch from Nish to Salonika which was to prove such a sore temptation to amateur strategists among the Western Allies during the war.[4] Further to the East, inside the Russian Empire, railway conditions were again very different from those of Western Europe. Industrialization had come late to Russia, and her railway development had been slow until Sergei Witte became Minister of Finance in 1892. During the next decade, with an increase in mileage of 46 per cent, the Russian system expanded more rapidly than that of any other country in Europe. But such comparisons do not help us much; the Russian expansion includes, for example, the whole length of the Trans-Siberian Railway, 5,500 miles from Moscow to Port Arthur—but still only a single track when war came with Japan in Manchuria in 1904. On Russia's western frontiers there was nothing to match eastern Germany's well-developed network; this was partly deliberate policy to hamper invaders, as was the retention of a 5ft gauge on Russian lines (compared with 4ft $8\frac{1}{2}$ inches throughout Europe). Despite everything, in August 1914 4,000 trains succeeded in assembling six Russian armies rapidly on the frontiers.

So the railway technology of the First Industrial Revolution went to war; but from the very beginning a new technology was also on display. In one important respect the British Army was ahead of all others in the application of the new power of movement supplied by the petrol-driven internal combustion engine. As early as 1911, unlike any other army, the British had motorized the section of the supply system between railhead and the troops themselves. This was a great step forward. In 1914 the six-division British Expeditionary Force possessed 1,200 lorries; by comparison, we may note that the five armies constituting the mobile right wing of the great German advance through Belgium had only 500 between them.[5]

These figures, however, do not give us the full story; for that it is necessary to look a short distance ahead. A famous incident of the war, sometimes blown up out of all proportion, is usually referred to as 'the taxis of the Marne'—the use of Paris taxis to rush forward French reserves to take part in the Battle of the Marne on 6 and 7 September 1914 (one of them is to be seen today in the *Musée de l'Armée*). This has taken its place as part of the legend of the 'miracle of the Marne'. The truth is less grandiose, but at the same time revealing; it shows us the French capacity for improvisation. The French Army quickly collected parks of civilian vehicles which, with military drivers, became available for supply or transportation. In Paris itself, before 6 September, the Military Governor, General Galliéni, had already formed a permanent reserve of some 150 taxis ready for instant use. To these, on that day, it was only possible to add ten at short notice, but the next day another 500 were assembled. Each of these 660 machines carried five or six soldiers, a total of about 4,000 (one brigade); in a battle involving about a million men on each side, it will readily be seen that their contribution to any 'miracle' must have been small. On the other hand, everything has to have a beginning: here we see the first of the lorried infantry who would soon be a familiar sight in war.

The idea was seized with alacrity; early in October the British Commander-in-Chief, Sir John French, asked the War Office for 300 buses to make his infantry more mobile. By the end of the month there were four bus companies in France, and by the beginning of 1915 there was a permanent park consisting of 324 buses and 271 lorries, capable of moving in one operation all the infantry and dismounted engineers of a division. In October 1914, however, for the transfer of the BEF from the Aisne to Ypres, the British borrowed enough buses from the French to lift 10,000 men (i.e. about 400 vehicles). On the other side of the line, the Swedish explorer Sven Hedin, visiting the German armies in the West, reported that they had 50,000 motor cars with them as early as September. This sounds like exaggeration (Sven Hedin was an ardent Germanophile and tended to accept uncritically anything that his hosts told him) but the Germans certainly bent every effort to making up the lack which they had so sorely felt during the long march from the frontiers to the Marne.

The motorization of transport, significant though it was, was by no means the chief contribution of the Second Industrial Revolution to the war. It will nevertheless be convenient to pursue this subject somewhat further before turning to larger matters. Naturally, as the war continued, motorization increased; the British experience may be taken as speaking for all. On mobilization in 1914, the British Army possessed 1,485 motor vehicles of all descriptions; at the Armistice, in all theatres (including Home Forces and India) this total had risen to 121,720. When war broke out there were no motor ambulances; in 1918 there were 7,045; 131 motor cycles in 1914 had increased to 34,865. A motor epic of the war took place at Verdun in 1916. When the Germans pressed home their furious attack on the fortified region in February, only two life-lines existed by which it could be supplied: a narrow-gauge railway line, and the road to Bar-le-Duc, second-class but recently widened. This fifty-mile stretch became known as the *Voie Sacrée* (the Sacred Way). In one week in March 25,000 tons of supplies were carried on it to Verdun; at the peak of fighting in June, 12,000 vehicles passed along it, one every 14 seconds; the equivalent of a whole division was permanently employed on maintenance. So the *Voie Sacrée* entered the military history of France, while the roads of France entered the military history of the world. But when, after three years of deadlock in the trenches, mobile warfare returned in 1918, not even the great expansion of motorization which had taken place proved capable of freeing the mass armies entirely from their railway lifelines. For that a new generation of vehicles would be required.

War, until the twentieth century, had been conducted on land and at sea; the Second Industrial Revolution added a new element—the air. For centuries, of course, flight had been the ambition of men in all lands. Levitation (rather than flight) became a practicality in the eighteenth century when great advances were made with balloons. The first record of the use of a balloon in war is by the French at the Battle of Fleurus in 1794. In the American Civil War General George B. McClellan's army used two balloons, with a regular establishment of two officers and about 50 other ranks—the first 'air force' in history. During the siege of Paris, 1870–71, as many as 64 balloons were wafted out of the city, bringing despatches and letters to the outer world. Always at the mercy of the wind, some came to grief, but the overwhelming majority made safe passages. With the coming of trench warfare, balloons reached their military apogee, and the line of the front was marked by the captive observation balloons all along it on both sides. Their value to the massed artillery below was inestimable, and when operations intensified, each side made the enemy's balloons a priority target; parachutes first came into general use as a means of escape for observers when their balloons were set on fire.

Real flight, however, is much more than the ability merely to rise into the air. The idea of a powered balloon which could be steered (a 'dirigible') was not long in coming, but it was due to the indefatigable courage, energy, and vision of a retired Württemberg cavalry officer, Count Ferdinand von Zeppelin, that dirigible airships first became a practical commercial (and military) proposition. On 2 July 1900, at Friedrichshafen on Lake Constance, Count Zeppelin's new airship made its first flight. She was a silvery, pencil-shaped giant, 420 feet long and forty feet wide. She was powered by two 16-h.p. Daimler motors, and flew for $3\frac{1}{2}$ miles, part of the distance against a headwind of 16 m.p.h. Her structure was rigid (a German preference), its strength deriving from a lattice of girders of aluminium—one of the light metals which also belong to the technology of the Second Industrial Revolution.

By 1914 37,250 Germans had actually flown in Zeppelin airships. On commercial flights Zeppelins had flown 100,000 miles with passengers, without a single accident. The future seemed to be theirs: they could travel far greater distances, they could lift incomparably greater weights, they could climb higher more swiftly than any known aeroplane. The only people who remained unimpressed were the Army and Navy chiefs. Admiral von Tirpitz, the Navy Secretary, was opposed to a dirigible programme because he feared that it would divert funds from the building of warships. The Army never perceived the strategic possibilities offered by Count Zeppelin's huge machines, treating them merely as mobile observation balloons for artillery spotting. Even their obvious potential for tactical reconnaissance (demonstrated by the Italians in Tripoli in 1911) was ignored; it did not fit in with the German system of war. The German people went 'Zeppelin-crazy' (indeed, 'air-crazy') in 1911, and the General Staff somewhat modified its rigid views, but the conversion was only skin-deep. As an American historian has said:

'By 1914 37,250 Germans had actually flown in Zeppelin airships.' LZ-7 coming in to land, 1910.

'The airplanes and dirigibles were maintained chiefly as a bit of gold braid on its uniform for the public eye.'[6]

At the outbreak of war in August 1914 the German Army had nine dirigibles, of which seven were usable; five of these were on the Western Front. The Navy (following disasters in 1912 and 1913) had only one. Three more were available from civilian sources, and thanks to long experience the production capacity of German industry was superior to any. But the key fact at this stage was that the German High Command had no plans for the use of airships—a matter which, if known, would have greatly shocked the German public and surprised Germany's enemies.

The French had plans, and they had as many airships as Germany in the West (five fit for use out of 15 in existence), but their machines were inferior, their crews less experienced, and the public less enthusiastic. The 'air-craze' in France had received its stimulus from the great progress made by heavier-than-air machines in a very short time. We have to remember that aeroplane flight itself dates only from December 1903, when the Wright brothers made their famous breakthrough at Kitty Hawk. During the next five years a band of talented (and brave) Frenchmen did for the aeroplane in France what Count Zeppelin had done for the airship in Germany. The names of Léon Levavasseur, the engine designer, Captain Ferdinand Ferber, Gabriel and Charles Voisin, Hubert Latham, Léon Delagrange, Henri Farman, Alberto Santos-Dumont, Robert Esnault-Pelterie and Louis Blériot are triumphant markers along the course of humanity's conquest of the air. When Wilbur Wright took his machine to Le Mans in 1908 Frenchmen were already setting up flight records; the superior performance of the American machine enabled Wright to break most of these—duration, distance, height. This gave French aviation another fillip, and awoke the public of all industrial countries to the possibilities of flight; a period of competitions, races and continuous record-breaking now began, with the Press offering what then seemed substantial prizes for encouragement. The *Daily Mail* offered £1,000 for the first flight across the English Channel, and this was duly collected by Louis Blériot on 25 July 1909. At the Reims Meeting a month later, 38 machines were displayed, 23 of them made over 120 take-offs in eight days, and 22 pilots flew. Henri Farman won the long-distance prize (112 miles), Hubert Latham attained the highest altitude (508 feet) with one of Levavasseur's *Antoinette* engines, and the American pioneer Glenn Curtiss won the speed record (48 m.p.h.); between them the three men carried off nearly £6,000 in prize money. But more important than the finance was the fact that during these eight days aeroplane-flying was seen to be far more than a fair-weather sport. There were days of rain, storm, and wind which would have grounded most airships; yet the aeroplanes flew—towards a future still obscure but soon to become certain.

The military reaction in France was at first similar to that in Germany. In 1909 Orville Wright demonstrated an aeroplane at the Tempelhof Field in Berlin, arousing the same enthusiasm that his brother had achieved at Le Mans the previous year. Yet a German general pronounced his demonstration 'merely a clever circus stunt without military value.' In 1910 General Ferdinand Foch, Commandant of the *Ecole de Guerre*, witnessing a similar display, remarked:

'That is good sport, but for the Army the aeroplane is of no value.'[7]

This verdict is all the more curious inasmuch as Foch was an artilleryman, and it was precisely as an adjunct to artillery that the French air arm made its first big impression. At the Châlons exercise camp in 1911 air reconnaissance was practised in co-operation with cavalry, and air control of artillery fire was first seen. Squared maps were used for fire direction, and experiments were carried out with signals, both direct and via captive balloons and by wireless telegraphy (of which more later). A perhaps somewhat over-enthusiastic British observer reported:

'Practice has made almost perfect a remarkable system which renders the efficient French artillery more efficient than ever.'[8]

Co-operation with infantry and aerial photography were also practised at Châlons; the Official British Air Historian was moved to say:

'In short, almost all the uses which later became commonplaces of the war were exemplified in the French manoeuvres of 1911.'[8]

The manoeuvres of 1912 marked the climax of development of French prewar military aviation, with 46 aeroplanes and two dirigibles taking part—a larger number than any yet seen for such a purpose anywhere.

And then, only five years after the great 'take-off', a decline set in. Partly this was due to errors in reorganization of the air service, dividing offices with corresponding division of responsibility and lessening of authority. Non-flying personnel began to take over the units; infantry-style drills interfered with actual aviation; bureaucracy took hold. At the 1913 manoeuvres only 36 aeroplanes took part—a substantial drop from the previous year; recruitment of aviators dropped from 1,500 in 1911 to 300 in 1912 and only 22 in 1913. Reorganization does not entirely account for this state of affairs; as in Germany, neglect of aviation was chiefly due to a profound change in the system of war which took place at this time, and which we shall consider when we come to the plans. Here it need only be added that when war came the French air service, which had been credited with possession of 200–220 aeroplanes in 1911, had only some 136 fit for use.

In both fields of aviation Britain made a late start, but nevertheless enjoyed some important advantages. The Royal Flying Corps, with a Military and Naval Wing, did not come into existence until April 1912; this gave it all too little time to prepare for the war which many could clearly see coming. On the other hand, it did mean that the British flyers enjoyed the creative satisfaction of building a new service in which they believed with whole-hearted dedication at a time when their French and German counterparts were enduring considerable discouragement and frustration. Furthermore, the cause of that frustration was absent in Britain; the British General Staff did not shackle itself to a theoretical system of war as the French and Germans had done. How could it? Imperial commitments compelled it to be pragmatic—the Army might have to fight (and soon did) on the North-West frontier of India, in the Middle East, the Sudan or southern or central Africa. No one told the British airmen that they would not be needed. On the contrary, after the 1912 manoeuvres we find Lieutenant-General Sir James Grierson (commander-designate of II Corps in the Expeditionary Force) referring to the 'continuous stream' of immediate reports which he had received from the airship *Gamma* (by wireless-telegraphy), and saying of aircraft:

'The impression left on my mind is that their use has revolutionized the art of war. So long as hostile aircraft are hovering over one's troops all movements are liable to be seen and reported, and therefore the first step in war will be to get rid of the hostile aircraft.'[9]

Soon he would go even further:

'. . . warfare will be impossible unless we have the mastery of the air.'[10]

Finally, of course, the late start enabled Britain to take advantage of foreign progress. The worst aspect of the British situation was the virtual lack of an aero-engine industry; for the first six months of the war Britain had to rely entirely on France for engines. On the other hand, the existence of the Royal Aircraft Factory (lineal descendant of the Balloon Factory) assured the future production of some of Britain's best aircraft types. In 1914 the Naval Wing of the Royal Flying Corps separated to become the Royal Naval Air Service, under full Admiralty control; already Britain's entire force of airships had been transferred to the Navy. When war broke out, the RNAS possessed 39 aeroplanes (but of virtually no military value), 52 seaplanes, of which 31 were serviceable, and seven airships of which six were serviceable. The RFC had 179 machines of one kind or another on its books, but when the first four squadrons flew to France in August, it was with difficulty that they mustered 12 useful aircraft each.

For action in August 1914 the combined British and French air services numbered some 184 aeroplanes. They were faced by some 180 machines of the German Army air service (out of a paper strength of about 230; but with some units not at full strength). Like the airships, the German aeroplanes had been caught by the chill wind of a changing system of war. They suffered, too, from design problems. The famous Rumpler *Taube* monoplane had made its début in a blaze of glory in 1910, but by 1913 it was clearly obsolete, and in 1914 German pilots demanded its replacement. The war, in fact, caught German design and manufacture at an awkward moment. As for the naval service, its plight was even worse: lacking money, material, and men, it scraped together some 35 seaplanes at the outbreak of war, but hardly 20 of them were fit for use. But the worst aspect of the service was undoubtedly, as Mr Cuneo says, that 'little was actually expected of it.'

Only Imperial Russia offered any challenge in 1914 to the lead established by France, Germany, and Britain. One of the great names in air design, Igor Sikorski (later noted for work on flying boats and helicopters) had produced a four-engined biplane in 1913—generally regarded as the first of its kind. An improved model, the *Ilya Mourometz*, in 1914 flew from St. Petersburg to Kiev, a distance of 1,600 miles. The Sikorski machines captured distance, weight-lifting and altitude records for Russia; by 1917 75 of them had been built, but their military effect was slight owing to the lack of an aero-engine industry in Russia and a chronic shortage of engine spares. It may be noted, however, that though they made many operational flights, only one was ever shot down by a German plane.

Thus the Second Industrial Revolution launched humanity into the air. It may seem to some that the launch, as indicated by the statistics quoted above, was pretty feeble. In terms of the time-span, however, the reverse is true. Only eleven years separated the first flight of the Wright brothers from the First World War; military aviation was only half a decade old. The British experience reveals what war can do to technology. As the Official Air Historian tells us:

'By the 1st of November (1910) the Royal Aero Club had issued twenty-two

Igor Sikorski's *Ilya Mourometz*. These giants captured distance, weight-lifting, and altitude records, but their military effect was slight owing to Russia's industrial backwardness.

certificates; that is to say, twenty-two pilots, some of them self-taught, and some trained in France, were licensed by the sole British authority as competent to handle a machine in the air.'[11]

Only eight years later, in November 1918, the Royal Air Force (less than one year old) had a total strength of 291,748, of whom some 28,000 were officers; it comprised 200 squadrons, with 22,171 aircraft on charge. It was the largest air force in the world.

Nowhere were the effects of the successive stages of Industrial Revolution more evident than in the world's navies. The first application of steam to movement on water came very early—in 1783, only two years after James Watt had produced his large engine. Robert Fulton demonstrated a steamboat two years before the Battle of Trafalgar; ten years *after* the battle, the first steam warship was launched, U.S.S. *Fulton* (38 tons). In 1841 the Swede, John Ericsson, designed and launched the first screw-driven warship, U.S.S. *Princeton*. The final defeat of the paddle was signalized in 1845 by the famous contest between the screw-driven H.M.S. *Rattler* and the paddle-ship H.M.S. *Alecto*, when the former towed the latter backwards through the water at a speed of 2.8 knots. The first all-iron warship came in 1860: H.M.S. *Warrior*.

War is always the great accelerator of technical change, and the American Civil War, as we have seen, provided the first example of what an industrialized nation could do under pressure. The first contest between ironclads took place in 1862: C.S.S. *Virginia* (*Merrimac*) v U.S.S. *Monitor* at Hampton Roads. Torpedoes of a primitive kind were in frequent use, producing a moral effect well beyond their destructive capacity. Admiral David Farragut's order in Mobile Bay in August 1864 gave the U.S. Navy a famous slogan:

'Damn the torpedoes! Full speed ahead!'

In the same year, however, a Federal warship, U.S.S. *Housatonic*, was torpedoed by a Confederate submersible. (Indeed all 'conventional submarines' are really submersibles; the only true submarines are the very latest—atomic-powered). The Confederate vessel was sunk by her own explosive (carried on the end of a long spar) with the loss of her whole crew of nine. Yet her feat, in conjunction with the effect of mines, marked a new stage in warfare that we shall look at more closely, and which by 1914 had laid a heavy hand on all admirals and admiralties.

The second half of the nineteenth century, as far as navies were concerned, was a sustained sprint of technology. At the very centre of events was the contest between guns and armour, with both contestants continually adding to the size and weight of warships, and calling for more and more powerful engines to propel them. So the giant modern battleships were born. By the 1890s, the latest British battleships carried 110-ton guns which could pierce $30\frac{1}{2}$ inches of solid wrought iron at 1,000 yards. The ships themselves were now displacing over 12,000 tons. Already such armaments as these, using steel plate instead of iron, and calling for ever-increasing sophistication in all branches of equipment, were becoming a heavy financial burden even for the richest countries. The 165 vessels of the Diamond Jubilee Review in 1897 represented a daunting display of naval might—but they also represented a daunting expenditure of money. What was so alarming was the possibility that much of it might be waste.

It was above all the combination of the Whitehead torpedo (prototype tested in 1867, and steadily improved) with the submarine that threatened the existence of the great battleships. The Confederate Navy may have scored the first 'kill' by a submersible boat, but it was the French who pioneered the underwater craft (with *Le Plongeur*, 1863) and maintained a lead in their development until the end of the nineteenth century. From very early days the torpedo was seen as a natural submarine weapon; the problem was the uncertain performance of both. At first, therefore, torpedo attack was envisaged as a function of fast surface vessels. In 1893 the Royal Navy introduced a new class of naval vessel altogether: the 'torpedo-boat-destroyer' (T.B.D.), itself carrying three torpedo tubes and four guns, with a speed of 28 knots. High-speed destroyers now became a feature of every navy; the Royal Navy witnessed a convincing display of the power of steam-turbine engines at the Diamond Jubilee Review, and took the lesson to heart; in 1899 the turbine-driven *Viper* worked up 37 knots, and held 34 knots for three hours.

Meanwhile the submarine was progressing. In the French naval man-oeuvres of 1898 and 1901 the submarine *Gustave Zédé* scored hits on battle-ships not only when these were at anchor, but even when under way. At this time France led the world with 14 submarines in commission and building; other nations took belated note. The United States Navy acquired its first submarine, designed by J. P. Holland, in 1900; at the end of the same year the British Admiralty decided to acquire five Holland boats which would be built in England by Vickers. Italy already had two submarines; Russia launched one in 1901 and by 1909 had 29, the world's third largest submarine force; Japan ordered five Hollands in 1904, when war broke out with Russia, but neither belligerent made operational use of the new weapon during that war. Obsessed by his dreams of a big-ship fleet, Admiral von Tirpitz opposed the building of submarines for the Imperial German Navy; not until 1905–06 was there any provision for such vessels in the naval estimates, and not until 1906 did Germany actually possess a U (*untersee*)-boat afloat, by which time France had 85.

As with aircraft, so with submarines: numbers were not, ultimately, the thing that mattered. What did matter was performance, which decided their rôle. The French submarine service, despite its numbers, was actually in decline in the decade before the First World War—but not before it had offered one last important gift to the new underwater arm. In 1899 M. Laubeuf's *Narval* was launched, marking a revolution in design and function. She was the first long-range 'overseas' submarine:

> *'the fore-runner of the many hundreds of so-called submarines which were to be built during the next fifty years, right up to the time when atomic power produced the true submarine with unlimited endurance submerged from a single set of machinery.'*[12]

Hitherto (and for a few years still) the submarine had been regarded by the world's navies as a defensive instrument—this, indeed, was a main reason for von Tirpitz's hostility as late as 1902—but now it was turning into an enemy capable of striking at fleets and bases far from its own coasts.

The capability became reality through the application of two more tech-

'The submarine was progressing': in 1900 the British Admiralty acquired five Holland submarines. No. 1 is seen here with full crew on deck.

nological advances, one German, one Austrian. Rudolf Diesel patented the engine that bears his name in 1892, and experiments at once began in several countries to find marine applications for it. The British *A13* had an experimental version in 1908, and the whole D class (1909) was diesel-driven; this became the standard means of propulsion for British submarines from then onwards. D-class boats had a surface speed of 14 knots and a radius of action of 1,250 miles; the E-class, larger, faster and better-armed, followed in 1912. Germany introduced diesel-driven submarines in 1913, and they were formidable. Their engines were superior to the British Vickers version and could develop 1,700 h.p.; they had a maximum surface speed of 15½ knots, but more significantly, they could travel 5,000 miles at 8 knots. These (and the British Es) were true offensive vessels carrying an offensive weapon which was now of great menace. From *U-18* onwards they carried 19.69-inch torpedoes; thanks to the Austrian, Ludwig Obry, who had first adapted the gyroscope for directional control of torpedoes in 1895, and his successors, these were more reliable than the British. So the submarine now had range and striking power.

By August 1914, Britain had 74 submarines built and 31 building; Germany had 33 built and 28 building. Significantly, of Britain's 74, only 18 (8 Es and 10 Ds) were 'overseas' boats; of Germany's 33, 28 were 'overseas'. What was their rôle going to be? The Germans themselves were uncertain; their relatively modest building programme (a target total of 72 by 1920) shows that they placed no great faith in their underwater fleet. One man, however, had no doubts about how the 'overseas' U-boat would be used; in June 1913 Admiral Lord Fisher wrote a famous memorandum predicting that it would be against merchant shipping, without regard for international law. The submarine, he said,

'cannot capture the merchant ship; she has no spare hands to put a prize crew on board . . . she cannot convoy her into harbour . . . There is nothing else the submarine can do except sink her capture, and it must therefore be admitted that (provided it is done, and however inhuman and barbarous it may appear) this submarine menace is a truly terrible one for British commerce and Great Britain alike, for no means can be suggested at present for meeting it except by reprisals . . . it is freely acknowledged to be an altogether barbarous method of warfare . . . [but] the essence of war is violence, and moderation in war is imbecility.'

The Government and the Admiralty were appalled at Fisher's memorandum. The Prime Minister, Mr. Asquith, refused to circulate it to the Committee of Imperial Defence; the First Lord of the Admiralty, Mr. Winston Churchill, told Fisher, 'I do not believe this would ever be done by a civilised power'; the First Sea Lord, Prince Louis of Battenberg, said that Fisher's otherwise brilliant paper 'was marred by this suggestion'; even Captain Roger Keyes, Commodore Submarines, discarded this form of warfare 'as impossible and unthinkable'. One powerful voice, however, joined Fisher's on the very eve of war; in July 1914, at the end of a furious controversy in *The Times*, the famous gunnery expert, Admiral Sir Percy Scott, wrote:

'Our most vulnerable point is our food and oil supply. The submarine has introduced a new method of attacking these supplies. Will feelings of humanity restrain our enemy from using it?'

Fisher and controversy were never far apart. Between 1904–10 his reforming zeal had done for the Royal Navy what the clear thinking and energy of Mr. Haldane had done for the Army. It is to these two men above all that Britain owed the preparedness of her Services for war in 1914. In Fisher's case, however, there is an ironic contradiction. He was one of the first important figures in the Royal Navy to appreciate the threats of torpedoes and submarines; in 1902 he was urging long-range gunnery because at conventional ranges 'the Torpedo will get in!' In 1904 he was demanding the addition of 100 submarines to the Navy. And at the same time it was Fisher who led the way in the development of the great battleship which caught and held the public eye, and led directly to the naval building race between Britain and Germany.

Fisher became First Sea Lord for the first time on Trafalgar Day (21 October) 1904; he immediately set up a committee under his own chairmanship to consider the design of a revolutionary battleship. In just under a year her keel-plate was laid; she was launched with the name H.M.S. *Dreadnought* in February 1906; in October she was ready for trials, and in December she was completed. The essential features of *Dreadnought* were gun-power and speed. Her armament represented the triumph of the all-big-gun school advocated by a number of modern designers: she carried ten 12-inch guns (no other battleship carried more than four guns of the largest calibres) and no other guns except 3-inch 12-pounder quick-firers to repel torpedo-boat attacks. She was the first battleship in the world to be turbine-driven, giving her a trial speed of 21.6 knots—more than 2 knots faster than any other battleship. She was protected by 11 inches of steel plate, and displaced 17,900 tons. She made every other battleship in the world obsolete including Britain's own huge pre-Dreadnought fleet (no less than 52 battleships laid down since 1891).

Naturally, voices were raised passionately enquiring whether this drastic abandonment of a long-cherished numerical superiority was justified. Was it sensible, the critics asked, to thrust the Navy into virtual equality with potential rivals in this precipitate manner? The answer to the critics was, quite simply, that the movement towards these ships was already well advanced in the United States and the German and Japanese Navies were considering them closely. Dreadnoughts were going to be, and soon; Fisher stole a march and gave Britain a lead which she never lost. In 1914 Britain had (besides the pre-Dreadnoughts) 20 of the new type in commission and 12 building, compared with Germany's 16 with 4 building. Not only that, Britain's building programme included the fast oil-fired *Queen Elizabeths*,

'. . . a profound revolution in naval technology': dreadnoughts of the Queen Elizabeth class, laid down in 1913, were oil-burning, capable of 25 knots, and carried eight 15-inch guns.

with their 15-inch guns and 25-knot speed. These began to appear in 1915, and remained in service with distinction throughout not only the First but also the Second World War.

More legitimate controversy centred around Fisher's second brainchild, the battle-cruiser. The first of the line was H.M.S. *Invincible* (launched 1907). Like *Dreadnought*, her essentials were speed and armament; her official speed was 25 knots and this she could maintain for days on end; she reached 26 knots at her trials and more than once even managed 28. She carried the same calibre guns as *Dreadnought*: eight 12-inch. Clearly, she was a very powerful, fast ship; but what was she *for*? Various rôles were suggested: penetrating the light screen of an enemy fleet to obtain information; hunting down armed merchant raiders (Germany's 23-knot transatlantic liners were mentioned); harrying an enemy battle-fleet. Was she a super-cruiser? Or was she a fast battleship? The design committee said: 'These Armoured Cruisers are Battleships in disguise'—but they did not have the armour which was essential for the battleship rôle. *Invincible's* main belt was only 6 inches thick, and while her gun turrets had 7 inches on the sides they only had 3 inches on their roofs to resist plunging shot. Clearly, as one who served in them said, 'on all counts these ships were not fit "to stand the line of battle".'[13] Nevertheless, in 1914, the British Navy had nine of them, with one building, while Germany, following the British lead, had six with two building.

Such was the alarming gift of advancing technology to naval warfare: a compound of the fruits of successive revolutions of technology. To the coal and iron of the first were now added the further powers of oil, electricity, and compressed air; to the original reciprocating steam engines were added the turbine, the internal combustion engine, and the diesel. Steel was replacing iron for many purposes; new metals—tungsten, chromium, nickel, manganese, etc.—provided special alloys; zinc and aluminium had arrived; chemistry gave the great guns ever more destructive ammunition; optics supplied the range-finders to place it on its target and the periscope which enabled the submarine to see; above and below the waves the sciences of navigation and combat were in constant transformation. To be a captain or an admiral in 1914 was to follow a profession whose future was full of mystery, full of questions which only practical experience of war could answer. Admiral Sir John Jellicoe took up command of the British Grand Fleet, the supreme repository of British sea power, at the outbreak of war. He was, as Winston Churchill said, 'the only man on either side who could lose the war in an afternoon.' Even more significantly, comparing Jellicoe with England's most famous admiral, he said:

'Nelson's genius enabled him to measure truly the consequences of any decision. But that genius worked upon precise practical data . . . He felt he knew what would happen in a fleet action. Jellicoe did not know. Nobody knew.'[14]

'Nobody knew'—those words may serve as the epitaph of the war itself.

There remains one last new dimension to consider, affecting all the elements of the war—land, sea, and air: communication. When Nelson commanded the Mediterranean Fleet in 1803 it was not uncommon for weeks and even months to pass with no communication from the Admiralty, no access to recent Admiralty intelligence, no indication of current plans. Admirals on station had to depend on their own judgment, formed by experience, and on constructive imagination, similarly based. Fortunately the officers of the Royal Navy had had a lot of war experience, and showed no lack of judgment and imagination. Generals in distant theatres and colonial governors faced a similar problem, and solved it according to their varying qualities.

Long-range communication, in the days of sail, was accepted as being normally altogether unreliable. The same was to a lesser extent true of intermediate-range communication. Flag-signalling enabled a fleet to communicate across a wide expanse of ocean—as long as there was reasonable visibility; in fog, storm, or at night, of course, there was none. On land, communication between armies, detachments, or fortresses was generally by courier only; its speed was that of the courier's horse; in enemy country man and horse were vulnerable, even if, lacking accurate maps, they did not simply lose their way. At close range, however, the admirals and generals of those times possessed advantages that the First World War generation might envy. Battles, at sea and on land, were fought within hailing distance; ships and regiments, squadrons and brigades, obeyed the voices of their commanders even amid the smoke of black gunpowder. Nelson, Collingwood, and Villeneuve at Trafalgar, Wellington on the ridge at Waterloo, and Napoleon on his observation platform, had the entire panorama of their battles under their eyes, and the means to communicate swiftly with every part. Such a luxury was virtually unknown between 1914–18.

It was in the first place the electric telegraph and the steamship which began to solve the long- and intermediate-distance problems. The electric telegraph was first used in the Crimean War; in the American Civil War it came into its own. By 1860 America 'was stitched together by some 50,000 miles of wire'. Such a network constituted a revolution of command in itself:

'*It brought commanders into close touch with each other and with their military and political superiors; it made possible a greater measure of direction and control from the centre.*'[15]

By the end of the war in 1865, the two sides between them had added some 15,000 miles of wire to the existing network, and about 1,000 telegraph operators were at work. Such men, tapping out their messages in Samuel Morse's code, would be central figures in the world's communication system for many decades.

From telegraphy to telephony the advance was not long delayed. Morse transmitted his first telegraph message ('What God has wrought!') in 1844; in 1876 Alexander Graham Bell uttered his first message by telephone (to his assistant: 'Mr. Watson, come here, I want you'). The military possibilities of both the new means of communication were readily appreciated. In the South African War (1899–1902) we find telephone networks linking the defence strongpoints to headquarters and to each other in Ladysmith and Mafeking. In the open field, both sides made use of the telegraph line; the British Army maintained 28,000 miles of land-line and laid 18,000 miles of new line during the course of the war. By 1904–05 the lesson had been so well taken in some quarters that we even see criticisms of the Japanese Army for over-dependence on telephone and telegraph at the expense of useful visual systems such as the heliograph.

A lesson quickly learnt was the vulnerability of communication by wire in more than one way. It was a simple matter to cut the wires—Sir Ian Hamilton in 1904 called them 'that reed so easily broken'; it was not difficult to tap them, and learn what messages they carried. Both these procedures were adopted, chiefly by the Confederates, in the American Civil War; in South Africa cutting and tapping were commonplace, codes and other deceptions were in regular use—the beginnings of electronic warfare.

Meanwhile telegraphy without wires had arrived, while radio-telephony waited in the wings. Signor Guglielmo Marconi took out his patent and formed a company in 1897; in that year he transmitted a signal across the English Channel. In the Royal Navy's manoeuvres of 1899 three ships were fitted with 'wireless' and a transmission range of 85 miles was achieved. In 1901 Marconi transmitted a signal across the Atlantic.

For armies there were problems; the early wireless apparatus was bulky, heavy, and cumbersome. The British Army had five sets in South Africa, carried in horse-drawn waggons and operated by Marconi personnel, but there is no evidence of their playing any significant rôle; hilly country interfered with signals, atmospherics were bad. The Navy, on the other hand, had already appreciated the possibilities of interception and even jamming, and in the 1902 naval manoeuvres jamming was used extensively. When Marconi dramatically increased the range of his transmissions, the value of shore stations became apparent, and in 1910 the Marconi Company submitted to the Colonial Office a plan to link the component parts of the British Empire by a world-wide chain of wireless stations. In March 1912 a

'Telegraphy without wires had arrived . . . By 1914 the Royal Navy had some 435 ships equipped with wireless . . .' The wireless cabin of R.M.S. *Olympic*, 1912, with a typical naval installation.

tender was agreed between the Company and the Post Office for the erection of the first six. By 1914 the Royal Navy had some 435 ships in service equipped with wireless and about 30 shore stations in operation; to these, thanks to the foresight of Admiral Sir Henry Oliver, were added in August directional stations which for a long time gave the Navy a great advantage in locating enemy vessels and movements.

It was probably to the infant air arm, however, that rapid development of this new means of communication was probably due. As early as 1907 a captive balloon received wireless messages at a range of 20 miles, which was a startling innovation. But it was not what an aircraft might *receive* that mattered, it was the information that it might transmit. In the French Army manoeuvres of 1911 and 1912 great attention was paid to methods of air control of artillery fire; there is mention of wireless, but the details are somewhat uncertain. The story of British development is clearer: Captain Lefroy, Royal Engineers, installed a transmitting apparatus in the army airship *Beta* in 1911, and was able to send clear messages to the ground station 30 miles away. He then gave his attention to installing similar apparatus in aeroplanes—a far more difficult matter, considering the small size of the planes and the large size of the sets. (It also meant, in single-seaters, that the pilot had to be a proficient wireless operator, and perform this work while flying the aircraft.) It was, in fact, the Naval Wing of the new-born Royal Flying Corps whose experiments with light sets first bore fruit; in June 1912 Commander Samson, in the first Short seaplane, sent signals up to 10 miles. In August of the same year came the breakthrough; two airships were to take part in the Army manoeuvres, one on each side. *Delta*, on the attacking side commanded by Lieutenant-General Sir Douglas Haig, broke down at once, but *Gamma*, for the defenders under Lieutenant-General Sir James Grierson:

'was an unqualified success. Her signals came in strong and loud from a distance of thirty-five miles to a station at Whittlesford fitted with naval service receiving apparatus. Speaking of the work of the aircraft, General Grierson . . . says: "the impression left on my mind is that their use has revolutionized the art of war."'[16]

General Haig, who was defeated in these manoeuvres, took the lesson to heart; from the very beginning of the war he paid great attention to air reconnaissance. The Royal Flying Corps itself profited from this demonstration of what its prime rôle should be. It entered the war with a far more realistic sense of purpose than either the German or the French air services—strategic reconnaissance was its explicit object.

What was still missing in every country—and 1914–18 would show how serious was the lack—was the blessing of voice communication. Nowhere would this be felt more acutely than at the shortest ranges—in actual combat. In 1915 a voice speaking in Arlington, Virginia, was carried by wireless to Paris and Hawaii, 4,000 miles away, opening up magical possibilities for the future. What was immediately needed in 1915, however, was the means of making a voice heard up to about 4 miles away amidst the heat of battle—and that kind of magic was not quite ready. This proved to be a tragic circumstance for multitudes of soldiers.

———————

Such (in brief) were the new dimensions of war that the First Industrial Revolution and its successors had created by 1914. From the first the pace of change had been brisk, but it accelerated as the nineteenth century drew to its end; as Major-General J. F. C. Fuller says:

'. . . the turn of the century witnessed an outburst of inventiveness which was destined to revolutionize war even more completely than had the introduction of the horse in the third millennium B.C.'[17]

Of all the novelties which crowded in upon this period the two most fateful, says Fuller, were the internal combustion engine and wireless telegraphy; the former, by solving the problem of flight, lifted warfare into a third dimension.

'The latter virtually raised it into the fourth dimension; for to all intents and purposes the wireless transmission of energy annihilated time as well as space. Thus two new battlefields were created—the sky and the ether.'[18]

For the generation which encountered this transformation, on the battle-fields, on the oceans, in the skies, and in the laboratories of 1914–18, the new dimensions would repeat what was, after all, only an old lesson; as Marshal Turenne once said:

'Speak to me of a general who has made no mistakes in war, and you speak of one who has seldom made war.'[19]

To which the Industrial Revolutions added:

'New capacity meant new complexity; new methods of making war meant new ways of making mistakes.'[20]

NOTES

1   Marshal Joffre: *Memoirs* translated by Col. T. Bentley Mott, i p. 6; Geoffrey Bles, 1932.
2   *Military Operations, France and Belgium* (the Official History, compiled by Brig.-Gen. Sir J. E. Edmonds; henceforth 'O.H.') 1914, i p. 31.
3   Major-General Sir C. E. Callwell: *Experiences of a Dug-Out*, pp. 4–5; Constable, 1920.
4   Sir Charles Callwell, who was Director of Military Operations in 1914, recalls a meeting with Mr. Lloyd George (Chancellor of the Exchequer) who was in a buoyant mood: 'He had made a discovery. He had found on a map that there was quite a big place—it was shown in block capitals—called Salonika, tucked away in a corner of the Balkans right down by the sea. The map furthermore indicated by means of an interminable centipede that a railway led from this place Salonika right away up into Serbia, and on from thence towards the very heart of the Dual Monarchy.'* The Allied forces landed at Salonika in 1915; the Germans referred to the expedition as 'the greatest Allied internment camp'.
    * Callwell, op. cit. p. 153.
5   Journal of the Royal United Services Institute, June 1978: 'Supplying an Army: An Historical View' by Martin Van Creveld, Note 59.
6   John R. Cuneo: *Winged Mars: The German Air Weapon*, i p. 133; The Military Service Publishing Company, Harrisburg, Pa., 1942.
7   B. H. Liddell Hart: *Foch: Man of Orleans*, i p. 58; Penguin Edition, 1937.
8   Walter Raleigh: *The War in the Air* (The Official History), i pp. 177–8; Oxford, The Clarendon Press, 1922.
9   Ibid., pp. 226–7.
10 Quoted in a lecture by Colonel H. S. Massy at the Royal Artillery Institution, 6 November 1913.
11 Raleigh, op. cit. pp. 110–11.
12 William Jameson: *The Most Formidable Thing: The Story of the Submarine from*

its earliest days to the end of World War I, p. 59; Rupert Hart-Davies, 1965.

13 Vice-Admiral B. B. Schofield: *British Sea Power: Naval Policy in the Twentieth Century*, p. 37; Batsford, 1967.

14 Winston Churchill: *The World Crisis*, (Odham's Edition, 1938) i p. 1034.

15 Peter J. Parish: *The American Civil War*, p. 130; Eyre Methuen, 1975.

16 Raleigh, op. cit. pp. 226–7 (see p. 30).

17 Major-General J. F. C. Fuller: *The Decisive Battles of the Western World and their influence upon history*, iii p. 184; Eyre & Spottiswoode, 1956.

18 Ibid., p. 185.

19 Quoted by Major-General Sir W. F. P. Napier, *History of the War in The Peninsula*, ii p. 208; Thomas & William Boone, 1862.

20 Parish, op. cit. p. 130.

CHAPTER II

Plans and Forces:
Interior Lines

GEOGRAPHICALLY, POLITICALLY, PSYCHOLOGICALLY, Germany stands at the centre of the First World War, as she does with the Second. The German war plan (that is to say, German strategy) gave the entire war its shape; the plan itself was shaped by German geography, and powered by the German Army, which may be called the 'motor' of the war.

The German Empire, it has to be remembered, was less than half a century old in 1914; its strategic preoccupation was precisely as old as the Empire itself, dating from the proclamation of the Reich in the palace of Versailles in the hour of triumph over France in January 1871. Even the imposition of what seemed to be a punitive peace[1] did not remove the fear of a French revival and all that was implied by the word 'revanche'. Worse still was the thought of a Franco-Russian alliance which would face Germany with the prospect of war on two fronts—the eternal dilemma of the 'interior lines'. This nightmare was a direct product of the Prussian-dominated Empire; it had never troubled the kingdoms, arch-duchies, electorates, and other states of pre-imperial Germany in the days when their foreign policies were their own. In 1894 the nightmare became a fact; the culmination of long-drawn-out negotiations was reached in the Dual Entente between France and Russia, with a military agreement as its centrepiece. This provided for mutual support and automatic mobilization by both countries in the event of either being threatened by the whole or parts of the Triple Alliance of Germany, Austria-Hungary, and Italy.

For one man the implications of the Franco-Russian Alliance now became an obsession: he was General Count Alfred von Schlieffen, who had become Chief of the General Staff in 1891. It has been said of Schlieffen that:

'no soldier has ever stamped his individuality and teaching more strongly upon the Army of which he was the Chief.'[2]

One may go further: Schlieffen stamped his individuality on the course of European history—with fearful effect. It is not necessary to discuss the plan evolved by Schlieffen in great detail; no military plan has ever been subjected to such scrutiny or been the subject of so much argument. Here we need only be concerned with its salient points; it could be said that the whole of the rest of this book, and any other history of the First World War, is the story of the outcome of the Schlieffen Plan.

Two thoughts were fundamental in the evolution of the plan: first, that Russian mobilization would be slower and less efficient than the French; secondly, that the French fortress system designed and carried through by General Séré de Rivières in the 1870s made direct attack on France hazard-

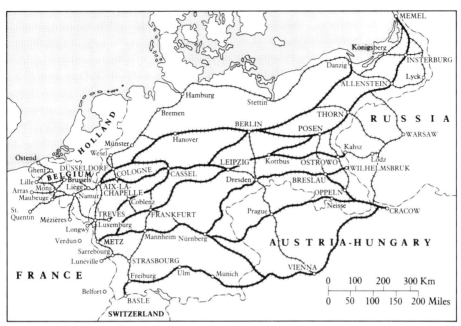

'Interior lines . . . Every main German railway line had a strategic rôle': the main systems, 1914.

ous and uncertain to say the least. From these propositions it followed that France should be attacked and defeated before Russian's masses could take the field; but that the attack on France must be indirect. There were two possibilities, both requiring the infringement of neutrality despite international guarantees to which Germany was signatory: a march through Switzerland or through the Low Countries. The former, given the mountain barrier and the resolution of the Swiss to defend it, was considered but promptly rejected. The latter, in the form of a massive sweep through Belgium (also using the awkward Maastricht Appendix, which is Dutch territory, for deployment) was the only remaining option.

It was the nature of this 'massive sweep' that gave the Schlieffen Plan its distinctive feature: with some 85 per cent of the German Army deployed in the West, leaving only a small fraction (plus the Austrians) to hold off a Russian advance, Schlieffen proposed to mass seven-eighths of that 85 per cent on his right wing for the great sweep, leaving what would amount only to a thin covering screen to face the main body of the French Army on the common frontier. No one has ever challenged the breath-taking boldness of this concept—though many have called it simply foolhardy. It stemmed from two linked ideas which dominated German military thinking at the time: the aim of a 'battle without a tomorrow'—a complete and decisive victory like Cannae in AD 216 or Sedan in 1870—which would be most likely to be achieved by fighting 'on reversed fronts', i.e. by a wide enveloping movement to bring the attack in upon the enemy's rear. This, of course, left one open to a similar riposte; it meant playing for the very highest stakes—the annihilation of one side or the other. But given sufficient strength Schlieffen considered the risk acceptable (and the provision of that sufficiency was one of his main concerns); a French offensive forcing back his weak left wing towards the Rhine could even be turned to Germany's advantage. Such a movement would be:

'like a revolving door—if a man pressed heavily on one side the other side would swing round and strike him in the back.' [3]

Such, then, was the plan as Schlieffen conceived it, and as it was accepted without serious demur by the Emperor, the Government, the General Staff, and the Army's higher command, irrespective of any outside consideration, political, psychological, or moral. According to General Erich Ludendorff, who was head of the vital Deployment Section, 1908–12, and who considered Schlieffen 'one of the greatest soldiers who ever lived', the plan:

'was based on the assumption that France would not respect Belgian neutrality or that Belgium would join France. On this assumption the advance of the German main forces through Belgium followed as a matter of course . . . Nobody believed in Belgium's neutrality.' [4]

This was basic German thinking; when a representative of Schlieffen, in May 1900, informed Baron von Holstein, a senior Foreign Office official, that the General Staff did not intend to be restricted by international agreements, and asked for his views, the reply was:

'If the Chief of the General Staff, particularly such a pre-eminent strategical authority as Schlieffen, considers such a measure imperative, then it is the duty of diplomacy to concur in it and to facilitate it in every possible manner.' [5]

General Sir Frederick Maurice sums up:

'The German plan was in conception bold, simple, and based on a careful abstract study of war. It was at the same time utterly ruthless and immoral in its cold-blooded contempt of national pledges and of the rights of the weak, and was fundamentally defective in its disregard of the psychology both of potential enemies and of possible allies. It was, in fact, a chef d'oeuvre of Prussian militarism naked and unashamed . . .' [6]

Schlieffen retired in 1905 and was succeeded by the younger General Helmuth von Moltke. Moltke has been accused of 'watering down' Schlieffen's concept to the extent of making it virtually unrecognisable. Recent research suggests that this view has been greatly exaggerated, and in fact one of the latest studies[7] pronounces that it was Moltke who, immediately on taking office, initiated 'the first realistic study of the supply and transportation problems of the great Plan.' Here we meet a major internal criticism: 'the logistic side . . . was not properly thought out'; 'Schlieffen does not appear to have come to grips with it at all.' On this analysis, Moltke's changes appear simply as rationalizations of what was from the first a thoroughly unsound logistical proposition; unfortunately for him, any alteration of such an edifice as this, no matter how sensible, was itself liable to cause new problems. The great accusation against Moltke is that he fatally weakened the right wing and allowed the left to assume a false importance. This ignores the fact that by abandoning the intention to cross Dutch territory he economized to the extent of the troops who would have had to face the Dutch Army. Equally, where Schlieffen had proposed to invest Antwerp with five army corps, Moltke used two. The striking wing was thus, if anything, increased; but the difficulty was that, by so narrowing the front of deployment, road congestion became chronic, with marching columns 80 miles long, and inevitable loss of contact between combat units and their logistical support. The contrast between this potentially chaotic situation beyond the railheads, and the scrupulously detailed planning (it has been called 'war by timetable') which brought the mighty German Army to its assembly points is indeed striking.

There was another problem, too, which Schlieffen had left unresolved and which Moltke just had to leave in that condition. As breath-taking as any other part of the great idea was its geographical scope. Schlieffen intended to fling his right wing right across Belgium—his own dramatic phrase was: 'the last grenadier on the right wing should brush the Channel with his sleeve'—before swinging south to encircle the French; then, crossing the Seine *west* of Paris, the German right would turn back eastward in a supreme demonstration of 'the battle of reversed fronts' to destroy the French Army against its own eastern frontier. And all this was to be done in 42 days—the limit of acceptability of the risks being taken on the Eastern Front. For the German *First Army* on the extreme right, a great mass of about a quarter of a million men, the march to the Seine was about 400 miles, and for this Schlieffen allowed 25 days, including days of battle. Clearly, he did not exaggerate when he said that these troops would have to make 'very great exertions'—beyond which he had no further suggestions. All that could be done was to prepare the men to some extent for the ordeal ahead of them. Foreign observers at German prewar manoeuvres had noted with surprise a tendency to overmarch the infantry as though speed was the only consideration:

'The condition of weary blankness to which it reduced the men was accepted as a necessary evil. What mattered was the punctual execution of the programme laid down at all costs.'[8]

In 1914 the reasons duly appeared.

Such, then, was the war plan of the world's most powerful military nation. Its fatal flaws were political and logistical—and they were irredeemable. The only means of correcting the logistical error was by compounding the political; from this there was no escape. Worst of all, however, this plan 'gave the

German strategy a rigidity which no other power possessed.'[9] Schlieffen's demands, even with Moltke's adjustments, placed a shackle not only on German strategy but on German policy:

'For it was only the German plan which involved an attack upon another power (France), whether or not the latter wished to become involved in the war; it was only the German plan which involved the violation of neutral territory simply to satisfy military exigencies; and—most important of all—it was only in the German plan that mobilization meant war.' [10]

With so much against it, what did the Plan have in its favour? Only the quality of the instrument by which it was intended to be carried out.

The German Army, at the turn of the century, was generally acknowledged to be 'the premier fighting force in Europe'.[11] Its last major wars had been triumphant: the overthrow of Austria in ten weeks in 1866 and of France in six months in 1870–71. In the two decades preceding the First World War its strength had been greatly increased and its equipment modernized; nobody seriously doubted the professionalism of its leadership. Its formidable peacetime strength (see p. 21) was based on the liability of every German male between the ages of 17 and 45 to military service. First enrolment was into the *Landsturm* (Home defence militia) at 17; at 20 the young man was called to the colours for two years' service (three in the cavalry and horse artillery) followed by five years in the active Reserve (four for cavalry and horse artillery) then eleven years in the *Landwehr* (territorial Reserve) and finally six years (39–45) in the second *Ban* (levy) of the *Landsturm*. Thus expressed, the military commitment of the male German citizen seems very heavy; however, with a population of some 65 millions in 1914, nothing like the numbers statistically available could be absorbed into the two Services. So we find, in 1911, that out of 1,271,384 men medically examined for service, 705,864 were, for whatever reason—health, business, special circumstances—not taken; this surplus was called *Restanten*. In 1913, although the number taken increased by over 50,000, the *Restanten* still numbered 705,659. The disposal of 20-year-olds in those two years was:

YEAR	AVAILABLE	TAKEN FOR COLOUR SERVICE	POSTED TO RESERVE	RESTANTEN
1911	563,024	106,249	22,821	433,954
1913	587,888	125,001	18,346	444,541

It will be seen that while Imperial Germany was indeed a militarized society, the degree of that militarization can easily be exaggerated.

Clearly, with an army so composed, the decisive factor would be the quality of the training imparted, and that, in turn, would depend on the quality of the leaders, the officers and non-commissioned officers. And equally clearly, that would reflect the social system and viewpoint of Imperial Germany. The Officer Corps did exactly that; its model was Prussia, militarily and politically dominant, but by any other standard in the Europe of 1914, distressingly backward (a twentieth-century Sparta). Prussia, in some important respects, had scarcely emerged from feudalism; in 1860, 65 per cent of officers in the Prussian Army were aristocrats, and the proportion was, if anything, criticized for being too low. By 1913, the proportion of aristocrats in the Imperial German Army had dropped to 30 per cent—but they continued to hold a firm grip on the most important posts and the most influential regiments. In the Prussian regiments, no less than 16 were *exclusively* officered by aristocrats, while well over half had more than 50 per cent aristocratic officers. The Württemberg regiments had a substantially lower proportion of aristocrats, yet even so 57 per cent of their cavalry officers were from that class. In 1909, out of 190 infantry generals in the whole Army, only 39 were non-aristocratic; in 1913 53 per cent of all officers of the rank of colonel and above were aristocratic. Even in the Great General Staff, the 'brain' of the Army, the proportion was 50 per cent. The German Officer Corps, in truth, was at an awkward transitional stage; the expanding size of the Army made it more and more dependent on bourgeois officers, and in the increasingly important technical branches (e.g. the artillery) they heavily predominated.

This was obviously a weakness; Imperial Germany had seen a tremendous burst of national energy, expressing itself in the fields of invention, industry, commerce, and education, and almost entirely owing to the bourgeoisie. The young, energetic, expanding German Navy was very largely officered by bourgeois; between 1899 and 1918, out of 57 admirals and heads of departments, only seven belonged to the nobility, and of these only three to the higher nobility. The Army, which was the epitome of German power, could only suffer by not making similar use of the most forward-looking element in German society; the nation could only suffer from the failure to harness these energies. The effects were what one might suppose: in the short run the German Officer Corps produced a large number of admirable regimental officers—brave, devoted, good trainers of men because in a conscript army with an annual contingent of raw recruits this was an essential and substantial part of an officer's work. The national characteristics of seriousness and industriousness enabled the cleverer of them to become excellent staff officers. The weaknesses began to appear as one approached the top; finding a large number of good commanders is always a difficulty, in any army at any time. Germany profited by making the army corps the basic unit—it was easier to find 25 competent corps commanders than 50 really good divisional commanders. Above that level the difficulties increased, and were compounded by a long-standing cult of individual initiative which had been appropriate under the elder Moltke, with his essentially empirical approach to strategy, but was less so with a plan so rigid and exacting as Schlieffen's. Furthermore, the High Command was inhibited by doctrines which had never been exposed to the test of active service:

'Over the course of years German military authorities had evolved a system of

warfare which recognized that campaigns must be fought in the fog of war. (The Army's) system of strategy therefore consisted of three features: a bold advance, an enveloping attack and full initiative in the commanders of minor units . . . In that type of warfare an energetic offensive replaced accurate information.'[12]

This was the reason for the neglect of the air service which we have noted above (p. 28); aircraft, according to this theory:

'were not needed. The lack of efficient aerial reconnaissance was not alarming. At the best it would only aid the execution of the German plans—and an army which believed itself invincible felt no need of help in that matter.'[13]

The technical invention and scientific progress which had contributed so much to Germany's position as a first-class power were distrusted by the German High Command. The 1913 Army Manual reaffirmed that reconnaissance would be supplied by massed cavalry rather than by airmen, and demanded an increase in the cavalry arm. From top to bottom, command was to be concerned with a relentless offensive at high speed and in great strength; all initiative was bent to that purpose. There was even a school which deprecated signalling as tending to weaken initiative by too-frequent reference back to superior officers. When the test came in August and September 1914, one of its most surprising aspects was the virtual lack of communication between Supreme Headquarters and the Army commanders at critical moments.

It was, however, in the long term that this very serious weakness of the German Officer Corps fully displayed itself. Heavy casualties in the early days of the war made deep inroads into the peace-trained officers; they could only be replaced by increasing commissioning of bourgeois candidates. It is impossible not to connect the breakdown of discipline and decline of quality of the German Army in the war's later stages with the earlier failure to identify the bourgeoisie more securely with officer functions. And worst of all was the spectacle at the top: from beginning to end Germany failed to produce a really first-class military leader of the stature of, say, Joffre or Foch or Haig. The best she could manage was Field-Marshal von Hindenburg, who was already 67 when the war broke out; in the true sense of command—originating and executing strategy—he was only a figurehead; yet he did exert that moral influence which is also an important attribute of command to an extent unmatched by his predecessors, Moltke and Falkenhayn, or by his First Quartermaster-General and famous collaborator, Ludendorff. As might be expected, the Germans produced some very able practitioners of battle—men like Mackensen and Hutier—but none conspicuously more able than the best on the Allied side, such as Pétain, Plumer, or Brusilov.

It is fair to say, then, that the best qualities of the German officers were seen at the intermediate staff levels and in the regiments, and in the latter they enjoyed the support of what was probably the most decisive element in the whole fabric of the Army—a body of some 100,000 non-commissioned officers. They consisted of what the British Army would call Warrant

Officers—*Feldwebels* and *Vizefeldwebels*, who wore swords with an officer's knot—and true NCOs—*sergeants* and *unteroffizers*. These were the men who drilled the annual conscript intake; it was they who maintained the active Reserve at a high level of efficiency; they who guaranteed the professionalism of the whole Army. When war came, they also played a part in battle leadership which surprised the British. It is probably fair to say that, as a nation, Germany was better educated than Britain in 1914, and this would enable the Warrant and non-commissioned officers of the German Army to display more initiative and in general play a more important rôle than their counterparts in the British Citizen Army. Indeed, it could almost be said that the land war was fought by—and against—these 100,000 true professionals. If the German Army was the 'motor' of the war (as I suggest), these were the men who made the motor work. While they were there to repair any damage, it continued to perform remarkably; not until they had been severely reduced did the motor begin to break down.

The characteristics of the 1914 German Army were not difficult to discern: thorough organisation, administered by the General Staff, and over and above that, 'simplicity and strength'[14]—a blunt instrument of great weight for the implementation of German policies. The weight was unquestionable: at the outbreak of war it expressed itself as an active force of:

> 8 Armies (7 in the West, 1 in the East) comprising
> 25 Army Corps (22 in the West, 3 in the East) consisting of
> 50 infantry divisions (44 in the West, 6 in the East) and
> 11 cavalry divisions (10 in the West, 1 in the East).

To this were added:

> 32 Reserve divisions (28 in the West, 4 in the East)
> 7 Ersatz (Supplementary Reserve) divisions (6 in the West, 1 in the East)
> 16 Landwehr Brigades (= 8 divisions; 14 in the West, 2 in the East).

(See Appendix I for composition of formations.)

In obedience to the further doctrine of the 'sudden immediate maximum', all the endeavours of the General Staff were directed towards making this impressive force at once effective. Within its totals were contained two great surprises: first, the presence of Reserve divisions (28 of them, formed into 14 army corps) alongside the active corps in the initial onset. This was what gave the Schlieffen Plan the invaluable surprise element; without this addition it would have been totally impracticable, and no military 'expert' dreamed that the Germans would use their Reserve divisions in this bold manner. The second surprise was the use of heavy artillery in the field; each army corps had a 'Foot Artillery' regiment, generally equipped with howitzers, chiefly the 150 mm. (referred to in British accounts as 5.9 in.) which many competent observers regarded as the outstanding artillery piece of the war. A regiment (2 battalions) comprised 8 batteries, each of 4 guns; the German corps would thus possess 32 of these heavy howitzers. The French at first considered such heavy artillery as totally unsuitable for field use; the British,

'The outstanding artillery piece of the war': the German 150 mm. (5.9 inch) howitzer, whose appearance and performance on the battlefield shocked the Allies.

warned by South African experience, had a battery (4 guns) of the excellent 60-pdr. with each regular division, giving 8 per army corps, which still meant that they were heavily outgunned. The Germans derived great advantage from this superiority, which went far to atone for the deficiencies of their field guns. They had made the mistake of re-equipping their entire field artillery with the 77 mm. breech-loader in 1896—a gun which was probably better than its equivalent in any other army. But in 1897 the French introduced the famous Puteaux 75 mm. quick-firer, which 'heralded a revolution in the design and capabilities of artillery.'[15] The British 18-pdr., introduced in 1905, followed this line; the Germans could only do their best by adapting their 77s, and in this important category were at a disadvantage throughout the war.

Such, briefly, were the qualities and defects of the German Army. It has to be added that it made a very marked impression on all who encountered it. A British regular officer who had that experience paid it this tribute, referring to its dark days in 1916:

'The commanders who had such troops to rely on in days of adversity were fortunate. It was almost impossible to ask or expect of them more than they were ready to give and capable of giving.'[16]

Never did it seem more formidable than in the first period of the war, its seemingly invincible advance in the West in 1914. But its strength was always in its sinews rather than in its head; and in that fact lay its ultimate downfall.

Whatever its faults, it was unquestionably the Army which provided the power-base on which German policies could be founded. In ironic contrast, the sister-Service contributed only to the undermining of German power. At the head of the Imperial German Navy stood the Secretary of State, Grand Admiral von Tirpitz; for all effective purposes, one could say that the Navy was as old as Tirpitz's term of office—he was appointed in 1897. As a student of Admiral Mahan, Tirpitz believed deeply in sea power; he was also convinced that Britain, by the exercise of her undoubted naval supremacy, was determined to prevent Germany from becoming a great world power. In the very month of taking office, Tirpitz stated in a profoundly significant secret memorandum:

'For Germany the most dangerous naval enemy at the present time is England.'[17]

To English eyes this statement appears to turn the true naval situation upside down:

'Sea-power played no part in the making of modern Germany, and was irrelevant to Germany's home defence. It was sought deliberately as an engine of conquest and as the only effective weapon with which Germany could win power abroad and above all dispute British supremacy.'[18]

And that, indeed, was the exact intention of the Navy Law which Tirpitz introduced in 1898, and which marked the beginning of the construction of a German battle fleet. In 1900 Tirpitz justified this policy by his famous—or notorious—'Risk Theory', the basis of which was that a powerful German fleet in home waters would force the British to weaken the naval forces protecting their overseas Empire to a dangerous extent; rather than take this risk, they would seek agreement with Germany on Germany's terms. In short, the German Navy was a weapon of blackmail.

Nowhere was Germany's nervously excited mood (*'Hurra patriotismus'*) more clearly revealed than in the naval enthusiasm which swept the country. The Kaiser, Wilhelm II—'our future lies on the water'—gave the new fleet his warmest personal blessing; a vociferous Navy League promoted it throughout the Empire. Cooler-headed politicians and army leaders might shake their heads—the latter muttering about wasted money and resources—but there was no doubting the approval of the German public for their new showpiece. In 1912 the Chancellor, von Bethmann-Hollweg summed it up:

'The fleet was the favourite child of Germany.'[19]

The Navy Laws followed each other steadily, all pointing the same way. Incredulous at first, the British soon took note; Admiral Fisher launched his famous naval reforms specifically with the German Fleet in mind. Fecklessly, without due consideration, Germany, already faced with the potential

'. . . sleepless nights at the Admiralty and Scapa Flow . . .': a squadron of dreadnoughts of the High Seas Fleet at sea. Thirteen of Germany's 23 battleships were dreadnoughts.

hostility of two great land powers, Russia and France, now added the certain enmity of the world's greatest sea power. In 1904 Britain and France reached their *Entente Cordiale*; in 1907 Anglo-Russian agreement turned the Dual Entente into a Triple Entente. But Tirpitz was undismayed; 'the evil genius of German foreign relations',[20] it was he who ensured that war, when it came, by drawing in the British Empire, would be world war.

As we have seen, Tirpitz was unimpressed by the potential either of the air arm or the underwater weapon. He grudged money spent on airships or submarines that could have gone instead to his favourite battle squadrons. In the High Seas Fleet (the German main fleet) in 1914 there were, besides the flagship *Friedrich der Grosse*, three of these, a total of 23 battleships, of which 13 were dreadnoughts, with three more dreadnoughts just about to join and four more building. In addition there were five battle-cruisers with one about to join and two more building. It was certainly a formidable force, calculated to produce sleepless nights at the Admiralty and at Scapa Flow, where the British Grand Fleet was based. By yet another irony, however, the real harm done to the British by the Imperial Navy would not be the sinking or damage of British battleships by Tirpitz's battle squadrons; it would be the torpedo threat by submarines and light craft which gave the British admirals a permanent sense of insufficiency of protective destroyers—precisely when these craft were most needed for convoy duties. The High Seas Fleet, when it chose to come out of harbour, could bring with it 88 destroyers; a nominal 110 destroyers and flotilla leaders in the Grand Fleet could only offer an *average* of less than 80 at any given moment. This was not the threat that

Tirpitz had planned, but as the naval war reached its grim peak in 1917 and 1918, it was as effective as any of his dreams.

Although, when war came, it was the German Army which gave it its dynamic, and the German Navy which ensured that the conflict would be world-wide, the war itself was not, in origin, a German quarrel. It was Germany's ally, Austria-Hungary, which brought Europe's uneasy peace to an end by her angry reaction to the murder of the heir to the imperial throne by Bosnian terrorists on 28 June. The Austrians blamed Serbia for giving aid and encouragement to the assassins, and on 23 July presented that country with an ultimatum which Serbia found impossible to accept. During the next few days the fatal link between the European system of alliances and the exigencies of Industrial Revolution war was revealed with awful clarity. The quarrel could not be confined: Russia backed Serbia, which meant that, by the terms of the Triple Alliance, Germany must back Austria—but as we have seen, Germany's war plan, on which her whole apparatus of mobilization was based, called for an attack not on Russia, but on France. Britain was now France's ally, with the obligation of coming to her aid; in the Liberal Government of 1914 there were men who, faced now with the precise meaning of policies which they had pursued without understanding for nearly a decade, tried to shy away from this obligation. The German plan allowed them no chance of escape; it was through neutral Belgium that the great mass of the German Army would march to the attack on France, and whatever divisions of opinion might have persisted over helping the French, on defending Belgium the British were substantially united. So the consequences of the murder of an Austrian arch-duke in distant Bosnia followed with absolute precision:

28 July	Austria declared war on Serbia; partial mobilization;
30 July	partial Russian mobilization;
31 July	full mobilization in Austria and Russia;
1 August	full mobilization in Germany and France;
	Austria and Germany declared war on Russia;
3 August	war between Germany and France;
4 August	war between Britain and Germany.

The war of masses had begun; six million men were moving to their appointed positions, most of them by rail; by the time this war was over, some 65 million would have put on uniform.

The rôle of the Austro-Hungarian Army in the war has never received the attention or the credit that it deserves; sarcastic remarks by German staff officers in 1914 about being 'fettered to a corpse' have been treated much too seriously. The truth is that considering its inherent difficulties and virtually insoluble problems, the Austro-Hungarian Army kept the field with amazing stubbornness, great courage, and no little skill until the very end of the war—which was something that no-one with knowledge would have cared to

'The Austro-Hungarian Army kept the field with amazing stubbornness, great courage and no little skill': Austrian infantry, covered by machine-guns, attacking Russian positions near Przemysl.

predict at the outset. The most serious defect of this army was, of course, its racial composition, drawn as it was from all parts of an empire which has often been called 'ramshackle' and which certainly was polyglot. Some 47 per cent of the imperial army was composed of Slavs, of six different ethnic groups: Czechs (15 per cent), Poles (9 per cent), Ruthenes (8 per cent) and Serbo-Croats (7 per cent) predominated. Only 29 per cent of the whole army were true German-speaking Austrians; 18 per cent were Magyars, faithful to the Emperor not as such, but as King of Hungary. Fierce Hungarian nationalism did nothing to improve general efficiency. It was Hungarian antagonism to the Slavs which made certain that the Empire would have to fight on at least two fronts, straining the loyalty of parts of the population to its limits. The Army's final ingredients were Rumanians (5 per cent) and Italians (1 per cent); they, too, would in due course find their allegiance divided. For the whole organism the *lingua franca* had to be German, and all words of command were given in that language; instruction, however, had to be carried out according to the racial composition of each unit. This was a problem which no other metropolitan army in Europe shared.

The fortitude which the Austro-Hungarian Army displayed throughout four and a half years of bitter and often disastrous warfare undoubtedly owed much to its officers. Their composition was far more democratic than that of their German counterparts; the great majority were middle-class or lower middle-class, with a high proportion from families which had for generations followed the military profession. As a result:

'the Austrian Corps of Officers possessed a well-founded reputation for professional knowledge, zeal and devotion, second to no similar body in Europe.'[21]

It was sad that, at the head of this long-suffering, much misjudged force there stood a man who was as obsessed as von Schlieffen, and capable of as much mischief. Of all the senior military figures of the period the only one who palpably deserves to be called a war-monger was General-Field-Marshal Conrad von Hötzendorff, the Austrian Chief of Staff. If Schlieffen was obsessed by the menace of Russia and France, Conrad was devoured by detestation of the Serbs and the Italians. He constantly urged preventive war against both (in 1907 he even wanted to take advantage of the Messina earthquake to crush Italy). Qualified historians have called Conrad 'the best strategist of the war'; strategy, however, like politics, is the 'art of the possible', and Conrad's grandiose offensive schemes appear at times to be very distant from the possible—a fault for which his unfortunate soldiers, and finally the Empire to which he was devoted, had to pay the penalty.

Like the German, the Austro-Hungarian Army was based on the army corps, and its district; the active Army contained 16 corps (33 divisions), and on mobilization backed these with 16 *Landwehr* (Hungarian *Honvéd*) divisions, giving a total of 49 infantry divisions, with 8 regular cavalry divisions backed by 2 *Honvéd* divisions (see Appendix I for composition). The whole Army was recruited by universal military service, as was the German Army, and also like the German Army it only took in a fraction of each annual conscript contingent (shortage of money plagued it at all times). Nevertheless, it could field some 1,800,000 men at the outset. Naturally, with a force so composed, the quality was variable; in general it showed remarkable loyalty to the House of Habsburg.

Its weapons—the infantry's Männlicher rifle and the simple, sturdy Schwarzlose machine-gun—were sound; if the field artillery gun, though efficient, was less good than the French or British versions, that was a fault shared with the Germans. Its very heavy howitzers (305 mm., firing an 858 lb. shell) made an early impression in the West, supporting the German Army in the bombardments of the Belgian forts. The air service, however, was backward by comparison with other great powers; on the main front, in Galicia, only a very small number of aircraft were available out of a total of no more than 42.

Austria-Hungary's strategic problem, like Germany's, was war on two fronts—the dilemma of the interior lines. Given the oppressive and aggressive attitudes of Hungary towards the Slavs; given Field-Marshal Conrad's hatred of Serbia; given also the steady rise of Slav nationalism; given, finally, the provocation of the annexation of the provinces of Bosnia and Herzegovina in 1909, war between the Empire and the kingdom of Serbia was always likely. But certainly after 1909, it was equally likely that such a war would immediately bring hostilities with Russia, the 'protector of the Slavs'. This meant that there would be a southern front on the Danube and an eastern front in Galicia; it was a problem that Conrad entirely failed to solve. Conrad had a half-promise of a German offensive in East Prussia, which might alleviate his Galician difficulty. It could only be half a promise, however, no matter how fervently expressed, since he knew quite well that the bulk of the German Army was going to march against France. He had

hopes of Rumanian support against Russia—but only hopes; he also had
hopes of Bulgarian support against Serbia—but only hopes. Clearly, his one
prospect of success was to strike down his smaller enemy, Serbia, while the
(supposedly) slow-moving Russians were assembling; and with hindsight
(though it was not too difficult to perceive at the time) it is equally clear that it
behoved him to stand on the defensive in the best possible positions in Galicia
until this was done. Instead, he attempted offensives on both fronts, with the
result that a strong army was lost to both: his *Second Army* found itself
imitating General d'Erlon's corps on 16 June 1815, marching all day between
the battles of Ligny and Quatre Bras, and taking part in neither. This
performance has generally been considered the nadir of Napoleonic strategy;
Conrad's in 1914 was equally fatal.

Against either Serbia or Russia, the Imperial Navy had no rôle; its designated enemy was Italy, though ostensibly that country was now Austria's

'*Schlanke* (slim) *Emmas*—a sardonic tribute to one of the stubbiest artillery pieces ever seen':
Austrian artillerymen with a Skoda 305 mm. (12 inch) howitzer.

ally. The Navy was based at Pola, at the head of the Adriatic; it contained 15 battleships, but of these only three were dreadnoughts (with one building) and of the rest only six were really battleworthy. There were two armoured and nine light cruisers, with three more of the latter building. From the Allied point of view in 1914 (especially the French, who had to bring substantial forces across the Mediterranean) the menace lay not so much in these heavier vessels as in the light craft: the 15 destroyers, 58 torpedo boats and six submarines. The possibility of a German squadron using the Pola base was also a disagreeable prospect.

NOTES

1 By the terms of the Treaty of Frankfurt (10 May 1871) France lost the rich provinces of Alsace and Lorraine, with the 'natural' Rhine frontier and the great fortress of Metz. She had to pay what was considered an astronomical indemnity of 5 milliard francs, and submit to a German army of occupation on French soil until this was done.

2 Marshal of the Royal Air Force Sir John Slessor: *The Great Deterrent*, p. 5; Cassell, 1957.

3 B. H. Liddell Hart: *History of the First World War*, pp. 68–9; Cassell, 1970.

4 Ludendorff: *My War Memories*, i p. 25; Hutchinson, 1919.

5 Quoted by Gordon A. Craig: *Germany 1866–1945*, p. 317; Oxford, 1978.

6 Maurice: *Forty Days in 1914*, p. 16; Constable, 1919.

7 Martin van Creveld: *Supplying War: Logistics from Wallenstein to Patton*, p. 119; Cambridge University Press, 1977.

8 *The Times History of the War*, i p. 226; *The Times*, 1915.

9 Paul Kennedy: *The War Plans of the Great Powers 1880–1914*, p. 10; Allen & Unwin, 1979.

10 Ibid., pp. 15–16.

11 David Woodward: *Armies of the World 1854–1914*, p. 33; Sidgwick & Jackson, 1978.

12 John R. Cuneo: *Winged Mars: The German Air Weapon 1870–1914*, i p. 132; The Military Service Publishing Company, Harrisburg, Pa., 1942.

13 Ibid.

14 *Times History of the War*, i p. 226.

15 Curt Johnson: *Artillery*, p. 50; Octopus Books, 1975.

16 Captain Cyril Falls: *The First World War*, p. 200; Longmans, 1960.

17 Quoted in full in *Yesterday's Deterrent* by Jonathan Steinberg, p. 209; Macdonald, 1965.

18 *Times History of the War*, i p. 55.

19 Quoted by Lord Haldane: *Before the War*, p. 117; Cassell, 1920.

20 Craig, op. cit. p. 310.

21 *Times History of the War*, ii p. 222.

Exterior Lines

WHATEVER DIFFICULTIES GEOGRAPHY and other circumstances might inflict upon them, the Central Powers did always have the inestimable advantage of being central—of operating on the interior lines. Time after time this would enable them to strike telling blows or avert seemingly imminent disaster. The Entente Powers enjoyed no such advantage; they were ranged along the exterior lines, geographically divided from each other by great distances and formidable barriers. As a consequence, throughout the war, their strategy remained individual and incoherent. For some, this was to prove fatal; the first of these was Serbia, that small country whose very existence many Austrians and Hungarians looked upon as an affront and a threat. This quarrel was the trigger of the war itself, and not surprisingly Serbia was the scene of the earliest action; what did surprise enemies and friends alike, however, was the brilliant success with which she managed the opening rounds.

Of all the war's cloudy areas, Serbia's part is one of the most heavily veiled. The reasons (and the same would apply to the Eastern Front) are not difficult to perceive: Austria-Hungary disintegrated at the end of the war, which meant that her side of the story remained very incomplete; Serbia was overwhelmed and overrun in 1915, with severe loss of records, and after the war she was swallowed up in the new Yugoslavia where it was not always politic to encourage Serbian vainglory. All that can safely be said about the country in 1914 is that every statement must be half speculative, and that nothing can be taken as exact.

Even the size of the Serbian Army is a matter of considerable doubt. Every male Serb was liable for military service, but economy limited the numbers taken; estimates of the Army's real strength vary from 180–200,000 up to half a million. Its organization is equally uncertain: one authority affirms that it consisted of four 'armies', regionally based, each containing four divisions with supporting arms, making, he says 'a grand total of 292,000 men.'[1] This organization, he claims, was complete by July 1914, and the armies fully equipped. A second authority divides the country into five divisional districts, each providing one regular and one Second Ban (reserve) division, with an independent cavalry division. His 'conservative estimate' of the strength of the regular army is about 130,000; admitting that 'it is not easy to estimate the numbers of the Serbian Army with any confidence', he finally concludes that 'a high but not impossible figure for its active first line would be 250,000 men.'[2]

Amid such large discrepancies it is evidently only possible to make a few broad statements with any assurance. First, it has to be remembered that Serbia had been at war in 1912 against the Turks, and in 1913 against the Bulgarians. The Serbs had been victorious on both occasions, which not only raised their national morale to a high level, but also provided them with a substantial proportion of experienced officers and soldiers; indeed, *The*

Times historian goes so far as to say that they were 'beyond question the most experienced of all the armies in the field.' Patriotic emotion, always a powerful force, was strengthened by the tide of Slav nationalism flowing through Eastern Europe at that time; all these elements combined to make the Serbs hard enemies to beat. On the other hand, 'the army was emphatically the army of a poor State.'[3] Its field artillery was armed with French 75 mm. quick-firers which did good service, but there was always a shortage of ammunition; Creuzot supplied useful mountain batteries and some heavy artillery, but not much. The first-line infantry carried modern Männlicher and Mauser rifles, but the equipment of the reserves was much inferior. Even the first-line suffered from a shortage of rifles on mobilization, with cases of regiments nominally 4,000 strong only able to arm 2,600 men, the remainder having to wait to take the weapons of fallen comrades. Nor did it help to have four types of rifle on issue. In all material respects the Serbian Army was seriously weak; 'its sanitary service in particular was painfully inadequate.'[3]

Worst of all was Serbia's strategic position, which was, quite simply, impossible. To begin with, the country was entirely land-locked; secondly, it contained only two main-line railways, both single-track—the Orient Express to Constantinople via Belgrade and Nish, and the branch line from Nish to Salonika (see p. 25); thirdly, it faced potentially hostile neighbours on its western, northern, and Eastern frontiers. The capital itself, Belgrade, epitomized the predicament of the whole state; it stood right on the frontier, at the junction of the rivers Danube and Sava. Looking across their waters the Serbs saw on the farther bank the territory of their most implacable foe, Hungary. To the west, across the Drina, stood Bosnia, annexed to the Habsburg Empire in 1909; to the east, behind a long frontier, was Bulgaria, smarting with the memory of defeat in 1913 and only prevented now from joining in the attack by fear of what Rumania might do. Against such a combination of enemies, courage, determination, patriotism, experience, mountain ranges, could not give indefinite protection. Serbia could have no strategy but hope: hope that the Russians would draw off enough of the Austro-Hungarian Army to make the rest a feasible opponent; hope that fear of Rumania and Allied diplomatic pressure would deter Bulgaria; hope that Germany would be too preoccupied to intervene. It all seemed rather far-fetched but, amazingly, for over a year these hopes were fulfilled, and this fulfilment, plus their own ferocious fighting ability, saved the Serbs for a time.

'Russia,' wrote Winston Churchill, 'is a riddle wrapped in a mystery inside an enigma.' He was referring to Soviet policy in 1939, which was, indeed, enigmatic. Imperial Russian policy in 1914 was superficially much clearer: it was determined by the Franco-Russian Treaty of 1894, with its military clauses, which we have noted on p. 44. Beyond that, however, and in the all-important area of implementation above all, we find ourselves again in the presence of riddles and enigmas, which nearly seven decades of dogma have rendered virtually insoluble.

We know that Imperial Russia collapsed in 1917; we know that between August 1914 and March 1917 Russia endured heavy defeats and suffered great casualties. It is natural and normal to connect the two very directly; to regard Imperial Russia as virtually on the point of collapse when she entered the war, and all that followed as an inevitable consequence. Informed studies suggest that this is not so; that the Russian Empire possessed greater economic and military strength than is normally supposed, and in fact squandered substantial assets not through backwardness in the economy or disaffection, but chiefly through simple inefficiency in administration.

Only nine years before the First World War Russia had been rocked by humiliating military defeat at the hands of Japan and revolution at home. The autocracy—'that peculiar apparatus of government for government's sake which nailed Russia into the coffin of her past'[4]—was forced to yield some political reforms. These were accompanied by what the most recent historian of Russia's war calls 'a period of unexampled economic growth'; he continues:

'After 1906, the country moved out of the depression that had bankrupted much of its industry at the turn of the century. Years of government railway construction and foreign investment began to pay off, as new markets, new sources of raw materials and labour, could be tapped. A series of good harvests, combined with high prices for grain—Russia's principal export—gave prosperity to the country as a whole . . . The new prosperity even enabled Russia to reduce her dependence on foreign capital. Foreigners lent much the same—indeed rather more—in terms of quantity, but their share of Russia's capital formation declined from one half in 1904–05 to one eighth just before the First World War . . .'[5]

It would have been surprising indeed if none of this activity had been reflected in military matters. The truth would seem to be that the whole period of 1908–1914, as well as being one of naval reconstruction (after the Tsushima disaster), was one of Army reform. It was in 1908 that General V. A. Sukhomlinov became Minister of War; he is firmly lodged in the demonology of World War I, a symbol of incompetence and corruption, 'a sort of uniformed Rasputin'.[6] Recent study suggests that Sukhomlinov was, in fact, a promoter of necessary reforms—increased use of reserve formations, more flexible field artillery organization, less reliance on fortresses, promotion of lower-class officers—though in such a system as Russia's any large change in an institution like the Army was bound to be slow, resisted by vested interest at every turn. Sukhomlinov, a 60-year-old ex-cavalryman, was himself part of the system; he would be no whirlwind. Yet the impression of action and change is strong, and nowhere more clearly indicated than in the steady increase of defence expenditure: 565 million roubles for both services in the annual budget for 1909–10, 581 million roubles for the Army alone in the budget for 1913–14, and 826 for the two services together. Altogether, the annual budgets of 1909–14 amount to an expenditure of 3,311 million roubles—and in addition there were substantial special grants: 700 million roubles (half each to Army and Navy) arranged in 1908–09, 800 million for the Navy in 1913, and another 432 million for the Army in 1914. Even accepting the drag of bureaucratic inefficiency and the fact that money bought less in the way of military supplies in Russia than elsewhere, it is clear that *something* was going on.

Certainly, the party most intimately concerned was impressed. France understood quite well that she would have to bear the brunt of a German onset at the opening of a war, and that therefore the relief that her Russian allies could bring her might determine her very survival. General Joffre, the Chief of Staff, visited Russia in 1913 and pronounced himself pleased with the growing efficiency of the Russian Army. The Franco-Russian Military Convention reached its final form in September of that year; the Russian Chief of Staff, Jilinski, promised that Russia would deploy an army of at least 800,000 men on the German frontier on the fifteenth day of mobilization. This was a handsome pledge; concealed behind it, however, was the chronic division of responsibility between the General Staff and the Ministry of War, and the lack of a strong figure to insist on a unified plan. Faced with two enemies, the Russian High Command fell between two stools; the concentration against Germany would simultaneously be accompanied by a concentration against Austria-Hungary. And for such a double task even the 'steam-roller' of the Russian Army was not strong enough.

It was, however, undoubtedly strong. In Imperial Russia the entire male population, regardless of rank, was legally liable for military service, but clearly with a total of over 160 millions, it was out of the question even to attempt to call up the whole annual levy. There were very numerous exemptions, which nevertheless permitted a peace strength of some 50,000 officers and 1,200,000 men. General mobilization in July 1914 produced a total of about 4,100,000. For war purposes this large number of men produced an army of some 114 infantry divisions and 36 cavalry divisions (see Appendix II for composition), by far the largest in the world. Numbers are not everything, but in the wars of the First Industrial Revolution they counted for much; it would clearly require some remarkable combinations of circumstances to make the Russian Army anything less than a very formidable foe. Russia, however, has a way of throwing up remarkable circumstances.

Responsibility for the quality of an army lies squarely upon its officers; in the very uneven quality of the Russian Officer Corps we may discover a large reason for the misfortunes that befell it. The truth is that the Officer Corps reflected the autocracy that it served and was shaped by it. It was not, like the German, an aristocratic body; in the decade before the war about two-fifths of officers below the rank of colonel were of peasant or lower middle-class origin; 'a great many more were only one generation removed from such origins.'[7] At the Alexis Military School in Moscow, whereas in the period 1864–69 81 per cent of cadets had been of noble parentage, by 1912–13 this proportion had dropped to 9 per cent; 5 per cent children of peasants in 1888–89 had risen to 19 per cent. The nobles kept their grip on the Guards, the cavalry and the higher ranks, but they had to struggle for it; the Officer

'The new Russian 76.2 mm. quick-firing gun was an excellent weapon': part of a field battery sited in a farm. As long as they had shells the Russian gunners gave a good account of themselves.

Corps was by no means a unified caste—on the contrary it was divided between 'patricians' and 'praetorians', which was no doubt convenient for the autocracy, but a fertile breeding-ground of personal dislikes and professional rivalries.

In the aftermath of the Russo-Japanese War there were clearly many lessons to be learned; unfortunately, there was no consensus on what these were, nor was there any strong guideline offered by the General Staff. The artillery was the crack arm of the Imperial Army, and the artillerists stood out against all reforming pressures in defence of theories that cost Russia dear. They clung to 8-gun field batteries when the advent of quick-firers taught other armies that 6- and even 4-gun batteries were now more effective. The new Russian 76.2 mm. quick-firing gun was an excellent weapon (better than the German 77 mm.) whose potential was not grasped by its users. The senior artillerists parted company with infantrymen on the matter of field howitzers (where the Germans had a decided advantage, as we have seen). They considered that artillery had far more important tasks than helping infantry to advance by means of high-trajectory fire; in consequence the Russian Army went to war with only 240 field howitzers—a ludicrous number. But this did not mean that Russia was short of heavy guns; it only meant that its strategy, and in particular its artillery policy, was guided by fortress-mania. The Russian fortresses contained no fewer than 2,813 modern heavy guns and some 3,000 of older vintage. Vast mountains of shells were piled up for these guns inside the fortresses (some 2 million were captured by the Germans in 1915) while the field artillery had to make do with a shell reserve per gun half that of the French and a third of the German.

It is impossible not to admire the Russian soldiers—and sympathize with them. The overwhelming majority were peasants, mostly illiterate; the long centuries of serfdom (only ended in 1861) had left their legacy of superstitious credulity and total lack of initiative (attributes shared by too many officers, especially in the lower ranks). As with all armies, tradition had much influence, sometimes to their advantage, sometimes not; a Russian tradition, curious to Western eyes, was that the infantry carried bayonets always fixed—the scabbards were left behind on active service. The reason for this was a saying of the famous Marshal Suvorov (who died in 1800): 'The bullet misses, the bayonet doesn't. The bullet's an idiot, the bayonet's a fine chap.' Many a peasant soldier was going to die, demonstrating that times had changed since the days of Marshal Suvorov.

There was a credit side: used to low standards of living, the Russian soldiers displayed amazing endurance. The reverse side of the lack of initiative—which often took on the look of sheer indifference—was a happy-go-lucky cheerfulness which sustained them in adversity. The majority, too, were upheld by deep religious feelings, by a powerful patriotic love of 'Mother Russia', and reverence for the Tsar, the 'Little Father'. As they had shown against Napoleon, and would show again between 1941–45, they had wonderful powers of recuperation:

'They might seem to be fought to a finish, hammered to a jelly. While the pressure was maintained they showed no signs of recovery, but if they were afforded half a chance through its slackening they were ready to batter away once more.'[8]

The ultimate enigma lay in the equation between these virtues (and the high skills displayed by some generals) on the one hand, and the dead hand of bureaucracy plus the insipid incompetence of the autocratic system on the other; how long could they balance each other out?[9]

For war purposes, Russia's dependence was entirely on the Army. Smashed to pieces by the Japanese in 1905, the Imperial Navy was only at the beginning of its recovery programme in 1913. It did possess a few modern ships—four dreadnoughts and one exceptionally heavily armoured cruiser in the Baltic—but most of its vessels were old if not obsolescent. Division between the Baltic and the Black Sea was a further weakening factor. The Navy's rôle could only be negative—the retention of a certain proportion of the German Navy in the Baltic instead of the North Sea. This aid to the Royal Navy was not to be despised, and soon, as we shall see, the Russian Navy made one further very significant contribution.

Russia had promised 800,000 men against Germany on the fifteenth day of mobilization; for her part, France promised to commence offensive operations on the eleventh day, with practically her entire army. Since France was generally considered (certainly by Germany) to be a first-class military power, this clearly implied the deployment of very considerable strength. And as it turned out, it would be the French Army which, for two sacrificial years, engaged virtually single-handed the main body of the German Army —the 'motor' of the war.

At the heart of France's military position in 1914, and constituting her fundamental problem, was that puzzling circumstance referred to on p. 7: the falling birth-rate. A comparative table vividly illustrates the significance of this in relation to Europe's most serious potential source of conflict:

YEAR	FRANCE (MILLIONS)	GERMANY
1875	36.9	42.7
1880	37.7	45.2
1890	38.3	49.4
1900	38.9	56.3
1910	39.6	64.9

It will be appreciated from almost all that has gone before that in the age of the Industrial Revolutions, waging war was not simply a matter of mass armies; there was also to be considered the mass production which would support them, and in the first half of the century this depended very much upon a mass work-force. Germany's advantage was thus twofold.

By 1905 the situation was already palpably serious; it was reckoned that peace-time army strengths gave Germany a superiority of over 100,000, which reserves would make even greater. Since 1871 France had in theory been subject to universal (male) military service, but successive laws had been lightly enforced; the 'Two-Year Law' of 1905 was very different. This sought to restore some sort of equality with Germany by placing on the French people a heavier military burden than that borne by any other European power. Service with the colours was reduced to two years, but service in the Reserve was increased to 11 years, followed by six in the Territorial Army, and then six in the Territorial Reserve. But the feature of this Law, what gave it its almost penal weight, was that there were no exemptions except on grounds of physical unfitness. By these means a peacetime army of 500,000 was aimed at, with reserves amounting to some 4 million men. Attempts were made by various means to mitigate the hardships involved, but clearly Alfred de Vigny's phrase, '*servitude militaire*', now had a meaning in France that it possessed nowhere else.[10] As the *Times History* says:

'*Thus did the need for self-preservation at last compel the French people to accept a system in which "military service was equal for all", and so to fulfil the principle of the law of March 4, 1791, that "the service of the Fatherland is a civic and general duty."*'

Yet even this was not enough; in 1912 substantial additions were made to the German Army, and now the calculation was that France's 567,000 peace effectives would be faced by 870,000. A new Army Bill was brought in in 1913: the 'Three-Year Law'. Now every Frenchman fit for service had to spend three years in the Active Army, 11 in the Reserve, then seven each in the Territorial and Territorial Reserve. As a palliative—some would say very

'The colourful regiments which had made much appeal since the Crimean War': these
Zouaves were photographed on manoeuvres in 1911. War was less kind to such panoply.

slight—service with the colours would now begin at 20 instead of 21, to
minimize disruption of a young man's future career. By these means France
added another 100,000 men to her Active Army and gave herself a total of
fully 4 million trained men. But this Law, as the Military Correspondent of
The Times percipiently remarked, 'was France's last card'.

The result of this painful effort was that when war came France was able to
field 61 infantry divisions (see Appendix II for composition) in the European
theatre—shortly increased by one more from North Africa. Of this total, 43
were Active divisions, four were Colonial or Moroccan, and 14 were Reserve
divisions. In the Colonial forces were to be found the colourful regiments
which had made much appeal to the general public since the Crimean War:
the Zouaves, four crack regiments (each of five battalions) of Frenchmen in
(basically) Turkish uniform, four regiments of 'Turcos' (*Tirailleurs
Algériens*) each of six battalions recruited from native Algerians, and also
wearing Turkish uniform, the *Légion Étrangère*, formed in 1831 and already
the most famous regiment in the world, *Chasseurs d'Afrique*, light cavalry
raised for North African service, *Spahis*, Arab light cavalry in long flowing
cloaks. In addition there was a division of Moroccans and some Senegalese
riflemen; in general, however, France drew very little on the manpower
reserves of her overseas empire in 1914—only in 1916, after two years of
murderous loss, did she turn to her colonies for large-scale support. Against

this background it is not difficult to estimate the importance she attached to the Russian alliance, the 'steamroller' at the far extremity of the exterior lines.

Naturally, as with any large organization, the quality of this army was variable; yet by and large, it is fair to say that France had possessed no such instrument of war since the heyday of Napoleon's Grand Army, 1805–12. Hindsight knowledge of the tragic destiny of the army of 1914 makes it difficult to assess objectively. Its image is deceptive: the cavalry (89 regiments) with cuirassiers and dragoons who looked as though they had come straight from the Battle of Waterloo, the infantry of the line in red *képis* and red trousers, looking almost exactly as it had looked in the Crimea and in 1870, the endless horse transport which blocked the roads behind the armies. A British officer wrote:

'*The aspect of the French infantry straggling forward anyhow had profoundly shocked me when I first saw the long columns sprawling all over the road, no two men in step, the capotes unbuttoned, looking much more like a mob than like disciplined men, but it quickly became apparent that although this infantry was not smart to look at, it got there all the same, and that the lack of polish was due more to badly fitting uniforms than to anything else. The French soldier, we were soon to learn, had lost nothing of the wonderful marching powers which had proved so disturbing to us in the days of the Peninsular War.*'[11]

The large majority of the French soldiers were peasants, sturdily built, hardy and strong, with powers of physical endurance which surprised friend and foe alike. They carried the long Lebel rifle, the first true magazine rifle at the time of its invention in 1886, but now outclassed by both German and British types. The cavalry firearm was a short carbine generally regarded by foreign observers (particularly British cavalrymen) as quite useless. In 1914 the French took into battle 2,500 machine-guns (2 per battalion); the Germans had 4,500.

The wonder-weapon of the French Army ('God the Father, God the Son and God the Holy Ghost' to its devotees) was the 75 mm. Puteaux field gun referred to on p. 52. Introduced in 1897, it was the first modern quick-firing gun, thanks to a recoil mechanism which was in fact the invention of a Krupp engineer, but had been rejected by Krupps and the German artillery authorities as 'impracticable for use in the field'—with the results that we have seen. The '75' was a trim, workmanlike, easily manoeuvrable gun (it weighed 2,513 lb.) throwing a 12 lb. high explosive shell or a 16 lb. shrapnel shell to a maximum distance of 7,500 yards. It could attain, in the hands of a well-trained crew, a maximum rate of fire of 25 rounds per minute—the '*rafale*' which French gunners were convinced would dominate the battle-fields of the future. There is little doubt that in 1914 the '75' was the best field gun in the world, and the French Army possessed 3,800 of them. Unfortunately, thanks to exaggerated doctrines carried to the point of absurdity, it possessed little else.

'God the Father, God the Son and God the Holy Ghost': the admirable Puteaux 75 mm. field gun with which French artillerists hoped to dominate the 1914 battlefields.

We have already noted the astonishing lack of howitzers and heavy field artillery in the Russian Army; the French Army was scarcely any better off. Marshal Joffre records how, from 1910 onwards in his capacity as Director of the Services of the Rear and later as Chief of Staff (Commander-in-Chief designate), he tried to remedy this lack. Manoeuvres revealed the limitations of the '75' in any kind of enclosed or hilly country: it was incapable of high-angle fire to search 'dead ground'. It was known that the Germans had introduced an effective 105 mm. field howitzer for just this purpose, in addition to the admirable heavy 150 mm. Joffre pressed for urgent action to remedy the French deficiency, but he made little headway against bureaucratic inertia and the stubbornness of an artillery priesthood as bigoted as the Russian. The Schneider Company submitted a 105 mm. howitzer in 1912, whose tests were quite satisfactory; credits for manufacture were blocked by the '75 mm. lobby'. An adaptation permitting the '75' to be elevated for higher trajectory was adopted instead, although this meant reduced range and a lighter projectile than the German. A 120 mm. howitzer which would to some extent counter the German 150 mm. was sanctioned in February 1914, and trials were carried out in July—the war was less than a month off, and 'found the French without a field howitzer.'[12] As for heavy guns, the French had only 104 Rimailho 155 mm. and about 170 Baquet 120 mm., now thirty years old; the Germans could put a total of 848 heavy guns into the field.

Such were the serious drawbacks of the French Army of 1914; they would require the utmost that the regimental officers and soldiers of all arms could offer in the way of courage and endurance, the utmost that commanders could summon up of moral resolution and intellectual adaptability, if they were to be overcome. And they all stemmed from the same deadly source: a false doctrine of war. It is not difficult to understand how that doctrine arose. The defeats of 1870 and 1871 had been deeply humiliating and nation and Army were at one in the determination that they should never be repeated. Analysing that disastrous experience, military theorists concluded that France had been beaten because she had departed from the true principles of war evolved by Napoleon: instead of always and immediately seizing the initiative in the Napoleonic manner, she had stood on the defensive, permitting the Prussians to develop their operations as they wished. The remedy was clear: to return to the tradition of the Revolution and of Napoleon—the headlong offensive to throw the enemy off balance from the very beginning, and hammer him into submission.

The chief apostle of this doctrine was Colonel Ferdinand Foch, who from 1895 to 1900 was Instructor and Chief Instructor at the *École Supérieure de Guerre*. 'The decisive attack,' said Foch, 'is the supreme argument of the modern battle.' With all his considerable teaching gifts, Foch inculcated the offensive spirit, and his influence was enormous:

'During Foch's six years at the Ecole de Guerre . . . more than 400 French officers passed through his hands. Assuming their average age to be 35, on the outbreak of war in 1914 the majority of them would be commanding divisions or brigades or holding senior posts. There is little doubt, therefore, that his doctrine of pursuing a vigorous offensive under all circumstances was largely responsible for the grievous casualties suffered by the French infantry in the opening battles of 1914.' [13]

When Foch's favourite pupil, Colonel de Grandmaison, became head of the *Troisième* (Operations) *Bureau* in 1908, the headlong offensive was formally written into the French war plan. In the preamble to the notorious Plan XVII, under the subheading, 'Intentions of the Commander-in-Chief', we find the sentence which for tens of thousands of men spelt death:

'Whatever the circumstances, it is the C.-in-C.'s intention to advance, all forces united, to the attack on the German armies.'

It was because of this—the worship of the *offensive à l'outrance* as preached by Foch and Grandmaison—that the French cavalry did not carry a useful firearm; it had no time for dismounted work; it was trained for the immediate charge. For the same reason the infantry was taught to avoid long-range fire and premature deployment into open firing-line formations:

'The final assault was to be delivered in mass upon the decisive point; rapidity and the bayonet rather than fire effect being relied on in this last phase of an action.' [14]

The use of cover was virtually ignored; entrenching was heresy—'the idea of a stationary defensive was not admitted.'[15] Progress in war technology was brushed aside; machine-guns, said the Inspector-General of Infantry, 'will not make the slightest difference to anything.' It was the spirit of the offensive which caused the lack of heavy artillery: 'Thank God we have none,' said a General Staff representative to a Parliamentary commission. 'The strength of the French Army is in the lightness of its guns.' When Joffre (himself a prisoner of the doctrine) tried to obtain some trench mortars— which the Germans were known to have—at the last moment in 1914, he was refused. The decline of the Air Service in 1912 and 1913 which we have noted (p. 30) was also a direct result of the doctrine; in the French Service Regulations of 1913 it was laid down that

'Information often comes too late; it is nearly always inadequate and is often contradictory. Hence, it is only by keeping firmly to the main lines of his plan, that a commander can carry out his task and impose his will on the enemy.'

As Mr. John Cuneo remarks, such a system of war 'which practically advocated a blind offensive, was not one under which aeronautics would flourish.'[16] Nor did they.

And finally, in the realm of strategy, the doctrine of the headlong offensive played straight into Germany's hands. If anything could remedy the grave defects of the Schlieffen Plan, it was this extraordinary embrace of lunacy by the French. It needed precisely this to provide the push on the revolving door of Liddell Hart's simile (see p. 46) which would give the Germans their desired 'battle on reversed fronts'. Plan XVII crowded the French armies in a dense mass on the common frontier; anyone who suggested that the Germans might intend to march in great strength through Belgium and so outflank the whole French array was laughed to scorn. Joffre's predecessor, Michel, was sure that this was what would happen; he was removed. Foch himself warned Joffre in 1911 'remember this, you will have to deal with 35 corps, with their right flank on the sea.' Joffre was an Engineer; he did not presume to argue with the Foch-educated strategists of the Operations Bureau. The Second (Intelligence) Bureau, discredited by the scandals of the Dreyfus Case, could offer him no guidance. The warning fell on deaf ears. Not until the very eve of war, 2 August, was any amendment at all made to Plan XVII. So the French marched to a catastrophe of their own making; nothing illustrates the high intrinsic quality of their 1914 Army better than the fact that it was able to survive and rise above this lethal dogma.

For France, like Germany, Austria-Hungary, and Russia, the pillar of defence was the Army; but unlike the other great continental powers, for over three centuries France had possessed an overseas empire, founded like all such on naval power. In the seventeenth and eighteenth centuries France had looked out from her Atlantic naval bases, Brest, Lorient, Rochefort, towards her vast possessions in the New World: Canada, Louisiana, and her Caribbean islands. In the nineteenth century she built a new empire in North and Central Africa; the Mediterranean crossing became a vital concern, and the key base was Toulon.

During the whole of this time (and until 1904) France's chief imperial and naval rival was Britain; the end of this rivalry was like the breaking of a mainspring. And with expansion of the Army placing heavy financial burdens on the nation, what was the argument now for naval spending? What use were battleships and commerce raiders against Vienna and Berlin? By 1914 France had dropped to fifth place among naval powers, overtaken by Germany, the United States and Japan. It would nevertheless be quite wrong to say that the rôle of the French Navy in the war was negligible: its concentration in the Mediterranean, as well as giving direct support to the Gallipoli landings in 1915, enabled the Royal Navy to concentrate in the North Sea and the Atlantic—a contribution for which it would be grateful.

In 1914 the French Navy had an effective strength of 23 battleships, 10 of them dreadnoughts, of which four were armed with twelve 12 in. guns (10-gun broadsides), a battery matching that of the latest German battleships. France had no battlecruisers, but 16 of her 24 cruisers were large vessels of over 8,000 tons, some carrying as many as fourteen 7.6 in. guns. In addition there were eight light cruisers, now obsolescent, 80 destroyers, many of them of modern construction and capable of speeds of 28–35 knots, 140 torpedoboats, and 50 submarines, all modern, the latest fitted with ten torpedo tubes.

The predestined victim of the Schlieffen Plan was Belgium. By the Treaty of London (1839) 'perpetual neutrality' had been imposed on Belgium by the agreement of five powers: Austria, Russia, Prussia, France, and Britain. (This was the treaty which the German Chancellor referred to in 1914 as 'a scrap of paper'.) Neutrality, for three quarters of a century, had been the dominant theme of Belgian policy, 'and a very great curse it was',[17] giving Belgians a sense of false security, preventing military agreements, even with neighbouring Holland, and leading politicians and people to regard defence as a waste of time and money. No soldier, not even Belgian, doubted that in the event of a major war the great highway of the Meuse valley would have the strategic significance that it had always had, and would have to be defended; but only in the last five years before the war did any substantial number of Belgians begin to appreciate that neutrality and independence might not be at all the same thing—indeed, that they might conflict with one another.

Until 1909 the Belgian Army, although ostensibly based on a limited form of conscription, was in fact a quasi-volunteer force, largely made up of substitute-conscripts and voluntarily re-enlisted men. Its peace strength was about 43,000 and its war strength potentially 130,000. In 1909 a new Army Bill at last established the principle of a national army, and the war strength potential rose to 210,000. All these figures, however, are to a certain extent misleading; Belgium placed her trust, for over thirty years, not in her field army but in her fortifications. Inspired by the genius of a distinguished Engineer, Brialmont, she had developed three major fortified areas: barrier systems (*forts d'arrêt*) at Liège (six large forts and six smaller ones) and Namur (four large and five small) and a great national 'keep' at Antwerp, whose latest additions were only completed in 1913. In that year, too, international tensions, and alarm at the progress of modern artillery, prompted a new Army scheme which laid down that on mobilization its strength should be:

Field Army	150,000
Antwerp garrison	90,000
Liège garrison	22,500
Namur garrison	17,500
Reserves	60,000
	340,000

At the outbreak of war this scheme had been in existence for only a year and a half, so the Belgian Army, like others, was caught in transition. Its Field Army was organized in six infantry divisions and a cavalry division (see Appendix II for composition). The field artillery was equipped with a Krupp quick-firer, less good than the French, Russian, and British models, but superior to the German; it possessed field howitzers, but of an old pattern. The fortress artillery was in process of modernization. The infantry weapon was a .301 in. Mauser of 1899 vintage; three types of machine-gun were in use, including the 'Berthier', a light gun often transported on a two-wheel cart drawn by dogs. Uniforms were old-fashioned and conspicuous—none more strange than those of the *Garde Civique*, an anachronistic survival of the citizen bands which had risen against the Dutch in 1830. This force num-

'Uniforms were old-fashioned and conspicuous': this very posed picture purports to show action during the retreat to Antwerp, but only underlines Belgian helplessness in the new warfare.

bered some 90,000; it did not come under War Department jurisdiction, but under the Ministry of Home Affairs. The German invaders in 1914 served notice that they would not consider the *Garde Civique* as a properly consti- tuted military force, but as irregulars, liable to be shot if caught.

Such was the Belgian Army, as it faced invasion in 1914: in the eyes of most informed observers, an instrument of doubtful worth. The country's sharp racial division, between French-speaking Walloons in the East and the Flemish-speakers of the Western provinces was another source of weakness which Germany could be depended on to try to exploit.

At Queen Victoria's Diamond Jubilee Review at Spithead in June 1897, the Royal Navy made

'. . . the greatest display of naval force the world had ever seen. It was more than a mere review or ceremonial pageant; it was a demonstration to the world of Britain's sea power as 165 modern fighting ships of all classes, the flower of the Royal Navy, passed in review before the Queen and her distinguished foreign visitors. There were thirty miles of ships in five lines, each over five miles in length. Not a single post abroad had been weakened to make the strong show at Spithead. Only the modern units in home waters were used.' [18]

In the years that followed the Diamond Jubilee Britain suffered shocks and scares about the condition of the Navy in relation to the new threat which had come into being across the North Sea. The 'Two-Power Standard' on which it had prided itself was allowed quietly to fade out of sight. The new technology—above all the quick maturing of the submarine, and the development of aircraft—threw many long-accepted beliefs into doubt. Yet the fact remains that the fleet which faced Germany in 1914 was incompar- ably stronger than the one which had amazed the world at Spithead seven- teen years earlier. And this was, almost entirely, the work of one man.

It was John Arbuthnot Fisher (1841–1920) who took hold of a navy grown complacent, running to fat and with much of its higher-level thinking in corsets of habit and tradition, who made it look squarely at its new enemy and consider what might be required to beat him. From Trafalgar Day, 1904, until January 1910, Fisher was First Sea Lord, and during that time accomplished a series of sweeping naval reforms without which it is hard to see how the Royal Navy could have coped with the First World War. It goes without saying that he made mistakes—some serious—and roused a lot of wrath. His career ended sadly; but during those six years of tearing, search- ing energy he had transformed an imposing Victorian navy into a modern instrument of war.

Fisher's most serious fault may be summed up in the simple phrase: 'his genius was not strategic'.[19] Such strategic ideas and plans as he had, he hatched privately, in complete isolation from the General Staff at the War Office and the Committee of Imperial Defence. Fisher did not believe in a

Naval Staff; the sailor, he insisted, did not need such an instrument of instruction; constantly at grips with the powers of Nature, he was perforce a realist. Thus, wrote Churchill, who became First Lord of the Admiralty in 1911, after a profoundly alarming revelation of the gap between Naval and General Staff thinking,

'when I went to the Admiralty I found that there was no moment in the career and training of a naval officer, when he was obliged to read a single book about naval war, or pass even the most rudimentary examination in naval history . . . The "Silent Service" was not mute because it was absorbed in thought and study, but because it was weighted down by its daily routine and by its ever-complicating and diversifying technique.' [20]

Such was the heavy pressure of the Industrial Revolution upon Britian's senior and most cherished Service. Under Churchill a Naval Staff at last came into being, but as he said, the knowledge of war problems without which even the greatest professional proficiency and devotion would be at grave disadvantage required at least fifteen years of consistent policy:

'Fifteen years! And we were only to have thirty months!' [21]

Such was the condition of the Royal Navy in August 1914; the weaknesses were well concealed from public view, at home and abroad, by a tremendous outward show of strength. To the 20 dreadnoughts which formed the core of

'A tremendous outward show of strength': twenty dreadnoughts formed the core of the Grand Fleet, seen here in 1914. Note the torpedo-net booms along each hull.

the Grand Fleet were added no less than 40 pre-dreadnoughts—34 in Home waters (see p. 54 for a comparison with Germany). There was nine battle-cruisers (four in Home waters), 32 armoured cruisers, 52 obsolescent 'protected cruisers' and 36 modern light cruisers. There were 270 destroyers—to which 249 would be added during the war; it seems a large number, but there were never enough—the latest of which, the 'M' (*Mary Rose*) class, were capable of 35 knots. Finally, there were 74 submarines in commission, of which 65 were in Home waters, and of these 54 effective for duty, but only 17 belonging to the 'overseas' category.

Thanks to wise and courageous initiative by the First Sea Lord, Prince Louis of Battenberg, supported by Churchill as First Lord, the Royal Navy was at its war stations by 1 August, three days before war was declared. 'At no time', wrote Churchill, looking back over the immediate prewar years, 'were we more completely ready.' Certainly, in 1914, there was no doubt about what made Britain a great power; the Government had none—in Lord Hankey's words, they 'put their money on sea-power.' As for himself,

'My belief in sea-power amounted almost to a religion.'[22]

The public, expecting 'Glorious First of Junes' and Trafalgars, was puzzled as the sea war developed its much quieter patterns; it may be as well, before passing on, to set down now what the overall record of the Royal Navy was going to be in the war. Some leading French generals, including Joffre and Foch, reported in 1913 by a British general who should have known better, 'did not value it at one bayonet'; well . . . here is the record:

> It was the Royal Navy that made possible the mobilization and deployment of $8\frac{1}{2}$ million men of the British Empire, coming from all parts of the world, and none lost at sea;
> among them were $5\frac{1}{2}$ million deployed and maintained on the Western Front, closely adjacent to the German Navy, without ever losing a man, horse or gun at sea;
> the Royal Navy was also largely responsible for the entirely safe arrival in France of some 2 million Americans;
> it enabled eight overseas campaigns to be conducted;[23]
> it maintained, even in the darkest hours of the U-boat war, the trade on which the British Isles depended for very life;
> it swept German trade from the oceans at once and totally;
> it established a blockade of the Central Powers whose slow, cumulative, deadly effect made a large contribution to victory;
> it exercised an immediate and lasting moral ascendancy over the German fleet.

The Royal Navy did not win the war; but it is impossible to see how the war could have been won without it.

The supremacy of the Royal Navy conferred upon Britain the status of a first-class power; it also permitted Britain to attempt 'to maintain the largest Empire the world has ever seen with military armaments and reserves that would be insufficient for a third-class military power.'[24] This contradiction, which was to cost the nation dear, was the result of Britain's devoted adherence to the principle of long-service voluntary enlistment for the Army—which her most distinguished soldier, Lord Roberts, called 'Conscription by Hunger', and Lord Esher called 'the Principle of Unequal Sacrifice'. It meant that, when war came, a people of over 45 millions was only able to put into the field the same number of divisions (one cavalry, six infantry—see Appendix II for composition) as Belgium, with a population of $7\frac{1}{2}$ millions; and even part of this tiny contingent was held back for a while through fears of invasion, despite naval supremacy. In the war of masses that now came, numbers were all-important; as a wise soldier-historian has remarked of 1914:

'Military critics talk airily of the superiority of small professional "armées d'élite" over "armed conscript hordes". Very good; but in the first place the main enemy had a magnificent army, and in the second small armies feel losses more sharply than big. "Armées d'élite" would be invincible if wars were fought without casualties.'[25]

Within this limitation, which for the first two years of the war was crippling, the British professional army of 1914 was nevertheless a remarkable instrument.

If, thanks to Fisher, the Royal Navy had made a traumatic entry into the twentieth century, so had the Army, thanks to quite different benefactors: first, the Boers against whom it had fought in South Africa from 1899 to 1902, and secondly, Richard Burdon Haldane (1856–1928) the Scottish philosopher and lawyer who became Secretary of State for War in 1905 and initiated or brought to fruition a series of reforms unparalleled in the Army's history. The Boers had held up a mirror to the Army in which it saw all its professional warts and debilities clearly reflected: vacillation and incompetence in too many generals, too much poor staff work, low professional standards among regimental officers (as Lord Esher said, 'gallantry is not competence'), poor shooting and lack of initiative on the part of the soldiers, unsatisfactory equipment, especially of the artillery. Altogether, this was a serious catalogue of faults, brought into the open by one of the most searching enquiries ever conducted, the Royal Commission under Lord Elgin which began its investigations in 1902 and reported with great clarity and frankness in 1903.

Thanks to the thoroughness and speed of the Elgin Commission, reform began to take place quickly after the South African War. Under Mr. St. John Brodrick the Committee of Imperial Defence was created in 1902 as a mastermind of all defence matters, but without the invaluable adjunct of a permanent secretariat. In the same year a new uniform was introduced so that the Army could train in the uniforms that it would wear to fight. A programme of barrack-building enabled the units to be more conveniently concentrated and better housed. Under Brodrick's successor, H. O. Arnold-Forster, the Committee of Imperial Defence received its secretariat and the Prime Minister became its permanent president—a great step forward. This was the first reform proposed by Lord Esher's Committee in 1904; others followed swiftly—the creation of an Army Council on the lines of the Board of Admiralty, and a fundamental reorganization of the War Office to create a true General Staff. When the Liberals swept to power in 1905 and Haldane took office, he found much valuable groundwork done which he gratefully accepted and acknowledged. His own contribution was enormous: the creation of the Expeditionary Force (involving large reorganization of the Army itself), the creation of the Territorial Army as the first line of Reserve, the introduction of Field Service Regulations, the extension of a unified military system to all parts of the Empire. Among his staunchest supporters and ablest helpers in all this was Major-General Sir Douglas Haig.

In this manner the entire higher direction of the British Army was modernized in the years before the war; as Haldane himself expressed it:

'A new school of officers has arisen since the South African War, a thinking school of officers who desire to see the full efficiency which comes from new organization and no surplus energy running to waste.' [26]

'. . . excellent 13-pdr. Horse Artillery counterpart': Royal Horse Artillery battery in action near Wytschaete (Ypres) in 1914; these were the guns which won the action at Néry, 1 September (p. 81).

In other words, a new professionalism was present, which could be traced right down the Army to the lowest rank, and was matched by an important re-equipment programme. In 1903 the Short Magazine Lee-Enfield rifle was adopted, a weapon suitable both for infantry and cavalry; the Mark 3 version, which was used throughout the First World War and into the 1950s, became standard issue in 1907. A new artillery programme was inaugurated in 1904 (though not completed until 1908); this introduced the excellent 18-pdr. quick-firing field gun with its 13-pdr. Horse Artillery counterpart, the equally excellent 4.5 in. field howitzer which was to prove invaluable (and continued in service until 1944), and the 60-pdr. medium gun whose only fault was its paucity of numbers in 1914 (the Mark 2 version of 1918 remained in service until 1941). Often found in gun lists, though actually an infantry weapon, was the machine-gun. The British Army had used 315 of these in South Africa, but against a normally invisible enemy on the defensive they had not been particularly useful. Their potential, however, was recognized, and there was considerable debate about how they should be used in future; by 1914 each cavalry regiment and infantry battalion had two guns—the same establishment as the French and German. The difference was that the Germans, whose infantry fought by regiments of three battalions (6 guns), gave to each regiment a reserve of 1 gun, making 7, or 28 to a division. The French could have done the same, but did not set much store by such a defensive weapon, so their divisions had only the basic 24. The British, fighting by battalions, thus had eight to a brigade, and like the French, 24 to the division. The guns of 1914 were Maxims of an early pattern in process of being replaced by the excellent Vickers version which was to remain in use until 1968, but whose production figures in 1914 were only 10–12 guns per week.

In 1908 the infantry received the serviceable webbing equipment which it used in two world wars, though the cavalry clung to leather. In the same year the efficient D-III Field Telephone appeared. On the debit side, due to chronic shortage of money, there remained a serious lack of heavy and medium artillery which could only be made up by use of obsolete types—a deficiency which would soon be acutely felt. In the Territorial Army there was a total absence of modern artillery, adapted Boer War guns having to be issued instead. Ammunition reserves were, of course, calculated in relation to the small Expeditionary Force; in particular there was a grave lack of high-explosive shell. Equally serious was the total lack of the siege-warfare weapons and stores which would prove essential for trench warfare (among them trench mortars and hand-grenades). There was also a shortage of wireless equipment, despite the considerable progress in that field by the Navy and the Royal Flying Corps which we have noted. On the other hand, we have also seen (pp. 25–26) the considerable step forward in motorization of transport which took place in 1911.

With the new weapons came new proficiency, inculcated by fresh ideas and systems of training. The Boers had taught the British Army something that no European army had yet grasped in 1914: the meaning of the modern

'Musketry prizes stimulated competition . . .': rifle instruction at the School of Musketry at Hythe, where Colonel Monro taught the British Regular Army his doctrine of fire and movement.

phenomenon of the 'empty battlefield', characterized by long distances made possible by the increasing range of firearms, an invisible enemy, thanks to smokeless powder and field entrenchments, and the wide extension forced upon all formations by the hitting power of the latest guns and rifles. The Army took the lesson to heart; as early as 1904 a German observer reported, in words that would be echoed over and over again ten years later:

'In their manoeuvres the British Infantry showed great skill in the use of ground. Their thin khaki-clad skirmishers were scarcely visible. No detachment was ever seen in close order within three thousand yards. Frontal attacks were entirely avoided . . . Volley firing is abolished . . .'[27]

It was time to bid farewell to the precision-volleys of Blenheim, Waterloo, Inkerman and Omdurman; instead, from 1901, the Army's shooting began to be ruled by the 'Monro doctrine', the combination of fire and movement taught by Colonel (later General Sir Charles) Monro as Chief Instructor and later Commandant at the School of Musketry at Hythe. From the same institution, when an increase in the number of machine-guns had been turned down for the usual financial reasons, came the extraordinary musketry skill of the 1914 British Expeditionary Force. Fifteen aimed rounds a minute became normal; a distinguished military historian has vivid memory to this day of watching, during the late 1920s, a demonstration by a Mons veteran:

'He started with a full magazine, one round in the breech, and a pile of char-gers—"clips"—holding 5 rounds conveniently placed to his right. He fired on the order for 60 seconds, timed by the captain. My memory is very clear. When he received the order "stop" he had hit the bull 29 times. One round had gone astray, into the inner ring . . .'[28]

Musketry prizes stimulated competition in infantry and cavalry alike; in the 11th Hussars, for example, thanks to the keenness and hard work of Lieutenant E. L. Spears and Staff Sergeant T. G. Upton, 26 marksmen in 1910 rose to 114 in 1913, 175 first-class shots in 1910 became 262 in 1913, and in that year the number of third-class shots was nil.

The decade before 1914 saw great advances in Army welfare and education. The brave but rather stupid soldier of the South African War, leaning on officers who were often little better educated professionally, was clearly an anachronism. The Voluntary Principle still forced the Army to recruit more than it should from the least educated sections of the community, but in the Army itself education took on a new significance. No-one could obtain even the lance-corporal's single stripe without at least a third-class education certificate; sergeants required at least a second-class. For the new open-order style of warfare, non-commissioned-officers with initiative were essential; under the new régime, in which the soldier was at last treated like a human being, these were forthcoming. The anecdotes of 1914 are full of the names of admirable NCOs; Corporal Parker of the 11th Hussars, Sergeant Langford of the 5th Dragoon Guards, Battery-Sergeant-Major Dorrell and Sergeant Nelson of 'L' Battery, Royal Horse Artillery, were all representatives of that invaluable stratum of the Army who distinguished themselves on the same day in the same action—1 September 1914, at Néry, where a British cavalry brigade defeated a German cavalry division. The German Kaiser called I Corps of the BEF. 'a perfect thing apart'; the same might have been said of the whole of the initial 1914 Force. But like so many perfect things, it was very small, and quite irreplaceable.

It remains to consider what was the intended function of the 'perfect thing'—what was the British war plan? The answer displays a matter of everlasting wonder: that the war planning of the world's greatest naval power was shaped entirely by the Army. It was by one of history's ironies that the Liberal Party, with its strongly anti-militarist tradition, came to office at the height of an international crisis. The Tangier Incident of 1905 was the first of a series of crises which led directly to the First World War, and it was also the first test of the new Entente Cordiale. Anglo-French Staff talks (*Army* staffs, of course) began in January 1906, and broad agreement was quickly reached that a British expeditionary force of one cavalry and six infantry divisions would take the field on the left flank of the French Army in the event of war. But co-ordination began and ended there; the fatal doctrines which guided the deployment of the French Army were never mutually examined. Nevertheless, it was never henceforth doubted by the General Staff that this was what Haldane's expeditionary force was for. Only the Government—

which had given its sanction to the Staff talks—remained oblivious to their implication: involvement in continental war. This, as Colonel Repington, *The Times* Military Correspondent, observed, was due to

'*the complete disbelief of both great political parties that such war would ever come, and their determination that we should never take serious part in it . . . if it came. The chance that such a war might be forced upon us by the aggression of a foreign power was too inconvenient to be considered.*'[29]

As the 1905 crisis died down, the urgency of translating the Anglo-French agreement into logistical reality diminished, but the respite was brief; international tension soon began to build up again. In 1910 the keenly francophile Brigadier-General Sir Henry Wilson became Director of Military Operations at the War Office, and detailed planning was initiated for the movement of the BEF, with timetables so exact that they would even include halts of '*dix minutes pour une tasse de café.*' In 1911 the Agadir crisis revealed to a startled Government that despite all the work of the Committee of Imperial Defence during the last six years, there was no meeting-point whatever of naval and military thinking. Deeply secretive and francophobe, Admiral Fisher (now retired) had evolved a private scheme for landing the Army on Germany's Baltic shore—totally ignoring the views of the General Staff, and equally ignoring the commitment to France: an extraordinary situation. Its immediate result was that Churchill became First Lord, with the creation of a proper naval staff as a priority mission—but as we have seen, it was very late in the day. The longer-term result was that Britain remained tied hand and foot to the French Army's strategy, for want of any other; and because her own contribution was so minuscule in relation to the French, she could have no effective voice in making or modifying that strategy. What this would mean in the event was that, when Germany seized the initiative, France would have to dance to a German tune—and so would her ally, Britain. That fact contains the inner strategic truth of the First World War; it was a high price to pay for such devotion to the Principle of Unequal Sacrifice.

Such was the line-up on the interior and exterior lines of the war. Such was the equipment, physical and intellectual, with which the powers of Europe faced the new dimensions of the Industrial Revolution. It was, in fact, the mixture as ever before and ever after: tradition seeking to keep in step with change, old and new ideas wearing the same uniforms, old principles and new techniques trying to find a proper balance. What was new, and unique, was simply that never before or after had there been so much change, all at once and in so short a time. That was the cross to which the 1914–18 generation found itself nailed with agony.

NOTES
1 H. W. Wilson & J. A. Hammerton: *The Great War*, i p. 353.
2 *Times History of the War*, ii p. 286.
3 Ibid., p. 287.
4 John Terraine: *The Mighty Continent*, p. 70; Futura Publications, 1974.
5 Norman Stone: *The Eastern Front*, p. 18; Hodder & Stoughton, 1975.
6 Ibid., p. 25.
7 Ibid., p. 21.
8 Cyril Falls: *The First World War*, p. 99; Longmans, 1960.
9 For the Russian Air Service see p. 31.
10 Alfred de Vigny's moving book, *Servitude et Grandeur Militaire*, was translated by Humphrey Hare and published under the title *The Military Necessity* by The Cresset Press in 1953.
11 Major-General Sir Edward Spears: *Liaison 1914*, pp. 87–8; Eyre & Spottiswoode, 1930 and 1968.
12 Marshal Joffre: *Memoirs*, ii p. 589; trans. Col. T. Bentley Mott, Geoffrey Bles, 1932.
13 General Sir James Marshall-Cornwall: *Foch as Military Commander*, p. 17; Batsford, 1972.
14 *Times History of the War*, i p. 94.
15 Ibid., p. 93.
16 John R. Cuneo: *Winged Mars*, i p. 167.
17 Colonel Repington: *Vestigia*, p. 246; Constable, 1919.
18 Arthur J. Marder: *The Anatomy of British Sea Power*, p. 281; Frank Cass, 1940.
19 Dr. P. Haggie in *The War Plans of the Great Powers*, p. 130; ed. Paul Kennedy, Allen & Unwin, 1979.
20 Winston Churchill: *The World Crisis*, i p. 69; Odham's edition, 1938.
21 Ibid., p. 70.
22 Lord Hankey: *The Supreme Command 1914–1918*, i p. 165; Allen & Unwin, 1961.
23 Salonika, Gallipoli, Egypt and Palestine, Mesopotamia, German West African colonies, German East Africa, German Pacific colonies, Archangel Expedition.
24 Wilson & Hammerton, op. cit. i p. 160.
25 Falls, op. cit. p. 16.
26 Dudley Sommer: *Haldane of Cloan*, pp. 169–70; Allen & Unwin, 1961.
27 Von Lobell's Reports for 1904; *Royal United Services Institute Journal* vol. xlix p. 1281.
28 Brigadier Shelford Bidwell, letter to the author.
29 Repington, op. cit. p. 256.

Part Two:

The Act

Main Events 1914

2–4 August	Declarations of war
12 (–25)	First Austrian invasion of Serbia
17	Fall of Liège
18 (–24)	West: Battle of the Frontiers
19	East: Battle of Gumbinnen
23 (–31)	East: Battle of Tannenberg
(–5 Sept)	West: Retreat from Mons
25	Fall of Namur
28	Battle of Heligoland Bight
31 (–3 September)	Battle of Lemberg
5 September (–29)	Second Austrian invasion of Serbia
6 (–10)	West: First Battle of the Marne
7 (–19)	East: Battle of the Masurian Lakes
15 (–20)	West: First Battle of the Aisne
21 (–12 October)	West: The Race to the Sea
1 October (–9)	East: Battle of Augustovo
10	Fall of Antwerp
15 (–23)	East: Battle of Warsaw
16 (–22 November)	West: First Battle of Ypres
29	Turkey enters the war
1 November	Battle of Cape Coronel
15 (–15 December)	Third Austrian invasion of Serbia
16 (–15 December)	East: Battle of Lodz
28 (–3 December)	East: Russian offensive in Galicia
3 December	East: Battle of Limanova
8	Battle of the Falkland Islands
12 (–end December)	East: Austrian counter-offensive in Galicia
14 (–24)	West: First Battle of Artois
16	German raid on British East Coast
20 (–15 January)	West: First Battle of Champagne
25	RNAS raid on Cuxhaven

CHAPTER I

The Clash of Battle:
Character, Style, and Action

THE WAR THAT CAME IN AUGUST 1914 lost no time in declaring its character: it was the sort of war that General Sherman had waged in Georgia and Carolina in 1864—total war, not just of fleets and armies, but of entire nations. Civil populations were as much part of the 'firing line' as men in uniform. This became clear at once when the first invasions began.

Austria's declaration of war on Serbia was made on 28 July; Belgrade was bombarded on 29 July; Austrian troops began to cross the frontier on 12 August. War in the Balkans—until recently a rebellious province of the Ottoman Empire—was never an elegant affair; even in peacetime the area was notorious for brigandage, blood feuds, and assassination. Serbia's ally, the little kingdom of Montenegro, had a particularly ferocious reputation for such practices, its people, according to *The Times* Correspondent, having 'led for centuries the typical life of wild frontier tribes, on a level of civilization not much above the standard of the Afridis and Pathans'. The Austrian Commander-in-Chief, General Potiorek, with his still-fresh memory of the Sarajevo assassination, frankly regarded the campaign against the Slavs as a punitive expedition against savages; in an Instruction to his troops he said:

'*For such a population any disposition towards humanity or kindliness would be entirely misplaced; it would even be fraught with danger . . . I therefore order that during the military operations everyone shall be treated with the greatest suspicion and harshness.*
In the first place, I will not allow persons armed, but wearing no uniform, to be taken prisoners . . .
In passing through a hostile village hostages . . . must be taken and kept until the last house has been passed, and they must be all killed if a single shot is fired at the troops . . .
Any person encountered outside an inhabited place, and, above all, in forests, must be considered only as a member of an irregular band who has hidden his arms somewhere.'

Since the whole of the Serbian Third Ban (Reservists of 38–45) was without uniform and the Montenegrins were essentially irregulars, as the Austrians well knew, this was a recipe for pure brutality and terror—which at once ensued.

For the German Army, with its tight march-schedule through Belgium (see p. 47), no obstruction by the civil population could even be contemplated. From the first, the Germans adopted a policy of 'frightfulness' (*Schrecklichkeit*)[1] designed to deter any guerilla or partisan or *franc-tireur* activity (such as had tied down some 25 per cent of their army to protect lines of communication during the Franco-Prussian War, 1870–71). All stray shooting, by rearguards or stragglers, was attributed to *francs-tireurs*, and followed by immediate reprisals: burning of towns and villages, shooting of hostages. The *Garde Civique* had to be disbanded under German threat (see p. 74). A trail of massacre and terror followed the German armies. On the quiet evening of 20 August, a British officer was sitting on a hill overlooking the industrial sprawl of Charleroi and the great plain of Belgium to the north, wondering by what sign he would know that the Germans had arrived:

'Then, without a moment's warning, with a suddenness that made us start and strain our eyes to see what our minds could not realize, we saw the whole horizon burst into flames. To the north, outlined against the sky, countless fires were burning. It was as if hordes of fiends had suddenly been released, and dropping on the distant plain, were burning every town and every village. A chill of horror came over us. War seemed suddenly to have assumed a merciless, ruthless aspect that we had not realized till then.' [2]

South, West, and East, the impact of war was the same: streams of peasant refugees in Serbia, fleeing from the Austrians and Hungarians; as the news spread, the roads of Belgium and northern France choked with more refugees, trying to escape the Germans; in East Prussia, when the Russian advance began, streams of Germans pouring westward to escape the dreaded Cossacks. There is no evidence that the Russian armies undertook any systematic brutality: on the other hand, many Russian soldiers were from a harsh and primitive way of life, and all soldiers when they are hungry, tired and afraid, are of uncertain temper. Everywhere, the loot of captured wine-vaults aggravated passions.

Everywhere, too, there was a tally of destruction which put the efforts of General Sherman quite in the shade: the trim, clean towns of East Prussia were gutted by fire and high explosive; ruins gaped to the sky right across Belgium, from Visé on the eastern frontier to Ypres in the west; famous French cities suffered the damage of modern artillery (the burning of the cathedral at Reims on 20 September provoked a—quite useless—French protest to the neutral powers). Before the war was a month old there was another ominous sign of things to come: a German aeroplane (inevitably referred to as a 'Taube' by a Press which seemed to know no other name) flew over Paris and dropped a few small bombs which killed one man; a second attack in October caused no casualties—but notice had been served on the civilians of the world of fresh ordeals in store. Not even the British, in their 'right little, tight little island' were immune; three German cruisers appeared off Yarmouth on 3 November and shelled the town without any significant effect for about 15 minutes. On 16 December, however, another squadron arrived further north and caused 113 deaths and some 300 wounded in the Hartlepools, 17 killed and about 80 wounded in Scarborough, and 3 killed, 2 wounded in Whitby, with much damage. It was a trifle compared with continental experiences, but for the world's supreme naval power it was very shocking, and the ensuing uproar was vociferous and undignified.

From the very first this war, so cruel to civilians, so destructive of all kinds of property, showed itself pitiless to the soldiers of all nations. The Germans declared war on Belgium on 4 August, and that same day their advanced forces appeared in front of the fortress system of Liège. The next day they tried to rush the forts, using the close formation prescribed by their current tactical doctrine; a Belgian officer described the scene:

'They made no attempt at deploying, but came on, line after line, almost shoulder to shoulder, until, as we shot them down, the fallen were heaped one on top of the other in an awful barricade of dead and wounded men that threatened to mask our guns and cause us trouble. I thought of the French saying, "C'est magnifique, mais ce n'est pas la guerre!" No, it was slaughter—just slaughter.'[3]

'. . . the machine-gun announced its battlefield potential': French dead on an early battlefield. Contrary to widespread belief, it was not the machine-gun but artillery that was the war's greatest killer.

So the machine-gun announced its battlefield potential, the German infantry its first victims. Soon it was the turn of their French opposite numbers, obeying the dictates of the 'offensive spirit' in the disastrous Battles of the Frontiers; in the words of Sir Edward Spears:

'the sense of the tragic futility of it will never quite fade from the minds of those who saw these brave men, dashing across the open to the sound of bugles and drums, clad in the old red caps and trousers which a parsimonious democracy dictated they should wear, although they turned each man into a target. The gallant officers who led them were entirely ignorant of the stopping power of modern firearms, and many of them thought it chic to die in white gloves.'[4]

By the end of August (which really means only some 12 days of fighting) the French Army's losses were 4,478 officers and 206,515 other ranks—a rate of loss never equalled during the war, and constituting, as Churchill said 'wounds which were nearly fatal and never curable'.

In the East the story was the same, with only this difference: that whereas with the Western Allies casualty figures are reasonably exact, on the Eastern front only broad generalizations are possible. The Austrians, who had fired the first shots of the war, made three attacks on Serbia in 1914; each one was defeated in bitter fighting; it is thought that battle against this small enemy alone cost Austria-Hungary some 227,000 casualties in that year. Her losses on the main front, against Russia, were, of course, far greater—according to her official history, some 350,000 by the end of September; a recent authority[5] says 400,000, and a total of over 1 million by the end of the year. Russian casualty figures are never precise, but were certainly on a matching scale: at Tannenberg in August the Germans claimed 92,000 prisoners, with 30,000 more in Masuria in September. A reliable authority puts the Russian loss in the *first month* of the war at 300,000; by the end of the year it cannot have been less than 1 million, but may well have been substantially more.

The Germans, in most respects so exact and methodical, have no clear record of their 1914 casualties on either Western or Eastern Fronts. Their efforts on both were prodigious, but we can only glimpse the cost by fragments—the heaps of dead before Liège, mass attacks 'shot flat' by British infantry at Mons, disastrous officer losses on the Marne, the 'Massacre of the Innocents' (the young Reserve volunteers) at Ypres (after one day of heavy attacks a single platoon of Gordon Highlanders counted 240 dead Germans on its own short front). On the Eastern Front it is a similar jigsaw: we read of 100,000 German casualties in September, another 100,000 (including 36,000 dead) in November, according to their official sources. All that we discover powerfully suggests that, barring certain freak occasions, the German experience in 1914 closely resembled that of their enemies and allies; for them, too, the war was pitiless—indeed, more pitiless, since they had to bear so much of its burden. Everywhere, man was now paying in flesh and blood the price of his new mechanical skills—and it was high.

When the war's 'motor' started, when the German Army crossed the Belgian frontier on 3 August 1914, the hand of the now dead Count von Schlieffen guided it towards an outcome which was decisive—though not in the manner that he had intended. The great sweep through Belgium and northern France was one of the most spectacular movements in military history; it failed in its purpose—which was to defeat France in 40 days—but it conferred a benefit on Germany which was not taken from her until July 1918. It gave her the strategic initiative of the war. 'Strategic initiative' is not just a piece of military jargon; between 1914 and July 1918 it meant that Germany dictated the course of events. Where the main German military effort was, there was the true seat of war: in the West in 1914, in the East in 1915, in the West again in 1916, remaining there until the end. If, therefore, the remainder of this book concerns itself chiefly with the Western Front, that is why: the Western Front, for most of the war, was the one that mattered, for two reasons. The first is crisply stated by Field-Marshal Sir William Robertson (C.I.G.S., 1915–1918):

'In the Great War the decisive front was fixed for us by the deployment of the enemy's main masses in France and Belgium . . .' [6]

Or as Marshal Joffre, commanding the most important and effective part of the Allied forces, put it:

'The best and largest portion of the German army was on our soil, with its line of battle jutting out a mere five days' march from the heart of France. This situation made it clear to every Frenchman that our task consisted in defeating this enemy, and driving him out of our country.' [7]

And as we have seen (p. 82) owing to Britain's military weakness, that meant every Englishman too, whether he liked it or not. When Lloyd George (Chancellor of the Exchequer) plaintively asked Winston Churchill in January 1915:

'Are we really bound to hand over the ordering of our troops to France as if we were her vassal?' [8]

the short answer was 'Yes, we are'—something that both Churchill and Lloyd George found it very difficult to swallow, especially in the light of Germany's initiative.

The second reason why the seat of war had to be chiefly in the West is ably stated by Major-General J. F. C. Fuller, who cannot be accused of subservience to High Command points of view; granted, he says, that the Allied aim had to be the defeat of Germany 'since her defeat would carry with it the collapse of her allies', the question arises:

'In what locality could Germany be most profitably struck? The answer depended

on the most practical allied line of operations, which, in turn, was governed by the location of the allied main bases. They were France and Great Britain, and in no other area than France could the ponderous mass armies of this period be fully deployed and supplied in the field. The main bases and the main theatre of war were fixed by geography and logistics, and no juggling with fronts could alter this.'[9]

The $5\frac{1}{2}$ million men who served in North-West Europe under General Eisenhower between 6 June 1944 and 8 May 1945 were obeying the same compulsions as the 6,432,000 of the Allied forces on the Western Front in November 1918. These were the disciplines of the wars of the mass armies of the Industrial Revolution.

STYLE

Field-Marshal Lord Haig, in his teaching as Chief of Staff in India (1909–11), pronounced that there would be four phases of future war:
   the manoeuvre for position;
   the first clash of battle;
   the wearing-out fight of varying duration;
   the eventual decisive blow.
He was wrong about the first; modern mobilization techniques placed armies in position in the very act of assembly. The manoeuvres which took place at the outbreak of war were not concerned with position as such; they were the preordained movements prescribed by the governing plan—or reactions to such a plan. Haig's next three phases, however, accurately describe the war.

1914 saw, on both fronts, the clash of battle. 'Clash' implies movement, and warfare in 1914 was war of movement in the West and in the East. In the latter the distances were greater, the movement more apparently dramatic, the pins on the maps of armchair strategists made gratifying leaps. But distances in the West, in 1914, were not negligible: Schlieffen demanded a march of some 400 miles from his right wing; Joffre, when he grasped the danger, swung his regrouping forces 200–250 miles across France; from Mons to its final halting-place the BEF retreated 136 miles as the crow flies—but more like 200 as the soldiers marched. The 'Race to the Sea' established a front 450 miles long. These things were not done by sitting still.

What became immediately and disconcertingly apparent in this war of movement was that the existing mobile arm—the cavalry—was no longer able to fulfil the rôles expected of it. These were, first, reconnaissance: locating and identifying the enemy's forces; secondly, exploitation: turning defeat into rout, making victory final. Against modern fire-power, especially the fire-power of machine-guns, the man on horseback was now seen to be incapable of doing either of these things: Russia's mounted masses, the dashing Magyar horsemen, the well-trained German regiments which had provided spectacular finales at so many pre-war manoeuvres, the French with their memories of Murat, Kellermann, Lasalle, and other heroes, all proved equally impotent. Only the British cavalry division, schooled by the Boers and armed with a rifle which it knew well how to use, proved really effective in 1914, and that was in a capacity which many of its officers scorned: as mounted riflemen, riding to battle but fighting dismounted.

Generals who had relied on their cavalry for information, neglecting their infant and untried Air Forces, found themselves groping in darkness; then they realized that the airmen could at least locate, even if they could not identify (it is difficult to read a helmet-number or a cap-badge from an aeroplane) and began to treat them with almost embarrassing deference, asking for more than the aircraft of the period could perform. Nowhere, neither East nor West, did cavalry in 1914 succeed in turning defeat into absolute rout, although it did manage some impressive round-ups of prisoners on the Eastern Front. This was a failure which persisted throughout the war, and to which only the last stages of the Palestine campaign against Turkey in 1918 proved any exception. The generals of both sides were, as a percipient historian has said,

'caught by a hiatus in the mobile arm: horsed cavalry had become obsolete and the blitzkrieg tank had not yet been developed.' [10]

It was an unenviable fate; it meant that, until technology made a further stride, generals were like heavyweight boxers with one leg in plaster—they could maul savagely, but they could never follow through to the clean knock-out.

For the world's infantry, also, there were grim shocks in store in 1914. We have noted the influence of the offensive doctrine; in France and Germany the combination of this with the tactical images of 1870–71 led to dense, vulnerable attack formations which made perfect targets for automatic or rapid fire. The resulting loss of officers and NCOs made it correspondingly difficult to loosen the assaulting waves, so casualties mounted inexorably and astronomically. As the French took up their positions for the Battle of the Marne, General Franchet d'Esperey, watching his Fifth Army go past, was heard to cry:

'Mais où sont mes officiers, où sont mes officiers?'

Well he might; the dreadful total of some 4,500 who had already fallen as the month of September began represented 10–11 per cent of the entire French Officer Corps. The consequences of this slaughter were profound; as Churchill says:

'The cadres of the whole French Army were seriously injured by the wholesale destruction of the trained professional element. The losses which the French suffered in the years which followed were undoubtedly aggravated by this impoverishment of military knowledge in the fighting units.' [11]

This was virtually a universal story:

'*The Prussian military aristocracy was not overthrown in November 1918. Its power in the army and the Empire was destroyed by the appalling sacrifice of life made in 1914 by the Prussian nobility in the great offensive on the Western Front . . . the old Bismarckian Germany was destroyed on the battlefield of the Marne.*'[12]

In Russia, Dr. Norman Stone tells us, officer casualties mounted to 60,000 in the first year of the war:

'*The 40,000 officers of 1914 were more or less completely wiped out.*'[13]

The sharp deterioration of quality in the Austro-Hungarian Officer Corps in 1915 indicates that their experience of war in 1914 was similarly murderous.

Europe's dead infantry officers and soldiers bear witness to over-concentration by staffs and instructors on the distant lessons of Gravelotte or Plevna, ignoring the informative examples of the Wilderness Campaign in Virginia in 1864, or the more recent battles of Liao-Yan and Mukden. The British infantrymen at least had their vivid recollections of Colenso, Magersfontein, and Paardeburg; when their turn to attack came—briefly—on the Aisne in September, they presented a spectacle in sharp contrast. A German officer wrote:

'*Stretched out across the broad expanse of meadows between us and the river was a long line of dots wide apart, and looking through glasses one saw that these dots were infantry advancing, widely extended: English infantry, too, unmistakably. A field battery on our left had spotted them, and we watched their shrapnel bursting over the advancing line. Soon a second line of dots emerged from the willows along the river bank, at least ten paces apart, and began to advance. More of our batteries came into action; but it was noticed that a shell, however well aimed, seldom killed more than one man, the lines being so well and widely extended. The front line had taken cover when the shelling began, running behind any hedges or buildings near by, but this second line kept steadily on, while a third and fourth line now appeared from the river bank, each keeping about two hundred yards distance from the line in front. Our guns now fired like mad, but it did not stop the movement: a fifth and sixth line came on, all with the same wide intervals between men and the same distance apart. It was magnificently done.*'[14]

The British professional infantry alone, in 1914, was capable of this open order advance, in what Europeans would call 'skirmish lines', but what South Africa had taught were the only possible attacking lines on the modern empty battlefield. In defence, the British infantry made their contribution to emptiness by vanishing under cover, and developing a great volume of fire-power from concealed positions. They were very good soldiers—but they were not immortal; they, too, were vulnerable to the war's chief destructor.

'"Emmas" and "Berthas" quickly brought about the surrender of Liège': here we see a German (Krupp) 305 mm. howitzer being prepared for action.

The war of 1914–18 was an artillery war: artillery was the battle-winner, artillery was what caused the greatest loss of life, the most dreadful wounds, and the deepest fear. Artillery fired the first shots of the war—at Belgrade, in July; in August, the French '75s' proved their destructive power—and would have done even better if they had not been too often sacrificed to the 'offensive spirit'; but the Germans made a profound impression on all their enemies by their use of the 150 mm. howitzer (the French called their shells the '*Gros Noirs*' because of the black smoke of the explosions, the British called them 'coal-boxes' or 'Jack Johnsons' after the negro heavyweight boxing champion). A British soldier interviewed in September 1914 said:

'*People who say that the German artillery fire is no good simply don't know what they are talking about. I can only figure it out as being something worse than the mouth of hell.*'

This sentiment would certainly have been echoed by the defenders of the Belgian forts at Liège and Namur. It was against these that the heaviest calibres of the German siege train were deployed: the 280 mm. (11 in.) howitzers which surprised observers by appearing on travelling carriages in the field, instead of requiring concrete beds, as expected; the 305 mm. (12 in.) Krupp and Skoda howitzers; (Austrian Skodas were known as '*Schlanke Emmas*'; '*schlanke*' means 'slim'—a sardonic tribute to one of the stubbiest artillery pieces ever seen); and the Krupp 420 mm. ('*Dicke*—Big', literally 'stout'—Berthas').[15] It was the arrival of the 'Emmas' and 'Berthas' which quickly brought about the surrender of Liège, after ten days of firm resistance. Namur, less strong, lasted only five days in all; it, too, is often written of as the victim of the very big howitzers, but acording to the Belgian commander this was not so. General Michel considered that it was the 280 mms. which did the real damage; typical is the case of Fort Suarlée, on the north-west side:

'The bombardment of Fort Suarlée commenced on Sunday morning, August 23, and it fell on the 25th at five in the afternoon. Three German batteries armed with the 28 cm. howitzer fired 600 shells each weighing 750 lb. on the 23rd; 1,300 on the 24th, and 1,400 on the 25th against it. These destroyed the whole of the massive structure of concrete and wrecked all the turrets, and further resistance was impossible . . . the German fire literally swept off the face of the earth forts and improvised defences, troops and guns.'[16]

These holocausts of destruction by high explosive would be the standard practice of battle for the next four years. One statistic tells the grim true story: of all wounds inflicted on British troops throughout the war, 58.51 per cent were by shell or trench mortar bomb; 38.98 per cent were by machine-gun or rifle bullet.

Evidently, only mechanization made possible the introduction of the very heavy calibres of guns and howitzers on to the battlefield. The Krupp 420 mm. required five vehicles, drawn by agricultural tractors, for transportation. The Skoda 305 mm. was transported on a 100 h.p. Daimler tractor with two trailers; the tractor carried the platform (weighing 10 tons) and most of the crew; the first trailer had the carriage and trail (also 10 tons), the second carried the gun itself ($8\frac{1}{2}$ tons). These, however, were the super-heavies; even such large weapons as the 150 mm. (like the British 60-pdr.) were horse-drawn, as were, of course, the 105 mm. field howitzers (British 4.5 in.) and the field guns of all armies. What this meant was that out of the 5,592 horses in a British infantry division, 3,814 belonged to the artillery. (The four-brigade Cavalry Division of 1914 had 9,815 horses, of which 1,576 belonged to the Royal Horse Artillery.) The slightly smaller German infantry division had some 4,000 horses, which means that the number with the divisions in the West was over 350,000, with another 56,000 for the cavalry divisions, and more again for all the troops attached to higher formations—corps, armies and the Supreme Command (OHL—*Oberste Heeresleitung*). It must never be forgotten that throughout the war, in the midst of all the technology of Industrial Revolution, the legs of man and beast provided the bulk of transportation in the battle areas. It is salutary to reflect that the animal introduced to the Babylonians in approximately 2100 BC was still, in the twentieth century AD, a vital ingredient of war; it continued to be so in 1939, when *Wehrmacht* divisions marched with 1,200 horse-drawn waggons each, in 1945 when the Red Army entered Europe with large numbers of men on horseback and a strange selection of animals drawing its supplies, and it is still well thought of, if a photograph in my files of Chinese cavalry exercising near the Great Wall in 1974 is anything to go by.

The limitations of the horse in an industrial and mechanical age scarcely need to be pointed out: first, its vulnerability to modern fire weapons, and secondly, its mountainous fodder requirements. General von Kluck's *First Army* alone had 84,000 horses, consuming nearly 2 million lbs. of fodder a day. To carry such an amount would have needed 924 standard fodder-wagons, which was clearly out of the question. During the great advance the German horses had to live off the country; the season of the year was favourable for this, but even so, by the time they crossed the French frontier the cavalry horses were showing signs of exhaustion. By the opening of the Battle of the Marne (6 September) the condition of much of the cavalry was serious, and the heavy artillery had fallen right behind the army. For every army, for the rest of the war, obtaining and transporting fodder supplies was a continuing nightmare.

ACTION

The war of movement rolled forward on the legs of men and horses and the wheels of machinery; the massive mobilizations proceeded smoothly, the huge armies assembled like so many toy soldiers exactly positioned by a giant hand. While the German strategic railways sprang into bustling activity, and the 'ghost' sidings and platforms came to teeming life, a strong advance guard entered Belgium before the declaration of war to open the way for the host that was to follow. This it did, practically to schedule, overthrowing the fortress systems in the manner we have seen, and pushing aside the Belgian

'. . . the German strategic railways sprang into bustling activity': the thirteen main rail lines carried 1,500,000 men in ten days to their starting-points for the great offensive.

field army. Under the firm, dignified leadership of King Albert, unprepared and inadequate as it was, the Army put up a good fight which propaganda inflated as hysterically as the denunciations of 1940 when the image of 'gallant little Belgium' was exploded. By the end of a fortnight, however, as the last resistance of Liège crumbled, it was clear that battle could not continue in the open field; the Army began to retire into the Antwerp 'keep' on 18 August, the day on which the German main body began its great movement. By the 20 August the Belgian troops were all in Antwerp, and the German *First Army* was marching through Brussels.

The fate of the forts startled governments, General Staffs, and public opinion alike. Namur's quick fall was particularly shocking. Soon it was followed by the capture of the second-class French fortress of Maubeuge; this place held out for a fortnight (24 August–7 September) but only five days from the arrival of the big German howitzers. When Antwerp's own turn came (28 September) it, too, lasted just under two weeks. There is a mystery surrounding all these events; the 'Big Berthas' and the 'Emmas' were such impressive-looking engines of destruction that they acquired almost a science-fiction aura. Photographs of smashed concrete, wrecked steel cupolas, and tales of shell-holes large enough 'to put a three-storey house in', excited and alarmed imaginations everywhere. But one authoritative German participant in the event said that the most spectacular damage was not caused by shell-fire but by dynamiting later, and a recent writer adds:

'This, coupled with the comparatively slight losses of the Belgian garrisons, seems to point to the fact that the Belgians simply lost their nerve and surrendered to a lot of noise, smoke and dust.'[17]

This may be going too far, but we have just noted that the vital destruction at Namur was done, not by the 'Berthas' and 'Emmas', but by the 280 mm. (11 in.) howitzers whose destructive powers had been seen as long ago as 1905 when the Japanese brought them into action against Port Arthur. There is positive evidence that the 'Berthas', at any rate, were present at Maubeuge from 2 September, and hastened its surrender, but that act is shrouded in so much curiosity that it is impossible to say exactly what their effect was. The Belgians insisted that they were the decisive factor at Antwerp, but even at the time there were doubts about this. *The Times History* says:

'. . . it is difficult to get positive evidence that they were in use there. The 28 cm. shell is such a formidable projectile—it spreads such havoc when it falls effectively—that it is easy for those who witnessed its effects for the first time to believe that it belonged to one of the very largest pieces.'

On the other hand, *The Times* admits that the range of some of the German shelling indicates a larger weapon, and suggests something 'intermediate in size between 28 and 42 cm.'—which would, of course, be the Skoda or Krupp 305s. Whatever the technical truths may be, the effect of the fall of these successive fortified systems on the General Staffs of the Allies was to make them very distrustful of fixed defences; French forts were stripped of their guns to provide heavy artillery for the field armies, and their garrisons were reduced or removed. This later proved unfortunate; our sceptic quoted above is on stronger ground when he refers to 'the unquestionable failure of the "Berthas" after the Belgian campaign'. He is referring—with reason—to Verdun, whose steel and concrete landscape fills one with awe to this day.

Two things are certain: first, that whatever their actual performance, the super-heavy howitzers gained a reputation in these early days which, by its daunting moral effect, became another weapon in Germany's arsenal. Secondly, heavy artillery, from the first, established a dominance on the battlefield which it kept throughout the war.

On the main front, in France, the war of movement also produced some surprises. The first of these was the sheer mass of the German armies, provided by their Reserve divisions as explained on p. 51. The second was the endurance and fortitude in adversity shown by the French infantry. Dash and élan in attack had always been a French quality; it was expected of them in 1914, and duly displayed—with sacrificial results. Undoubtedly, under the terrible stress of their baptism of fire, some French units gave way; there were panics and routs, worsened by the loss of officers. But the Army as a whole did not collapse; the advancing Germans took no large numbers of prisoners (except the garrisons of fortified areas such as Longwy and Maubeuge when these capitulated). Instead, the French soldiers, despite their crushing losses, despite their equally crushing disappointment, and despite their fatigue under the hot August sun, rallied and returned to the battle time and again.

Their Commander-in-Chief displayed equal resolution. If Joffre has to bear responsibility for much of the unreality of French strategic and tactical doctrine before the war; if he at first found it difficult to believe how wrong the General Staff had been—difficult, indeed, to believe the evidence of his own eyes as what should have been sledgehammer offensives in Lorraine, in the Ardennes, and on the Sambre turned into bloody defeats and retirements—he and he alone must be given the credit for taking hold of disaster and turning it into victory. At first he thought that the Army itself had failed—that the soldiers were simply not fighting well. Then he concluded that the officers must be to blame, especially the senior officers, many of whom he knew to be due for retirement—he had intended a considerable weeding-out in 1914, but the outbreak of war prevented it. Now he had to carry it out in the midst of battle—never a pleasant prospect. By 6 September he had already removed 50 generals: two army commanders, one cavalry and nine infantry corps commanders, five cavalry and 33 infantry divisional commanders. In this tough action he was fortified by the Minister of War, M. Adolphe Messimy, who told him on 24 August:

'The only law in France today is to win or die. I repeat my formal request, that you place in the highest positions only men who are young, energetic, and decided to

win at any price: eliminate the old fossils without pity.'[18]

These were strong words, brave words, but as Joffre (who had to carry out the instruction) says:

'. . . never in the course of my whole career did I ever have to perform a duty more difficult or more disagreeable than that of relieving from their commands generals—some of them my friends, all of them perfectly honourable men—whose force of character had proved unequal to the rough test of war.'[19]

Dismissing generals was no doubt a necessary act; in itself, however, it would not turn the tide of war. It was in this time of dire adversity that Joffre showed his real quality. Stage by stage he worked out what needed to be done—and did it. Following a week of harrowing events and demoralizing crises, on 25 August after much thought and debate (prompted by the wide swing of the German right wing, whose envelopment threat had just driven the BEF from Mons) Joffre concluded that the only correct answer was to create 'on the outer wing of the enemy a mass capable, in its turn, of enveloping his marching flank'. This thought he embodied in his *Instruction Générale No. 2* of that date, which may be regarded as a turning-point. A distressing interview with Field-Marshal Sir John French the next day reinforced his conviction that he had to have, on his extreme left, an army to which he could give direct orders—which, of course, he could not do to an ally. Out of these considerations was born the French Sixth Army, commanded by General Maunoury, whose intervention began the Battle of the Marne on 6 September. As we have seen (p. 21) Joffre, an Engineer officer, was a firm believer in railways as an instrument of modern war; some 300 trains were now required to bring across the necessary divisions from right to left to build up Maunoury's army. As the Germans continued to plunge southward towards Paris, it became a race with time; it was fortunate that Joffre had seen the light when he did. He alone was responsible for the existence of this new army in the right place, because he alone possessed the information on which the decision to create it was based, and the authority to implement that decision.

The qualities of Joffre in 1914 are never more apparent than when we contemplate his opponent. As Joffre's stature grew, General von Moltke's diminished. By 25 August, he had made a number of fatal mistakes. Lodged far away from the shifting battle-front at his Supreme Headquarters 200 miles distant in Coblenz (not for him the indefatigable travels of Joffre up and down his front) his grip on events had never been strong; as early as 19 August he had permitted his two left-wing armies (*Sixth* and *Seventh*) to take the offensive, contrary to all the teaching of the Schlieffen Plan; now he convinced himself that 'the great decisive battle in the West had been fought and decided in Germany's favour'. He actually considered moving six army corps from the Western to the Eastern Front, where matters were looking critical; in the event only two went, starting next day. Moltke's original intention (bad enough) was that these should come from the *Seventh Army*; instead, he sent the two released by the fall of Namur, which should have supported his right. 'I admit that this was a mistake,' he said afterwards, 'and one that was fully paid for on the Marne.' These two corps, like the Austrian *Second Army* (see p. 58) were condemned to float between two great battles, taking part in neither. It was not long before Moltke followed the French generals whom Joffre had dismissed; by mid-September he had become a mere figure-head at OHL; his formal dismissal came in November. By then the Schlieffen Plan was ancient history.

Never has the phrase 'the fog of war' been more apt than during this period on the Western Front. In Coblenz, Moltke and his staff conducted their war in almost unalleviated ignorance; blinded by the failure of the cavalry, the German Army Commanders were little better off, although much closer to the fighting line. Kluck, in the key position, was particularly in the dark; after the rearguard action of the British II Corps at Le Cateau on 26 August, his Army virtually 'lost' the BEF. The *First Army* zigzagged across north-western France, occasionally bumping into small British detachments (such as the 1st Cavalry Brigade at Néry on 1 September), or leading units of General Maunoury's army, assembling in the Amiens area, never understanding who its enemies were, or in which direction it ought to strike. Its neighbour, General von Bülow's *Second Army*, was equally in the dark, and suffered a sharp setback at Guise on 29 August, when the French Fifth Army counter-attacked under Joffre's eye. He, on the other hand, was increasingly fortified by the tonic of reliable information.

The reason for this state of affairs is not difficult to discover, and lies in the new technology of war and the different attitudes towards it. Although Allied troops were constantly alarmed by the sight of German aeroplanes, whose appearance, they were convinced, was certain to bring down a storm of artillery fire with devastating accuracy, the truth is that the German air weapon had completely failed in its most important rôle. This was not the fault of the airmen—the quality of the German flyers was always high—but of the High Command, which had no idea how to use them. The case of the Zeppelins is revealing; as we have seen, the Germans had five of these available in the West in August 1914, and with the experience of flying that their crews possessed this should have been an invaluable instrument of long-range reconnaisance. No such use was made of them; instead, one of the latest was thrown away by sheer stupidity. Following the failure of the attempt to storm Liège on 5 August, the next day Z-6 was ordered to bomb the forts. The sheer fatuity of this mission can only be grasped when it is realized that at that stage no such thing as aerial bombs existed. She could only drop artillery shells, and of these she probably carried about four. As Mr. Cuneo says,

'To send one airship to accomplish with a few shells what constant bombardment by artillery had failed to achieve is hardly what one would expect from trained general-staff officers.'[20]

And he adds: 'the result was hardly surprising'. The shells could add little material damage to the Belgian positions; on the other hand, they did overload the Zeppelin, which became a target for Belgian artillery, machine-gun, and rifle fire. *Z-6* was holed in several places, failed to reach its base, and was completely wrecked in attempting to land near Bonn. Thereafter OHL appeared to forget the very existence of the Zeppelins.

It has to be admitted that the French, although they had a detailed plan for the use of airships in the long-range reconnaissance rôle, did no better. This was due, as we have seen, to the inferiority of their machines—and they, too, had a *Z 6*-type disaster, due this time to the foolishness of soldiers rather than staff officers. The dirigible *Montgolfier*, stationed at Maubeuge, set out on a mission on 21 August, and was promptly and enthusiastically shot down by French troops. Where the airships failed, the aeroplanes did no better; largely because they were sent off in the wrong direction, they completely failed to observe the entry of the great German masses into Belgium and their march westward. The Royal Flying Corps was, of course, better placed, and it is not surprising that the first useful information about the great German sweep came from the British flyers. It was soon confirmed by the Cavalry Division, but although Sir John French was himself a cavalryman and now had information from two sources, he preferred to trust French Intelligence reports, which were at that stage useless. The resulting débâcle bred a corresponding distrust which unfortunately persisted when the French Air Service at last began to be effective. This came about in the last stages of the retreat to the Marne. While the German commanders were receiving almost no help at all from their air arm—it appears to have completely missed the large transfers of French troops from right to left—the Allied aircraft were playing an increasingly vital rôle. On 31 August the RFC reported an important change of direction by the German *First Army*—not the famous turn to the south-east which later exposed its flank, but a useful forewarning to General Maunoury. On 2 September French airmen warned General Galliéni, Military Governor of Paris, of impending danger to the capital. On 3 September, first French then British flyers observed and reported the critical German swerve south-eastwards; the telegram to Galliéni from the Head of the French Mission with the BEF said:

'*Definite and unconflicting reports show the entire German First Army except the IV Reserve Corps . . . are going southeast to cross the Marne between Château Thierry and La Ferté sous Jouarre to attack the left of the Fifth Army. Without doubt the heads of the columns will arrive at the river this evening. GQG. [Grand Quartier Général: the French GHQ] and the Fifth Army are being duly warned.*'

Galliéni and Joffre were thus both in possession of the information essential for a successful counterstroke. The former, nearer to the critical point, wanted to strike at once; Joffre, with the wider perspective of the whole battle from Verdun on the right to Paris on the left, preferred to allow the Germans to develop their perilous movement a little further. But not much further: on 5 September the decisions were taken which turned the Allied retreat into advance, and that night Maunoury began the battle which spread along the whole line next day. This vital information-gathering was a striking début for the most strikingly novel part of the Industrial Revolution's contribution to modern war.

Less immediately impressive because less visible was another contribution of the new technology. Generals do not commonly like to say much about their Intelligence sources; normally these would consist chiefly of field observations by the troops, information obtained by interrogating prisoners, and reports by secret service agents. Joffre mentions all of these (as well as diplomatic sources) in his account of his attempts to pierce the fog in that critical first month of war. And to them the air added something more than aerial reconnaissance—valuable though that was. It offered now, for the first time in war, what Ronald Lewin has referred to as 'the enchanted loom', the

'infinite patterns constantly woven throughout space by the incessant radio signals of . . . High Commands, their armies, navies and air forces, their diplomats, their secret establishments.'[21]

So began the indiscreet clatter of distant invisible voices which would henceforward be a prime source of military Intelligence; indeed, it had already became so before the war was a month old. As Joffre says:

'The German wireless stations were one of our most precious sources of information.'[22]

Thus supported, Joffre won his battle; it was not an easy matter—beating German armies is never an easy matter—but after hard fighting and some alarming crises by 11 September he was able to report to the Minister of War:

'The Battle of the Marne is an incontestable victory for us.'

It was also a decisive victory, because it determined the character of the war. It meant the failure of the Schlieffen Plan—Germany's only plan; that, in turn, meant that this would not be a short war, but a long one; and that meant that it would become ever more savage, ever more destructive, as the new technology discovered ever new ways for human beings to kill and damage each other. Some of these now made a very prompt appearance.

The German armies fell back to the line of the River Aisne, and along the heights on the precipitous north bank (known, between Soissons and Reims, as the *Chemin des Dames* Ridge—the 'Ladies' Road'—soon to acquire dreadful fame) they halted and turned at bay. To check the Allied advance they adopted an old and familiar expedient which modern technology now made fatally effective: they dug field entrenchments, as Marshal Villars had done to oppose the Duke of Marlborough at Malplaquet, as the Duke of Wellington had done to check Marshal Masséna at Torres Vedras, as Confederates

'The Germans had built up substantial supplies for siege warfare': a consignment of barbed wire arriving behind the front, a heavy mallet for staking, long-handled spades, and mortar bombs in basket containers can also be seen.

and Union troops had learned to do automatically on every new position by 1864, and as the Boers had done to trouble the British in South Africa. In this style of war the Germans had a decided advantage: implicit in all Schlieffen's thinking was the consideration that substantial parts of the German Army—the *Eighth Army* on the Eastern Front, and the left wing in the West—would be standing on the defensive while the great mobile mass advanced. Clearly, this defensive against what were expected to be heavily superior forces would require every kind of technical aid to make it effective. The Germans had therefore built up substantial supplies of the kind required for siege warfare (in which they also expected to be engaged): entrenching tools, various types of timber, hand- and rifle-grenades, searchlights, flares (fired from pistols), periscopes, trench mortars. These last, modern versions of a long-familiar instrument of war, were another surprise of 1914. We have seen how Joffre had failed to obtain authorization for them (p. 71); the British had none either. General Haig, commanding I Corps, visited the 4th (Guards) Brigade on 24 September and found the brigadier

'somewhat dispirited owing to an occurrence this afternoon . . . the enemy had thrown a huge bomb estimated at 120 lbs of high explosive into a trench held by the Grenadiers, and killed and wounded a whole platoon numbering forty or fifty men. This form of attack is novel and seems difficult to deal with . . . Such large bombs are terribly demoralizing . . .' [23]

They certainly underlined the frailty of even the finest and best-trained soldiers in the face of the new technology; the high explosive did not pause to enquire the name and traditions of the regiment on which it was falling. Haig noted that in this respect as well as others,

'*Our troops are certainly now fighting at a great disadvantage in not having*
    (*a*) *large bomb-throwers (Minen Werfer)*
    (*b*) *small effective hand bombs with mechanical safety catch arrangements.*'

Experiments to remedy the deficiency were at once begun by I Corps Royal Engineers' Workshops.

Both sides dug themselves in along the crest of the Aisne heights; peace-time practice had taught the Germans to construct better trenches, zig-zagging so as to avoid enfilade fire, and traversed to limit the effects of shell bursts. Protective aprons of barbed-wire entanglements, on the models displayed in South Africa and Manchuria, checked attempts to rush them; well-placed machine-guns took heavy toll of attackers caught in the wire. Like the mortars, the machine-guns did not ask the names of the regiments they slaughtered. Only heavy artillery offered any solution to this problem of trenches, machine-guns, and barbed-wire—and the Allies as we have seen, were badly deficient in heavy artillery. Here, again, the Germans were at an advantage; the French could at least take guns from their numerous forts; the British had to fall back on semi-obsolete weapons of Boer War vintage. Haig remarked on 16 September:

'. . . *so the enemy's big guns possess a real moral superiority for some of our gunners! In fact, our gunners cannot "take on" the enemy's heavy batteries.*'[24]

The pattern of the artillery war was becoming clearer every day, and already one of its greatest problems had appeared. Before the month of August was out, the advancing Germans, beset by supply difficulties of every kind, were learning what it meant to feed modern quick-firing guns with ammunition. The *First Army*, at the extreme edge of the front, was the first to experience a real shortage; fortunately, however, as Martin Van Creveld says,

'*consumption fell very sharply after the battle of Le Cateau on 26 August. Had this not been the case, the supply service would, in all probability, have broken down.*'[25]

By mid-September the shortage was being felt all along the German front; the French faced a similar situation—Joffre calls it 'agonizing'. When General Foch (commanding a new Ninth Army) sent a staff officer to plead for more ammunition, Joffre gave him a cool reception:

'*To ask for more ammunition was, in a way, as bad as cutting off one of his legs. "Come up," he said curtly.*

Once in his office he poured out his heart:
"What has come over you all, to keep asking me for ammunition I don't have? At the end of October, we shall be producing five thousand shells a day. Today is only the 27th of September. For a month, therefore, we'll have to do some faking. Three shells per gun! Tell Foch to stop bothering me.""[26]

Foch accepted the position loyally: 'Obviously Joffre cannot give what he does not have.' But, an artilleryman himself, he added with a flash of insight: 'The siege war is only beginning. It will last for years.'

So, briefly, the war of movement halted in stalemate. Neither side was in any doubt about what to do in these circumstances. 'To my mind,' wrote Joffre,

'there could be no question of our beginning a general action, for it would cost us heavy losses and use up most of our ammunition. My intention was, while maintaining an aggressive attitude which would keep the enemy constantly under the threat of a general attack . . . to undertake a powerful action with my left against the German right . . .'[27]

The Germans had anticipated this strategy; as General von Falkenhayn, now effectively Chief of Staff, said, their right wing 'was hanging in the air'. To avert this danger, and at the same time turn the tables on the French, the *Sixth Army* was ordered from Lorraine to the right flank. So now the war of movement resumed in the form of steady prolongations of the German right and the French left, to Noyon on the River Oise, up to Péronne on the Somme, to Arras on the Scarpe, to Armentières on the Lys, to the Yser at Dixmude, and so, finally, to the Channel coast. The great manoeuvre was called—misleadingly—'The Race to the Sea'; it was nothing of the kind. The trench warfare which soon afterwards began and continued to rule the Western Front until 1918 is often written about as though the General Staffs of the world, in their dullness and folly, had elected with one accord to abandon mobility. The truth is that these September and October weeks witnessed their desperate attempts to preserve it. Unfortunately, although the Germans were said always to be 'twenty-four hours and an army corps' ahead of the Allies, the balance of force was such that by the time both sides came to the sea, both had equally failed to fulfil their intentions to turn the flank, and thus keep movement going.

A significant part of the last manoeuvre began on 1/2 October: II Corps of the BEF came out of the line on the Aisne, and started to move towards the left. On 9 October (the day the Germans entered Antwerp) II Corps reached Béthune, halfway between Arras and Ypres. III Corps took position three days later on its left, and on 19 October I Corps came to Ypres. So the most famous, the most enduring and the bloodiest of British battlefields came into existence. In point of numbers engaged and length of front held, in the First Battle of Ypres which now began, it was not really a 'British' battlefield; as Foch (now commanding this northern sector) points out, by 31

'The BEF fought magnificently'—but its losses were irreplaceable. These men are
Light infantry, resting behind a wall during the First Battle of Ypres.

October—the second crisis—the French were holding 15 miles of front
there, the British 12, and by 5 November the French held 18 miles, the
British 9. On the extreme left, stretching to the sea at Nieuport, the Belgians,
supported by French Marines and Territorials, held another 15 miles. It was,
in fact, in the Belgian sector along the Yser that the battle began, with
extremely heavy fighting at Dixmude, held by a French Marine brigade. But
numbers and measurements apart, 'First Ypres' acquired a significance for
Britain that was unique. For now the penalty of depending on a small élite
army was paid. The BEF—barring inevitable incidents—fought magnificently; it is invidious to single out any part of it—the artillery, hoarding its
scanty shells, the cavalry, a splendid mobile reserve, Guards, Highlanders,
infantry of the line, Royal Engineers, trying to construct defence lines
without material—all performed like heroes. One unit must stand for all,
displaying the qualities of the whole in the moment of crisis on 31 October, as
the Germans crashed down the Menin–Ypres road and threatened breakthrough at Gheluvelt:

*'In this war of Army Groups, Armies, Army Corps, Divisions, this war of
impersonal masses, one battalion, the 2nd Worcestershire Regiment, about 350
strong, retook Gheluvelt, and the German attack was stopped. It was the last time
that such a handful would be able to produce such an effect—the last flourish of the
old British Regular tradition.'* [28]

The penalty had, nevertheless, to be paid: the cost of these sometimes superhuman efforts was 58,000 officers and men. Already there was a serious drain on the Regular Reserve; this loss brought the total for the war so far to 89,000. By continental standards this was trifling, but in the British context calamitous; in the words of the Official History, 'The old British Regular Army was gone past recall, leaving but a remnant to carry on the training of the New Armies.' It is to this fact that the disappointments and tragedies of 1915 are chiefly due.

Because the British losses were so high in proportion to their strength, and because they possessed this sombre significance, an equally tragic experience is often lost to view. In mid-August, with belief in quick, decisive victory in the West still undiminished, the German High Command ordered the creation of six new Reserve army corps for use as an army of occupation, releasing trained formations for the East. The manner of raising these constituted a heavy draught upon Germany's future resources: 75 per cent of them were untrained volunteers. Four of these raw corps went in October to form a new *Fourth Army* in Flanders, whose new mission was, quite simply, to win the war:

'*It included the flower of the youth of Germany, middle- and upper-class students, flaming with patriotism and enthusiasm, ready for sacrifice. They had little power of manoeuvre because their training had been so scanty, but they were absolutely determined to win or fall. For the most part they fell.*'[29]

This was the 'Massacre of the Innocents' (see p. 90); a German officer, watching them go singing into attacks as vain as they were costly, wrote:

'*There is no doubt that the English and French troops would already have been beaten by trained troops. But these young fellows we have, only just trained, are too helpless, particularly when the officers have been killed.*'[30]

The special tragedy for Germany was that a large proportion of these young men who fell were themselves potential officers. Already a severe shortage of junior officers was being felt; it would persist for the remainder of the war. The further tragedy was that Britain, her Regulars expended, would soon be found repeating the German experience; the Germans, at least, learned by their mistake and never recruited by such wasteful means again.

The First Battle of Ypres began as an encounter battle; the Allies, in Foch's words, determined 'to exploit the last vestige of our victory on the Marne'; the Germans equally determined to smash the Allied left. Like the war itself to date, it displayed an ominous balance of force, threatening a long, grim future ahead; and also like the war, it dealt out credits and debits to both sides with a distressingly even hand. The Germans had a substantial advantage of numbers, and the quality of their peace-trained units was very high; the Belgians fought well for the last patch of their native soil, but leaned heavily on Allied support (chiefly French); the French also, for the most part, fought well—surprisingly well, considering the appalling losses they had already endured and their great exertions. The BEF, especially II Corps, was hampered by lack of numbers despite its high quality. The Germans possessed an unquestioned material advantage over all the Allies, especially in artillery, and above all the heavy calibres whose deafening explosions were so destructive and shattering to the nerves. They complained of an ammunition shortage—real enough, no doubt, in view of the ever-increasing demand, but nothing like as real as it was for the Allies; the British, by the end of October, were down to nine rounds per gun per day; shell production for the French 75s was now picking up, and that was just as well, for once again they were depending on these guns.

On the German debit side we have to place the misuse of the young volunteers and certain other command failings. Brigadier-General Charteris, Head of Intelligence in Haig's I Corps, noted on October 25

'an accommodating German Corps Commander who sends out constant messages and orders to his units by wireless, without coding them. I suppose he thinks we do not know any German! . . . God bless him! I'll give him a drink if ever I see him when the war is over.'[31]

It took all combatants some time to learn that the air itself had ears.

Other command faults were also noted; the German officer quoted above observed a brigadier who,

'when he was snowed under with reports, when his troops were having the hottest time, when they were in the most dire need of calm, clear orders, when everything depended on his doing something decisive . . . cried to his Brigade Major in a state of terrific excitement, "The horses, my dear L. Come, let us fling ourselves into the battle!"'[32]

In the various crises of this battle, when strong, determined leadership was essential, it was noted that the Germans failed; their intermediate commanders displayed caution and want of enterprise against very thin defences; they seemed 'paralysed by the thought that fresh British forces might appear at any moment from the shelter of the woods and surprise them.'[33]

On the Allied side, command effectiveness varied as one might expect. In what rapidly became a 'soldiers' battle', a modern Inkerman, brigadiers were very important; the brigadiers of the BEF were a mainstay of the defence of Ypres, as the tally of death and wounds attests. The divisional commanders were also busy men. Major-General Lomax (1st Division) was mortally wounded, and Major-General Monro (2nd Division) badly stunned as they conferred close to the front line at Hooge Château. Major-General Capper (7th Division) displayed all the energetic qualities which led to his death in 1915. At the moment of crisis on 31 October, Lieutenant-General Haig did much to restore confidence by personal example, calmly riding at the head of his staff towards the enemy down the Menin Road. But his more significant contribution was in keeping a cool head and forming realistic views when those above him—GHQ and Foch—appeared to dwell in clouds of ill-founded optimism. Among the French, Admiral Ronarc'h, commanding the Marines at Dixmude, conducted an epic struggle; General Dubois (IX Corps) proved himself a loyal and unselfish ally; and Foch himself, whatever his misjudgments of the strategic situation, stood out as an admirable coalition general—a rare quality.

In the end, however, it is the infantry soldier, and particularly that superbly trained infantryman of the BEF, with his 'mad minute' rifle fire which persuaded the Germans that they faced lines of machine-guns, who emerges as the hero of this battle. Thanks to him and his allied comrades—those enigmatic paladins of 1914—all the German attacks were held. By November *Hauptmann* Binding was writing:

'*Everything on the front is rooted to the same spot. I don't call it a success when a trench, a few hundred prisoners, are taken. They have always cost more blood than they are worth. The war has got stuck into a gigantic siege on both sides. The whole front is one endless fortified trench. Neither side has the force to make a decisive push.*'[34]

He added: 'This proves that generalship is lacking.' He was speaking, of course, chiefly for his own side, but undoubtedly there were many among the Allies who would have agreed with him. But it was not a fault of generalship that brought the war of movement to an end. The final assault on Ypres came on 11 November—a date of destiny; with its failure the war of the trenches took over the Western Front for three hard years—a long-drawn-out *impasse* due to a lethal combination of geography and technology.

NOTES

1 See Terraine, *The Smoke and the Fire*, pp. 22–30; Sidgwick & Jackson, 1980.
2 Spears, op. cit. p. 106
3 Wilson & Hammerton, op. cit. i p. 151.
4 Spears, op. cit. p. 36.
5 Stone, op. cit. pp. 91, 122.
6 Field-Marshal Sir William Robertson: *Soldiers and Statesmen 1914–1918*, i p. 75; Cassell, 1926.
7 Joffre, op. cit. ii p. 327.
8 Martin Gilbert: *Winston S. Churchill*, iii, Companion Volume i p. 472; Heinemann, 1971.
9 Fuller: *The Conduct of War 1789–1961*, pp. 161–2; Eyre & Spottiswoode, 1961.
10 Brigadier C. N. Barclay: *Armistice 1918*, p. 90; Dent, 1968.
11 Churchill, op. cit. ii p. 952.
12 Arthur Rosenberg: *The Birth of the German Republic*, pp. 116–17; Oxford, 1931.
13 Stone, op. cit. p. 166.

14   Walter Bloem: *The Advance From Mons*, pp. 181–2; Peter Davies, 1930.
15   Liliane and Fred Funcken: *The First World War*, Part 2 p. 114; Ward Lock, 1974.
16   *Times History*, i p. 459.
17   Johnson, op. cit. p. 55.
18   Joffre, op. cit. i p. 186.
19   Ibid., p. 156; M. Henri Isselin in *The Battle of the Marne*, Elek, 1965, says Joffre also dismissed 90 brigadiers, making a total of 140 generals.
20   Cuneo, op. cit. ii pp. 14–15.
21   Ronald Lewin: *Ultra Goes To War*, p. 20; Hutchinson, 1978.
22   Joffre, op. cit. i p. 289.
23   Haig Diary; author's papers.
24   Ibid.
25   Van Creveld, op. cit. p. 127.
26   André Tardieu: *Avec Foch (août–octobre 1914)*, Paris, 1939, quoted by Richard Thoumin: *The First World War*, pp. 104–5; Secker & Warburg, 1963.
27   Joffre, op. cit. i p. 282.
28   Terraine: *The Great War*, p. 54; Arrow Books.
29   Falls, op. cit. p. 59.
30   Rudolf Binding: *A Fatalist at War*, p. 19; Allen & Unwin, 1929.
31   Charteris: *At GHQ*, p. 50; Cassell, 1931.
32   Binding, op. cit. pp. 24–5.
33   *O.H. 1914* ii p. 301.
34   Binding, op. cit. pp. 20–1.

CHAPTER II

The Clash in the East

IN THE EAST, as in the West, geography and technology governed the conduct of the war and guided it to similar conclusions. The geography of the Eastern Front was, of course, very different from that of the West, and itself contained sharp variety. In the north, from Memel on the Baltic to Lublin in southern Poland, the land is low-lying, with vast areas at or even below sea-level (like western Flanders); this is the great north European plain, and unlike Flanders much of it is covered by vast coniferous forests, pitted with chains of lakes and wide stretches of windswept marsh. Then comes the Carpathian range, a 500-mile loop of mountains slung round Hungary, rising to 8,737 feet where it faces north towards Warsaw and 7,562 in the east where it looks down on Bukovina. Behind the mountains, to the west, lies the plain of Hungary, beyond it, to the east, the rolling plateaux of the Ukraine. In 1914 the strategic feature of the Eastern Front was the great bulge of Russian Poland, legacy of the partition of 1795 and the 1815 settlement. Taking this projection into account, the Front itself, from the Baltic to the Romanian frontier, measured some 750 miles as the crow might fly, more like 900 in reality.

Such a length clearly ruled out a continuous trench line—the curse which soon lay upon the Western Front. In consequence, in the East there were always flanks to turn, which meant that there was always freedom of movement (except in the very depths of winter; though it was amazing how both sides managed to overcome quite appalling conditions). The opportunity for decisive action thus seemed readier and more tempting, and all armies accordingly undertook huge, impressive manoeuvres. Yet these always ended, just like the Western struggles for ruined hamlets or for a few hundred yards of trench, in stalemate. Geography had won another victory; it was not the length of the front that ultimately counted, but the immense distances on either side of it. It was these that swallowed up the armies (as they had done to Napoleon in 1812) and reduced them to an impotence as absolute as that which reigned in Flanders or Picardy or Champagne. In Churchill's lapidary phrase:

'In the West the armies were too big for the country; in the East the country was too big for the armies.'[1]

Technology added its contribution to human misery by permitting, by use of railways, the assembly of the masses. The Russians did not fulfil the pledge which they had made a year earlier, to put 800,000 men in the field against Germany on the 15th day of mobilization (see p. 63). Nevertheless, their northern group of armies (First Army, General Rennenkampf; Second

Army, General Samsonov) amounted to about half a million men. Further south, against Austria, four Armies were assembled, totalling some 1–1,200,000. And simultaneously, largely thanks to the new railways, all over the Tsar's sprawling empire reserves and new formations were gathering to back the leading units, something like 4 million men in all. Friends and enemies were equally surprised by this achievement; as General Joffre said, 'Russia was surpassing all our expectations.'

Similar scenes unfolded on the other side. The main body of the Austro-Hungarian Army was deployed in Galicia: a total of some 900,000. Probably 300,000 more were in the south, facing the Serbs; another 500,000 were being collected and distributed by the railways of the empire, as the reservists reported to their depôts. Only the Germans, in obedience to Schlieffen's doctrine, were at this stage comparatively weak: General von Prittwitz's *Eighth Army* in East Prussia faced the Russian invasion with no more than about 25,000 men. War games, however, carefully based on railway timetables, had already taught the German staffs how numbers can be multiplied by movement, and the railway system of East Prussia gave them the instrument they needed.

The Polish salient dominated strategy. Schlieffen's intention had always been to stand on the defensive in the east (even, if necessary, abandoning East Prussia) until the decisive victory had been won in France, and then to use Germany's main strategic railway lines to straighten the account. The hazard was the salient. Russian Poland projected westward some 200 miles; northward, at its nearest point, the Baltic coast was only 75 miles away, offering the Russians the chance of cutting off the whole *Eighth Army* and the fortress of Königsberg; westward, Berlin itself was only 180 miles distant. Southward, there was less temptation for a Russian advance from the salient; Austria-Hungary lay secure behind the Carpathian shield. On the other hand, there was every temptation for an Austrian thrust northward *into* the salient, in the direction of Lublin, especially if combined with a German thrust southward towards Syedlets. This offered a splendid encirclement of Russian field armies and the isolation of an important section of their fortress system. To a lively mind like Conrad's, this strategy was both obvious and irresistible; it became his theme song, pressed upon Moltke and Prittwitz from the earliest days and blinding Conrad himself to more significant realities.

For the next three years the war of movement in the East took the form of great pendulum swings, beginning in East Prussia, where General Jilinski's northern Army Group opened its offensive on 17 August—only two days behind the schedule of the 1913 Franco-Russian military agreements. The Russians faced a serious obstacle: 30 miles inside the German frontier ran the chain of the Masurian Lakes, 50 miles long, running due north–south from Angerburg almost to the Polish frontier. Any army trying to penetrate this maze of waters would be exposed to defeat in detail. North of Angerburg the country was open and accessible, though the Germans had not neglected field fortifications and behind them stood Königsberg. Clearly, there was no great

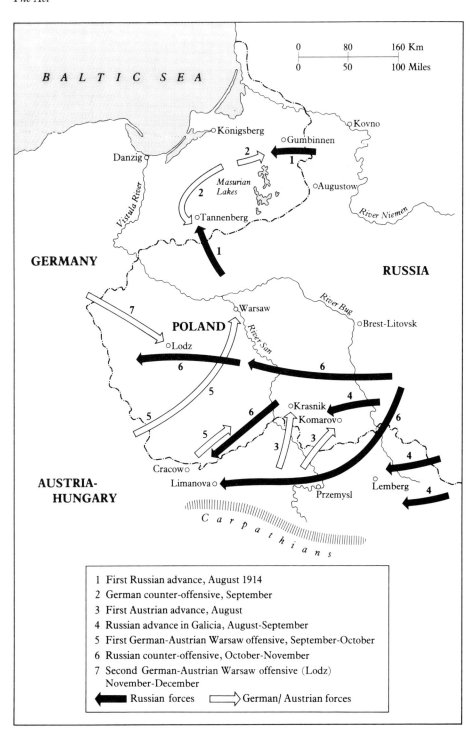

1 First Russian advance, August 1914
2 German counter-offensive, September
3 First Austrian advance, August
4 Russian advance in Galicia, August-September
5 First German-Austrian Warsaw offensive, September-October
6 Russian counter-offensive, October-November
7 Second German-Austrian Warsaw offensive (Lodz)
   November-December

■→ Russian forces   ▷ German/ Austrian forces

'. . . war of movement in the East took the form of great pendulum swings . . .'

'The Russian cavalry proved quite useless for reconnaissance': the photograph illustrates both Cossacks and regular cavalry. Their enemies did little better, except in rounding up prisoners.

scope for decisive manoeuvre in this direction; the temptations of the Polish salient became accordingly more alluring. So Jilinski adopted a plan which was obvious enough, but potentially deadly: a pincer movement. While Rennenkampf distracted the Germans north of the Lakes, Samsonov would strike northwards from Warsaw, to envelop the *Eighth Army* and cut off the whole province of East Prussia from Germany.

The fault of the Russian plan was the 'Russian disease'—that blanket of lethargy and inefficiency, of corruption, nepotism, jealousy, and sheer ignorance which suffocated every right endeavour under the autocracy, even in its reformed days after 1905. Russia, in a word, was still unfit to undertake modern war; that she survived for three years is astonishing; her achievements were a miracle; but from beginning to end she was a giant bleeding to death. The clash of battle which began on 17 August, and swelled to tumult in the days that followed, set the irrevocable pattern of the eastern war.

Correctly, Prittwitz and his staff judged that, because distances were shorter and railway facilities better, it would be Rennenkampf who posed the first threat. The bulk of the *Eighth Army* was accordingly held in the north, with only one corps and some supporting units to watch the approaches from Warsaw. Rennenkampf crossed the frontier on the 17th, brushing aside the German covering forces, and made a leisurely advance (only some 20 miles) to Gumbinnen, where he arrived on 20 August. It was a momentous day: in the West the Germans were entering Brussels and inflicting the first defeats on the French in the Battles of the Frontiers. In Serbia the Austrians were reeling back from their own first, horribly unexpected defeat, known as the Battle of the Jadar. The main Russian armies were on the move towards Galicia, and Conrad, fortified by dubious German promises, was beginning his cherished advance into Poland towards Lublin. And on this day, so heavy with distant consequences, the fortune of war dictated that the first important victory on the Eastern Front should be gained by the Russians—the Battle of Gumbinnen.

'Very few people', wrote Churchill in 1931, 'have even heard of Gumbinnen, and scarcely anyone has appreciated the astonishing part it played' in the development of the First World War. The Russian victory was not an easy one, but it was quite definite; there was a panic in one German army corps, and 7,000 prisoners were left in Russian hands; General von Prittwitz was severely shaken, and informed Moltke that he intended retiring behind the Vistula, perhaps even further. This meant abandoning East Prussia, as Schlieffen had contemplated, but Moltke now refused to do. His immediate reaction was to remove Prittwitz, the first of the war's senior failures; in his place came the 67-year-old Field-Marshal von Hindenburg with General Erich Ludendorff as his chief of staff. They arrived on 23 August, by which time Prittwitz and the *Eighth Army* staff, inspired by Colonel Max Hoffmann, Head of the Operations Section, had taken a firm grip on the situation. But already the consequences of Gumbinnen were in train:

'*It induced Prittwitz to break off the battle . . . It provoked Moltke to supersede Prittwitz. It inspired Moltke to appoint Hindenburg and Ludendorff, and thereby set in motion the measureless consequences that followed from that decision. It procured from Hoffmann and the staff of the Eighth Army the swift and brilliant combination of movements which dictated the Battle of Tannenberg. It imparted to the Russian Command a confidence which was in no way justified. . . . It lured Jilinski to spur on Samsonov's marching army. It lured Samsonov to deflect his advance more to the West and less to the North, i.e. farther away from Rennenkampf . . . It persuaded Rennenkampf to dawdle for nearly three days on the battlefield in order to let Samsonov's more ambitious movement gain its greatest effect, and it led Jilinski to acquiesce in his strategic inertia.*'[2]

Nor was this all: the even more far-reaching effects of Gumbinnen were, first, to rob Conrad of German support in his march into Poland, and secondly, to alarm Moltke so much that he ordered that fatal transfer of forces from the decisive point in the West that we have noted on page 102.

'. . . staff was improvised; few had prepared for the work they had to do.' This 1914 photograph is a perfect illustration of episodes in Alexander Solzhenitsyn's *August 1914*.

And this was still not the full reckoning for 20 August. For it was on that day that Samsonov's Second Army at last reached the frontier—indeed, it was airmen's reports of this advance that had so unnerved Prittwitz (virtually the only significant contribution of the air arm of either side to these opening manoeuvres in the East). But what the airmen did not reveal was the condition of Samsonov's army, which was now fully in the grip of the 'Russian disease'.

The catalogue of disorder is impressive, even by Russian standards. First, the general himself: Samsonov was considered a 'soldier's general', which does not normally suggest profound study of war; he had held a political post for the last five years, and was actually on sick leave when war broke out. It did not help that he and Rennenkampf had physically come to blows in a public altercation during the Russo-Japanese War. His staff was improvised; few of them knew each other, or had prepared for the work they had to do. The supply organization of the army was chaotic, with catastrophic shortage of transport. Sixty per cent of the men in some units were reservists, whom one corps commander called 'peasants in disguise whom it was necessary to train'; they were, he told Samsonov, quite incapable of undertaking mobile operations—yet Jilinski was urging 'the energetic execution of the advance.' To top it all—and this was particularly serious for an army operating on a wide front in an area practically devoid of road and rail communications—there was virtually no Signal organization in the Second Army.[3] For the whole army there were only 25 telephones and one primitive and uncertain teleprinter; complete cipher keys had not been issued to the corps, so that wireless messages had to be sent in clear (the shortage of trained operators would probably have ensured this in any case). This Russian practice was to confer wonderful advantages on their enemies along the whole Eastern Front in 1914. For Samsonov it would soon spell ruin.

Though Prittwitz was filled with alarm at the news of Samsonov's arrival on the frontier, sharper-eyed staff officers, in particular Hoffmann, noted three significant features of it: first, its wide separation from Rennenkampf, secondly, its slowness in relation to the First Army, thirdly, its long extension westward. Prewar study of the railway timetables now delivered its reward: Hoffmann urged that while Rennenkampf lingered, the bulk of the *Eighth Army* should be swung round by rail to roll up Samsonov's extended left, and trap him in a decisive counter-encirclement. Hindenburg and Ludendorff had formed the same plan, and when they arrived they found the bold manoeuvre already in progress. It was a remarkable example of 'the German General Staff system, institutionalized excellence, which had caused two individuals with extremely different personalities—Ludendorff and Hoffmann—to analyze a military situation thoroughly and objectively, so that the same set of facts led both of them to identical solutions.'[4]

So came about the famous Battle of Tannenberg (26–30 August), a classic of military history, a brilliant example of the mobile warfare of the Industrial

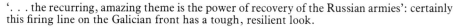

'. . . the recurring, amazing theme is the power of recovery of the Russian armies': certainly this firing line on the Galician front has a tough, resilient look.

Revolution at that stage. It was a battle made possible only by the railways of East Prussia, and the knowledge of how to use them possessed by the German General Staff. They were, however, immensely assisted by the Russian wireless indiscretion; on the eve of action they were happily reassured by the certainty 'that Rennenkampf's army could not take part in Samsonov's battles'.[5] And from top to bottom of their forces engaged, the Germans enjoyed the superiority of organization and equipment which distinguishes a modern, developed industrial country from a backward one. The Germans lacked only numbers; as Dr. Stone says, 'The Tsarist army was not crippled by its inferiority in artillery or men; it was crippled by its inability to use its superiority.'[6] The result was devastating: the Germans claimed 92,000 unwounded and 30,000 wounded Russian prisoners (the number of dead is unknown, but must have been high because fighting was often fierce) and 500 guns.[7] Samsonov, in an agony of remorse, walked off into a wood and shot himself. But Tannenberg spelt more than the human and material losses sustained; as Alexander Solzhenitsyn says, 'it was the *first* defeat which set the tone of the whole course of the war for Russia.'[8]

Tannenberg marked the end of the first pendulum-swing; no sooner was the battle over than the reverse action was prepared. Reinforced now by the two army corps which Moltke had sent from the West (too late for Tannenberg, too soon for the Marne) the German High Command re-deployed their forces by the familiar rail lines to demolish Rennenkampf. They were much helped by the dense fog of war which existed on the Russian side. Reliable news of what had happened to Samsonov was slow in coming in; the Russian cavalry proved quite useless, despite its great numbers, for reconnaissance; the few aircraft were unusable, either because of mechanical faults, or because the Russian soldiers shot at them on sight. Jilinski's orders, says Churchill, 'dealt largely in phantom armies and with an imaginary situation. They were brushed aside by reality.' During 5–7 September, the Germans took up their new positions, their chief feature being once more a wide turning movement by *I Corps*, commanded by the fiery and audacious General von François. It was his corps, after a march of 77 miles in four days, which opened the main action on 9 September, playing, as Churchill says, 'a part on this day as decisively and brilliantly successful as at Tannenberg.' Rennenkampf, unlike the irresolute Samsonov, recognized defeat when he saw it and reacted instantly; 'he fled and he flew'. Covered by sacrificial rearguards, the First Army made off by forced marches (55 miles in 50 hours) for the fortress of Kovno and the Niemen line. By 14 September it was all over; Rennenkampf had lost 45,000 prisoners, 200 guns, perhaps 100,000 casualties all told—but at least the First Army was still in being. Three days later Jilinski joined von Prittwitz in the ranks of what the French called the '*limogés*' (Limoges was the posting of generals who had been dismissed); Rennenkampf's turn would not be long delayed.

While the northern pendulum swung from east to west and back, the southern was in reverse motion. There it was Conrad who struck first, into south Poland, where his left flank armies won the first battles, Krasnik

(23–26 August) and Komarov (26–30 August). Once again, the striking feature of the action was the impotence of the cavalry of both sides; Austrians and Russians blundered into each other, each missing the main movements of the other. Aircraft appear to have played only one brief, disastrous rôle. At Komarov, Conrad was within an ace of a Tannenberg-style encirclement, but an airman's false report on one flank and one equally misleading from the cavalry on the other robbed him of his triumph. And meanwhile the Russian advance in Galicia was making its measured progress, with two armies (Ruzski's Third and Brusilov's Eighth) against one Austrian, the *Third*, with a wide gap on its right where the *Second* should have been instead of dallying to no good purpose on the Serbian front. What is extraordinary is that the Austrians could completely miss the approach of Brusilov's whole army of four corps on a front of about 60 miles. In this region of practically non-existent railways and few roads, the marching columns were 25–30 miles long. Logistically, this means that the rear of each column was about two days' march behind its head; strategically, it means that they presented an unmistakable spectacle, if only there were eyes to see. But there were none; such aircraft as Austria possessed (like the French in Lorraine) were looking in the wrong direction—northward.

The result was precisely what one might expect: an Austrian catastrophe surpassing that which had overtaken the Russians in East Prussia. The critical fighting began on 26 August (when Conrad's attention was all on Poland); the first stage is known as the Battle of Zlotchov, the opening of the great Battles of Lemberg which continued until 11 September. As the Russians stage by stage deployed their preponderance of strength, suddenly it was Conrad's armies that faced encirclements from which they were only rescued by the further indiscretions of the Russian wireless which gave them just time enough to retreat. The large commercial and cultural centre of Lemberg fell on 3 September; on the 11th Conrad gave orders to retreat to the River San, where stood the great fortress of Przemysl. But by now his armies were in such a deplorable condition that there was no question of their standing here. Back they had to go to the line of the Carpathians and the River Dunajec, which pursues its course to the Vistula some 130 miles west of Lemberg, and here at last they stood on 26 September.

Such was the southern pendulum: war of movement indeed. The armies of the Habsburg Empire had 'fought the greatest, bloodiest and most exhausting battles in the history of the dynasty.'[9] Out of some 900,000 troops involved, the Austrian Official Account admits a loss of 250,000 dead and wounded and 100,000 taken prisoner. Churchill comments:

'This mutilation of the Austro-Hungarian army in the terrible battle of two nations called Lemberg ranks with the turn at the Marne as the most important and irrevocable result of the war in 1914. It is the supreme condemnation of Conrad's narrow military creed. . . . Of all the armies that have ever existed since Hannibal marched into Italy, the Austro-Hungarian army needed the most careful handling. Conrad broke their hearts and used them up in three weeks.'[10]

And still there was more to come; for now the Germans, freed of anxiety on their own frontiers, could take into account the lamentable condition of their ally. Now at last—when Austria was virtually on her knees in Galicia, and locked again in stubborn, indecisive struggle in Serbia—the Germans announced themselves ready for combined action against the Polish salient. Once more the railways hummed and rattled; the *Eighth Army* was stripped of four of its corps, which went to form a new *Ninth Army* (commanded by Hindenburg) on the left of the Austrians north of Cracow. On 28 September (only a fortnight after their victory in East Prussia) the Germans launched their offensive against Warsaw, and the pendulum was swinging again. By 12 October General von Mackensen's corps was within 12 miles of the Polish capital; the Austrians had relieved their besieged fortress of Przemysl on the 9th, and the line of battle stood along the line of the rivers San and Vistula—and there the pendulum stuck.

In all these narratives of the Eastern Front, the recurring, amazing theme is the power of recovery of the Russian armies (see p. 65). Their immense reserves of manpower refilled the ranks, reconstituted the shattered units; their immense endurance carried them back to battle. The tragedy was that, due to mistaken purchasing policies and bureaucratic incompetence, even rifles were in such short supply that the depôts could only arm one man in ten. Yet they came on; by October the Second Army was back in the field and new Ninth, Tenth, and Eleventh Armies were either formed or forming. The Grand Duke Nicholas, commanding in chief, even contemplated an advance from the Polish salient into Germany, and moved three armies northward from Galicia for the purpose. So it came about that the four corps of the German *Ninth Army*, almost unaided by their Austrian allies, found themselves faced by four Russian armies in south Poland—an indication, says Churchill, of 'the ratios and values already established on the Eastern Front'.

In stubborn fighting, the *Ninth Army* lost 40,000 men; on 17 October the back-swing of the pendulum began—the Germans began a 150-mile retreat to the frontier, and there *that* swing also stopped. On 1 November they learned from the Russian wireless that the pursuing armies were exhausted; they had a breathing-space. What should they do with it? Hindenburg gave the answer by a simple gesture at the conference that decided the matter: he raised his left hand. He meant that, as the right-hand blow had failed, they must try again with the left—another attack on Warsaw, this time from the north. So once again the railways hummed, and the iron soldiers, who seemed not to know fatigue, prepared themselves for yet another battle. It was called Lodz; this was where, by 18 November the Germans had 150,000 men of the remade Russian Second Army as well encircled as Samsonov's original had been at Tannenberg. But this time there was a rescue: the Grand Duke Nicholas brought his Fifth Army across the rear of the Second to attack the left pincer of the encirclement, General von Scheffer-Boyadel's *XXV Reserve Corps*. This critical sub-battle opened on 21 November, and on the same day fresh Russian forces drawn from their First Army to the north-east began to press on Scheffer's rear. Now it looked as though 60,000

Germans faced encirclement; the Russians were so sure of the outcome that they ordered up trains from Warsaw to take away the prisoners. But as Churchill says, 'a sharp knife will cut wood'; *XXV Reserve Corps* was the knife and Scheffer was the man to use it. By 25 November he had cut his way through the Russians and rejoined the *Ninth Army*; his losses were light, and he brought back with him 16,000 Russian prisoners and 64 guns. 'It was an almost unbelievable feat, one of the greatest of the war, and of all military history'.[11]

Nevertheless, the second German offensive against Warsaw had failed, as the first had done. And meanwhile their allies were in serious trouble again. The Russian counter-offensive in Galicia had carried them back to Przemysl (besieged once more on 1 November) and on towards Cracow; by 25 November they had reached the crests of the Carpathians; at the end of the month they captured the Dukla Pass and stood only 15 miles from Cracow. And then the Austrians did the unbelievable: they struck back on 3 December at Limanova and halted the Russian tide. At last the pendulum of 1914 came to rest; snow, ice, and sub-zero temperatures brought a brief interval to these battles of giants in their enormous landscapes. After all this movement all that had been proved was that movement itself proves nothing.

Only two footnotes need to be added to this epic. While the Russians were developing their Galician threat, a gleam of light at last appeared for Austria on the Serbian front. On 19 November General Potiorek's forces captured the important centre of Valievo, and on the 28th they won what seemed to be a decisive victory at Lazarevatz; the Serbs were exhausted, obviously near the end of their tether. On 2 December the Austrians entered Belgrade. And then the impossible happened yet again. The very next day all the Serbian armies counter-attacked with a ferocity beyond all that had gone before; the 70-year-old king himself entered the firing-line, rifle in hand; and everywhere the Austrians were routed. On 15 December the Serbian Army was back in Belgrade; the Austrians were flung back across the frontiers for the second time, leaving behind over 40,000 prisoners, 133 guns, and large quantities of stores. Potiorek was dismissed, and deep humiliation was added to the grief of the Habsburg Empire at the terrible losses that only five months of war had brought.

For Russia, too, despite the recovery in Poland and the successes in Galicia, the year ended in shadow. A new belligerent had entered the war: Turkey. The significant acts of the war against Turkey began to unfold in 1915, but in the last month of 1914 they took the form of a Turkish advance towards Russian territory in the Caucasus. Russian forces here had been weakened by substantial detachments to Galicia, and as the Turkish *Third Army* came forward into the mountains there was grave alarm. The new year would soon show that this was unfounded, but for the time being the Turkish threat was one more weight in an already almost intolerable burden.

NOTES

1 Winston S. Churchill: *The World Crisis: The Eastern Front*, p. 83; Thornton Butterworth, 1931.
2 Ibid., pp. 183–4
3 For this catalogue see Lieut.-Gen. Sir Geoffrey Evans: *Tannenberg 1410:1914*, pp. 78–9; Hamish Hamilton, 1970.
4 Col. T. N. Dupuy: *A Genius for War: The German Army and General Staff 1807–1945*, p. 155; Macdonald & Jane's, 1977.
5 Churchill, op. cit. p. 195.
6 Stone, *The Eastern Front*, p. 58.
7 Evans, op. cit. p. 156; he notes that Lieut.-Gen. N. N. Golovine (*The Russian Army in the World War*, Yale University Press, 1931) says that the number of guns lost was 'between 180 and 190'; Stone (p. 66) says 'nearly 400').
8 Alexander Solzhenitsyn: *'August 1914'*, p. 399; trans. Michael Glenny, The Bodley Head, 1971.
9 Edward Crankshaw: *The Fall of the House of Habsburg*, p. 431; Cardinal Edition, 1974.
10 Churchill, op. cit. pp. 220–1.
11 Dupuy, op. cit. p. 158.

CHAPTER III

The Clash at Sea

M ODERN SEA WARFARE, in 1914, was all mystery; as suggested above, the words 'Nobody knew' might serve as the epitaph of the whole war, but to no part of it more exactly than the sea. Above all, of course, it was that new element, under water, which contained the core of the mystery. It did not take long to declare its presence. On 5 August the British light cruiser *Amphion*, with two destroyers in company, on a sweep in the North Sea came upon the minelayer *Königin Luise*, which was promptly sunk by the British force. So the Royal Navy had drawn first blood; but what the price of admiralty might be was quickly revealed. The very next day *Amphion* struck two mines (presumably some of those laid by *Königin Luise*) and sank with a loss of some 150 officers and men. So straight away the mine danger placed its shackles on the navies of the world; on 27 October it claimed a prize victim— the battleship *Audacious*, off the north coast of Ireland. Never again would ships move freely in restricted waters in time of war.

'First times'—first experiences of new techniques and new perils —abounded; the submarine services provided a handsome quota. Here the Germans, of course, had a great advantage: virtually the monopoly of targets, since their commerce vanished from the seas with the outbreak of

The sinking of the *Audacious*: H.M.S. *Audacious* was a modern dreadnought (1912; 23,000 tons, 21 knots; 10 15-inch guns) and therefore a serious loss.

war, and their High Seas Fleet remained resolutely in harbour. Nevertheless, it was once again the Royal Navy that drew first blood—on 9 August,
when H.M.S. *Birmingham* rammed *U-15* in the North Sea, cutting her clean
in half. This was the first action between surface and under-surface craft in
history, the first case of a submarine being sunk in such action. The first
sinking of a warship by a submarine in action at sea followed on 3 September:
the light cruiser *Pathfinder* sunk by *U-21* off the Firth of Forth.[1] The first
sinking by a British submarine came ten days later: the cruiser *Hela* by *E9*.
The next 'first' was the destruction of a submarine by another submarine: *E3*
by *U-27* on 18 October. Then came an omen: the first merchant ship to be
sunk by a submarine—the British steamer *Glitra* by *U-17* on 20 October.
The U-boat captain (Lieutenant-Commander Feldkirchner) gave *Glitra's*
crew ten minutes to abandon ship, and then towed the boats several miles
towards the English coast. Less fortunate was the French ship *Amiral
Ganteaume* on 26 October: she was sunk without warning by *U-24*
(Lieutenant-Commander Schneider) while carrying Belgian refugees. Some
40 lives were lost. 'It was a new and exceedingly unpleasant happening in the
war at sea.'[2]

Such was the onrush of novelties in the first three months of war. What I
have listed are the historic 'firsts'—all of them containing matters for every
admiralty in the world to ponder with alarm. Yet the most dramatic stroke by
underwater craft, the one which made the most serious impact on naval and
public opinion, was not one of these. It occurred on 22 September, in waters
constricted on one side by the neutral Dutch coast and on the other by a
German minefield: the sinking in quick succession of the old cruisers
Aboukir, *Hogue*, and *Cressy* by a single submarine, *U-9* (Lieutenant Otto
Weddigen). The ships mattered little; they were obsolete. The loss of nearly
1,500 officers and men, mainly Reservists, married with families, was a
tragedy. What made it worse was that *Hogue* and *Cressy* were hit while trying
to pick up survivors—they were sitting ducks. Clearly, the new mysterious
styles of war were going to take some getting used to. Meanwhile, in the
words of the Official History,

*'Nothing that had yet occurred had so emphatically proclaimed the change that had
come over naval warfare, and never perhaps had so great a result been obtained by
means relatively so small.'*[3]

For the Royal Navy, for the German High Seas Fleet, for the British and
German publics at large, these were bewildering times. In both countries,
says the Official History,

*'of recent years, by a strange misreading of history, an idea had grown up that (a
fleet's) primary function is to seek out and destroy the enemy's main fleet. This
view, being literary rather than historical, was nowhere adopted with more unction
than in Germany, where there was no naval tradition to test its accuracy.'*[4]

When no such thing happened, admirals, captains, ordinary seamen, newspaper editors, and newspaper readers all felt cheated; something must be 'wrong'. It was natural that the Germans should seize upon the successes of their U-boats for consolation—equally natural that the British should be highly pleased by a smart incursion into the Heligoland Bight on 28 August by light cruisers and destroyers, backed by Vice-Admiral Sir David Beatty's battle-cruiser squadron. Three German light cruisers and a destroyer were sunk (a loss of over 1,000 men); no British ship was lost, 35 men were killed and 40 wounded. The moral effect, for both fleets, was in proportion. On 22 October there was further satisfaction for Britain: a North Sea action in which the Royal Navy sank four German destroyers with a loss of over 200 men, the British ships receiving only superficial damage and having one officer and four men wounded.

Yet by early November there was deep discontent with the Admiralty and the Navy itself. People were reminded that back in early August the German battle-cruiser *Goeben* and the light cruiser *Breslau* had escaped from a superior British force out of the Mediterranean to Constantinople; on 29 October they reappeared in the Black Sea, under the Turkish flag, to bombard the Russian port of Sebastopol. This meant the entry of Turkey into the war on Germany's side—a definite *coup*. German raiders—the light cruisers *Emden*, in the Bay of Bengal, *Karlsruhe* in the Atlantic, and *Königsberg* in the Indian Ocean—were doing damage to trade and communications with apparent impunity. Then came the sickening loss of the three cruisers. Winston Churchill, the First Lord, was strongly criticized (particularly by those who knew very little about it) for his personal intervention with naval brigades at Antwerp; the fall of that fortress on 10 October seemed to underline another major error. Attempts to conceal the loss of the *Audacious* (although this had been witnessed and photographed by the passengers on the liner *Olympic*) added to the prevailing distrust and annoyance. The final blow was the sinking of the two elderly cruisers, *Good Hope* and *Monmouth*, in the Battle of Coronel off the Chilean coast on 1 November.

It was on that same day that Lord Fisher returned from retirement as First Sea Lord, replacing Prince Louis of Battenberg; it is easy to see the reappointment of this 74-year-old firebrand as a turning point in the naval war—easy, but superficial and incorrect. What shortly followed seemed to be a thorough vindication of one of Fisher's most controversial policies; the truth is that he had already received a truer vindication before he resumed office. Let us examine the facts.

The victor of Cape Coronel was Vice-Admiral Maximilian von Spee's East Asiatic Squadron, a cruiser force whose hard core was the two modern armoured cruisers, *Scharnhorst* and *Gneisenau*, 11,600 tons, with eight 8.2 in. and six 5.9 in. guns (a formidable armament) and capable of speeds of about 23 knots. These were crack vessels, famous for their gunnery; they were

'*among the finest of their breed in the world, fast enough to escape from any*

'. . . the high qualities of the Imperial German Navy': the armoured cruiser, *Scharnhorst*, flagship of Admiral von Spee's squadron; a crack ship, she was famous for her gunnery.

battleship, a match for any enemy cruiser, and destructible only by the newer, bigger and faster battle-cruisers which had entered service since the German ships had first been commissioned.' [5]

Three modern light cruisers completed the squadron (including the *Emden*, whose feats on detached duty in the Bay of Bengal were already becoming legendary). The mere presence of this powerful force in Eastern waters vindicated Fisher's prewar policy of withdrawing weak or old vessels from distant stations and scrapping them—a policy which had drawn forth howls of rage. The superiority of *Scharnhorst* and *Gneisenau* to virtually anything that the Royal Navy could easily produce after North Sea demands had been met was fully recognized. Spee's squadron posed a most serious threat, and his destruction of Rear-Admiral Sir Christopher Cradock's two weaker ships at Coronel merely dotted the i's and crossed the t's.

Yet all the time there hung over Spee precisely the threat which he himself posed to the weak British detachments in the Pacific. Somewhere to the south would be H.M.A.S. *Australia*, a battle-cruiser of 18,800 tons which had reached 25.8 knots at her trials and carried eight 12 in. guns. All naval theory taught that this single ship was capable of destroying Spee's entire squadron at ranges which would ensure that she herself received no damage. And in company she would most likely have H.M.A.S. *Sydney* and *Melbourne*, two strong, modern ships displacing 5,400 tons, capable of 25.7 knots and carrying eight 6 in. guns (compared with ten 4.1 in. on each of von Spee's light cruisers). When Japan entered the war on the Allied side on 23

August, she could contribute two large, modern Dreadnought battle-cruisers capable of 27 knots, and four smaller ones with speeds of 20.5 to 22.75 knots. To Spee their presence in the north, and that of the Australian Navy in the south, had the look of iron jaws which might close at any moment. At the same time, the Japanese attack on Tsing-tau robbed him of his only defended base. Hence the move across the Pacific which brought him to Coronel.

The Battle of Coronel fluttered the Admiralty dovecots (at first they refused to believe the news) and horrified the British public; to this day it exercises a morbid fascination. Yet the truth was very different from the appearance of German triumph on 1 November. From the very beginning of his cruise Spee was, in Churchill's words, 'a cut flower in a vase; fair to see, yet bound to die'. Being a highly professional and intelligent man, he himself had no illusions; when he was presented with flowers by the rapturous German colony in Valparaiso after the battle, he said: 'They will do for my funeral.' This was not long delayed. On 6 December Spee's squadron[6] set course for the Falkland Islands, with the intention of destroying the British base at Port Stanley (with its important coal stocks) and the wireless station. At 8 am on 8 December *Gneisenau*, with *Nürnberg* in company, was approaching Port Stanley, the advance guard of the East Asiatic Squadron; Commander Johann Busche, senior gunnery officer of *Gneisenau*, was observing from the control top. It was he who made the dreadful discovery—not quite so dramatically or immediately as Churchill tells it, but the effect was the same:

'. . . *a terrible apparition broke upon German eyes. Rising from behind the promontory, sharply visible in the clear air,*[7] *were a pair of tripod masts. One glance was enough. They meant certain death.*'[8]

In other words, the battle-cruisers which Spee had been avoiding since August had arrived: *Invincible* and *Inflexible*, borrowed from the Grand Fleet, each of 17,250 tons, able to do 25 knots and armed, like *Australia*, with the overwhelming 12 in. guns. There could be no reasonable doubt of the outcome, and there was none. After a long, hard chase *Scharnhorst* and *Gneisenau*, with the two light cruisers *Nürnberg* and *Leipzig* and two tenders were all sunk—a loss of some 2,000 officers and men. Only *Dresden* escaped—to meet her end some three months later. Damage in the British squadron[9] was light, and the total of casualties was about 30. Such is the grim law of naval arithmetic.

Naturally, there was public jubilation in Britain when the news of this Nelsonian finale was released. In naval circles there was relief, mixed with concern (there was also some regrettable backbiting, stemming from Fisher's splenetic feud with the victorious admiral, Sir Doveton Sturdee). The concern was at the fact that it had taken some nine hours for the two great battle-cruisers to sink their far less powerful opponents; by that time *Inflexible* had only 30 rounds left for her 12 in. guns, *Invincible* only 22. This suggested poor handling by the admiral and captains; the truth, reflected in the infinitesimal casualties (nil in *Invincible*; one man killed, 2 slightly wounded in *Inflexible*) was more probably that this was the penalty of fighting at very long ranges—another first experience of the war. The true misfortune was the euphoria about battle-cruisers in general produced by Sturdee's victory. What it had demonstrated was only the familiar naval precept that good big ships will normally defeat good smaller ones. It added nothing to knowledge of what the British battle-cruisers might be capable of in pitched battle against other capital ships. *Australia* and the Japanese had displayed the strong deterrent effect that this class could have upon commerce raiders; the unwisdom of asking more of them would be displayed in the haunting spectacle of *Invincible* twenty months later, her fore and aft ends projecting separately from the sea at Jutland.

The Battle of the Falkland Islands seemed to underline a turning-point in the war at sea under the Fisher régime. The truth is somewhat different: it is that despite setbacks and alarms the main tides of the naval war had been flowing from the very first without serious check. All those significant processes listed on p. 76 were in full operation; they did not make sensational headlines, they did not often even make news—but they were shaping the pattern of the war. And some of those of which the public was least aware were the ones of most profound effect. It was on 26 August that the German light cruiser *Magdeburg* ran ashore in the Gulf of Finland and was destroyed by Russian warships; the Russians found the body of a German petty officer with the cypher and signal books of the Imperial Navy clasped in his arms. In October these were brought to London, and early in November an organization was set up in the Admiralty to bring this insight to bear upon the war—another new dimension.

Wireless itself had been a factor from the first. All the German harbours and the ships inside them were under radio surveillance—indeed, it was said that the Germans could not move a picket-boat without the Admiralty knowing of it. The *Times History* relates that, for example, on 19 August the Press Bureau had 'announced that "a certain liveliness" was noticeable in the North Sea' and remarks

'*In what manner it was discovered that the enemy was on the move, that cruisers, submarines and destroyers were "showing a certain liveliness", we have not been told . . .*'[10]

The answer, of course, was that the manner of discovery was wireless, already the vigilant monitor of all naval movement—though many naval officers themselves were slow to realize this. Wireless stations became important targets. German stations at Kamina (Togoland) and Duala (Cameroons) were destroyed in August and September; their Pacific stations were eliminated one by one; *Emden* was sunk after damaging the British cable and wireless station at Cocos Keeling Island, and as we have seen, the wireless station was one of the objectives of Spee's last foray to the Falklands.

Wireless communication, monitoring and jamming were all now standard practices of war. And all this, too, was new.

And there was more besides. It was the Royal Naval Air Service, rather than the Military Wing of the Royal Flying Corps, which was first to envisage a combatant (as distinct from reconnaissance) rôle for aircraft. This was the more remarkable in view of the virtual inability of seaplanes to carry bomb-loads and their general clumsiness in flight, and the Navy's shortage of useful aeroplanes. Nevertheless, the RNAS was first to carry out an air raid—two, to be precise, two machines each attacking the Zeppelin sheds at Düsseldorf and Cologne on 22 September. All returned safely, which is the most that can be claimed for this adventure, except that it was a portent. The second attempt, on 8 October, was more successful. Two Sopwith Tabloids set out from Antwerp (on the eve of its fall) towards the same targets, piloted by Squadron Commander Spenser Grey and Flight Lieutenant R. L. G. Marix. It was the latter who flew to Düsseldorf, found the Zeppelin shed and dropped his mighty armament of four 20 lb. bombs right on it from 600 feet. The result was most gratifying: flames rising to 500 feet showed that he had caught a Zeppelin at home—it was, in fact, the *Z-9*, and she was completely gutted. Flight Lieutenant Marix's Tabloid was damaged by enemy fire, but it carried him back to within 20 miles of Antwerp; he then borrowed a bicycle and re-entered the fortress area, which was occupied by the Germans next day. Squadron Commander Spenser Grey found mist at Cologne, which prevented him from locating the airship sheds, so he dropped his bombs on the main railway station and returned safely to Antwerp. These raids made a strong impression in Germany, as well they might, for they were omens of things to come.

In November the RNAS went even further afield: it launched a bold attack on the very birth-place of the Zeppelins—Friedrichshafen on Lake Constance, close to the Swiss frontier. This made it an awkward place to attack with the low-endurance aircraft of 1914. Careful planning by Lieutenant Pemberton Billing, RNVR, a pre-war flying enthusiast, enabled three

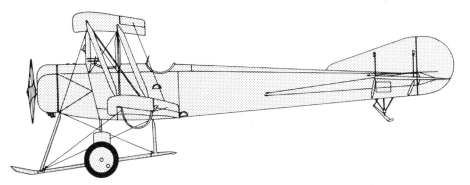

'. . . a raid which destroyed one Zeppelin and did considerable damage': the Avro 504, which attacked Friedrichshafen in November 1914, was an outstanding aircraft, remaining in production until 1933.

'. . . converted cross-Channel steamers': the seaplane-tender H.M.S. *Engadine*, which took part in the R.N.A.S. attack on the Zeppelin sheds at Cuxhaven, 25 December 1914.

Avro 504b single-seaters to take off from Belfort in Alsace on 21 November, and carry out a raid which destroyed one Zeppelin and did considerable damage to the sheds. Once more there was deep consternation; this raid

'struck right at the almost sacred heart of the whole great Zeppelin venture . . . The place had been untouchable, almost a scientific shrine. After the raid nothing seemed safe from British Naval bombs.'[11]

Two of the airmen (Flight Commander J. T. Babington and Flight Lieutenant S. V. Sippe) returned safely to Belfort; the third, Squadron Commander E. F. Briggs, was brought down inside Germany by machine-gun fire. On landing he was attacked by civilians and badly injured; but the military treated him with great respect and gave him every care in hospital. The air war was cruel and destructive, but it quickly evolved a chivalry which went some way to redeeming it.

Christmas Day saw the last of the naval novelties of 1914, and it was impressive. Once more Zeppelins were the target; considering that they had so far made no attack on England, this preoccupation with them shows what a grip the huge airships had upon professional as well as public imagination. On this occasion it was the sheds at Cuxhaven, at the mouth of the River Elbe, that were to be attacked, and it was hoped that in the process useful information would be gathered about the dispositions of the German fleet. The method was entirely new: the attack was to be made by seaplanes[12] carried in three converted cross-Channel steamers, *Engadine*, *Riviera*, and *Empress*, to a position close to the target. Two of the nine aircraft involved failed to get off the surface; the others flew to Cuxhaven, but could not locate the sheds; however, the reconnaissance of the German fleet proved valuable, and so disturbed the German command that they at once moved a number of vessels. The battle-cruiser *Van der Tann* was badly damaged in the process.

Meanwhile, more history was in the making. The British supporting squadrons, light cruisers and destroyers under Commodore R. Y. Tyrwhitt, were attacked by two Zeppelins (*L5* and *L6*) and a number of German seaplanes—the first air attack on naval forces at sea. It was beaten off with comparative ease, and *L-6* very nearly became a casualty, returning home with great difficulty due to over 600 bullet holes in her gasbags. No hits were made on the British ships, though there were a number of near-misses. Commodore Tyrwhitt reported:

'I am quite convinced that, given ordinary sea-room, our ships have nothing to fear from seaplanes and Zeppelins.'[13]

For the remainder of that war he proved to be correct. Three of the British seaplanes used on Christmas Day returned to their carriers; three more pilots were picked up by submarine *E11*, and the last by a Dutch trawler.

So the year ended: five months of naval war full of surprises, full of perplexities. Not the least of the surprises was the apparent inactivity of the two main fleets, the Grand Fleet under Admiral Sir John Jellicoe, and the High Seas Fleet under Vice-Admiral Friedrich von Ingenohl. For the Grand Fleet this passivity was more apparent than real, for a very serious reason. None of the British North Sea bases was completed in August 1914; Scapa Flow, the main base of the Grand Fleet, was particularly insecure against underwater attack. There were repeated scares of submarines inside the anchorages which caused the whole fleet to put to sea with undignified haste. In October, with the sinking of *Aboukir*, *Hogue*, and *Cressy* still very fresh in mind, Jellicoe was so disturbed by one of these that he took the entire Grand Fleet round to Lough Swilly on the northern coast of Ireland. Nobody could regard that as a favourable position from which to intercept a foray by the High Seas Fleet. It was in these waters that *Audacious* was mined and sunk; the British public, of course, was not told what she was doing there, which was perhaps just as well.

Jellicoe was 55 years old in 1914, a prime of life (Admiral Sir Andrew Cunningham was 56 when he became C-in-C of the Mediterranean Fleet in 1939.) His opponent, von Ingenohl, was 57. Spee was 53 when he went to his death, Cradock was 52 and Sturdee the same age as Jellicoe, 55. For all these officers, and all their colleagues, the five months of 1914 brought strains more severe than those of the whole of the rest of their lifetimes.

They brought, also, a revelation: the Royal Navy, absolutely supreme for over a hundred years, had found a worthy foe. The British officers and sailors acknowledged freely the high qualities of the Imperial German Navy: the great bravery of ships' companies which refused to surrender even against hopeless odds; the high skills of commanders like Spee or Müller of the *Emden*; the proficiency, especially at gunnery, displayed by ships like *Mainz* beating off destroyers at Heligoland, *Scharnhorst* and *Gneisenau* in dreadful conditions at Coronel. A lot of complacency evaporated very swiftly in the sea air of 1914.

NOTES

1   Technically, *U.S.S. Housatonic* was the first warship to be sunk by submarine action, on 17 February 1864, when anchored off Charleston (see pp. 32-3). There is, however, a very substantial difference between the sinking of a ship at anchor by a submersible craft which perished in the explosion of its own weapon, and that of a vessel in movement at sea, the attacker remaining invisible and making a clean escape.

2   Jameson: *The Most Formidable Thing*, p. 133.

3   Sir Julian Corbett: *Naval Operations*, i p. 177; Longmans, Green and Co., 1920.

4   Ibid., p. 2.

5   Richard Hough: *The Pursuit of Admiral von Spee*, p. 35; George Allen & Unwin, 1969.

6   *Scharnhorst*   armoured cruiser   flagship, Vice-Admiral von Spee
    Gneisenau   ,,   ,,
    Nürnberg   light cruiser
    Leipzig   ,,   ,,
    Dresden   ,,   ,,

7   Richard Hough, op. cit. p. 139, says 'Dense clouds of black smoke rose high into the air' above Port Stanley.

8   Churchill: *The World Crisis*, i p. 392.

9   *Invincible*   battle-cruiser   flagship, Vice-Admiral Sturdee
    Inflexible   ,,   ,,
    Carnarvon   armoured cruiser   flagship, Rear-Admiral A. P. Stoddard

    Cornwall   ,,   ,,
    Kent   ,,   ,,
    Glasgow   light cruiser
    Bristol   ,,   ,,
    Macedonia   armed merchant cruiser

10 *Times History*, ii p. 8.

11 Kenneth Poolman: *Zeppelins over England*, p. 207; Evans Brothers, 1960.

12 These were all Short aircraft: three Type 74, two 'Folders' and two Type 135.

13 Raleigh: *The War in the Air*, p. 204.

CHAPTER IV

Making Mass Armies

In his final despatch (21 March 1919) Lord Haig wrote:

'The feature of the war which to the historian may well appear the most noteworthy is the creation of our new Armies.'

As regards the British historian certainly, that is correct. When war broke out in 1914 there were, in the whole British Empire, only two effective land forces. These were the British Regular Army, 247,432 officers and men (see p. 21) and the Indian Army, totalling 159,134. Of the British total, 75,000 were in India, and 43,486 stationed in other parts of the Empire.[1] The Indian Army had only 34,767 reserves; its real function was the defence of India's frontiers, and the truth about it was that it was 'never organized for any bigger undertaking than a second-class war.'[2] Taking into account these limitations (and an invasion scare in the nervous early days of war) the net result was that at the outset the British Imperial contribution to the war of masses was, in the words of its Commander-in-Chief, 'approximately 100,000 men.' In November 1918 the British Empire had under arms 5,336,943 officers and men, of whom 3,226,879 were serving in the various expeditionary forces. From first to last the Empire had mobilized 8,654,467 men; these were the 'new armies' of whom Haig spoke. They did indeed constitute a 'noteworthy' feature of the war. The manner of their creation was peculiarly British.

Field-Marshal Lord Kitchener was appointed Secretary of State for War on 6 August 1914; he had few illusions about the situation facing both himself and the country. 'There is no Army!' was his first remark, and in terms of the task ahead this was no more than the simple truth. The Regular Army had some 200,000 reservists, whose function was to bring units up to war strength and replace casualties (about 60 per cent of the men in the ranks of the first BEF were reservists); casualties on a 'First Ypres' scale, of course, would very soon swallow up this reserve. Beyond that, the only available force of any note whatever was the Territorial Army created by Lord Haldane. This had a theoretical establishment of 316,094, but its actual strength in August was 268,777, and it had no reserves at all. Worse still, it was specifically a Home Defence force which was not intended and did not expect to serve abroad. Neither its equipment nor its training fitted it to take the field in a continental war; its very statutes insisted on a period of six months' training on embodiment *after* war was declared. Territorials could only be sent overseas if they volunteered to go, and in the foolish optimism of the early days there was not much incentive to do that. Only when it was realized that things were going badly did whole units—to their great honour—proclaim their willingness to go wherever needed. But willingness and readiness were not by any means the same thing.

So Kitchener had to start from scratch. He had no doubt that the war would be a long one (at least three years) and said bluntly that it would be the 'last million' men, not the first, that would win it. He set a target of 70 divisions—an unheard-of array. He appealed for the 'First Hundred Thousand' recruits on 7 August, and the result was staggering:

August	298,923
September	462,901
October	136,811
November	169,862
December	117,860

—a total of 1,186,357 by the end of the year. This set the course of Britain's progress towards a war of masses: 1915 produced another 1,280,362 volunteers, 1916 produced 1,190,075. Out of that British Empire total of over 8½ million which I have quoted above, the United Kingdom supplied 5,704,416, of whom no less than 3,621,045 were produced by the Voluntary system. Such were Britain's New Armies, and it is small wonder that the ardent volunteers of 1914, 1915, and 1916 were generally known as 'Kitchener Armies' and are referred to as such to this day.

It was, of course, a dreadfully wasteful and inefficient way of doing things; it exercised, as Lord Esher said, a

'pernicious influence and disorganizing effect on the nation at large, by taking all the finest, physically and morally, from the mass of youth available in the first bunch, and indiscriminately plucking out from important industries their captains—the very men who under a rational and fairer system would have been ordered to remain at their posts. These objections and dangers lay at the root of the voluntary system.'[3]

It is probable—Churchill, for one, believed that it was so—that if Kitchener had demanded conscription immediately on becoming Secretary of State, he would have obtained it. In the end, of course, it had to come—but by then the waste had been tragic. It is impossible not to regret, with our hindsight not only of that war but the next as well, the decision that Kitchener took; nevertheless one has to agree with Lord Esher that

'since it was conceded that the War should be fought under a system of voluntary enlistment and unequal sacrifice—a concession for which England was destined to pay, and is still paying (1921) a heavy price—it is more than doubtful whether armies could have been raised by any method other than the one he chose . . .'[4]

The amazing rally of the British Isles in 1914 was, of course, only part of a

'The first Canadian contingent arrived in England in October 1914: these men are repairing rifles in camp on Salisbury Plain. The Canadians were equipped with Ross rifles, excellent for range firing, less good for active service.

generally amazing picture. Outside India, with its small army of regulars, the land forces of the British Empire in 1914 were virtually non-existent: Canada had 3,000 regulars and a voluntary Militia of some 55,000; following the Imperial Defence Conference of 1909, Australia and New Zealand were ahead of Britain inasmuch as they brought in compulsory military training, but like Canada, their forces were no more than part-time militias; the Union of South Africa went further—compulsory military *service* (as well as training) for all white males between 17 and 60 in time of war—but its permanent force was only about 2,500 strong. Such were the tiny beginnings of a mighty effort: by November 1918, Canada had raised 628,964 men, Australia 412,953, New Zealand 128,525 (the highest in proportion to population, next to Britain) and South Africa 136,070.

The first Canadian contingent (31,200 officers and men) arrived in England in October 1914; out of this a first division was formed which crossed to France in February 1915. It was a portent. In due course four Canadian divisions appeared on the Western Front, formed into an army corps which by 1917 was firmly established as an élite formation by any standard; in June of that year it received its first Canadian corps commander, Lieutenant-General Sir Arthur Currie. The Australians and New Zealanders assembled first in the Middle East, grouped in a formation which gave a new word to the English language: the Australian and New Zealand Army Corps (ANZAC). In 1916 they came to France, where they, too, rapidly established themselves as élite troops. By 1917 there were five Australian divisions; in November they were designated an army corps (though they did not all fight side by side until August 1918) under an Englishman, Lieutenant-General Sir William Birdwood; at the end of May 1918 they, too, received their own native-born commander, Lieutenant-General Sir John Monash. Under that outstanding soldier, the Australian Corps became the spearhead of Allied victory. Under another very fine general, Sir Andrew Russell, the New Zealand Division upheld a superb reputation to the end. In a scene of understandable European deterioration after four years of war, and palpable amateurishness on the part of the newly-arrived Americans, these ten hardened divisions from the British Dominions stood out more and more as crack units in the last days of the war, producing effects out of all proportion to their numbers.

All of this—the mobilization of the United Kingdom, the rally of the British overseas—has a look of the miraculous; but there is one more miracle to relate. The Indian Army in 1914 totalled 239,561; this included the 159,134 officers and men with the colours, the reservists and the non-

'First to take their place beside the British regulars were the Indians': the Indian Corps arrived at Ypres in November 1914. These are Baluchis, preparing to defend the still undamaged village of Wytschaete.

combatants (always a high proportion because of caste-occupations; Rudyard Kipling has immortalized one Indian non-combatant, 'our regimental *bhisti* [water-carrier], Gunga Din'). Recruitment in India during the war totalled 1,440,437, of whom 563,369 were non-combatants. By any reckoning, this was an extraordinary phenomenon in an alien sub-continent whose loyalty to Britain was doubted by many. What made it the more so was, first, that the whole response was voluntary, and secondly, the time-span in which it was accomplished.

By late 1916, incredible though it seems, only three battalions had been added to the order of battle of the Indian Army. Then General Sir Charles Monro arrived as Commander-in-Chief. He was a Western Front Army Commander, of acknowledged professionalism but no startling reputation; he was now about to display administrative talents of the highest order:

'It is from the autumn of 1916, when General Monro arrived in India, that the development of a new system of recruiting, the consequent expansion of the Indian Army, and the great increase in India's share of the Empire's burden should be dated . . . As a result of (Monro's) methods the supply of recruits increased enormously. In 1917 nearly as many recruits were taken as had come in up to the end of 1916, and in consequence the number of additional battalions rose to over 50 before the end of the year . . . The expansion of the Indian Army by another 50 battalions between March and May 1918 allowed of the "Indianization" of the bulk of the Egyptian Expeditionary Force . . . and at the end of the war India was the one portion of the British Empire whose effective man-power was still increasing.' [5]

Such was the manner in which the British Empire made its contribution to the war of masses. First to take their place beside the British regulars on the Western Front were the Indians: an army corps which began embarkation on 24 August 1914, began disembarkation at Marseilles on 26 September, and entered the line on 23 October south of Ypres. The Indian Corps remained in France until the end of 1915, then went to join India's main effort—the war against Turkey. Replacement of regulars by Territorials in overseas garrisons (including India) permitted the formation of five new regular divisions. In addition, seven Yeomanry regiments and 23 Territorial infantry battalions joined the BEF in 1914, the first to see action being the London Scottish, whose testing baptism of fire was on 31 October. Much hampered by competition with the New Armies for every category of very scarce war material, the Territorial Army was nevertheless able to place 4 complete divisions on the Western Front by the end of April 1915, the first to assemble being the 46th (North Midland) on February 27. The Canadians were already present, the New Army soon followed—three divisions by the end of May, the first to arrive being the 9th (Scottish) on 9 May. By 31 January the strength of the BEF was 347,384; by September it counted 28 infantry divisions,[6] a total of 916,605 men. At that stage the Empire as a whole (excluding India) had mobilized 2,572,455. In February 1916 the BEF itself passed the million mark: 1,037,600.

The dead Schlieffen cannot really be blamed for not foreseeing that this astonishing rally would be a consequence of his bold march through Belgium in quest of a short war; nobody foresaw the reality of such a thing, though some had foreseen the need. It was indeed an extraordinary phenomenon, and Haig did not exaggerate when he said:

'To have built up successfully in the very midst of war a great new Army on a more than Continental scale, capable of beating the best troops of the strongest military nation in pre-war days, is an achievement of which the whole Empire may be proud.'[7]

NOTES

1   Figures quoted on pp. 134–39 are from *Statistics of the Military Effort of the British Empire during the Great War 1914–1920*, H.M.S.O., 1922, (henceforth *Statistics*).

2   General Sir George Barrow: *The Life of General Sir Charles Carmichael Monro*, p. 142; Hutchinson, 1931.

3   Lord Esher: *The Tragedy of Lord Kitchener*, pp. 142–4; John Murray, 1921.

4   Ibid., p. 37.

5   C. T. Atkinson in *The Empire at War* (ed. Sir Charles Lucas) vi; O.U.P., 1921.

6   Compared with Germany's 102, France's 98, and Belgium's 6 (see *O.H. 1915* ii p. 133, f.n.1).

7   *Sir Douglas Haig's Despatches*, ed. Lieut.-Col. J. H. Boraston, p. 346; J. M. Dent, 1919 & 1979.

Main Events 1915–17

1915
19 January	First Zeppelin raid on England
24	Action of the Dogger Bank
31	East: Battle of Bolimov: first use of gas
2 (–22) February	East: Winter Battle in Masuria
19	Gallipoli: First naval attack
22 (–end September)	First U-boat campaign
10 (–13) March	West: Battle of Neuve Chapelle
18	Gallipoli: Second naval attack
22 April (–25 May)	West: Second Battle of Ypres
25	Gallipoli: landings at Cape Helles and Anzac Cove
2 May (–September)	East: Battle of Gorlice-Tarnow and pursuit
9 (–18)	West: Second Battle of Artois
23	Italy enters the war
29 June (–7 July)	First Battle of the Isonzo (ten to follow, ending September 1917)
5 August	East: Germans enter Warsaw
6	Gallipoli: landing at Suvla Bay
18 September	East: Germans enter Vilna (end of offensive)
25 (–15 October)	West: Third Battle of Artois
(–8 October)	Battle of Loos
11 October	Bulgaria enters the war; invades Serbia
2 December	Central Powers occupy Serbia
19	West: General Sir Douglas Haig becomes British C-in-C

1916
7–8 January	Gallipoli: evacuation completed
21 February (–18 December)	West: Battle of Verdun
18 March (–30 April)	East: Battle of Lake Naroch
29 April	Mesopotamia: Turks capture Kut-el-Amara
14 May (–3 June)	Italy: Austrian offensive in Trentino
31	Battle of Jutland
4 June (–September)	East: General Brusilov's offensive
1 July (–18 November)	West: The Battle of the Somme
27 August	Rumania enters the war
12–16 September	General Allied offensive
15	First use of tanks

6 December	East: defeat of Rumania; Germans enter Bucharest
7	Mr. Lloyd George becomes British Prime Minister
12	West: General Nivelle succeeds General Joffre as French C-in-C

1917

1 February	Unrestricted U-boat warfare begins
12 March	First Russian Revolution
16	West: Germans begin withdrawal to Hindenburg Line
6 April	United States of America enter the war
9 (–4 May)	West: Battle of Arras
16 (–20)	West: Second Battle of the Aisne
29	West: General Pétain succeeds General Nivelle as French C-in-C
25 May	First 'Gotha' raid on England
7 (–14) June	West: Battle of Messines
25	West: First American contingent arrives in France
31 July (–10 November)	West: Third Battle of Ypres
23 October (–1 November)	West: Battle of Malmaison
24	Italy: Battle of Caporetto
8 November	Bolshevik Revolution
20 (–6 December)	West: Battle of Cambrai
9 December	British enter Jerusalem

CHAPTER V

Deadlock:
The Problem

HUGE LOSSES IN 1914, huge expenditure of munitions costing unbelievable fortunes in money, material damage on a scale that could scarcely
be grasped, all this had produced precisely nothing; victory and defeat doled
out with unprofitable evenness to both sides, an advantage here always
counterbalanced by a setback there; deadlock. On the battlefronts themselves it was hardest of all to grasp; commanders and commanded alike had
the sense of being caught in some grotesque improbability, some ghastly bad
joke that must end soon (when the winter was over, perhaps . . . when spring
returned). 'If we had only had more guns . . .', '. . . more shells . . .', '. . .
more high explosive . . .', 'if it hadn't been for that machine-gun . . .', 'if we
could get hold of some mortars . . .', '. . . hand-grenades . . .', '. . . better
training for this sort of business . . .', 'better observation'—the little
remedies, the correctives for particular disappointments, were not hard to
perceive, not hard (with a little patience) to obtain. And it was not as though
the soldiers were not brave—indeed, often they were *too* brave; hence their
losses. It was not even that they were (in most cases) not properly trained; the
battlefield is a great educator. And it was not, as some came to suppose, that
all the generals, everywhere, were suddenly afflicted by some mental collapse
into imbecility; on the contrary, they were finding solutions to new problems
every day. The trouble was that all the little remedies, necessary though they
were, were only part of a much larger remedy: a new stage in technology, a
new stride which would not be made at the front, or at headquarters, or in
Government councils. It would be made in laboratories, at drawing-boards,
in workshops, and factories.

The problem, in a nutshell, was the 'hiatus of the mobile arm' (see p. 93).
Modern technology had entirely solved the problems of bringing the mass
armies to their battlefields; now what was needed was a means of moving
them *on* the battlefields. The horse was still invaluable in the last stages of
approach to the fire zone, but *inside* the fire zone, for the reasons set forth on
pages 92–93, the horse was helpless and useless. And there was nothing else.
So, while statesman and general publics looked for 'great captains' who
would dismiss the problem by 'thunderbolts of war', the soldiers awaited
the new key which only technology could provide to unlock their prison.

Meanwhile, to save themselves from massacre by the means that technology had already provided, they remained in their trenches. In the West the
trench systems on both sides took on ever-increasing complexity: forward
saps projecting from fire-trenches, backed by second and third support lines

'. . . trench systems took on ever-increasing complexity . . .': this German trench displays
lavish use of sandbags, a good high parados, strong firing-step, duck-boards (for drainage),
and substantial wattle revetment for solidity.

(sometimes more) which an earlier age called 'parallels', linked by communication trenches ('zigzags'). On maps the Western Front is usually shown by a continuous line which in 1915 was 475 miles long. It was never quite as continuous as the maps suggest: flooded areas, rivers, swampy river valleys (the Somme bottom is mostly marsh, in places three-quarters of a mile wide) and abrupt declivities interrupted the lines. Nor was it of uniform character: where the water-table was high, trenches could not be dug downwards, instead they had to be built up by sand-bag breastworks—which meant, in effect, creating a new landscape. French trenches were generally less elaborate and less sanitary than British (though the French were better at making themselves comfortable in their rear positions); the Germans, being basically on the defensive in the West from the spring of 1915 until the spring of 1918, had more occasion and better opportunity than the Allies for sophistication. It was they who made the most lavish use of concrete, for deep shelters and covered ways, and later the ferro-concrete blockhouses, loopholed for machine-guns, which the British Army christened 'pill-boxes'. When the great bombardments swept across these systems, they were often pulverized out of recognition, and the red or blue lines on maps have to be interpreted as small groups of men or individuals crouched in shell-holes or mine-craters, unable to move, unable to communicate, trying just to stay alive until darkness brought relief.

So the humble spade became a master-weapon. No armies have ever liked digging, but the lead-storms of 1914–1918 taught them to dig as they had never dug before. They did not only dig trenches and gunpits to protect their teeming infantry and the ever-increasing guns behind them; they also dug offensively. Mining is one of the oldest arts of war—its history must be almost as long as the history of fortified places.[1] Extensive mining in the field, on the scale practised on the Western Front, was a novelty, attributable to two causes: the proximity of the opposing lines, and the length of time that they were held. Here, as in so many matters, the Germans had the initial advantage; it was slowly wrested from them in an underground war which lends an extra dimension to a scene already full enough of horrors. The British Army had no provision at all for this activity when war broke out; by the end of 1915, however, the BEF had 21 Royal Engineer Tunnelling Companies, and in due course it was the British front which saw the most dramatic mining exploit of the war: the 19 huge mines, which blew the top off the Messines Ridge in June 1917. In the BEF the underground war brought with it a mine rescue organization similar to that of collieries, mining schools to instruct in tactics, and an entirely new Intelligence process through underground listening which acquired an extraordinary degree of precision when modern technology contributed the geophone.

The technical aids and weaponry of trench warfare multiplied, though never as fast as the front-line troops desired and demanded. Barbed wire uncoiled by incredible mileages; telephone wire, on which communication overwhelmingly depended, did the same. Trench mortars, crude improvisations on the Allied side at first, no match for the German *minenwerfer*,

'. . . flame-projectors, throwing jets of blazing liquid accompanied by dense clouds of black smoke . . .': this fore-runner of napalm was chiefly useful as a weapon of terror.

supported by variations on the mediaeval catapult and bow, became standard equipment, invaluable but intensely disliked by the infantry because of the retaliation which they invariably invoked. Eleven types of mortar (light, medium, and heavy) came into use in the British Army, total production reaching 19,096; of these the overwhelming majority (11,241) were of the simple, sturdy 3-inch type invented by Mr. Wilfred Stokes in January 1915 and rescued from War Office rejection by the intervention of Haig, then commanding the First Army. There were Bangalore torpedoes to blow gaps in enemy wire (not a notable success), flares to light up the night scene, rockets for signalling. Further extreme unpleasantness for front-line soldiers was provided by flame-projectors, throwing jets of blazing liquid accompanied by dense clouds of black smoke to distances of about 40 yards. These would seem to have been used first by the French as early as the autumn of 1914. However, when the British encountered them in July 1915, they were described as an 'inhuman projection of the German scientific mind'. In fact, they were simply a modern version of a device used by the Byzantines as long ago as the eighth century A.D.,[2] and regarded as standard in the Second World War. The latest version of incendiary war—napalm—thus has a long ancestry.

These were all 'small remedies'; they met pressing needs, but neither singly nor in conjunction did they in any way solve the problem of trench warfare. And by an extra irony, the one weapon which did present to all armies a plausible solution in fact made the problem more difficult. Artillery promised to slash gaps in the enemy's wire, smash in his trenches, blow his machine-guns to pieces and even hammer his own artillery into quiescence. And as the guns multiplied, as the gunners became more skilful, as new ranging techniques and instruments came into existence, together with more deadly explosives and more sensitive fuses, the artillery of both sides proved able to do all these things. It did more: it even curtained the advancing infantry with 'creeping' or 'rolling' *barrages*—the word is French, and it means a barrier, like a dam in a river.[3] A defensive barrage was a curtain of bursting shells, barring an enemy attack; a 'creeping' barrage was a moving curtain, nailing the enemy into his deep shelters until the last moment when the attacking infantry was virtually on top of him, then moving on to the next objective to repeat the performance. An accurate preliminary bombardment (for a big battle in the West, this might last 10 or 14 days) to destroy defences, dumps, and communications, followed by an equally accurate barrage with well-trained infantry behind it, could generally, from early 1915 onwards, be guaranteed to capture an enemy position. But then it invariably encountered its own penalty: the devastation of the landscape, in particular the destruction of roads, paths, or tracks, which made all movement across it, especially of guns and supplies, impossible.

The first British offensive battle worthy of the name conveniently illustrates the repeated experience of the next three years. This was Neuve Chapelle, in March 1915—a very minor affair indeed, by comparison with what was happening and continuing to happen on the French front, or about to happen in the East. Yet Neuve Chapelle supplied a blueprint of trench battle which even the French and Germans considered worthy of study. The attack was to be carried out by IV Corps (Lieutenant-General Sir Henry Rawlinson) of the First Army (General Sir Douglas Haig). Tactically, strategically, and psychologically there were good reasons for attacking at Neuve Chapelle, sufficient to outweigh in the mind of Field-Marshal Sir John French the two even better reasons for not doing so. The First Army's line ran through the water-logged meadows of the Lys valley, dominated to the east by the Aubers Ridge, only 40 feet high, but nevertheless offering drier ground and observation over the flat lands for many miles in all directions. The village of Neuve Chapelle, captured by the Germans in October 1914, lay in a salient about 2,000 yards across, giving the opportunity of converging fire; the Ridge lay only a mile beyond the village. The temptations were obvious—and only a little further lay the strategic prize of Lille, so near on the map, but over $3\frac{1}{2}$ years away in terms of 1914–18 realities. Finally, there was the psychological bait: the very evident facts that the Germans had an undoubted sense of superiority on the British front (following disastrous attempts to advance without proper equipment or preparation in December) and that the French clearly regarded the BEF as 'second-class citizens' for all offensive purposes. The combination of these arguments overbore the critical circumstances that even with a better flow of equipment (especially artillery) the BEF still had no capacity for a sustained offensive effort without French help, and that such help would not be forthcoming.

So Neuve Chapelle would be a British battle, a test of British ability to wage offensive war—and the British had everything to learn. Haig had two ideas firmly in mind from the first: the essential need for surprise and, as he told Rawlinson, that 'success depends upon methodical preparation'. Such was the British ignorance of these matters at that stage that even from an officer who would later play as distinguished a part in the war as Rawlinson, he had the greatest difficulty in extracting a plan at all. And when one did appear, it proposed to take two days over the capture of Neuve Chapelle, which meant, as Haig remarked, that 'there would be no element of surprise on the second day, but the enemy would be ready for us'. Bit by bit, however, a plan was worked out; the surprise element (which also had the advantage of being economical of still-scarce ammunition) was a 'hurricane' bombardment of only 35 minutes duration, using the unprecedented number of 66 heavy guns—more than the whole BEF possessed in the First Battle of Ypres. Still over two years off were such deployments as the Second Army's 819 heavy guns and howitzers at the Battle of Messines, or the Fifth Army's 752 for 'Third Ypres'.

Nevertheless, the artillery contribution to Neuve Chapelle offered a strong hint of things to come; but so did much else. Haig insisted that 'every man must know exactly what his duty was'; accordingly, officers familiarized themselves with the ground over which they would attack and the assaulting infantry were rehearsed in their tasks—standard drill later, but this was the first time. 'Forming-up trenches' were dug, and dummy trenches for deception; advanced ammunition and supply depots (dumps) were established; roads were improved for battle traffic, and a light railway laid—all these were 'firsts'. So, too, was the issuing of artillery timetables, giving each battery its exact targets for each stage of the action, a most important innovation. Gun platforms were devised to give stability in the soft muddy ground. Aerial photographs built up a map showing the network of German trenches—the novelty of this is indicated by the fact that efficient air cameras did not arrive until February. Each of the two corps involved[4] received 1,500 copies of this map. Secrecy was carefully preserved in all the preparations. To exploit a success, five divisions of cavalry were brought up behind the offensive front; this also would continue to be standard procedure. Occasion after occasion on the Western Front would show, until the changed conditions of the very last days, that cavalry were quite incapable of performing this function; but a general who made *no* provision for taking advantage of victory would be a very poor general indeed.

The British bombardment opened, with an exhilarating crash, at 7.30am on 10 March. At 8.05 the infantry attack went in; 45 minutes later Neuve Chapelle was captured, and very soon the first objective was gained along the whole central part of the 8,300-yard front. Only on the flanks were there serious difficulties. It was all most promising—but then, in the words of one of Haig's staff, 'for some reason not yet explained, the whole machine clogged and stopped. It was maddening'.[5] The battle would continue for three days, but all the ground won was won in the first three hours. The British penetration was 1,200 yards deep on a front of 4,000. Their casualties for the whole battle were 583 officers and 12,309 other ranks. German losses were estimated at about 12,000, of whom 30 officers and 1,637 other ranks were taken prisoner.

'The whole machine clogged and stopped'—the words sound like an epitaph, the epitaph of so many gallant, doomed endeavours in 1915, 1916, and 1917. If the techniques employed in the British preparation for Neuve Chapelle provided a blueprint for the future, so, sadly, did the miserable outcome. The reason is not far to seek: it lies, as I have said on p. 41, in the need for some means of making a voice audible in battle. Meticulous preparation for battle was clearly essential, but something more was also required; as General Sir Hubert Gough, brother of Haig's chief-of-staff, expressed it:

'The problem is controlling events when you have gone beyond the plans which are cut and dried.'[6]

It was a problem that was never solved in that war—though it could be, in a sense, bypassed. Yet by and large the words of another baffled officer remained true to the end:

'. . . *once troops were committed to the attack*, all *control was over.*'

The reason was, quite simply, that the First World War

'was the only war ever fought without voice control.'[7]

The implications of this were, of course, devastating, chief among them being, as I have said elsewhere, that generals everywhere 'became quite impotent at the very moment when they would expect and be expected to display their greatest proficiency.'[8] And so, on the French fronts in Artois and Champagne, at Ypres and at Loos, on bloody fields in the East, and at Gallipoli, throughout that year and the next and most of the next, 'the whole machine clogged and stopped'. More than anything else, it was this sheer inability of commanders and commanded to communicate information and fresh orders that swelled the awful casualty lists of the war.

The chief instrument of generalship throughout the war was, of course, the telephone. In quiet times, on quiet sectors, visual signalling was possible, and various forms were used: flags, semaphores of different types, rockets, lamps (the French provided a useful electric version). But all visual systems were vulnerable to weather conditions, and the dust and smoke of battle. Only the telephone, the uncertain, temperamental telephone of the second decade, gave generals any real power of command. A vast, intricate net of cables linked the trenches to command posts all along the fronts; generals

'Command in battle was restricted to what the telephone permitted': a Royal Engineers signal dugout in October 1915.

had to be at the nodal points of this net—'the ONLY place where it was possible to know what was going on was at the end of a wire'[9]—and even such a fire-eating commander as General Charles Mangin had to accept that during a battle, if he left his headquarters and 'went marching about the front line, I would be commanding no more than one or two companies.'[10]

So command in battle was restricted to what the telephone permitted—which was, in turn, very much a matter of what the cables permitted. Cables on the surface were vulnerable to all passing traffic, to the thieving propensities of unscrupulous soldiers,[11] and above all to enemy shelling. Burying cable became standard practice; to give but one example, the Canadian Corps buried 420 miles of cable 6 feet deep in the Kemmel area between 1 April and 30 June 1916. Six feet down was secure against all but very heavy shells (though the Germans advocated 10 feet), but was clearly not always possible. In action, it was not uncommon for Signallers to have to repair 40 or 50 breaks in a cable in one day, a dangerous, arduous, and frustrating duty calling for much courage and much skill. When all else failed, the legs of men were called upon: 'runners', carrying verbal or written messages. As the British Official History tersely comments, this system was 'slow and expensive in men, requiring the best and bravest of a battalion.'[12]

'The "fullerphone" scrambler of 1916': these men are using the device which enabled field telephones to be used without giving away information to the enemy.

One more hazard calls for mention in this war of endless novelty. As early as June 1915, British Intelligence reached the conclusion that the Germans were somehow overhearing telephone conversations in the forward area. The French faced the same problem, and a listening post of their own found itself able to overhear some German conversation. The problem was badly insulated telephone lines laid on or in the earth, which acted as a conductor. Full security restrictions, then as ever, proved virtually impossible to enforce, despite the introduction of codes and call-signs. Once more technology had to provide the answer: the 'fullerphone' scrambler of 1916 and its counterparts. Even so, such was the ever-increasing sophistication of listening devices that, in March 1918, the German High Command forbade the use of telephones within 7 miles of the front before their great attack on the British Army. The sophistication that everyone longed for, however, was deferred for another war; although wireless communication made great strides towards the end, there was never, between 1914–18, anything approximating to the 'walkie-talkie' sets which restored command to its function in the Second World War.

1915 was the year when deadlock clenched its grip upon the war, despite all the efforts of both sides to break it by orthodox or unorthodox means, on land and at sea.

NOTES

1 Richard Humble's *Warfare in the Ancient World*, (p. 64; Cassell, 1980) raises the question whether Joshua's dramatic capture of Jericho (*circa* twelfth century B.C.) was not accomplished by 'intensive mining operations'.

2 Mr. Jim Bradbury, in *History Today*, May 1979, in an article entitled 'Greek Fire in the West', says that at that time 'they developed a device that enabled them to project an inflammable mixture from a tube that could be directed against enemy ships.'

3 It is likely that the first 'barrage' of the war was fired by the highly trained gunners of the Royal Artillery (65th Field Howitzer Battery) in support of a French infantry attack at Vermelles on 14 October 1914.

4 The Indian Corps attacked alongside IV Corps.

5 Brig.-Gen. John Charteris, *At G.H.Q.* (Cassell, 1931) p. 81; letter dated March 12.

6 Quoted in *Goughie*, by Anthony Farrar-Hockley, Hart-Davis, MacGibbon, 1975, p. 152.

7 See Terraine *The Smoke and the Fire*, p. 179: Lieut.-Col. C. F. Jerram (GSO 1, 46th Div.) quoted by General Sir Alan Bourne in a letter to the author.

8 Ibid.

9 Ibid.

10 Mangin: *Lettres de Guerre 1914–1918*, Librairie Arthème Fayard, 1950, p. 120: July 4 1916.

11 See Terraine *To Win a War* (Sidgwick & Jackson, 1978) p. 166 for a case of a cavalry unit cutting out some 100 yards of cable serving a divisional headquarters for use as a picket line for the horses.

12 *O.H. 1916* i p. 71.

CHAPTER VI

Trial and Error:
Unorthodoxy 1. *Submarine*

T HE DEADLOCK DISGUSTED BOTH SIDES; in 1915 continuous efforts were made to break it, three by the Germans, three by the Allies, one rudimentary, but pointing ways forward for both. Three of these (all German) involved major unorthodoxies, significant new departures in the conduct of war.

The weight of traditional British naval power, displayed at the Falklands in December 1914, was seen again in the North Sea in January. At the Dogger Bank action on the 24th, Vice-Admiral Sir David Beatty's squadron sank the armoured cruiser *Blücher* with heavy loss of life and inflicted serious damage on the battle-cruiser *Seydlitz*; in the British squadron the flagship, *Lion*, was badly damaged, as was the destroyer *Meteor*; but no British ship was lost, and casualties totalled 13 dead and 22 wounded. Informed naval opinion believed then, and continues to believe, that more resolute action after Beatty had dropped out of the fight in the damaged *Lion* should have accomplished the sinking of the other two German battle-cruisers, *Derfflinger* and *Moltke*. Nevertheless, the result was unmistakable, and the more impressive in that Beatty had signalled for a speed of 29 knots (*Lion* actually attained 28) and opened fire at 20,000 yards. Yet even such a spectacular development of surface warfare as this was not the true revelation of the new dimension of war at sea.

On 4 February 1915 history confirmed the prescience of Lord Fisher and Sir Percy Scott before the war (see pp. 35–6): the German Admiralty issued a declaration stating:

'*All the waters surrounding Great Britain and Ireland, including the whole of the English Channel, are hereby declared a war zone. From February 18 onwards every enemy merchant vessel found within this war zone will be destroyed without its being always possible to avoid danger to the crews and passengers. Neutral ships will also be exposed to danger in the war zone . . .*'

So the first deliberate submarine campaign against merchant shipping began (last-minute misgivings delayed the actual starting-date until 22 February). Ironically, it was a direct result of Britain's Dogger Bank victory, which had caused the replacement of Admiral von Ingenohl by the Chief of the Naval Staff, Pohl. Pohl strongly backed the demand that submarines should be used to counter the already highly effective British blockade of Germany; the mood of the submarine lobby is indicated by this memorandum from the High Seas Fleet:

'The first deliberate submarine campaign against merchant shipping': this is U-38—one of the undersea fleet which bore out Fisher's 1913 prediction and earned the title 'the most formidable thing'.

'We can wound England most seriously by injuring her trade. By means of the U-boat we should be able to inflict the greatest injury . . . A U-boat cannot spare the crews of steamers, but must send them to the bottom with their ships . . . The gravity of the situation demands that we should free ourselves from all scruples . . .'[1]

An instruction to U-boat captains added significantly:

'The first consideration is the safety of the U-boat.'[2]

The Naval Staff assured the Kaiser that 'Great Britain will capitulate six weeks after new commercial war begins if from thence onwards it is found possible to employ with energy every kind of warlike resource.'[3] This, then, was the first attempt to break the deadlock of the war by means of new technology, because although the word 'capitulate' must be read here to mean 'end the blockade of Germany' rather than 'sue for peace', it is unthinkable that, having achieved such a large result by these means, the Germans would not have used them to obtain the highest prize of all—victory—as, indeed, they did, nearly two years later. And the attitude displayed in the passages quoted above shows clearly that, although 'unrestricted' U-boat warfare is associated with the campaign of 1917, it was in fact in existence from the very first.

What is amazing is that rational men guiding the destinies of a great nation should have committed themselves to such a drastic policy (with all its political implications, above all with America) when the instrument to hand was so feeble. A perspicacious U-boat commander (Lieutenant-Commander Blum), estimating the requirement for a blockade of the British Isles, placed the number at 222. That is precisely twice as many as Germany had available in January 1917, and 44 more than the number she surrendered at the Armistice. So Blum was not far wrong. But in February 1915 Germany had only 21 U-boats, and eight of those were pre-diesel. With this slender force she now proposed to ruin the commerce of a nation whose ports saw arrivals and departures often aggregating nearly 1,500 a week.

It is not surprising, then, that the first U-boat campaign is generally written off as a failure. Winston Churchill dismissed it with the words:

'No substantial or even noticeable injury was wrought upon British commerce by the first German submarine campaign.'[4]

The truth is not quite so rosy. By the end of September, when the campaign definitely ended, some three-quarters of a million tons of British and Allied shipping had been sunk. This was out of a total British tonnage alone of over 20 million tons, so that the loss amounts to less than 4 per cent of just British capacity. However, the full picture of the U-boat campaign cannot be quite so crudely framed. As William Jameson pertinently remarks, 'war puts a tremendous demand on merchant ship tonnages'[5] He points out that some 25 per cent of merchant shipping was requisitioned for use as armed merchant cruisers, transports, or store ships, and was thus not available for normal work. No fewer than 2,180 small vessels (yachts, trawlers, drifters, motor boats etc.) were drawn directly into anti-submarine work in 1915; all these had to be manned, maintained and directed, over and above the substantial effort of the Royal Navy itself. If one adds to these drains sinkings of over 100,000 tons a month (as in May, June, and July) it is not surprising to find that 'the tonnage position was becoming serious' from a shipbuilding point of view.

The point is that all this was done with only 21 U-boats, to which nine were added during the campaign from new construction. Twelve ocean-going U-boats and four smaller ones were lost from all causes during the campaign, which supplies in itself a sufficient reason for calling it off—sheer shortage of vessels. But there were more on the stocks and improved types waiting to come forward, and such exploits as those of *U-38*, under the ruthless Lieutenant-Commander Valentiner, which sank 75,000 registered tons (three sailing vessels, five trawlers, and 22 merchant ships) in the course of one 25-day cruise in August, persuaded the U-boat lobby that this offering of technology had fully proved itself. Maybe the U-boats would have done better without this rehearsal; but the rehearsal could only give encouragement to those who believed in them.

Yet technology is a deceitful magician. The U-boat rehearsal was also, of course, a rehearsal of anti-submarine methods (which we shall discuss later), and an impulse to make technological thrusts in new directions (mines, depth-charges, hydrophones, etc.). Worse still, the most spectacular success obtained by the 1915 U-boats proved to be a powerful factor in Germany's ultimate undoing. On May 7 *U-20* (Lieutenant-Commander Schwieger) sank the great Cunard liner *Lusitania* off the southern coast of Ireland, with the loss of 1,198 lives of men, women, and children, including a considerable number of Americans. This deed deeply shocked American opinion, already much disturbed by the U-boat campaign. Not only did American opposition to British blockade methods now greatly diminish, but at this point we may safely discern the beginning of the frame of mind which ultimately brought America into the war as one of Germany's enemies.

So the first unorthodox assault upon the deadlock came to a fruitless end.

NOTES

1 Jameson: *The Most Formidable Thing*, p. 137; quoting Admiral Scheer, *Germany's High Seas Fleet in the World War*, Cassell, 1920.
2 Ibid., p. 154, again quoting Scheer.
3 Ibid., p. 156, quoting *Der Krieg Zur See, 1914–1918, Der Handelskrieg Mit U-Booten*, edited by Rear-Admiral Arno Spindler.
4 Winston Churchill: *Thoughts and Adventures*, p. 88; Odhams Press, 1932.
5 Jameson, op. cit. pp. 171–2.

Unorthodoxy 2. *Chemistry*

MAKING WAR BENEATH THE WAVES added a new element to human conflict; Germany's further essay in unorthodoxy threatened to deprive human beings of an essential element of life itself—the very air they breathed. The first weapon of mass destruction now made its dubious début.

The selected victims were the Russians, trying to recover from the terrible battles of 1914. To distract attention from the initial moves of a new on-slaught in Masuria, the German *Ninth Army* made an attack at Bolimov, some 30 miles south-west of Warsaw, on 31 January. 'For this purpose,' says Ludendorff, as though it was the most ordinary thing in the world, 'our General Headquarters placed eighteen thousand rounds of gas shells at our disposal.' He merely remarks that at the time this seemed an exceptional amount; German scientists confidently predicted that the contents of these shells (chlorine) would produce wholesale asphyxiation of the opposing Russians. In the event no such thing occurred, for a very simple reason which the Germans had not realized: the intense cold prevented the gas from diffusing. The Germans won a small tactical success which certainly did not justify their disclosure of a potentially devastating weapon. On the other hand, their strategic aim—diversion—was fulfilled.

The sheer ineffectiveness of the first use of poison gas helped to preserve its surprise effect when it next appeared. In truth, however, the German High Command seemed unconcerned about whether it achieved surprise or not. Exactly when the decision was taken to use gas on the Western Front is not known, but it would appear to have been shell shortage that persuaded the Germans to use cylinders. Once the decision to use cloud gas from cylinders was taken, the next question was, of course, the direction of prevailing winds. Meteorologists (themselves a new element in the military hierarchy) predicted southern winds in the Ypres sector in the coming season; a front facing more or less north was therefore required, and the south-eastern face of the Ypres Salient (the 'Hill 60' sector) was accordingly chosen. Cylinders were dug in along a narrow front by mid-February; despite successive widenings, preparations for a gas attack in this area were completed by 10 March. As the British Official History remarks, 'the German meteorologists were strangely mistaken'[1] in their wind predictions. However, a second sector for a gas attack was authorized on 25 March, this time facing virtually due south (Bixschoote to Poelcappelle). Preparations were completed by 11 April. Even here, however, the wind proved disobliging for nearly another fortnight; six weeks thus elapsed during which there was always a possibility of the Allies discovering what was afoot.

The Allies did, in fact, receive several warnings. If the British Official History is to believed,[2] the Germans actually used some gas shell in the Battle of Neuve Chapelle (10–12 March), but in the smoke and general stench it was not noticed. On 14 April a prisoner taken on the French (northern) sector gave detailed information of gas preparations there, and on the 16th there was more from Belgian sources. On 17 April fierce fighting flared up at Hill 60, and next day the British troops there reported gas shelling. There is no corroboration of this from the German side, but there is, of course, the possibility that some of their cylinders were damaged and leaking. Inscrutably, however, on 20 April, they did fire 60 gas shells at Hill 60—what purpose this number could achieve (other than to alert the British) it is impossible to imagine. Perhaps even more significant, however, was the report of the Wolff News Agency on 17 April that 'yesterday east of Ypres the British employed shells and bombs with asphyxiating gas'.[3]

All doubts were dispelled on 22 April—'a glorious spring day'.[4] At 5 o'clock in the afternoon the Germans began a furious bombardment of Ypres (the bottleneck of all communications with the famous Salient) with heavy artillery. Very shortly great agitation was observed on the front of the French 45th (Algerian) Division at Langemarck, on the left of the British. Men started abandoning their trenches and running back, evidently in a state of panic, many clutching their throats, coughing and retching. A French doctor described the scene:

'. . . *as we looked to our left, we saw a thick, yellowish-green cloud veiling the sky like a cloud of vapour. We were already affected by the asphyxiating fumes. I had the impression that I was looking through green glasses. At the same time, I felt the action of the gas upon my respiratory system; it burned in my throat, caused pains in my chest, and made breathing all but impossible. I spat blood and suffered from dizziness. We all thought we were lost . . .'*[5]

This was the effect of chlorine; as the Official History more frigidly states, it

'has a powerful irritant action on the respiratory organs and all mucous membranes exposed to it, causing spasms of the glottis, a burning sensation in the eyes, nose and throat, followed by bronchitis and oedema of the lungs. Frequently there is evidence of corrosion of the mucous membranes of the air channels and of the cornea. Prolonged inhalation or exposure to a high concentration of the gas will cause death by asphyxia, or, if not fatal, produce cardiac dilatation and cyanosis (blueness of the skin) as a result of the injury to the lungs.'[6]

Naturally, the impact of this terrifying weapon was tremendous. The Germans were comprehensively denounced; *The Times* called this an 'atrocious method of warfare . . . this diabolical contrivance . . . will fill all races with a horror of the German name.'[7] The troops at the front—French Territorials, Canadians, and British were all soon exposed to the same afflictions as the

'. . . a thick yellowish-green cloud veiling the sky . . .': cylinder gas rolling forward in preparations for a German attack. More menacing in aspect, this use of gas was far less effective than gas-shell.

unfortunate Algerians—were roused to unusual anger by this style of war, for a reason stated by a distinguished soldier-historian with definitive clarity:

'In the face of gas, without protection, individuality was annihilated; the soldier in the trench became a mere passive recipient of torture and death. A final stage seemed to be reached in the whole tendency of modern scientific warfare to depress and make of no effect individual bravery, enterprise and skill.'

As he says, the soldier on active service has to be a fatalist:

'But his fatalism depends upon the belief that he has a chance. If the very air which he breathes is poison, his chance is gone: he is merely a destined victim for the slaughter.'[8]

Such was technology's new contribution to civilization and progress. Used in this crude manner, it did not do the Germans much good: the Second Battle of Ypres settled down into a hard, grim slogging-match on familiar lines until the end of May. By the end of it the British alone had suffered 59,275 casualties, many of them attributable to inexperience and lack of equipment; they had lost more than half of the Salient, but they clung to Ypres and its immediate surroundings, and continued to hold that stretch of blood-soaked ground for the rest of the war.

The first gas attacks at Ypres (a second fell upon the Canadians on 24 April) found the Allied soldiers entirely unprepared; they had no respirators; no anti-gas measures of any description were in hand. The best that could be done at first was to cover the nose and mouth with a wet cloth—a handkerchief, piece of towelling, or of a cotton bandolier, or in privileged cases a gauze pad. This was wetted with water or, as the Official History dryly says, 'any liquid available in the trenches'. And that was all. Yet even with such primitive protection as this, history records the first failure of a gas attack on 1 May. The men who defeated it were the British 15th Brigade (5th Division), by sheer courage and determination. If any unit should be singled out, it would be the 1/Dorsetshire, who maintained rapid fire from their trench, ignoring the gas swirling round them; for this they paid a price—90 men dead of gas poisoning in the trenches, 207 more admitted to dressing stations, of whom 46 died almost at once, and 12 more after long suffering. Out of 2,413 British gas cases admitted to hospital during this period, 277 died.

Technology, of course, was soon busily overtaking itself. Respirators were improvized by the Army, and experiments were conducted behind the fighting fronts. The scientists faced no light task:

'It was imperative to design a respirator that would give complete protection for several hours, was easy to put on and comfortable to wear, afforded good visibility,

'Respirators were improvized . . .': these French troops, awaiting a gas attack in 1916, illustrate the dehumanization of war by advancing science.

allowed speech, required no maintenance, would withstand the roughest conditions and could be quickly assembled by unskilled hands from parts produced by the million to close tolerances from readily available materials. Even for wartime this was an unusual specification and created great difficulties.'[9]

A Newfoundland Medical Officer devised an impregnated flannel bag helmet with a celluloid window; by July the whole BEF was issued with this. An improved version came out in November; in 1916 the box respirator appeared, with special patterns for such particular cases as artillerymen, whose work required great exertion. The French and Germans progressed similarly, the Germans always with the advantage of being the originators of this chemical warfare.

Technology, countertechnology, counter-countertechnology: the chemical warfare services were everywhere hard at work. Lacrymatory gas made its appearance in June 1915, phosgene (in conjunction with chlorine) in December. Phosgene produced similar effects to chlorine, but was considered more dangerous because it was less perceptible; low concentrations could be inhaled for a considerable time, but still be fatal. In April 1916 a very strong concentration of chlorine—so strong that the smell was noticed 15 miles away and every blade of vegetation in the path of the gas was withered—took the British 16th Division by surprise. There were 1,260 gas casualties, of whom 338 died. What was most alarming was that 'the helmet was obviously insufficient protection against the strong concentration of gas which the enemy was able to produce.'[10] In 1917 Mustard Gas ('Yellow Cross'—dichlorethal sulphide) arrived:

'The symptoms were severe pains in the head, throat and eyes, vomiting and bronchial irritation. The affection was in many cases extremely painful . . .'[11]

Mustard gas is a liquid: ground or objects soaked with it could cause blistering even days after its delivery. On the other hand, it was rarely fatal; only 2 per cent of 'Yellow Cross' cases died. By November 1918 63 different kinds of poison gas had been used, successfully or otherwise. By that time the United States had added its technological resources to those of the Allies; its chemical warfare service, although a very late comer, was engaged in no less than 65 'major research problems', which included eight gases more deadly than any hitherto used. Among them was one which rendered soil barren for seven years; a few drops of it on a tree-trunk would cause the tree to 'wither in an hour'.[12] No less than 48,000 men had been allotted to this useful work.

More significant than these futuristic nightmares was the developing proficiency in the matter of delivery. Gas clouds looked dramatic, and could occasionally produce alarming results. A weapon which depended entirely on the vagaries of wind could not, however, be taken entirely seriously. Soon the Germans went back to their original idea, and others followed suit; by 1918 all the belligerents except the British (who never entirely overcame their munition problems) were delivering over 90 per cent of their gas in the form of shell. (Such was the scale of shell expenditure that this represents only 5 per cent of all the ammunition fired.) What this meant was that gas could be delivered with great precision; battery positions, in particular, could be deluged with it, seriously reducing the effectiveness of the opposing artillery. Sneezing gas and mustard gas made the Steenbeek valley, just behind the front line before the Passchendaele Ridge, virtually uninhabitable in the autumn of 1917. In March 1918 the Germans pumped 120,000 gas shells into the Flesquières Salient in the course of three successive nights, inflicting some 7,000 casualties on the 2nd and 63rd Divisions. There was no longer anything haphazard about gas; it could be placed exactly where it was intended to be. This consideration, linked to the capabilities displayed by the German Gotha bombers of 1917 and the British Independent Air Force in that year and the next, presented bleak prospects to the mass populations of great cities in the coming decades. At the front, between 1914–18, the fear of gas was often far greater than its actual effect; the fear of gas, delivered from the air, lay heavily on the post-war generation. Mass-extermination seemed not far away. Meanwhile, the deadlock endured.

NOTES

1 *O.H. 1915* i p. 188 f.n.2.
2 Ibid., p. 165 f.n.1.
3 Ibid., p. 164 f.n.1.
4 Ibid., p. 176.
5 General Mordacq: *Le Drame de l'Yser*, quoted in *The First World War* by Richard Thoumin, p. 175; Secker & Warburg, 1960.
6 *O.H. 1915* f.n.3.
7 *The Times*, 29 April 1915. It is interesting to see how men's minds in different places move towards the same ideas; some six weeks before the German use of gas at Ypres Haig recorded in his diary (11 March): 'Lord Dundonald arrived from England, he is studying the conditions of the war in the hopes of being able to apply to modern conditions an invention of his great grandfather for driving a garrison out of a fort by using sulphur fumes. I asked him how he arranged to have a favourable wind.' It was not a bad question.
8 C. R. M. F. Cruttwell: *A History of the Great War 1914–1918*, pp. 153–4; O.U.P., 1934.
9 L. F. Haber: *Gas Warfare 1915–1945: The Legend and the Facts*, p. 7; Bedford College (University of London), 1976.
10 *O.H. 1916*, i p. 196.
11 *O.H. 1917* ii p. 137 f.n.4.
12 *Foreign Affairs—U.S.A.*, July 1922, quoted in *Falsehood in War-Time* by Lord Ponsonby of Shoulbrede; Allen & Unwin, 1928.

Orthodoxy 1. *Sea Power*

Turkey's entry into the war held out for many frustrated strategists a delusive promise—a brilliant return to the familiar, traditional British system of exercising decisive pressure by the use of sea power. The 'lessons' of naval enterprise in the long wars with France were recalled. As the new armies began to form, naturally the question arose: how should they be used? Important voices questioned whether it was at all sensible to commit them to the deadlocked trench line in France. Lord Kitchener himself wrote to Sir John French on 2 January 1915:

'I suppose we must recognize that the French Army cannot make a sufficient break through the German lines to bring about the retreat of the German forces from Northern Belgium. If that is so, then the German lines in France may be looked on as a fortress that cannot be carried by assault and also that cannot be completely invested, with the result that the lines may be held by an investing force, whilst operations proceed elsewhere.'[1]

This superficially reasonable point of view was shared by many. The reasonableness was only superficial, for two clear reasons: first, because in terms of land warfare Britain was the junior partner of France, and for France, as we have seen (p. 91), there was only one possible strategy—to throw the invader off her soil, and also out of Belgium. So for Britain the only real choice was whether to stand by France through thick and thin, or to risk the break-up of the alliance and French defeat. It was very simple—but it took some swallowing.

The second reason for doubting the reasonableness of Lord Kitchener's proposition lies in the phrase, 'whilst operations proceed elsewhere'. Where? Germany had only two coasts: a stretch of some 200 miles of the North Sea between neutral Holland and neutral Denmark, protected not only by the High Seas Fleet but by one of the most perilous complexes of shoal water in the world; and the Baltic, whose sole entry point is through the Skaggerak. The Admiralty devised several tentative plans in 1915: an attack on the Ruhr via Holland—unfortunately Holland remained neutral and the British Government remained understandably reluctant to treat her as Germany had treated Belgium in 1914; capturing the island of Borkum as a base for attacking the port of Emden, and from there marching on Berlin; capturing the island of Sylt, possibly infringing Danish neutrality also, in order to seize the Kiel Canal and thus win access to the Baltic in order to land a Russian army on the Pomeranian coast. It is difficult to believe that anyone took any of this seriously. Lord Fisher, however, had always been a believer in the possibility of attacking Germany's Baltic coast, and remained one. There cannot have been many people who shared his optimism; even the gallantly handled British submarines found the Baltic a difficult sea to penetrate (though once inside they did some very useful work). As for Austria-

Hungary, she had only one coastline, in the Adriatic—the rugged Dalmatian littoral, with a hinterland virtually devoid of communications, protected by the naval base at Pola, and to which (until Italy entered the war) the nearest Allied base was Malta. Even the most confident arm-chair strategists balked at this. On the other hand, there *was* the railway leading to the 'very heart of the Dual Monarchy' from Salonika which so cheered Mr. Lloyd George (p. 42 Note 4). The only snag about that was that Salonika is in Greece, and Greece, too, remained obstinately neutral.

So it turned out that the 'lessons' of the French wars were not entirely helpful when it came to making war on Europe's Central Powers. The entry of Turkey, however, considerably changed the picture. Turkey offered to the Central Alliance simultaneously an accession of strength and weakness. The strength is generally estimated, in military terms, at 36 infantry divisions of varying numbers and quality; one has to say 'estimated' because, as the *Times History* remarks,

'*No Government by skilful artifice could be more successful in baffling the curiosity of the outsider than is the Turk by the simpler means of statistical incompetence and a natural disinclination to make practice march with theory.*'[2]

It was believed that the Turks had some 500,000 more or less trained men in the Army, with another 250,000 in the depôts. What their value would be in

'500,000 more or less trained men': Turkish infantry in 1915. Their fighting qualities surprised the British wherever they met them, and won sincere respect.

action, no one could tell; on the one hand, German advisers and instructors had already made some obvious progress; on the other, Turkey as a whole was far from fresh—she had been almost continually at war since 1911[3] and had suffered some demoralizing defeats. Yet it was a sobering thought that, by contrast, the whole might of the British Empire at the end of 1914 could only put 11 divisions in the field.

Turkey's weakness, obvious enough, was the sprawl of her empire in the Middle East. Not only did it contain disaffected populations—Christians, Armenians, and many of the Arab provinces—but its coastlines were virtually indefensible. They ran round Asia Minor all the way down to Sinai, then followed the Red Sea to Aden and reappeared in the Persian Gulf. This huge stretch—to say nothing of well over 600 miles of Black Sea littoral—presented distinct possibilities for naval action and naval pressure which were not lost upon Turkey's enemies. Of these, the most important and persistent was Britain's First Lord of the Admiralty, Winston Churchill.

Ironically, Churchill had been a lone voice in Government circles before the war, demanding better relations with Turkey, which he had visited in 1910. The advent of the Young Turks and the steady rise of the pro-German Enver Pasha (Minister of War in 1914) changed his views, and this change was put to the test at the very opening of the war. The Turkish Government, in 1911 and 1913, had ordered two battleships in British shipyards; the money for these was largely raised by patriotic public subscription—the only trouble was that Turkey did not possess suitable docks for such ships. Armstrong Whitworth and Vickers offered to build the necessary installations, and signed an agreement with the Turks in December 1913. Meanwhile the ships proceeded towards completion in England, and by the end of July 1914 they were ready to sail to Turkey. Five hundred Turkish sailors had arrived in the Tyne to man the *Sultan Osman I. Reshadieh*, the more powerful of the two (23,000 tons, 21 knots, with a primary armament of ten 13.5 inch guns) had a 14,800 lb. broadside, superior to that of any ship in the Grand Fleet. Churchill and the Admiralty were much disturbed at the thought of such a ship going to a state whose neutrality was by no means certain. On 1 August Britain comandeered the Turkish vessels; compensation was naturally offered, but the Turks were bitterly disappointed, and regarded the transaction as an act of piracy. Since Britain was not at war, even with Germany, their attitude is understandable.

How much effect the Admiralty's swift move had on Turkish policy—as opposed to Turkish emotions—must remain a matter of doubt. German influence had been increasingly powerful for some time, and on 2 August Enver signed a secret treaty which confirmed it completely, while Germany promised support in the event of a Russo-Turkish war. These negotiations were evidently in progress while the British Government was deciding what to do with the *Sultan Osman* (fourteen 12 inch guns, broadside 12,900 lb.) and *Reshadieh*. In the circumstances, it was just as well that they were added to the Royal Navy with the new names *Agincourt* and *Erin*.

On 10 August the Turks incurred the further displeasure of the British

Admiralty: they gave permission for *Goeben* and *Breslau* to pass through the Dardanelles Straits (see p. 126) and the next day the two German ships arrived at Constantinople, were bought by Turkey and renamed *Jawuz Sultan Selim* and *Midilli*. The German crews remained aboard. For Churchill this was decisive; a Cabinet meeting on 17 August found him 'in his most bellicose mood',[4] at another on 21 August he was 'violently anti-Turk'.[5] This frame of mind hardened as Turkey held to uneasy neutrality for a few more weeks. As he later said,

'I had convinced myself that Turkey would attack us sooner or later.'[6]

His mind, therefore, was already on countermeasures, and one of these stood out pre-eminently; in his own words:

'It is obvious that the ideal action against Turkey, if she came into the war, was at the earliest possible moment to seize the Gallipoli Peninsula by an amphibious surprise attack and to pass a fleet into the (Sea of) Marmora . . . the Gallipoli Peninsula, giving access by water to Constantinople, exposed, if taken, the heart of Turkey to a fatal stroke.'[7]

This was no novel proposal; the General Staff and the Admiralty had considered the problem of forcing the Dardanelles in 1904, in 1906, in 1908, and again in 1911. The 1906 investigation, which according to one of its chief participants, Major-General Sir C. E. Callwell (Director of Military Operations in 1914), 'was practically accepted by the Committee of Imperial Defence as governing the military policy of the country with respect to attack on the Straits in the event of war',[8] dismissed the project as an unfeasible military operation. The 1908 enquiry concurred, and in 1911 Churchill himself informed the Cabinet:

'. . . it is no longer possible to force the Dardanelles . . . nobody would expose a modern fleet to such perils.'[9]

By September 1914, however, this clear picture had become somewhat blurred. It was above all the speedy collapse of the Belgian fortresses, Liège and Namur, followed by Maubeuge (see p. 98) which caused Churchill and other enquiring minds to ask whether modern artillery and ammunition had not fundamentally altered the factors in the old equation of ships versus forts. It had been axiomatic since the bombardment of Alexandria in 1882 (and there were later examples) that ships would always be at a serious disadvantage in such action; now, however, 'fortresses reputed throughout Europe to be impregnable' were collapsing in a few days. Churchill, always deeply impressed by the might of the new naval guns, allowed his imagination to take wing. And with such an imagination as his, it could be relied on to fly in more than one direction; as with certain other British politicians (notably Mr. Lloyd George) the idea of a Balkan League, welded together by hatred of Turkey, which it would soon overthrow as it had done in the First Balkan War, and then turn on Austria-Hungary, made a deep appeal. Serbia was already in the war; Bulgaria had no love for the Turks. In September Churchill prompted the British Admiral, Mark Kerr, who commanded the Greek Navy, to discuss with the General Staff the possibilities of Greece joining in a war against Turkey, and in particular attacking Gallipoli. At the same time he set on foot yet another examination of that project by Admiralty and War Office representatives; once more it was pronounced not feasible, but on second thoughts General Callwell considered that Greek help might make the difference. It would still be 'an extremely difficult operation of war', but he thought (possibly under pressure of Churchillian rhetoric) that it might be done. Later he admitted an important oversight:

'. . . *the Greeks had no howitzers or mobile heavy artillery worth mentioning, and any ordnance of that kind that we disposed of in the Mediterranean was of the prehistoric kind.'* [10]

But this was academic; Admiral Kerr's report came through on 9 September. The Greeks, he said, believed that they had sufficient force to take Gallipoli, *'if Bulgaria does not attack Greece.'* And this was the rub:

'It is not sufficient guarantee for Bulgaria to undertake to remain neutral. They will not trust her unless she also attacks Turkey with all her force.' [11]

This was not surprising; it was only just over a year since Bulgaria had treacherously turned upon her allies, Serbia and Greece, and started the Second Balkan War. As Churchill later gloomily pronounced:

'This warlike and powerful Bulgaria, with its scheming king and its valiant peasant armies brooding over what seemed to them intolerable wrongs, was the dominant factor in the Balkans in 1914 and 1915.' [12]

So there matters rested, in an atmosphere increasingly hostile on both sides, until 29 October, when the one-time *Goeben* and *Breslau* struck without warning at Russia's Black Sea ports (see p. 126; Nikolayev and Odessa were attacked as well as Sebastopol). British reactions, largely naval and attributable to Churchill's long-standing deep suspicion of Turkish behaviour, were very prompt indeed. On 1 November two British destroyers sank a small Turkish warship in Smyrna harbour; the next day, the light cruiser *Minerva* shelled the unmanned fort and put a landing party ashore at Akaba. A far more significant gesture followed on 3 November: an Allied squadron under Vice-Admiral Carden bombarded the forts at the entrance to the Dardanelles Straits, causing extensive damage in one of them by a shot which hit the magazine. This bombardment later drew much criticism upon Churchill and his advisers; it was said to have alerted the Turks and caused them to strengthen their defences. However, fuller investigation showed that no seri-

'*Goeben* and *Breslau* struck without warning': these are the two ships which attacked Russia's Black Sea ports in October 1914 and brought Turkey into the war.

ous work was done on these fortifications between November 1914 and April 1915. They had no invasion to fear, because no military force existed for such a purpose; and in any case, as Martin Gilbert says,

'*The Dardanelles was so obvious a point of attack for any enemy wishing to crush Turkey that it did not need a brief Allied bombardment to stress the importance of defending this one sea access to Constantinople.*'[13]

One thing the bombardment did, however: it reminded the British Government that an actual declaration of war might be in order. This duly followed on 5 November, just in time to anticipate yet another stroke against Turkey which would have far-reaching consequences—and once again the hands of the Royal Navy and the First Lord were very visible. So also was the everlasting influence of technological change. Very shortly after his appointment as First Lord, Churchill had presided over a profound revolution in naval technology; as he tells us:

'*The three programmes of 1912, 1913 and 1914 comprised the greatest additions in power and cost ever made to the Royal Navy . . . (except for 2 battleships) they did not contain a coal-burning ship.*'[14]

He adds:

'To change the foundation of the Navy from British coal to foreign oil was a formidable decision in itself.'[15]

This may stand as one of the great understatements of history.

To ensure an adequate supply of the Navy's new fuel, the Government in June 1914 acquired a controlling interest in the Anglo-Persian Oil Company (set up in 1909). The Company's refinery at Abadan, at the head of the Persian Gulf, was supplied by a pipeline from the oilfields 150 miles to the north-east. The capacity of the pipeline was 350,000 tons per annum; the refinery was able to deal with 1,000 tons of crude oil a day. The supply, said *The Times*, 'seems illimitable'. On the other hand, it was very vulnerable; Abadan itself stood on the very border of Turkish territory. A military expedition from India arrived off Abadan on 23 October, but as Turkey was still neutral it remained on board its ships. On 6 November, however, the Turkish defences were bombarded, and on 7 November the troops went ashore. Just over a fortnight later they were in Basra. Such were the origins of a campaign which, under the title 'Mesopotamia', would from first to last give employment to 889,702 British and Indian soldiers.

Finally, as we survey these stirrings of naval bellicosity with their unmistakable pointers to future action, we should note a small but significant event on 18 December. The light cruiser *Doris* arrived off the port of Alexandretta, which is the hinge linking Asia Minor with Turkey's great possessions in the Arab lands to the south. A landing party from *Doris* cut the railway line from Anatolia, and derailed a train. Next day a railway bridge was destroyed. Threatened by the cruiser's 6 inch guns, the Turks agreed to destroy railway material and stores, but having no explosives they had to ask the Royal Navy to supply some. This was duly done, and the ludicrous spectacle ensued of British sailors laying explosive charges while Turkish officials supervised their detonation. It was all very entertaining, but its sequels were not; Churchill said later:

'What kind of Turk was this we were fighting? . . . I must say that it was always in my mind that we were not dealing with a thoroughly efficient military power . . .'[16]

With what we know, we can only observe these successive encouragements to underrate Turkish strength with prickles of foreboding.

In the event, it was neither a naval nor a British crisis which brought about the great traditional riposte of sea power to the land deadlock. We have briefly noted (p. 122) how at the very end of 1914 the Turks launched an offensive against Russia in the Caucasus. This extraordinary act of suicidal folly was the inspiration of Enver Pasha himself, possibly prompted but certainly unrestrained by German advisers. Starting on 21 December, a Turkish army of some 95,000 men in summer clothing, without coats or blankets, tents or fuel, advanced through a mountain region nowhere less than 3,000 feet above sea level, mostly above 6,000 feet rising to over 10,000, scourged by bitter winds, snow, and night temperatures of 20° below freezing point. By mid-January they had met utter defeat at the hands of the pitiless climate and Russian counter-attack; their army was almost totally destroyed. But for a short space of time it had given the Russians a great shock. On 30 December the Grand Duke Nicholas told the Chief of the British Military Mission with the Russian Army, Major-General Hanbury-Williams, that the Turkish threat in the Caucasus was serious, and asked for British help to reduce the pressure. This was passed on by the Ambassador as a request 'for Lord Kitchener to arrange for a demonstration of some kind against Turks elsewhere, either naval or military'. This reached Kitchener on 2 January and he immediately sent it on to Churchill. They met at the Admiralty, both most eager to help the Russians; Kitchener suggested a demonstration at the Dardanelles; Churchill pressed for combined naval and military action. But when Kitchener returned to the War Office to examine the question, he very soon found himself confronted by the stark bedrock fact that, at that stage, the British Empire had no troops available for such a purpose. He wrote to Churchill:

'I do not see that we can do anything that will very seriously help the Russians in the Caucasus . . .
We have no troops to land anywhere . . .
The only place that a demonstration might have some effect in stopping reinforcements going East would be the Dardanelles—particularly if as the Grand Duke says reports could be spread at the same time that Constantinople was threatened. We shall not be ready for anything big for some months.'[17]

So we see how Russia's premature call for help provided 'the germ of the Dardanelles expedition.'[18]

This is not the occasion to recount the often-told tale of the stage-by-stage development of the operation famous in history as 'Gallipoli'; it is certainly not the place to re-examine the well-threshed question of who was 'to blame'. The plain truth is that the idea of opening up a new front to escape the deadlock in the West was working in many minds at once; that all shared a thought expressed by Sir Maurice Hankey, Secretary to the War Council, in his powerful 'Boxing Day Memorandum':

'Has not the time come to show Germany and the world that any country that chooses a German alliance against the great sea power is doomed to disaster?'[19]

Russia's request simply provided the reason and pointed the way.

It will be convenient, however, departing from chronology, to look a little further at the Russian influence. Dominating, for many months, the whole question of action at the Dardanelles was that sheer lack of troops of which Lord Kitchener was so gloomily aware. Once more the notion of bringing in the Greeks recommended itself, and it was known to have the warm support of Eleutherios Venizelos, the Greek Prime Minister. On 1 March Venizelos made a definite offer to support an attack on the Gallipoli peninsula with a Greek corps of three divisions; the next day the British Military Attaché in Athens reported optimistic discussions with officers of the Greek General Staff. At last, it seemed, a military operation was entering the realms of reality. And then came the body-blow. On 3 March the British Minister in Athens reported a conversation with his Russian opposite number who had said that 'in no circumstances will they allow Greek soldiers to enter Constantinople'.[20] And the following day the British Ambassador in Paris confirmed this; the French Foreign Minister had told him:

'Russian Government will not at any price accept co-operation of Greece in Constantinople expedition'.[21]

And that was that; as Martin Gilbert says: 'The Russian veto on Greek participation was final and absolute.'[22] Considering that it was Russia's plight that had brought the Allies to the point of launching this great enterprise, one must agree with Cruttwell's uncompromising verdict:

'History in its long record of the short-sighted selfishness shown by individual members of coalitions, devoted in lip-service to a common cause, can hardly provide a more fatal example.'[23]

For sundry reasons the Gallipoli campaign has never ceased to exercise fascination; indeed, it is very likely that the revival of interest in First World War studies, after long and untoward neglect, began with Alan Moorehead's *Gallipoli* in 1956. The theatre of war, with its classical associations—the Plains of Troy and the 'polyphloisbic, wine-dark' Aegean Sea[24]—and the sense of high adventure, the individual tragedies epitomized by the death of Rupert Brooke, the strange, fey character of General Sir Ian Hamilton, the illustrious début of the Australians and New Zealanders immortalized in the name 'Anzac'; the gallantry displayed in such feats as the 'six VCs before breakfast' of the 1/Lancashire Fusiliers at Lancashire Landing or Lieutenant-Commander Bernard Freyberg's DSO at Bulair; the sorrowful success of the evacuation, the sense of vast opportunity missed, all contribute to make Gallipoli an eternally poignant name. Dispassionate assessment is not easy, and when arrived at tends to be merciless.

'Gallipoli' is generally spoken and thought of as the great combined operation of the First World War. It was not so at first—the lack of troops at the beginning of 1915 made certain that if anything was to be done in the Dardanelles area, the Navy would have to do it. As a naval operation it gained credibility not only from the startling, swift collapse of the Belgian and French forts mentioned above, and the range and power of modern artillery, but also from an entirely new and at the same time ephemeral element of naval strength. As Churchill points out, until 1905 alteration of the type and value of British capital ships from year to year was negligible: minor improvements upon a uniform basic design. The coming of HMS *Dread-*

nought (see p. 36) changed everything, and

> '*once the Dreadnoughts began to multiply, all relation between the oldest and newest was lost. Every year had seen a large new construction. Every year had seen an immense advance . . . In guns, mechanism, armour, speed, subdivision, this advance was so great at each step that no proportion held between the oldest and the newest ships.*'[25]

This meant that Britain, in 1915, possessed a large fleet of battleships which were quite unfit for modern battle; in fact, they were due to be scrapped in that year. Nine *Majestics* built between 1894 and 1896, six *Canopuses* (1897–99), four *Formidables* (1898–99; six built, two already lost) and five *Duncans* (1901) were all marked for the breakers' yards; yet they remained, in themselves, powerful instruments of war. Was there no use for them? Obsolete they might be for naval battle, but at least they were contemporary with the Turkish forts, and this, as Churchill wrote,

> '*was a new fact in regard to all bombarding operations . . . In 1905 no one would have risked them in trying to force the Dardanelles. They were our latest vessels and all we had. In 1915 they were surplus and moribund. Yet related to the forts their strength was unimpaired.*'[26]

It was this surplus—itself an irony at a time of desperate shortage of virtually all necessities—this curious surplus created by the speed of technological advance, that seemed to make a purely naval penetration of the Dardanelles possible. When to this was added (at Fisher's instigation) technology's latest product, the Navy's most powerful vessel, *Queen Elizabeth*, with her eight 15 inch guns and 25 knot speed, the success of such an attack seemed not merely possible but practically certain.

The naval attack was approved by the War Council (predecessor of the 1917 War Cabinet) on 28 January, and it may be said that from the moment of that approval faith in it entered a decline. By mid-February Admiral Sir Henry Jackson (soon to succeed Fisher as First Sea Lord), Captain Richmond (Assistant Director of Operations at the Admiralty), Hankey, and finally Fisher himself had come to a conclusion succinctly expressed by Richmond:

> '*the bombardment of the Dardanelles, even if all the forts are destroyed, can be nothing but a local success, which without an army to carry it on can have no further effect.*'[27]

The final converts were Churchill and Kitchener. Nevertheless, the purely naval attack went ahead; two bombardments of the four forts at the entrance to the Straits on 19 February and 25 February succeeded in silencing them, and landing parties completed the destruction of their guns. It looked deceptively as though a Combined Operation might not be needed after all, but preparations for a military expedition as a back-up operation, using the Australians and New Zealanders training in Egypt and a Naval Division with a Regular division from England, continued. The Greeks obligingly contributed the island of Lemnos as a base.

Mid-March brought the sad awakening; until then, as Churchill says, 'no serious risks have been run, no losses have been sustained, and no important forces deeply engaged.' With the outer forts now helpless, the time had come to attempt the passage of the Straits, forcing a way through the Narrows at Chanak, where they are little more than a mile wide. This involved, first, the silencing of the inner forts, and then the sweeping of the minefields liberally sown in these restricted waters. The dangers were manifest, but past experience suggested that they were not insuperable. On 18 March, accordingly, the Allied Fleet (now under Vice-Admiral de Robeck, Admiral Carden's health having broken down) re-entered the Straits. Fourteen British and four French battleships, organized in two divisions, prepared to engage the Turks; eight of the British vessels had been launched between 1895–1901, four more between 1903–06 and were of pre-*Dreadnought* design. The others were the battle-cruiser *Inflexible*, of Falkland Islands fame, and the mighty *Queen Elizabeth*, 27,500 tons, whose total broadside was approximately

'. . . mobile howitzer batteries . . .': Turkish weapons, supplied by Germany, were good but never plentiful. The Gallipoli campaign is a story of Turkish endurance against great odds.

16,000 lb. At 11.30am the leading line of ships, which included the two dreadnoughts, opened fire at 14,000 yards.

The position from which de Robeck's fleet began the action, Eren Keui Bay, was defended by Turkish mobile howitzer batteries, difficult and elusive targets which proved very effective against all classes of ship, and minefield batteries whose task was to deter the sweepers. In addition, of course, there were the mines, and in particular, in Eren Keui Bay itself which was believed to have been swept clear, a new line laid by the Turks ten days earlier. These mines, remarks Churchill wryly, 'played a recognizable part in the history of the Great War.' They did indeed.

By 1.45pm the distant forts appeared to have been overcome; the howitzers were still troublesome, but although they had scored a number of hits they had inflicted less than 40 casualties on the ships' crews. The time had come for the minesweepers to clear the Narrows, and the second division of battleships to follow them for the kill. It was at this moment of seemingly clear success that disaster began. The French battleship *Bouvet*, retiring to make way for the second division, struck a mine and blew up with the loss of nearly her entire crew. As the minesweepers pushed slowly up towards the Narrows the forts came to life again, but by 4 o'clock they had been practically silenced once more, and the mobile batteries driven off by the secondary armament of the ships. Then, at 4.11pm, *Inflexible*, which had taken some severe punishment by gunfire earlier, reported having struck a mine; it was apparent that her condition was dangerous—and this was a prime fleet unit. It is only surprising that the fatal contact had not occurred before; she had been operating in the new minefield virtually throughout the action. Three minutes later the *Formidable* class (1898) battleship *Irresistible* was also seen to be listing heavily and apparently unable to move; it was soon learned that she, too, had hit a mine. Admiral de Robeck decided, very reasonably, to break off the action and withdraw. But the tale of loss was not yet complete.

Inflexible, surrounded by a destroyer screen, by excellent seamanship and devoted work in the engine-room was brought to Tenedos; she was out of action for six weeks. The *Canopus* class (1898) battleship *Ocean* was ordered to try to tow away *Irresistible*, whose crew had been taken off by destroyers. The task was peculiarly difficult, and while attempting it *Ocean* herself also hit a mine. Her crew was saved but the ship, together with *Irresistible*, had to be abandoned in a sinking condition; both went down in the night, 'and no man knew their resting-place'.[28] And this was still not the full tally: in the French squadron the battleship *Gaulois* was so seriously damaged by gunfire that it was for some time doubted whether she could be saved, while *Suffren* also required major repair. So the final reckoning was three capital units sunk and three more put out of action—one third of the fleet:

'*The great attempt to force the Narrows with the fleet had ended in what could only be regarded as a severe defeat.*'[29]

It is an illustration of the curiosities of naval war—its 'all-or-nothing' quality—that despite this very considerable material loss, British casualties were only 61 killed and wounded, while the French were almost all in the *Bouvet*—about 600. Furthermore, for the British, at any rate, the lost ships could easily be replaced; on 20 March Churchill informed de Robeck that two more *Formidables*, *London* and *Implacable* (both 1899) and two 'improved *Formidables*', *Queen* and *Prince of Wales* (1902), were on their way to join him. The French also agreed to replace *Bouvet*. Yet 18 March proved to be the death-knell of the purely naval effort, and the true starting-point of the Combined Operation.

The phrase 'Combined Operation' must be understood: it in no way implies anything remotely resembling the sophisticated activities of the command of that name which operated under Lord Mountbatten in the Second World War. The 1915 operation was 'combined' because it was conducted by the Navy and the Army together—just that. The last time they had performed such a task was the landing at Walcheren in 1809; other examples were supplied by Abercromby's expedition at Aboukir Bay in 1800 and Wolfe's capture of Quebec in 1759. No doubt Admiral de Robeck and General Sir Ian Hamilton, who had been appointed to command the Allied military force, found those campaigns to some extent instructive—the value of very intimate co-operation, and of rehearsal are both well illustrated—but they could do little to solve the new problems of long-range, quick-firing artillery, hidden machine-guns, and barbed wire on the beaches.

It must not be thought that preparations for the 1915 attack were 'slap-dash' or naïve—much criticism was aroused when it was later learnt that transports arriving in the Aegean from England were not what the later war would call 'tactically loaded'; the critics ignored the fact that when the transports set out there was no intention of making an assault landing. A sounder criticism is that Hamilton and his Chief of Staff, Braithwaite, did not make sure of taking out with them the various studies made during the last decade, especially that of 1906. But within their limitations the naval and military staffs grasped the complexities of the daunting problem that faced them with all due professionalism; what they lacked was the right equipment, and the lack was total.

Hamilton's tactics were correct: landings in several places to confuse the defence, with a convincingly large feint attack for good measure. Covering fire was to be supplied by the guns of the substantial fleet: 18 battleships, 12 cruisers, 24 British and five French destroyers. It was an impressive array; but 1940–45 experience would show that it was nothing like enough. And absolutely none of the special equipment and devices evolved through the landings in Sicily, at Salerno and Anzio for the Normandy landing in 1944 existed in 1915: the diversity of landing-craft, the amphibious tanks, the command ships etc., etc. all lay in a future nearly 30 years distant. There *were* some landing-craft, lighters holding about 500 men or 50 horses and capable of 5 knots under their own power, ordered by Fisher for his favourite Baltic schemes; they were retained in home waters. The nearest that Hamilton's

'The nearest that Hamilton's stormers came to sophistication . . .': there is nothing sophisticated about the look of the *River Clyde*. Beached too far out, soldiers were shot down in scores trying to land from her.

stormers came to sophistication was a converted collier, the *River Clyde*, holding 2,000 infantry; the idea was to ground her as close in as possible, then a floating pier would be run out to the beach, the soldiers would pour out of sally-ports cut in her side and rush ashore. It hardly needs to be added that on the day a wide gap separated intention and reality.

'On the day': the day was 25 April, and that date itself constitutes the most significant fact about 'Gallipoli'. As we have seen, it was precisely three days previously that the Germans had opened the Second Battle of Ypres with their gas attack, and that battle would grind on until the end of May with 59,275 British casualties (see p. 158). During this period the BEF experienced its most acute shortages; pressed by Joffre and Foch to extend its front, attacked by the Germans at its most sensitive point, its divisions, though increasing in number, were short of every kind of munitions, but above all the guns and ammunition required for the artillery war. In April and May Sir John French's field guns had available 10.6 and 11 rounds per gun per day, against a requirement of 50 rounds per day. The Second Army had only eight of the excellent 60-pdrs, the bulk of its medium artillery consisting of 44 converted naval 4.7s of South African War vintage; for these there were only 4.2 and 4.3 rounds per gun per day, against a minimum need of 25. And the 4.7 had already earned the name 'Strict Neutrality' because of its uncertain shooting. When two new British Regular divisions took over a stretch of the French front they found that the French had held it with 120 75 mm. field guns and 30 heavies; the British could only muster 72 18-pdrs between them. In the face of these dire needs on the main front, what chance did Sir Ian Hamilton have of a properly equipped force? His leading four divisions had an establishment of 306 pieces of artillery; instead they contained only 118. This shortage persisted throughout the campaign, and with it a dearth of ammunition and, indeed, of everything else that was needed. The simple truth was that, hard pressed to maintain even one major campaign in 1915, the British were quite incapable of two.

It is not necessary to repeat the heroic, tragic story of 'Gallipoli', the bloody landings, the lost opportunities, the stubborn, courageous Turks, handfuls of determined men hanging on in the face of enormous odds and bringing every enterprise of the British, Australians, New Zealanders, Indians, and French to nought. Within a fortnight the bitter truth about 'Gallipoli' was becoming plain; it was clearly expressed to Churchill in a letter from his younger brother, Jack, who was serving on General Hamilton's staff, on 9 May:

'Fierce fighting has continued and the real result has been most disappointing. Progress has been made—but at heavy cost, and where we hoped to gain miles we have advanced a few yards. It has become siege warfare again as in France. Trenches and wire beautifully covered by machine gun fire are the order of the day. Terrific artillery fire against invulnerable trenches and then attempts to make frontal attacks in the face of awful musketry fire, are the only tactics that can be employed . . . We shall have to fight every yard and to do this we must have lots more men.' [30]

In other words, the deadlock had simply been transferred—to the far end of

'It has become siege warfare again . . .': the deadlock at Gallipoli was as rigid as in France, but with only the narrow space between the trenches and the sea to hold all the paraphernalia needed. This is a corner of Anzac Beach.

the Mediterranean, a most inconvenient place. Jack Churchill's cry for 'lots more men' was answered, stage by stage; in the event, the expedition employed from first to last 410,000 British Empire and 79,000 French troops. The theatre of war imposed its own peculiar hazards: out of 213,980 British casualties, 145,154 were due to sickness, with dysentery heading the list (29,728 cases), diarrhoea next (10,373); and enteric fever (9,423). For the benefit of those who, like the Prime Minister,[31] thought of the Mediterranean as 'the gorgeous East' and vastly preferable to muddy Flanders, November produced a blizzard which caused 15,000 casualties by frostbite.

And it was all for nothing. Evacuation, in two stages, was carried out with much heart-searching, in December and January. There were natural fears that this might prove, in the face of a vigilant enemy, to be a ruinous business, but by a final irony meticulous planning and skilful deception made it the most successful endeavour of the whole campaign. Lord Fisher's motor lighters, christened 'beetles' by the troops, a few of which he had belatedly released, were very helpful; but as with so much else, another 25 years would have to pass for this kind of vessel to come to fruition.

The Dardanelles campaign was the classic example of what Major-General J. F. C. Fuller would later call the 'strategy of evasion'—the deep desire of people like Churchill and Lloyd George to evade the hard fighting and heavy loss of the Western Front. Fuller says:

'What they were unable to appreciate was, that should another locality be found in which the enemy's resistance was less formidable than on the Western Front, it could only be a matter of time before the same tactical conditions prevailed. It was the bullet, spade and wire which were the enemy on every front, and their geographical locations were purely incidental.'[32]

For Britain 'Gallipoli' held another, even more serious meaning: this was the last attempt in British history to exercise absolute naval supremacy in the traditional manner. Since the British Empire was founded upon naval might, one may say that the Gallipoli failure marked the beginning of the end of that Empire.

NOTES
1 See *O.H. 1915*, i p. 61.
2 *Times History of the War*, iii p. 55.
3 Italy declared war on Turkey on 29 September; it was in this war that she gained the great province of Libya. It continued until 18 October 1912, by which time the First Balkan War was already in progress (Montenegro, Serbia, Bulgaria, and Greece against Turkey). This ended in May 1913. The Second Balkan War began on 30 June, and Turkey re-entered it in July to win back a fair amount of what she had lost to Bulgaria in the First War. Peace was signed on 10 August.
4 Martin Gilbert: *Winston S. Churchill*, iii p. 195.
5 Ibid., Companion Volume i p. 49.

6   Churchill: *The World Crisis*, i p. 445.
7   Gilbert, op. cit. pp. 200–1
8   Callwell: *Experiences of a Dug-Out*, pp. 88–9.
9   Gilbert, op. cit. p. 220 f.n.1.
10   Callwell, op. cit. p. 89.
11   Gilbert, op. cit. p. 209.
12   Churchill, op. cit. p. 440.
13   Gilbert, op. cit. p. 218.
14   Churchill, op. cit. p. 102.
15   Ibid., p. 101.
16   Gilbert, op. cit. p. 222.
17   Ibid., pp. 232–3.
18   Cruttwell: *History of the Great War*, p. 132.
19   Hankey: *Supreme Command 1914–1918*, i p. 248.
20   Gilbert, Companion Volume i p. 623.
21   Ibid., p. 631.
22   Gilbert, op. cit. p. 328.
23   Cruttwell, op. cit. p. 209.
24   Rupert Brooke, letter, quoted in *Gallipoli* by Alan Moorehead, p. 109; Hamish Hamilton, 1956.
25   Churchill, op. cit. p. 537.
26   Ibid., p. 538.
27   Gilbert, op. cit. p. 287.
28   Corbett: *Naval Operations*, ii p. 222.
29   Ibid., p. 223.
30   Gilbert, Companion Volume ii pp. 852–5.
31   H. H. Asquith to Venetia Stanley, 26 February, having attended a review of the Royal Naval Division, in which his son 'Oc' and Rupert Brooke both served: 'How lucky they are to escape Flanders and the trenches and be sent to the "gorgeous East."'
32   Fuller: *The Conduct of War 1789–1961*, p. 161.

Orthodoxy 2. *Change of Direction*

NOWHERE WAS THE SHORTAGE OF SOLDIERS so acute as in Britain, but everywhere, after the murderous battles of 1914, a shortage was felt. Even the great German Army was affected; in February 1915 it numbered 143 infantry divisions of all categories, a very large force indeed, but even so the High Command was conscious of a lack of reserves which nullified the initiative which Germany had seized. The 1914 conscript class was exhausted, as was practically the whole of the trained *Landsturm*, so clearly the need could only be supplied by unusual methods. These were made possible by the unusual circumstances of trench warfare.

The Allies faced some unpalatable truths; it was not only in the material sense that they were unprepared, they were also unprepared psychologically for the trenches. All that carefully cultivated élan of the French was now mud-bound and buried, with the result that 'contrary to all expectations (they) did not distinguish themselves at all.'[1] The British also underwent the painful experience of having delusions swept away; a soldier acquaintance told the historian F. S. Oliver:

'The remarkable thing . . . is this—that when the war began we were all prepared for the Germans to be successful at first owing to their study of war and scientific preparation, but we argued that very soon we should become much better than they, not being hide-bound by a system. The exact contrary has been the case. The Germans with their foundation of solid study and experience have been far quicker to adapt themselves to the changed conditions of war and the emergencies of the situation than either we or the Russians have been—possibly even more so than the French.'[2]

It was this that offered the German General Staff a solution to its manpower problem; as Falkenhayn says:

'The moral and technical superiority of the German soldier over his opponents which was daily becoming more evident, also offered a way out of this difficulty. It turned out to be so great that it was possible to entertain the suggestion of the Director of the General War Department, Colonel von Wrisberg, to reduce by about 25 per cent. the strength of the fighting units, the divisions, without doing any harm to their effectiveness . . .'[3]

What this meant was that one 3-battalion regiment could be removed from each division, and these could then be grouped (with the addition of new artillery, machine-guns, mortars, etc.) to form new divisions. In March and April 19 divisions were raised in this way; with the addition of some entirely new regiments, by August the German Army had risen to 170 divisions.

The question (as with the Allies) was how to use this accession of strength. Falkenhayn himself was a dedicated 'Westerner'; he believed:

'No decision in the East, even though it were as thorough as was possible to imagine, could spare us from fighting to a conclusion in the West.'[4]

Indeed, he doubted very much whether a decision of any kind *could* be arrived at in the East, and was most reluctant to attempt one; 'Napoleon's experiences did not invite an imitation of his example.' Yet, like his Allied counterparts, he found himself forced to submit to inexorable pressures; he would readily have echoed Kitchener's gloomy remark to Churchill after facing some of these:

'We cannot make war as we ought; we can only make it as we can.'[5]

It was that extraordinary revival capacity of even the most seemingly shattered and miserably under-equipped Russian armies which constituted the chief pressure upon the doubtful Falkenhayn. We have briefly noted

(p. 122) how they returned amazingly to the offensive after heavy defeats in November 1914; they penetrated to the crests of the Carpathians and re-entered East Prussia. How much more they could have done is open to question, but what they undoubtedly had done was to cause much alarm in Berlin, sufficient to cause Germany's last reserves to be sent East to take part in what became known as the 'Winter Battle in Masuria'. This was fought under indescribable conditions in February; once again the Russians were driven out of East Prussia, their Tenth Army lost 110,000 prisoners and 300 guns, with at least another 100,000 casualties, so that it 'ceased to exist as an effective fighting force.' But the Germans themselves, especially their partially trained Reserve formations (similar to those which had gone singing to their deaths at Ypres), were completely exhausted by these exertions. Writing of the 'Winter Battle', Hindenburg says:

'The name charms like an icy wind or the silence of death.'

More significantly he adds:

'We could not achieve a decisive result. The superiority of the Russians was too great.' [6]

Max Hoffmann summed up the situation at the beginning of April: 'We are stuck fast on the whole front.' [7]

So the East, like the West, presented an intolerable deadlock—with certain more dangerous attributes. The build-up of Allied naval strength in the eastern Mediterranean emphasized the need for the Central Powers to open up some corridor of direct communication with their Turkish ally; Falkenhayn considered an attack on Serbia as a step towards this, but Conrad had had enough of Serbia. He had far more pressing preoccupations. In March the tireless Russians resumed their Carpathian attacks, threatening an incursion into Hungary; on the 22nd they captured Przemysl, freeing further forces for this advance. Once more Austria-Hungary's plight was desperate; once more she had to appeal for German help. But this time the strategist in Falkenhayn, despite his hesitations, was able to perceive substantial merit in the proposals which his ally, Conrad, put before him. They did, in fact, contain the substance of one of the vastest and most dramatic strokes of the war.

Conrad pointed out the interesting possibilities of the 30-mile stretch of front in Galicia between the otherwise undistinguished localities of Gorlice and Tarnow. A blow here, between the Carpathians and the Vistula, could bisect the Russian front; if successful, it would divide their armies in Poland and the north from those in Galicia and Bukovina, rolling up the latter and eliminating once and for all the Carpathian front. It would require two things: first, a total abandonment of the traditional Austro-German strategy of encirclement, and adoption of the French aim of penetration (*percée*). Secondly, it would have to be carried out by a German army; that much had

'Austria-Hungary's plight was desperate': a machine-gun section 'somewhere in Galicia'.

become humiliatingly apparent. Falkenhayn concurred. He did more; he actually doubled the German contribution which Conrad had somewhat timidly asked for—he threw in his whole strategic reserve, the *Eleventh Army* of eight seasoned divisions drawn from the Western Front. He had decided to play for the highest stake that he believed attainable: 'the permanent crippling of Russia's offensive powers.'

Great secrecy and deception surrounded the German preparations; even Conrad himself was not informed of the full scope of Falkenhayn's intentions until the last moment. A diversionary attack from East Prussia on 16 April forced the Russians to retreat some 75 miles into Lithuania and served to draw attention away from Galicia. On the 22nd came the attack at Ypres, suggesting that the Western Front was still the true centre of German attention. The apparent half-heartedness of some of their advances in this sector stems from the fact that they were, after all, only feints to cover the big blow in the East; there were no reserves left for any sustained endeavour in the West. (It nevertheless remains a puzzle why they chose to introduce such a weapon as gas for what was only a secondary operation.)

By 28 April the *Eleventh Army*, under General von Mackensen with the very able Colonel von Seeckt as his Chief of Staff, was in position: eight German and three Austrian divisions, with one Hungarian cavalry division, supported by the Austro-Hungarian *Fourth Army* of five divisions with one German and a cavalry division. Falkenhayn tells us:

'They were provided as abundantly as was possible with artillery, even with the heaviest calibre, which had scarcely been used at all in the open field till then, with ammunition and trench-mortar batteries. Numerous officers who were intimately acquainted with the incisive modern methods of war on the Western front were detailed to them.'[8]

Statistically translated, this meant 352 field and 146 heavy guns in the *Eleventh Army* and 350 field and 103 heavy in the Austrian *Fourth*: a field gun to about every 45 yards of front and a heavy gun to every 132 yards. The opposing Russians had only 141 field and four heavy guns. The Germans also brought up 96 *minenwerfer*, of which the Russians had none at all. By Western Front standards this assembly of Austro-German artillery was not particularly remarkable—the French were at this very time collecting 293 heavy and 780 field guns for their Artois offensive on a front of less than 10 miles—but on the Eastern Front it constituted a crushing novelty. The Russian positions, outposts shallowly entrenched with very little wire and no dug-outs, could not possibly withstand such a weight of metal.

The artillery registration began on 1 May, developing in intensity through the afternoon and night; at 6am on 2 May it swelled to maximum intensity for four hours, with trench mortars joining in. The Russian defences were smashed to pieces. At 10 o'clock the mortars ceased firing, the artillery lifted on to the Russian back lines, and some 30–40,000 infantry advanced at a rapid pace. 'The troops,' says Falkenhayn,

'freed from the fetters of trench warfare, swept the unwieldy enemy before them in the exuberant joy of the attack.'[9]

Making all allowance for a staff officer's somewhat elevated view of what can never fail to be, to some extent, a bloody business, he had good reason to be pleased. This was a real breakthrough at last; the Russian Third Army was practically annihilated—the Germans claimed 140,000 prisoners and 100 guns by 4 May; the arrows on the headquarters' maps at last appeared to have some meaning.

The exploitation was as dramatic as the breakthrough: as predicted, the whole Russian front in Galicia began at once to crumble. On 3 June Przemysl was retaken, and on 22 June Lemberg, where Austria's troubles had all begun. On 30 July the Austrians entered Lublin; at its furthest point the new front was now 150 miles beyond its start-line. Warsaw fell on 5 August, a shattering blow to Russian pride, but militarily even worse was the surrender of the fortress of Novogeorgievsk on 20 August, with 1,600 guns and nearly a million rounds of the precious ammunition whose shortage was constantly

'The Germans claimed 140,000 prisoners . . .': a group of Russian prisoners under guard. In 1915 alone Russia suffered 2 million casualties, half of them prisoners and missing.

being proclaimed. Four days later the Germans were in Brest Litovsk. By the end of September the offensive had come to a halt along a practically straight line from the eastern end of the Carpathians to Riga in the north; this represented a maximum advance of over 300 miles—movement indeed.

Yet this great, unprecedented campaign was a failure. By the end of the year it is estimated that the Russians had lost about one million casualties (killed and wounded) and another million prisoners or missing. Three thousand guns had also been lost. Nevertheless, they were counter-attacking; the 'permanent crippling of Russia's offensive powers' which Falkenhayn had sought had not been achieved—as the next year would devastatingly show. And once more there was deadlock, East and West.

––––––––––––––––––

One thing, however, this great straightening of the front permitted: the thorn in the south could now be nipped. An Austrian and a German army, both under the command of Field-Marshal von Mackensen, were brought across to the Serbian frontiers. On 5 October they began to cross the Save and the Danube; Belgrade fell on 9 October. Two days later, by prearranged agreement, Bulgaria entered the war, striking at the flank and rear of the Serbs with two more armies. All that was left for the hard-fighting Serbian Army was retreat, and this was carried out with great loss and suffering in bitter winter conditions. The remnants finally escaped through the mountains of Albania and were in due course taken off by the Allies to reform in Corfu. A feeble attempt by an Allied force to bring relief by advancing from Salonika was forced to retire into what the Germans would later call 'the greatest Allied internment camp'[10] of the war.

NOTES
1 General Erich von Falkenhayn: *General Headquarters 1914–1916 and its Critical Decisions*, p. 42; Hutchinson, 1919.
2 F. S. Oliver: *The Anvil of War*, p. 113; Macmillan, 1936.
3 Falkenhayn, op. cit. pp. 43–4.
4 Ibid., p. 56.
5 Churchill: *The Eastern Front*, p. 271.
6 Field-Marshal von Hindenburg: *Out of my Life*, pp. 137–8; Cassell, 1920.
7 Falls: *The First World War*, p. 100.
8 Falkenhayn, op. cit. pp. 81–2.
9 Ibid., p. 87.
10 Cruttwell: *History of the Great War*, p. 234.

Orthodoxy 3. *War on Two Fronts*

NOTHING IS MORE MISLEADING, in the historiography of the Western Front, than the concept of great individual battles, like Waterloo, or Gettysburg, or Sedan—clear, separate episodes, contained within a day, or a few days, with starts and finishes reasonably clearly perceptible. There *were* such battles in the First World War, on all fronts, but they do not give us any kind of true picture of the texture of fighting on the Western Front, which by mid-1915 had become apparent. The great German offensive in the East had begun on 2 May, and continued into September. The orthodox strategic response, obvious enough even to a very young cadet, was to take advantage of this German preoccupation in the East by hitting them as hard as possible in the West. But what do we see?

The launching of the attack at Gorlice-Tarnow found the Second Battle of Ypres (the German diversion) in full flood. Officially, 'Second Ypres' ended on 18 May (though some of those present might have found that hard to believe); already, on 9 May, the French, with some willing but not very effective British help, had begun the Second Battle of Artois, which continued at varying intensity until 18 June—according to High Command directive. 'Second Artois' was a major endeavour, involving 18 infantry and three cavalry divisions supported by the powerful artillery which we have noted on p. 182. The main point of attack was the Vimy Ridge, flanked on the northern side by the Lorette Ridge, which, according to one who knew it well,

*'from the south looked harmless enough, as a house may look until you are told it is
haunted by dreadful ghosts. It must have been haunted indeed, for at no point from
the sea to Switzerland were there more dead on so narrow a space of ground . . . It
contained gullies no bigger than a back garden, no farther from the front line than a
man could throw a heavy stone, into which whole companies had dashed with a
cheer, and whence not a man, not a single man, had ever come back. All that was
known of them was that shouting had been heard, heavy firing, and then perhaps
screams long into the night. Then they too had ceased and all had been silent
again.'*[1]

Forty thousand Frenchmen lie in the cemetery of Notre Dame de Lorette,
the great war-shrine of France that matches Verdun; the deadlock of 1915
was responsible for most of them.

The French bombarded the German positions for five days before their
infantry attacked—'the first real bombardment of the war'.[2] It was also the
first, but by no means the last, of the great artillery disappointments. To a
generation which had never before witnessed and heard a great modern
artillery bombardment, a continuous thunder, hour after hour for days and
nights on end, rising to crescendos from time to time to deceive the enemy
into expecting immediate attack and manning his parapets, this unleashed
power seemed overwhelming. The whole enemy line appeared to be engulfed
in flame and smoke, with débris, human and material, flying into the air.
'Nothing could live through it'—such beliefs die hard, as the Second World
War, Korea, and Vietnam have taught us. In May 1915 the French endured
an almost total disappointment; their centre corps advanced $2\frac{1}{2}$ miles and
almost reached the crest of Vimy Ridge; elsewhere there was less progress.
Reserves were too far back; on the second day there was virtually no progress
at all; by the third day the great attack had become just a series of bitter,
costly trench combats as the German supports came up. 'The operations
were brought to an end on 15 May', says the Official Historian.[3] Joffre tells us
that they were resumed on 15 June to give aid to the hard-pressed Russians.
But the records show that there was hard fighting in Artois on 20 May, 22
May; (*'réaction violente'*), 23, 24 May; (*'combats acharnés'*), 25, 26, 30, and 31
May; 2, 3, 4, 9 June; (*'lutte acharnée'*), 10 and 11 June. They also tell us that
during this time there was fierce fighting between French and Germans in
Champagne, Alsace, the Argonne, Picardy, the Woevre, and the Vosges,
while the British fought at Ypres. That was what the Western Front was like.

And this was the very clench of the deadlock: At this stage in the war there
was no hope of making a Gorlice-Tarnow-style break in an enemy front in the
West (at *no* time was a Gorlice-Tarnow-style exploitation possible). In 1915
the multiplying guns were still too few; artillery registration was a slow,
revealing business which annulled surprise; there were smoke candles to
mask attacks, but these, like gas, depended on the wind—smoke-shells were
coming, but not just yet (the British did not have them until 1917); there
were no mechanical devices for overcoming barbed wire and machine-guns.
So the two sides bickered expensively, with little to show for their losses on

'. . . a great modern artillery bombardment . . .': this is a German 210 mm. howitzer. The outstanding feature of the artillery war was the multiplication of the heavy-calibre pieces in all armies.

either side; the Germans themselves were the originators of much of this activity, seeking to disguise the absence of their main reserves in Russia. The great battle in Artois supposedly ended on 18 June, but fighting flared up there later in the month and in early July. The Argonne was seldom quiet for long; July saw much activity in the Woevre; throughout the whole year there was a swaying struggle in the Vosges mountains, with the name of Hartmannswillerkopf, a 4,000-ft. height north of Thann, overlooking the Rhine valley towards the Black Forest, constantly repeated as it repeatedly changed hands. This was the battleground of France's famous *Chasseurs Alpins*, highly trained mountain troops who, like all the Allied forces, found themselves well matched on those steep, rocky slopes. In July it was chiefly the French who were making progress—for a while. And in that month, at Ypres, the British made their acquaintance with liquid flame projectors (see p. 145).

Clearly it is quite wrong to say that the Western Allies were doing nothing while Russia bled. On the other hand, these costly exchanges of battered, blood-stained trenches were equally clearly doing Russia very little good.

General Joffre well understood that what was needed was a really big stroke by both the French and British Armies. He hoped to perform this in early September, and accordingly encouraged a quietening down of the whole front during August to allow preparations to be made—a laborious business, beginning far back on the lines of communication with large road repairs and improvements, and then the assembly of the mountains of supplies of all kinds, but especially ammunition, that would be required for a big battle. Finally, there were the troops themselves to be brought in; they would need tents and huts, training areas, food, drink, and specialized equipment, to say nothing of ambulances and hospitals. In the event, it proved impossible to complete all this before 25 September, on which day the greatest action of the Western Front since the Battle of the Marne was launched.

For the French, this took the names of the Third Battle of Artois (in the north) and the Second Battle of Champagne (in the south); here 35 French divisions stood ready to attack, with another 18 in Artois, supported by 12 British. Joffre told his troops:

'Three quarters of the French forces will engage in the general battle. They will be

'. . . the troops would need tents, huts, food, drink . . .': these are British field kitchens in 1916. British troops took their food supplies for granted, a silent tribute to good administration.

supported by 2,000 heavy and 3,000 field guns . . .'[4]

This meant, in Artois, 35 heavy guns per mile of front, in Champagne 47, or one to every 37 yards (the British could manage no more than 19 per mile). Already the Gorlice-Tarnow concentration, which had proved so devastating, was thoroughly outclassed. This time, surely, there could be no mistake—at least on the main front in Champagne. A great sense of confidence possessed the French Army, despite everything that it had been through in over four hundred days of war. Joffre's final Order of the Day, on 23 September, proclaimed:

'Thanks to your fellow-men, who have worked night and day in our factories, you will be able to advance to the assault behind a storm of shell-fire, along the whole of the front, and side by side with the Armies of our Allies. You will carry all before you. In one bound you will break through the enemy's defences and reach his artillery.
Give him neither rest nor pause until victory is gained . . .'[5]

The brave words penned in the calm of *GQG* found their echo amid the clamour of the front; an infantry officer put down his emotions on 25 September:

'My body, now invulnerable, has become an instrument of destruction with infernal powers. These peals of phosphorescent thunder, these cataclysmic concussions, this frenzy of devastation—all these chaotic energies galvanize and intoxicate me. I draw them into myself as a steel point attracts the lightning in a stormy sky. There's sulphur in my head, high explosive in my legs, saltpetre shaking my chest . . . the notion that nothing will stop us . . . nothing . . . En avant!'[6]

And once more it was all delusion; once more the great endeavour miserably took on 'that rhythm which came to be inseparably associated with the great trench battles. First a frantic intensity during the first twelve hours, never afterwards attained.'[7] The French assault penetrated some 3,000 yards into the German first position, only to find that the real defence was in the second position, on reverse slopes where they had little observation. They had given the Germans a bad shock, taking, according to one authority, 25,000 prisoners and 150 guns, but 'strategically nothing had been gained'.[8] The exhaustion of even the masses of ammunition that had been gathered together brought the offensive to an end on 6 October. French casualties were 143,567.

In Artois the French attacks were a complete failure, costing another 48,200 casualties. In the previous battle, reserves had been held too far back; this time they were brought well forward—and caught by the enemy's artillery. The British, on the left of the French, attacked in the uninviting low ground of the Loos sector. Their bombardment was necessarily weak, owing to lack of ammunition; they relied on gas mixed with smoke, which proved as always a dubious asset, blowing back in places on the attackers. However, they had the advantage of surprise and a 7 to 1 superiority in numbers, which enabled them to gain a footing in the German line. Sir John French, however, held back his reserves as the French had done in 'Second Artois'; they came up late and, being absolutely raw troops, in great confusion; the initial advantage was lost. The Battle of Loos dragged on into early November, finally costing the British 48,267 casualties; it also cost Sir John French his position as C.-in-C. On 19 December he was succeeded by General Sir Douglas Haig.

Worst of all was that none of this, none of the effort, none of the loss, had done Russia any good; the German offensive there was over. Nor did it help the Serbs, now enduring their martyrdom. It was distressingly plain that no such thing as an effective coordinated Allied strategy for war on two fronts existed; indeed, it would only exist once, briefly, in the whole course of the war, and that occasion was a year away.

Meanwhile, deadlock in the war of masses was taking its toll. By October 1915 admitted German casualties were over $2\frac{1}{4}$ million; Austria-Hungary's were past computation. Russia, as we have seen, suffered over 2 million in 1915 alone. France, however, was the chief sufferer: out of her much smaller population, by 31 December she had lost 1,961,687. British casualties on all fronts at this stage numbered 512,420. For the Germans there was a special regret: whatever Falkenhayn himself might say, many recognized that the 1915 strategy had been a total failure:

'There is no doubt as to what the proper course should have been in the spring of 1915. The Regular British Army had suffered heavily in the battles of 1914, and could only be reinforced gradually by volunteers from the United Kingdom and the Dominions, hardly trained as soldiers. The British Army should have been so defeated that it could never develop into an efficient "million army". It should have been like a newly-sown field struck by a heavy hailstorm, which never recovers to bear a full crop . . .'[9]

Instead, thanks to Falkenhayn, Conrad, and the false, showy brilliancies of Gorlice-Tarnow, Haig was able to note on 13 January 1916 that his forces numbered 987,200. By 6 February this total had risen to 1,037,600; Britain's 'million army' had arrived, and from now on would assert its influence on the land war.

Deadlock persisted, unbroken by any stratagem; but perhaps deadlock itself was a means of making war.

NOTES

1 Sir Edward Spears: *Prelude to Victory*, p. 297; Jonathan Cape, 1939.
2 *O.H. 1915*, ii p. 42.
3 Brig.-Gen. Sir James E. Edmonds: *A Short History of World War I*, p. 94; O.U.P., 1951.

4   Ibid., p. 138.
5   Joffre: *Memoirs*, ii pp. 359–60.
6   Jacques d'Arnoux: *Paroles d'un Revenant*, p. 19, quoted by Lt.-Col. J. Armengaud, *L'Atmosphère du Champ de Bataille*, pp. 142–3; Charles-Lavauzelle, 1940. Author's translation.
7   Cruttwell: *History of the Great War*, p. 164.
8   Ibid., p. 165.
9   *O.H. 1915*, i p. 25, quoting General von Moser, *Das militärisch und politisch Wichtigste vom Weltkrieg.*

Unorthodoxy 3. *War in the Air*

IN 1915 THE GERMAN NAVY found a use for Count Zeppelin's spectacular invention, which the Army, after the loss of *Z-6* (see p. 102), shortly followed by the similar fates of *Z-7* and *Z-8*, had neglected. Anger at the British blockade of Germany, frustration at the impotence of the High Seas Fleet, annoyance at the efforts of the RNAS (pp. 130–132), all pointed in the same direction: attacks on England, preferably on London. The Kaiser gave reluctant permission for bombing raids on 9 January, but the North Sea winter season was uncooperative. Not until ten days later did it clear sufficiently for take-off, and even then remained uncertain with much mist. However, three airships, *L-3-(Kapitän Leutnant* Fritze), *L-4* (*Kapitän-Leutnant* Freiherr von Platen) and *L-6* (*Oberleutnant* Freiherr Trensch von Buttlar-Brandenfels) set out on the morning of 19 January in the direction of the English coast. *L-6* turned back with engine trouble, but at twenty minutes to seven that evening the other two were seen coming in towards Norfolk like 'two bright stars moving, apparently thirty yards apart.'[1] These were the navigation lights of *L-3* and *L-4*; soon they separated, and proceeded to drop bombs indiscriminately wherever they saw clusters of lights through the mist. Between them they did some £7,740 worth of damage; they killed 2 men and 2 women, and injured 15 civilians including 2 children.

In the nervous, hysterical home atmosphere of Britain in 1914–15, reactions were out of all proportion to these actual results. The ridiculous (and quite baseless) spy-mania which had gripped the British public in September and October 1914 broke out afresh; an impossible number of cars were reported 'signalling' to the raiders with their headlights, and similar nonsense. Coming so soon upon the East Coast naval raids, the Zeppelins grimly underlined the end of island security, though the real meaning of that transition was yet to be seen.

There were 20 Zeppelin raids on Britain in 1915. The first raid on London was carried out by an Army ship, *LZ-38*, under *Hauptmann* Linnarz, coming from Belgium on the night of 31 May. On this occasion the casualties were 7 killed and 35 injured. Far more serious was the last raid of the year, on 13/14 October, when five Zeppelins crossed the coast. Only one, the new *L-15*

'. . . counter-measures multiplied . . .': 'barrage' balloons with cable aprons—a useful device in two world wars.

under *Kapitän-Leutnant* Breithaupt, penetrated to central London; its bombs accounted for most of the 54 civilians killed and 107 injured on this night. Anti-aircraft defences in 1915 were rudimentary; no Zeppelins were lost through enemy action, though weather and accident took their usual toll. The year's civilian casualties due to them amounted to 188 killed and 499 injured.

It will be convenient to summarize here the rest of the Zeppelin campaign. They were the pathfinders of long-range aerial bombardment, showing what might be done with the right weapon. Despite steady improvements, they themselves were not the right weapon; all told, they accounted for 498 civilian deaths (and 58 military) with 1,236 civilians injured (121 military). During 1916 and thereafter, counter-measures multiplied: anti-aircraft guns of improved design, searchlights, balloons with cable 'aprons', and what a later war would call 'night fighters', using tracer and incendiary bullets. Hampered by their slow rate of climb and weak armament, the aeroplanes found Zeppelins difficult to bring down; the first success of the Royal Flying Corps was obtained by Lieutenant W. Leefe Robinson on the night of 2/3 September.

In all, 130 airships were built or acquired by the German Army and Navy by the end of the war; only 15 survived at the Armistice, 31 having been deleted and broken up. Weather, by itself, surprisingly (in view of their apparent vulnerability to wind and storm) only accounted for 7; accident (including those occurring on return from operations) for 38, of which 27 were lost by the Navy. Enemy action caused 39 losses, the majority (22) once again being Navy vessels, and another majority (22 again) being at the hands of sea or ground forces. Air action, either attack in the air or bombing of sheds, was responsible for 17 losses, all at the hands of either the RFC or the RNAS. 1916 was their last year of important service (they only attacked Britain six times in 1917, only four times in 1918); in 1916 they tied down 17,340 officers and men in anti-aircraft defence in Britain, as well as 12 squadrons (110 machines) of the RFC. But above all, they struck terror. Their huge size, their virtually silent progress at any operational height, their ability to hover, spying on the land below, all gave an impression of sinister monsters with miraculous powers. Certainly they anticipated the dictum later propounded by Sir Hugh Trenchard: 'the moral effect of bombing stands to the material effect in a proportion of 20 to 1'[2] (see p. 275).

The future of war in the air, however, lay not with airships but with aeroplanes. We have seen (pp. 102–3) how the Royal Flying Corps and the French Air Service influenced the Battle of the Marne; the effect of this was deeply significant:

'*From a supplementary means of information relied upon principally for confirmation, the air weapon had begun to become the principal means of operational reconnaissance—an important factor in forming army commander's decisions . . . (it) had taken a step towards becoming one of the dominant features of warfare.*'[3]

Every aspect of technological advance between 1914–18, however, displays the same pendulum characteristic: initial advantage, countermeasure; new advantage, new countermeasure. Nowhere is this better illustrated than in the air war after 1914.

As soon as the importance of air reconnaissance was recognized, the importance of denying it to the enemy was also seen. This was the foundation of the concept of 'air supremacy', the prize for which the air forces of both sides contended for the rest of the war. Naturally, it implied air combat; but, as Mr. Cuneo says, 'no nation entered the war prepared for air combat'.[4] This is a subject which lends itself peculiarly to myth and legend, the most powerful myth of all at the time being the profound belief of both sides that the other, by fiendish ingenuity, had stolen a march and thus obtained 'unfair' advantage. Massive preparedness for air warfare seemed such an obvious concomitant of massive preparation for war on the ground that scarcely anyone in France or Britain could believe (nor bring themselves to believe for decades after) that their air forces were not hopelessly outnumbered and outclassed in the first months of the war. One reasonably authoritative British writer in 1914, for example, credited Germany with 'about 700 qualified pilots' with a reserve of civilian pilots to back them. These existed only in imagination, as did the great strides attributed to the German aircraft industry. The exact contrary was true; when mobilization came, it found the German industry quite unprepared for the Army's demands:

'Discarded machines had to be recommissioned and privately owned airplanes were purchased. As a result most of the airplane sections appeared ready when the order for mobilization came. However, the poor quality of much of the newly acquired material, the lack of replacements and spare parts were portents that the air arm could not stand more than a short campaign without collapsing.'[5]

The truth—and this would have astonished the Allies—was that the German Air Service was at a very low ebb, both materially and morally (in air warfare the two are very intimately connected; nothing saps an airman's morale more than a sense of the inferiority of his machine). Pilots lost all confidence in the *Taube*, which had to be scrapped at the end of 1914, and industry took time to replace it. Nothing illustrates the poor morale of the German airmen at this stage more clearly than their firm conviction that all French aircraft were carrying machine-guns. This, too, was pure illusion. In fact, it was the British who won the first air victories— Sir John French claimed five German machines destroyed 'by actually fighting in the air' during the retreat from Mons. This may be an exaggeration, but the first successful fight is documented: the pursuit of a *Taube* by three machines of No. 2 Squadron on August 25. The German machine was eventually 'driven down to the ground':

'Lieutenant H. D. Harvey-Kelly and Lieutenant W. H. C. Mansfield landed near it and continued the chase on foot, but the Germans escaped into a wood.'[6]

The French did not win an air victory until 5 October, and their total of wins in 1914 was small, yet it was them whom the Germans feared most. Possibly this was because the French aircraft were mostly pusher models (the airscrew placed behind the cockpit to push the machine through the air like the propellor of a ship; the British and Germans had more tractor types, with the airscrew forward, pulling the machine through the air); their clear view and field of fire in front encouraged the French pilots and observers to be more aggressive. Whatever the reason may be, the opening of 1915—in particular the First Battle of Champagne in February—'found the German Air Force practically non-existent'.[7]

It was a year of constant innovation and experiment in air warfare. At Neuve Chapelle the RFC (see p. 147) made a major contribution by photo-

'French aircraft were mostly pusher models . . .' A Voisin Type 10, fitted with flotation bags under the lower wings, showing the clear field of fire forward.

graphing the entire German trench system in front of the British First Army; photo-reconnaissance henceforth became the basis of all offensive planning. With it, of course, came the denial of this advantage to the enemy—the attempt to create an 'air blockade' by the continuous flying of defensive patrols. This system was soon discredited, but meanwhile provided a fruitful source of combats in the air (to which we shall shortly return). It was soon after Neuve Chapelle that the RFC attempted to overcome that fatal breakdown of communication in battle which, as I have said on p. 148, was to haunt the whole war. For the attack at Aubers Ridge (9 May, supporting the French in Artois) three radio-equipped aircraft were detailed to report the progress of the infantry; the latter were to display white linen strips, 7 feet long by 2 feet wide, as they reached successive lines in the German defences. Unfortunately, they did not reach those lines, and the airmen, in the smoke and dust of battle, found the tiny earth-coloured figures of friend and foe beneath them impossible to distinguish. The aircraft sent 42 messages, but they were of little value. This, too, was a 'first time'; soon 'wireless' reports from aircraft became an essential element in artillery programmes, and bad visibility was to be regarded as virtually fatal to chances of success.

By September, the time of the great autumn offensives, yet another advance had been made. Hitherto, barring only freaks of luck, attempts at bombing by the fragile, primitive aircraft of the period, had been almost entire failures. Out of 141 bombing missions carried out by the RFC between 1 March and 20 June, only 3 were definitely successful. On 24 July all such missions were suspended, except on direct orders from GHQ. What was lacking, of course, was a real bomb-sight—without which it was practically impossible for a pilot to know when to release his bomb unless he accompanied it almost all the way down in order to do so. Then two young RFC officers, 2/Lieutenant R. B. Bourdillon and 2/Lieutenant G. M. D. Dobson produced a bomb-sight which actually worked. It arrived in time for the Battle of Loos and enabled the RFC to mount the first successful offensive against enemy rail communications. Between 23 and 28 September, 82 100-lb. bombs and 163 20-lb. bombs were dropped; railway lines were broken in 15 places, five trains were damaged (including an ammunition

'. . . railway lines broken in 15 places, five trains damaged . . .': a photograph from a British aeroplane making a low-flying attack.

train, with spectacular results), much damage done to sheds at Valenciennes station, and more besides. Only two aircraft were lost. To the Germans these were, admittedly, mere annoyances, but in the history of warfare they are immensely important, marking the first possibility of tactical air offensives, of isolating a battlefield as was so brilliantly done by the 'interdiction' programme in Normandy in 1944. The RFC and its French allies were on the right lines; unfortunately, they were far too few in number (there were only 12 RFC squadrons in France in October) to isolate a battle area in 1915; even the heavy French superiority over the Germans in Champagne (200 to 60) was insufficient for that, though enough to make the German air service largely ineffective.

Small as it was, the Royal Flying Corps played a major part in the development of air warfare during the year; the French and German contributions were chiefly in the matter of combat. Despite wild suppositions on both sides, for the first few months this was almost entirely carried out with a strange and unsuitable collection of weapons: revolvers, rifles, carbines, hand grenades, and even steel arrows. There was little doubt that machine-guns would be far better for the purpose, but they were both in short supply and in great demand for ground forces. Furthermore, they were not all of suitable type for air use; there were obvious difficulties in mounting them, and (as stated above) in firing them forward in tractor machines. There were also production problems; the RFC had ordered the Lewis gun in 1913 (it was to become the most numerous of the Army's automatic weapons) but delivery to squadrons in France only began in September 1914. However, in February 1915 a French airman, Roland Garros, and the designer Raymond Saulnier together designed a means of firing a machine-gun through a propellor circle, so that the gun could be aimed by simply pointing the aeroplane at the target. They estimated that some 7 per cent of bullets fired would hit the propellor blades; their answer—admittedly crude—was to fix a deflector plate to each blade at the correct distance to intercept the bullets. This had the effect of slowing up the machine; sometimes the impact of the bullet broke the blade; the ricocheting bullet was an obvious menace. But Garros could fire a fixed machine-gun forward. It was a turning-point.

His career was brief: he won his first victory on 1 April, another on 15 April, and another on 17 April. On 18 April he was forced down in German territory, and the secret of his successes was revealed. It was shown to the young, talented Dutch designer, Anthony Fokker, and he was asked to adapt the Garros system for use by the German Air Service. Fokker did better; two of his engineers, Heinrich Lubbe and Fritz Heber, reminded him of a synchronizing device patented by a Swiss, Franz Schneider, in 1913, and turned down by the German authorities. Schneider's system was quite different and far better than the Garros/Saulnier: it was based upon interruption, not deflection, so that the gun only fired when the two-bladed propellor was horizontal, and thus out of the line of fire. Within 48 hours Fokker fitted this device to one of his M5 monoplanes and tested it successfully. This marked the real beginning of what was later known as the 'Fokker scourge'.

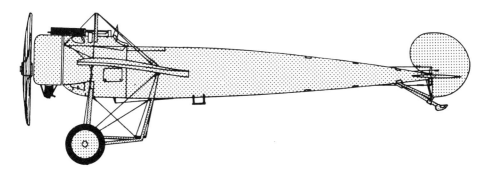

'. . . the E-III version corrected the faults of earlier types . . .' The diagram shows the
simple lines of the Fokker *Eindecker*, begetter of the 'Fokker scourge' of 1916.

Here, once more, we have to pick a wary course through much mythology.
It has often been asserted that the Fokkers immediately brought about a
revolution in air combat, but that is not so. Both the E (*eindecker* = monoplane) I and E-II versions proved to be difficult machines to fly except in very
skilful hands; two pilots crashed in training in July and another in August,
causing the Inspector of Aviation Troops to forbid the use of Fokker fighters.
Moreover, production was slow: in mid-July there were only 11 on the whole
of the Western Front. Their first 'kill' was on 1 August, when *Leutnant* Max
Immelmann shot down an unarmed British biplane. He and *Leutnant*
Oswald Boelcke (both members of Field Aviation Section 62) became the
chief exponents of the new style of air fighting which, in those days of
all-purpose aircraft, certainly entitles the Fokker to be called the first pure
fighter. Its disconcerting characteristics quickly gave it legendary qualities
far beyond its true performance; it was not, in fact, until the E-III version,
which corrected the handling faults of the earlier types, began to appear at
the end of the year that really heavy losses were inflicted on the Allied air
forces. Even then, there were only about 40 Fokkers on the whole front, but
such was the aggressiveness and skill of the best German pilots that they gave
the sense of being ubiquitous, and the RFC in particular took heavy punishment with corresponding damage to morale.

It was the arrival of the true fighter which, in turn, gave birth to the air
'ace'. The aces belonged to a phase of warfare which was, in fact, very short,
though their fame projected far beyond it. This was the 'romantic' period,
when flying and single combat in the sky stood out in vivid contrast to the
dirty, mud-bound, anonymous war of the masses down below. The 'aces'
—and their devoted ground crews—chalked up their 'kills' with a grim
satisfaction which was often poles apart from their true feelings. Captain
Albert Ball, killed before he was 21, with 43 enemy planes to his score, wrote
in one of his last letters:

'Oh, it was a good fight, and the Huns were fine sports. One tried to ram me, after he was hit, and only missed by inches. Am indeed looked after by God, but oh! I do get tired of living always to kill, and am really beginning to feel like a murderer. Shall be so pleased when I have finished.' [8]

Not all felt like that; Major Edward Mannock, Britain's greatest 'ace', according to one who flew with him, 'hated the Huns and he wanted to kill all of them'.[9]

Mannock's final score was 73, closely followed by W. A. Bishop (his predecessor in command of No. 85 Squadron) with 72; the greatest of all was Baron Manfred von Richthofen, with 80, and the next highest German was Ernst Udet with 62 (the famous Immelmann only had 15); the best of the French was René Fonck, with 75, followed by Georges Guynemer with 54; Austria-Hungary's Godwin Brunowski had 40, Belgium's Willy Coppens 37, Italy's Francesco Baracca 34, and America's Edward V. Rickenbacker 26. Between them, they and their fellows built up a mystique of aerial war which amounted almost to a religion; famous and frightening though the aces were, they soon became anachronisms as air warfare left the mystical phase and entered the phase of numbers and scientific method. Formation flying was born out of the successes of the early 'aces'—mutual protection to counteract their prowess. Many of them, particularly the highly individualistic French, did not like it:

'The Royal Flying Corps played a major part in the development of air warfare . . .': it took some time, however, for British industry to meet its needs. These are French 'Morane Parasoles' in service with the R.F.C., September 1916.

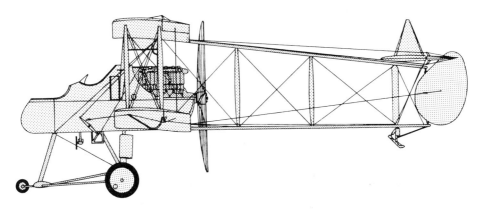

'Two British "pushers" . . .': the FE-2b, despite its primitive appearance, served with credit throughout the war. Originally designed as a fighter, it ended its career as a night bomber.

'To fly in groups smacked of cowardice (besides detracting from their individual publicity and glory). As a result, the commanding officers had difficulty in forcing them to abandon their fanciful notions and to recognize the prosaic demands of modern warfare . . .'[10]

Formation flying became standard practice in the RFC in January 1916; it was laid down:

'as a hard and fast rule that a machine proceeding on reconnaissance must be escorted by at least three other fighting machines. These machines must fly in close formation and a reconnaissance should not be continued if any of the machines becomes detached.'[11]

In February, this doctrine reached a peak of application when one reconnaissance aircraft ordered to observe railway activity in Belgium was escorted by 12 combat aircraft. As usual, however, it was counter-technology—the production of new types by the Allies—which put an end to the 'Fokker scourge'. Two British 'pushers'—the FE-2b and, in particular, the DH-2 —were the first to arrive and redress the balance; the French Nieuport XVII, one of the outstanding aircraft of the war, appeared in March, and at once asserted its superiority over Fokker's *eindeckers*. By June (the eve of the Battle of the Somme) the Allies once again had unquestionable air supremacy:

'Fokker pilots found fault with their monoplanes and longed for biplanes. When Lieutenant Immelmann's machine fell apart during an aerial combat on June 18 it was symbolic of the state of the German air weapon. The German air service was not only rendered impotent by the superior tactics and quality of the Allies but it was swamped by superior numbers.'[12]

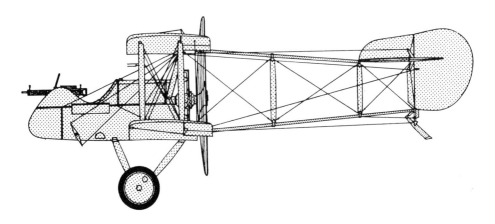

'Two British "pushers" . . .': the de Havilland DH-2, another primitive-looking aircraft which nevertheless played a great part in defeating the 'Fokker scourge' in 1916.

The tactics in question had been worked out by Colonel Trenchard (commanding the RFC in France) and Commandant de Peuty of the French Air Service during the dark days of the 'Fokker scourge'. They had concluded that, whatever the odds, whatever the technological disadvantage, the only true way of protecting the aircraft performing the essential work of army co-operation was to fight the enemy as far away from them as possible—ie. over the enemy's own airfields. 'An aeroplane', said Trenchard, 'is an offensive and not a defensive weapon'; he firmly advocated 'a policy of relentless and incessant offensive.'[13] This meant that, then and for the remainder of the war, the RFC (and RAF later) fought almost entirely over on the German side of the line—with the inevitable result that any aircraft shot down meant a total loss, including crew, whereas many German crews were saved by being within their own lines, and some German aircraft could even be repaired and returned to duty after being brought down. The Trenchard policy has been called 'the strategic offensive', which is an unhappy term, as Trenchard himself showed when he became the inspiration of a true 'strategic offensive' in 1918; it would be better to call it a 'tactical offensive', since it was so intimately connected with the essentially offensive posture of the Army to which the Royal Flying Corps at that time belonged. Whatever its true name, however, it was at least as important as the new aircraft:

'The recovery of the RFC was also due to great persistence in the principles of the strategic offensive as laid down by the conferences between General Trenchard and Commandant de Peuty in the fall of 1915.'[14]

The pattern of the battle for air supremacy was thus established, and it will again be convenient to summarize what followed. Technology, naturally,

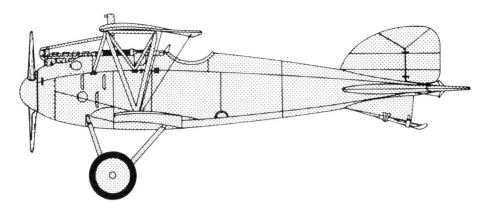

'. . . advantage, countermeasure; new advantage, new countermeasure . . .': no sooner had the DH-2s and Nieuports won an advantage than the Germans produced their business-like *Albatros* D III, another of the war's great aircraft.

always exercised the supreme influence. The Allied supremacy did not last long; in September 1916 the Germans produced their new *Albatros* fighter, another of the war's great aircraft, and the D III version, supported by the *Halberstadt*, gave the Allied air forces some very bad months. 'Bloody April' of 1917, when the new young pilots of the RFC measured their life-spans in days, was the lowest ebb of all; the French air service never really recovered from this time (partly for internal, administrative reasons). However, 1917 was also the year in which the British aircraft industry after a slow start, began to produce the right war-winning goods. The Sopwith '1½-Strutter' was a great standby; the Royal Aircraft Factory's SE-5a became for some 'the best fighter produced by Britain in the First World War',[15] and also from Sopwith came the famous 'Camel', the aircraft which brought down the legendary Richthofen in April 1918.

With these aircraft, once again, the RFC was able to make its comeback, and in truth it never faltered significantly for the rest of the war. Admittedly, in April 1918 Anthony Fokker (whose triplane had won great renown in the previous year) produced his splendid D-VII, which has been called 'one of the great combat aircraft of all time'.[16] But in September Sopwith (admirable firm) produced the Snipe which was at least as good. On 27 October a Snipe piloted by Major W. G. Barker unhesitatingly took on 15 Fokker D-VIIs, and survived; this type remained in RAF service until 1927.

Most air fighting was, strictly speaking, part and parcel of what a later generation would label 'army co-operation'; the real advance of air warfare, following the path blazed by the clumsy Zeppelins, came elsewhere, in 1917 and 1918. We shall return to that at a later stage.

NOTES

  1 Poolman: *Zeppelins over England*, p. 39.
  2 *The War in the Air*, vi (H. A. Jones) p. 136.
  3 Cuneo: *Winged Mars*, ii p. 94.
  4 Ibid., p. 159.
  5 Ibid., p. 158.
  6 *The War in the Air*, i (Raleigh) p. 329.
  7 Cuneo, op. cit. p. 158.
  8 W. A. Briscoe & H. R. Stannard: *Captain Ball V.C.* p. 267; Herbert Jenkins, 1918.
  9 Sholto Douglas: *Years of Combat*, p. 311; Collins, 1963.
10 Cuneo, op. cit. p. 227.
11 Ibid., p. 230.
12 Ibid., p. 262.
13 Quoted by Douglas, op. cit. p. 138.
14 Cuneo, op. cit. p. 233.
15 Douglas, op. cit. p. 195.
16 Bill Gunston: *The Encyclopedia of the World's Combat Aircraft*, p. 83; Salamander Books, 1976.

CHAPTER VII

The Wearing-Out Fight:
Western Version

WITH THE END OF 1915 and the failure of all attempts, by orthodox means or otherwise, to break the deadlock of the mass armies, the war entered the phase by which it is best known, and adopted the style which has given it such evil remembrance—indeed, from some accounts, one might suppose that there never was any other phase or any other style. It is the phase which Haig anticipated, and called the 'wearing-out fight' (see p. 92)—'the period of real struggle in which the main forces of the two belligerent Armies are pitted against each other in close and costly combat.'[1] Generally, it is known as the period of the 'war of attrition', which is not totally accurate, but serves to point up the feature which has so horrified successive generations in most countries: the human cost. Lacking for a long time the knowledge that this cost would be very greatly multiplied in the next Industrial Revolution war, and failing to see any helpful analogy with previous wars, politicians, soldiers, historians, and the public at large have recoiled from the spectacle of the 'wearing-out fight' to the point of actually *refusing* even to understand it. Haig, who had to conduct the British part of it (a melancholy duty which he neither relished nor shirked) understood it very well and explained it with great clarity:

'In the stage of the wearing-out struggle losses will necessarily be heavy on both sides, for in it the price of victory is paid. If the opposing forces are approximately equal in numbers, in courage, in moral(e) and in equipment, there is no way of avoiding payment of the price or of eliminating this phase of the struggle.

In former battles this stage of the conflict has rarely lasted more than a few days, and has often been completed in a few hours. When Armies of millions are engaged, with the resources of great Empires behind them, it will inevitably be long. It will include violent crises of fighting which, when viewed separately and apart from the general perspective, will appear individually as great indecisive battles. To this stage belong the great engagements of 1916 and 1917 which wore down the strength of the German Armies.'[2]

This interpretation is amply confirmed by German accounts.

Attrition was the strategy adopted by General Ulysses S. Grant in 1864 to tie down and render impotent the main army of the Confederacy under General Robert E. Lee, while his lieutenant, General W. T. Sherman, executed a dramatic movement against the Confederate flank and rear. To General George Meade, whose Army had to carry out the attrition, Grant gave clear and explicit orders:

'Lee's army will be your objective point. Wherever Lee's army goes, you will also go . . .'

In the First World War, as in Grant's war, attrition (or 'wearing-out') consisted precisely in this making the enemy's army the target, rather than any geographical or political prize. It was the strategy adopted in 1916, and introduced not, as many have believed, by the British under Haig, but by the Germans under Falkenhayn. He, too, is quite explicit on the matter. Viewing 'England' as Germany's most implacable foe, he describes at length the reasoning which drew him towards the decision on how she should be attacked. He dismissed out of hand (with full naval agreement) any idea of an invasion of the British Isles; he then also dismissed all thoughts of trying to seek a decision in subsidiary theatres (Mesopotamia, Egypt, Salonika); warned by the Allied experience in 1915, he rejected the notion of a mass breakthrough on the Western Front as being beyond Germany's powers. What then was left?

'As I have already insisted, the strain on France has almost reached breaking-point—though it is certainly borne with the most remarkable devotion. If we succeeded in opening the eyes of her people to the fact that in a military sense they have nothing more to hope for, that breaking-point would be reached and England's best sword knocked out of her hand.'[3]

He concluded that in order to knock out France a mass breakthrough ('in any case beyond our means') would not be necessary:

'We can probably do enough for our purposes with limited resources. Within our reach behind the French sector of the Western Front there are objectives for the retention of which the French General Staff would be compelled to throw in every man they have. If they do so the forces of France will bleed to death—as there can be no question of a voluntary withdrawal—whether we reach our goal or not.'[4]

So was conceived the 'mill of the Meuse' at Verdun in which, according to Falkenhayn, three fifths of the entire French Army was ground by August 1916:[5] attrition pure and simple.

No part of the First World War has been more copiously described in every harrowing detail than the 'wearing-out struggle' of 1916–17, embraced within the trinity of the three great battles, Verdun, the Somme, and 'Third Ypres', and including the bloody supplements of Arras and the 'Nivelle Offensive' in Champagne in 1917. It is therefore unnecessary to fight over that blood-soaked ground again, stage by stage and yard by yard. Certain salient features and certain important results of this phase nevertheless need to be pointed out. Verdun, from its very opening on 21 February 1916, displayed the force which was to make all of the 'wearing-out struggle' so brutally expensive in human life and limb. The artillery war, now supported by ceaselessly developing war industries, began to come into its own.

'"The mill of the Meuse" . . .': a French stretcher-party bringing back a wounded comrade through the shell-torn landscape of a classic artillery war battleground.

For the initial German assault, says Falkenhayn, 'an extraordinary amount of artillery of the largest calibre was allotted'. Verdun was a fortress system, with a ring of twenty steel-and-concrete forts around the ancient town; these, after 1914, had been 'down-graded'—stripped of their artillery to supply the field armies, and their garrisons withdrawn. Nevertheless, to the Germans they still presented a serious obstacle, and Falkenhayn assembled no less than 542 heavy guns on the 8-mile front of attack to deal with them and the surrounding defences. Of this formidable total, 13 were 'Big Berthas', the 420 mm. howitzers which had been so effective against Belgian and French forts in 1914; in addition there were 2 380 mm. (15 inch) long-range naval guns, 17 Austrian 'Emmas' (305 mm.), large numbers of 210 mm. (8 inch) howitzers and even more of the famous 150s which had already firmly set their mark upon the war. In all, including field artillery, the Germans deployed 1,220 pieces; this was the 'mill', the mincing machine through which the French Army would be made to pass. 'This compression of power and concentration of artillery on narrow sectors made them veritable hells,' wrote Cyril Falls. 'For sheer horror no battle surpasses Verdun. Few equal it.'[6]

What was endured by the French (and later the German) infantry at Verdun was to become the classic battle bombardment experience along the whole Western Front, increasing in weight, developing in sophistication, but unvarying in terror. A French survivor, wondering at being still alive, described it:

'*We listen for an eternity to the iron sledgehammers beating on our trench. Percussion and time fuze, 105s, 150s, 210s—all the calibres. Amid this tempest of ruin we instantly recognize the shell that is coming to bury us. As soon as we pick out its dismal howl we look at each other in agony. All curled and shrivelled up we crouch under the very weight of its breath. Our helmets clang together, we stagger about like drunks. The beams tremble, a cloud of choking smoke fills the dugout, the candles go out . . .*'[7]

A British soldier, somewhat later in the war, said the same, more tersely:

'*I lost all count of the shells and all count of time. There was no past to remember or future to think about. Only the present. The present agony of waiting, waiting for the shell that was coming to destroy us, waiting to die.*'[8]

Tersest of all, speaking for hundreds of thousands of frightened heroes on both sides of the line, is another Briton:

'*There's too much fuckin' artillery in this bloody war.*'[9]

There was (and in the next there would be even more). The landscapes of the battlefields of the artillery war took on nightmare aspect. The wounds inflicted were horrible. Lethal, brutal, shell-fire was also hideously demoralizing:

'*Never before, despite my capacity for fear, had I felt myself for so long in the grip of a terror so absolute. All around us was the continuing threat of instant death. Yet I saw no one fall. I saw men crying, and would have cried myself had I the tears. The company that night was in the grip of a sort of communal terror, a hundred men running like rabbits. I prayed that I would never see its like again.*'[10]

The novelist-turned-Gunner Gilbert Frankau caught the elemental, dehumanized savagery of the artillery war in his poem, '*The Voice of the Guns*':

'*We are the guns, and your masters! Saw ye our flashes?*
Heard ye the scream of our shells in the night, and the shuddering crashes?
Saw ye our work by the roadside, the shrouded things lying,
Moaning to God that He made them—the maimed and the dying?
　　　　Husbands or sons,
Fathers or lovers, we break them. We are the guns!

We are the guns and ye serve us. Dare ye grow weary,
Steadfast at night-time, at noon-time; or waking when dawn winds blow dreary

Over the fields and the flats and the reeds of the barrier-water,
To wait on the hour of our choosing, the minute decided for slaughter?
     Swift, the clock runs;
Yea, to the ultimate second. Stand to your guns!
     .   .   .   . '[11]

Frankau was a Gunner, deeply proud of his terrible arm, proud to be proficient in it. The developing proficiency of the artillerists was a feature of the war which is too often neglected; it is hardly too much to say that it was the ultimately decisive feature. In every army, the artillery suffered heavy losses on particular occasions; but the turnover of personnel in artillery units was never on the scale of infantry losses, so that experience and expertise survived to grow in value. But it is not only in the ranks of the artillery regiments of the belligerent nations that we must look for artillerists: besides such outstanding Gunners as Germany's famous Colonel Bruchmüller, or Britain's Major-General H. C. C. Uniacke, officers from other arms also won the accolade of 'master gunners'—among them, outstandingly, General Pétain and General Sir Herbert Plumer. Pétain was, by origin, an infantry-man, but long before he arrived to command the French defence of Verdun in February 1916 he had reached the conclusion 'that artillery now conquers a position and the infantry occupies it.'[12] Colonel Repington of *The Times*, visiting him in March, observed:

'*Pétain has a genius for heavy guns, which he manages now with great facility, and their feu d'écrasement (obliteration fire) is believed to do much damage. Pétain also uses the feu de barrage (barrage fire) with great effect . . . he had gone all out for the guns, and had, above all, tried to make his heavy guns* supple *so that they could quickly concentrate their fire on different objects and destroy them by the feu d'écrasement. He owed his successes to following this principle.*'[13]

Under Pétain a notable artillery general came to the fore at Verdun: General Robert Nivelle. And under Nivelle another non-artilleryman also became a convert: General Charles Mangin, who explained his assault system in typically racy terms.

'*I box in the first line with 75s; nothing can pass through the barrage; then we pound the trench with 155s and 58s (3-inch mortars) . . . When the trench is well turned over, off we go. Any Boches who are still there are ours. Generally, they come out in groups and surrender. While this is going on, their reserve companies are pinned in their dugouts by a solid stopper of heavy shells. Our infantry waves are preceded by a barrage of 75s; the 155s help to bang down the cork on the reserve companies; the tides of steel join up with the poilus*[14] *70 or 80 yards behind. The Boche gives up . . . You see, it is all very simple.*'[15]

Two costly, frustrating, heart-rending years of the wearing-out struggle would teach even the ebullient Mangin that it was *not* 'all very simple'.

"'Whatever you do, you lose a lot of men'". French infantry, widely spaced out, attacking a German position amid the craters—a glimpse of the forlorn loneliness of the front line.

The statistics of the artillery war reveal its destructive power, and are staggering. For their initial attack at Verdun the Germans brought up 2,500,000 shells, using for the purpose some 1,300 trains. By June the artillery of both sides had grown to about 2,000 guns, and it was calculated that in just over four months of battle 24 million shells had been pumped into this stretch of dedicated ground. The famous Fort Douaumont, captured by the Germans by surprise on 25 February, was finally retaken by the French on 24 October in an action which employed 711 guns (more than half of them heavies) on a front of just over 3 miles. A notice in the fort informs us that 1,000 shells were used for every square metre of the Verdun battlefield by the time the battle ended in December. Casualties, by then, amounted to some 700,000, almost equally divided: the British Official History gives them as 362,000 French and 336,831 German.[16] Unsuccessful attacks, persisted in, are always costly; on the other hand, as both sides experienced, the defensive, in the face of a well-prepared attack lavishly supported by artillery, could be horribly costly too. General Mangin was a natural attacker, and at times his men suffered severely, for which he was criticized; but noting the casualties suffered by neighbouring divisions while standing on the defensive, he came to a conclusion which may stand as the epitaph not only of Verdun, but of the whole wearing-out struggle in the artillery war:

'Quoi qu'on, fasse, on perd beaucoup de monde.'
(Whatever you do, you lose a lot of men.)[17]

Verdun has gone down in history as a blood-bath, an epitome of the savagery of the static battles of the First World War. Their static quality did, indeed, lend them a peculiar horror, because men had to live, day in day out for years on end, in the landscape of the artillery war, surrounded by its corpses, covered in its slime and afflicted by its stench. The Battle of Verdun lasted until 15 December—298 days, practically 10 months, during which the combined losses mounted to their total of around 700,000. It is a fearful figure; but for perspective (and certainly to correct the idea that it was the static quality that made Verdun and other battles of the First World War so expensive) we should compare with the losses of the German Army *alone* in 172 days ($5\frac{1}{2}$ months) of *blitzkrieg* in Russia in 1941: 22 June to 10 December, 775,078 (not counting the sick).[18]

On the 132nd day of the Battle of Verdun the BEF, now just under $1\frac{1}{2}$ million strong, launched its offensive on the Somme. As originally conceived, this was to be, once more, a mainly French battle, with a larger British supporting element than ever before. But as the French Army was drawn, division by division, into the 'mill of the Meuse', the rôles became reversed; the Somme became a British battle, the first of the war on the Western Front, with, nevertheless, a much larger French share than is generally recognized.

In the initial planning of Allied operations in 1916, of which what came to be called the Battle of the Somme formed the main Franco-British contribution, there was, says Joffre,

'one dominant idea; this was that we must seek to obtain a decision through simultaneous offensives on the Russian, Italian and Franco-British fronts.'[19]

It did not require a great strategic mind to see that a coalition wages war least effectively when its efforts are disconnected, and most effectively when they are co-ordinated. Strategically, the significance of 1916 is that this was, for various reasons, the only time that such a conjunction was arrived at by the Allies. In theory, the combined and simultaneous efforts of four such powers as Russia, France, Britain, and Italy (she had joined the Entente in May 1915) should have brought the war to a victorious end—but in practice they did not. That is the tragedy of 1916. But it is impossible to understand the Battle of the Somme except in the light of the intention and the attempt.

The battle was not conceived as attrition; what Joffre intended was 'to endeavour to break through the enemy's line by a general offensive'[20]—in other words, a repetition of his efforts in the autumn of 1915 in even greater force, with even more artillery. The tragedy and disappointment of the first day, 1 July, which cost the British Army 57,470 casualties—its worst single day in history—ruled out the break-through. On the other hand, one day's experience, no matter how appalling, could not possibly justify the British calling off the action on the 133rd day of Verdun—particularly as the Russians were by now well launched upon their most amazing enterprise of the war (see below). So the battle continued on its 4½-month course; it took on the character of murderous attrition on 2 July, when Falkenhayn told General von Below, commanding the *Second Army* on the Somme front:

'. . . *the first principle in position warfare must be to yield not one foot of ground; and if it be lost to retake it by immediate counter-attack, even to the use of the last man.*'[21]

This was interpreted by Below in an Order of the Day of 3 July as follows:

'*We must win this battle in spite of the enemy's temporary superiority in artillery and infantry. The important ground lost in certain places will be recaptured by our attack after the arrival of reinforcements. For the present, the important thing is to hold our present positions at any cost and to improve them by local counter-attacks.*

I forbid the voluntary evacuation of trenches. The will to stand firm must be impressed on every man in the Army. I hold Commanding Officers responsible for this.

The enemy should have to carve his way over heaps of corpses . . .'[22]

And so it was. What Below and Falkenhayn did not then know, but the latter ruefully admitted later, was that this was going to develop into the *matériel-schlacht*, the 'war of *matériel*', in which 'hitherto unexampled masses of artillery' would be employed with increasingly devastating effect. In July the British Fourth (Rawlinson) and Reserve (later Fifth, Gough) Armies deployed 2,029 guns of all types on the 14-mile frontage of the Somme; of these 452 were heavies. This meant 32.2 heavy guns to the mile, compared with 25.5 at Loos the previous autumn. To gunners who had been starved of both guns and ammunition for almost two years, it seemed a tremendous number; in the eight-day preliminary bombardment they fired off 1,732,873 rounds, an amount which, they were sure, must be annihilating. They assured their infantry colleagues that all that would be required of them would be to walk over and take possession of the pulverized enemy positions. They were not to know, at that stage, that owing to growing pains in Britain's brand-new munitions industry, about a third of the shells they fired were 'duds' which failed to explode; an observer visiting the Somme battlefields the next April said that there were so many unexploded British shells lying about that one could hardly take a step without treading on one—and they continue to appear to this day. But even if this weight of shell-fire had been fully effective, it would have been nothing like enough. The French, attacking on the right of the British, used 700 heavy guns on an eight-mile front—87.5 to the mile. At Messines, the following year, in a preliminary bombardment of similar duration, the British artillery fired 3,258,000 rounds.

By August the French had 1,200 heavy guns in action—but their frontage had increased to 16 miles, so that their density actually dropped to 75 per mile. By the end of the battle, the British Fourth and Fifth Armies had 807, a density of 57.6 per mile. Haig wonderingly confided to his diary the information that in 153 days of preliminary bombardment and battle his guns had fired 27,768,076 rounds, or 181,491 rounds per day—alternatively, 3,951 tons of ammunition a day, requiring 13 trains for transport. This—plus what the French were doing—was the punishment that the German Army was enduring on the Somme. It was under this deluge of increasingly effective artillery fire (as production faults were corrected) that the army tried to carry out the instructions of Below. The battle will not be understood unless one takes into account no less than 330 German attacks or counter-attacks against the British and French on the Somme—126 of them in September alone, the climactic month.[23] It was this combination—the crushing weight of Allied artillery, and the devoted courage of the continuous counter-attacks—that made the Somme 'the muddy grave of the German field army'.[24] It was this that caused Field-Marshal Prince Rupprecht of Bavaria to say: 'what still remained of the old first-class peace-trained German infantry had been expended on the battlefield'.[25] It was this, plus Verdun, in other words, that wrecked the 'motor' of the war. Falkenhayn suffered the penalty of the unsuccessful: dismissal on 29 August. Surveying Germany's grim situation at the end of the year, his successor, Field-Marshal von Hindenburg, remarked: '1916 spoke a language which made itself heard.'[26] And Ludendorff, now First Quartermaster-General, dotted the 'i's' and crossed the 't's': 'The Army had been fought to a standstill and was utterly worn out.'[27] The 'wearing-out struggle' was having its effect.

Attrition, of course, is unlikely ever to be entirely one-sided. No one knows what the German losses on the Somme were; no one can give a precise statistical meaning to 'the grave of an army'—for the simple reason that the losses were so great that the German High Command resorted to deliberate concealment during this battle. There is no reason whatever—especially in the light of the counter-attacks—to suppose that they differed to any significant extent from the Franco-British total. And that was dreadful enough. The French, in addition to what they lost in the 10 months of Verdun, lost another 204,253 on the Somme—an even higher rate than the 'mill of the Meuse'. The year ended at Verdun on a note of triumph for them: on 15 December they carried out an attack planned by General Nivelle which produced 11,103 prisoners and 115 captured guns. The delighted Mangin pronounced:

'Nous tenons la méthode et nous avons le chef. C'est la certitude de la succès . . .'
('We know the method and we have the Chief. Success is certain . . .')[28]

Nivelle succeeded Joffre as French Commander-in-Chief full of the confidence of a man who has found a winning system. Others, however, were less cheerful; the President, M. Poincaré, told Lord Esher that the French 'are at the end of their tether as regards manpower'.[29] It is scarcely to be wondered at, since one eminent French authority puts their total losses since the beginning of the war at 3,285,000 by the end of 1916. Cool observers concluded that despite the euphoria of the new C.-in-C. it was unlikely that the French Army would have the stomach for more than one more big battle—and it had better be successful!

British losses during the battle were 419,654, and during the year on all fronts totalled 607,784. This included the whole Empire, and brought the total for the war to date to 1,120,204. It may be compared with Germany's *admitted* total of 1,400,000 for 1916 alone[30]—and, of course, the fearful French total. The British public, unaware of these comparisons, was naturally much distressed at this entirely new experience. One soldier, on the other hand, one of that great host which had answered Lord Kitchener's call to arms, spoke proudly for many when he said:

'We were not intimidated by the war of attrition . . .'[31]

One thing was absolutely clear to every educated soldier on either side: if the effect already produced by the Allied offensives of 1916 was not to be lost, if the price paid for it was not to be thrown away, they must strike again as soon as possible in 1917. There might then have been a possibility of that year seeing Haig's final phase: 'the eventual decisive blow'. The new tragedy was that no such thing happened; the German Army was given time to make a recovery and evolve new tactics, while a major ally, Russia, collapsed in revolution. Instead of a decisive blow, 1917 saw merely the continuation of the wearing-out struggle. There were plain reasons for this, some avoidable, some not: utterly unavoidable was the dreadful winter of 1916–17, one of the worst in recorded European history. Changes of government and changes of military command on the Allied side were avoidable at least in theory; General Nivelle's plan of operations, by which he promised to make a decisive break through the German line in 48 hours, was certainly responsible for much confusion and delay. The German withdrawal to the 'Hindenburg Line'—whose very existence was a measure of their defeat on the Somme, since it spelt a complete reversal of all previous war doctrine—created further disruption along a considerable front of projected Allied attack. Nivelle's offensive, though it did the Germans considerable damage, was a complete failure in terms of its own intentions, and this caused great harm to morale in the French Army for the rest of the year. It also meant that the heavy losses (159,000) incurred by the British in their supporting attack at Arras (9 April–17 May) were largely wasted, while their own major effort, the Third Battle of Ypres ('Passchendaele') was seriously weakened and delayed.

That is, from the Allied point of view, the negative and tragic aspect of 1917, one of history's cruel years; it has had many chroniclers.[32] There is another aspect which deserves attention, though those living through these dire events may be forgiven if they found it hard to perceive. 1917 was, in

'1917 was when some very helpful techniques began to be understood.' This classic photograph from the Arras front displays co-operation of all arms: infantry advancing past an 18-pdr. Field Artillery battery, a tank in middle distance, cavalry beyond.

fact, the period when some very valuable lessons and some very helpful techniques, first adumbrated in 1916, began to be understood and applied. These are most obvious when we look again at the artillery war, for one thing is not in doubt: 1917 was the year of the guns, because it was artillery that was going to dominate the battlefields of 1918, and 1917 was when it learned how to do so.

It was, above all, the increase in quantity and quality of the British artillery which would have the greatest effect. This was not because it, at any time, matched its ally in numbers—on the eve of the spring offensives the BEF had a total of 5,658 guns and howitzers, 1,492 of them heavy; France had 4,970 heavies alone—but simply because from May 1917 to May 1918 it was the British who would be chiefly engaging the German Army. For their attack on 9 April (Easter Monday) at Arras, the British First and Third Armies employed 963 heavy guns on a frontage of 13 miles—more than twice as many as on 1 July 1916 on a larger frontage. For the attack on the Vimy Ridge bastion, the Canadian Corps (supported by the heavy artillery of I Corps) had 377 heavy guns on a frontage of just over 4 miles—a density of 1 heavy for every 20 yards of front, and in addition 1 field gun for every 10 yards.

These are impressive statistics, and there are more: 2,687,653 rounds fired in the preliminary bombardment (25 March–8 April), 4,261,500 fired in the period of most intensive fighting, 9 April–16 May. What is more important, however, than this sheer pumping out of projectiles in enormous quantities was the purpose and the method. Taught by the Somme, the British artillerists now understood that any attempt to crush by weight of fire the entire enemy defensive system was just not going to work; one had to be more selective, more scientific. The Canadian Official History describes the two-week preliminary bombardment at Vimy:

'By day the programme called for observed fire on the enemy's trenches, dugouts, concrete machine-gun emplacements and other strongpoints, and on his ammunition and supply dumps, on road junctions and other key-points in his communications. Both by day and night there would be harassing fire on all known approaches; and machine-guns would engage targets previously dealt with by artillery in order to prevent or hinder reconstruction.' [33]

The intensive phase of this bombardment began on 2 April; one German account describes this as 'the week of suffering'. Fifty thousand tons of shells reduced the sector to 'a pock-marked wilderness of mud-filled craters.' At the right time of day, a slanting light still reveals them, lip to lip.

At many points trenches were completely demolished. German ration parties, which had formerly reached the front line in fifteen minutes, now often took six hours to get forward along the broken and shell-swept communication trenches. Rations arrived cold and spoiled, and many of the front companies were without fresh food for two or three days at a time. German accounts afterwards cited this breakdown in the food supply as a major cause of weakness in the defence.' [34]

During 1916, on the Somme and at Verdun, the technique of the 'creeping barrage' to cover an infantry attack was steadily improved (see p. 146). No one knows who 'invented' this method—probably no one, that is to say, no individual; it is most likely that it was spontaneously and simultaneously evolved out of identical experience in several places. The very first use of such a device may have been as early as October 1914, by a British heavy battery supporting a French attack. Some credit General Nivelle with the idea, at the recapture of Fort Douaumont in October 1916. Others attribute it to General Sir Henry Horne, an artilleryman, commanding XV Corps on the Somme. In 1917 he commanded the First Army, to which the Canadian Corps belonged when it attacked Vimy. On the other hand, an officer of the 9/King's Own Yorkshire Light Infantry tells us that his battalion was trained to work with a barrage before the Battle of the Somme even opened, and that on 28 June, when the officers gathered for a final drink before going into action, one gave a toast 'which has never been forgotten':

'Gentlemen, when the barrage lifts . . .' [35]

For the main (Third Army) attack at Arras on 9 April, the creeping barrage was provided by the 18-pdrs., of which there were 858. A standing barrage by 4.5 in. (276) and 6 in. howitzers (220) was put down on the German support line; when the creeping barrage reached it, this lifted on to the next objective. The chief function of the heavy artillery (6 in., 9.2 in., and 12 in. guns, 8 in., 9.2 in., 12 in., and 15 in. howitzers) was also a novelty, first seen in rudimentary form on the Somme and brought to a high pitch of precision in 1917: counter-battery—destroying or neutralizing the enemy's artillery. In the later stages of the war gas shell proved most useful for this purpose, directed against batteries, command posts, telephone exchanges, and dug-outs; the British never had enough of it.

When the attack was delivered, it was usual for the Germans to disclose a number of batteries whose existence had been kept secret by careful camouflage. It was very important to locate and engage these as quickly as possible. The best instrument for that purpose was clearly the Royal Flying Corps, and the air contribution is inseparable from the proceedings of all the battles of the artillery war. By November 1916 (the closing stage of the Somme) Haig noted that there were 543 ground stations for disseminating wireless messages from aircraft to the artillery. This liaison also steadily improved throughout 1917; at Messines on 7 June the gunners received 200 'Now Firing' (N.F.) calls identifying new targets; at Ypres on 31 July bad visibility prevented any such calls being received, and the gunners felt as though their eyes had been put out.

Blinding the enemy was, of course, as important as giving sight to the British artillerymen. Trenchard's offensive policy always aimed at fighting the air battle over the German lines and keeping the German airmen out of 'British sky'. It included constant attacks on the observation balloons which fringed every battlefront—deceptive targets which were never so easy to destroy as they looked from ground level. All the preparations for the Battle of Arras and most of the battle itself were carried out at the lowest ebb of the Royal Flying Corps, when its machines were seriously outclassed, and the boy pilots fell like pigeons to the German hawk-aces. In just five days, 4–8 April, 75 British aircraft were shot down; the full month cost 316.

These, then, were the broad outlines of the artillery war. There were, however, some new and important details added in 1917. The wicked foe of all attacking infantry was barbed wire; a main purpose of the long prelimi-nary bombardments was to cut the thick belts of wire which protected every trench system. This, of course, made surprise impossible, and also had the effect of cratering the ground so that even the infantry had difficulty in crossing it, and moving guns forward to support an advance was often wellnigh impossible. At Arras, General Allenby (commanding the Third Army) and Major-General A. E. A. Holland, his artillery adviser, argued for a hurricane bombardment of only 48 hours; they were overruled by GHQ, chiefly on the ground that this would not be sufficient to cut the German wire. The Official History says that General Holland was 'ahead of his time'—and since short preliminary bombardments or even none at all

'. . . plotting by RFC observation . . .': air combat gave the RFC its glamour, but artillery co-operation was its chief task—and there were more ways of coming to grief than being shot down. This RE-8 simply made a bad landing.

became the rule in 1918, this is clearly so. What made this tactic possible was, naturally, further advances of technology. A new instantaneous percussion fuse (the '106') made its first appearance at Vimy, and proved highly satisfactory, splintering on impact in the wire without cratering. It was at once 'evident that it was destined to have a definite effect on battle tactics'[36] — but for some time to come it would lie under the familiar curse of 'short supply.' The same affliction inhibited the use of another novelty which would come into its own in 1918: smoke-shell. Natural fog always helped the attacker; smoke was artificial fog which could be turned on or off at will—a profoundly important element once it could be produced in quantity. The British had no smoke shell in 1916, not enough in 1917.

No novelty of the artillery war, however, was more significant than predicted shooting, first experimented on the Somme, but not brought to full effectiveness by the Germans until the Battle of Riga in September 1917, and by the British at the Battle of Cambrai in November. Until then, as artillery massed behind a front attack, battery after battery would 'register' its targets, thus giving away its own position, and advertising the intention to attack. It was an able artilleryman, Brigadier-General H. H. Tudor, commanding the artillery of the 9th Division, who proposed that this practice should be abandoned, and reliance placed instead on topographical survey. Obviously, similar thoughts had occurred to Colonel Brüchmuller and other

German gunners, and on the British side they had occurred also to a talented Engineer, Major B. F. E. Keeling, commanding the Third Army Field Survey Company. And it was, in fact, the work of these Companies, formed in March 1916, that made the new breakthrough possible. With the aid of the RFC, the Royal Engineers built up an excellent survey of the Western Front on the scale of 1:20,000; this was the basis of the 'artillery boards' supplied to all batteries, mounted maps on which targets were plotted so that range and bearing could be easily read off. Counter-battery targets were partly identified for plotting by RFC observation, partly by the now well-advanced technique of 'flash-spotting' (taking bearings on the flash of enemy guns) and sound-ranging (made possible by a remarkable new electronic device which separated the sound of a gun firing from the rest of the noise of battle, 'identified the gun by type, and fixed its position on the ground'.)[37] Both these systems were functions of the Survey Companies.

With all these aids, most artillerymen still considered that the only way to ensure any real accuracy was by registration; in November 1917, however, General Sir Julian Byng, now commanding the Third Army, was determined to achieve complete surprise at Cambrai, and absolutely forbade registration. In this bold decision he was fortified by the strongly-expressed advice of Major Keeling—himself fortified by knowledge of another developing technique which promised to double the value of the survey maps: calibration. Briefly (and somewhat crudely) calibration was the application of carefully measured study of each gun's individual characteristics to its battle performance; to this was added 'scientific calculation of the corrections of range necessitated by variations of thermometer, barometer and wind, even taking into account such factors as the distortion of the paper on which the battery map was printed.'[38] This clearly indicated a large stride towards the precision shooting which, in 1918, would virtually eliminate 'area bombardment'. It owed its progress to the increasing numbers of heavy guns, manned by the Royal Garrison Artillery, who had learned their method from the Royal Navy. They were known as 'slide-rule gunners', as opposed to the 'galloping gunners' of the Royal Horse and Royal Field Artillery. The artillery war was very much, and increasingly, a slide-rule war. The famous bombardment which opened the Second Battle of El Alamein on 23 October 1942 marked a return to this style, long-neglected in the interval, and evolved by much pain and grief in 1916–17.

The guns were never silent in 1917. No sooner had the thunders of Arras died down than the roar of Messines was heard: 2,266 guns and howitzers on a nine-mile front, supporting General Plumer's brilliant capture of the ridge on 7 June. During the preliminary period, according to Lieutenant-General Sir Noel Birch (GHQ Artillery Adviser), 'The Germans definitely set out to defeat the British artillery, and there were some anxious moments until 2 or 3 days before the battle, when it definitely established its superiority. During the actual battle, the enemy's guns gave us but little trouble.'[39] These artillery duels were now a regular feature of set-piece battles, watched by the infantry with the close attention of men who knew that their lives depended on the outcome.

The preliminary bombardment for the Third Battle of Ypres opened on 17 July and continued until 30 July. This time the attack was conducted by the Fifth Army (General Sir Hubert Gough); including the French First Army on the left, and supporting action by the Second Army on the right, 3,091 guns and howitzers were deployed on a 15-mile front—according to the Official History, a 'zenith':

'Both the number of guns employed and the ammunition expended established a record.'[40]

In the preliminary bombardment the Royal Artillery fired 4,283,550 rounds, at what then seemed the unbelievable cost of £22,211,389 14s 4d. Once again the German artillery disputed the mastery fiercely, and there were heavy losses both of guns and gunners; the outcome favoured the British, but less decisively than at Messines. Nevertheless, a German report spoke of the opening barrage on 31 July as being 'as if Hell had opened'.[41]

Haig, in his Final Despatch, noted a significant new fact about this kind of war:

'In the preliminary bombardment 4,283,550 rounds . . .': a 60 cm. gauge light railway delivering shells to one of the innumerable dumps behind the British battery positions at Ypres.

'In the opening attack on the 31st July our artillery personnel amounted to over 80 per cent of the infantry engaged in the principal attack on our front . . .'[42]

This meant, of course, that a heavier proportion of loss would fall on the Royal Artillery. One divisional history tells us:

'During the two months spent in the Ypres salient from June to August 1917, the 8th Division RA actually suffered greater casualties than they had incurred in the whole of the preceding period since their landing in France in 1914!'[43]

The opening stages of 'Third Ypres', while containing no disasters even remotely comparable to 1 July 1916, were disappointing; this was partly due to abominable weather, partly to incorrect tactics by General Gough. On 25 August Haig transferred control of the battle to Plumer, who at once began preparation for a methodical, stage-by-stage advance, with every part of the proceedings dominated by artillery. His main thrust was to be against the vital Gheluvelt 'Plateau', behind which sheltered a great mass of German guns. Plumer planned to capture the plateau by four successive steps, at intervals of six days (to enable the artillery to advance to new positions and bring up ammunition), each 'bite' to be approximately 1,500 yards deep. For the narrow assault frontage of 4,000 yards he asked for 1,339 guns and howitzers and actually received 1,295 (575 heavy). Compared with the attack made in the same area on 31 July, he was using double the force on half the frontage.

The first 'step' was taken, after a seven-day preparation, on 20 September: the Battle of the Menin Road Ridge. It provided a blueprint of what was to follow: the feature of the assault itself was the new-style barrage—no longer a single 'standing' line of shell-bursts on the enemy support line, while another single line crept in front of the infantry. Plumer's barrage was 1,000 yards deep, in five belts:

A: shrapnel, fired by 18-pdrs immediately ahead of the infantry, 200 yards deep;

B: high-explosive, fired by 18-pdrs and 4.5 inch field howitzers, 200 yards;

C: 240 machine-guns, to keep the German supports in their shelters (this offensive use of massed machine-guns was now standard practice);

D: high-explosive fired by 120 6-in. howitzers, 50 per cent of shells fitted with the 106 fuse;

E: 60-pdrs and very heavy howitzers, also using 106 fuses for 50 per cent of shells.

Such was the remorseless engine of destruction which swept across the German lines. Zero hour was at 5.40am; by midday the Second Army had taken all its objectives. And now, in classic German fashion, would come the counter-attacks which had dashed so many hopes after promising starts during the last two years. They were catered for in the British artillery programme, and with good weather permitting 394 wireless messages from aircraft, prompt action could be taken to break up the German formations. On the front of the 1st Australian Division, the artillery responded within half a minute to an SOS signal, the machine-guns in a matter of seconds. The counter-attack was crushed before it was even made.

Two more similar blows followed, on 26 September (Polygon Wood) and 4 October (Broodseinde; 'the black day').[44] On this occasion Haig noted that the artillery personnel amounted to as much as 85 per cent of the infantry engaged. The Second Army deployed 796 heavy and medium and 1,548 field guns and howitzers; in the dawn light the high explosive barrage looked like a 'wall of flame', and once again German defences and counter-attacks alike were crushed. New defensive tactics evolved to cope with this style of war proved a failure; the German Official Account says frankly:

'The Army High Command came to the conclusion that there was no means by which the positions could be held against the overpowering enemy superiority in artillery and infantry.'[45]

The Australian Official Historian says of this period during which his compatriots and the New Zealanders played such a leading part:

'An overwhelming blow had been struck and both sides knew it . . . This was the third blow struck at Ypres in fifteen days with complete success . . . Let the student, looking at the prospect as it appeared at noon on 4 October ask himself, "In view of three step by step blows, what will be the result of three more in the next fortnight?"'[46]

One Australian leader certainly had no doubt about the answer; Major-General John Monash, commanding the 3rd Division, wrote on 7 October:

'Great happenings are possible in the very near future . . .'[47]

It was not to be; instead, the rain which had marred the opening of the battle now returned to wreck its end—'our most effective ally', as Prince Rupprecht of Bavaria called it. The campaign foundered in a nightmare landscape of water-filled craters separated by patches of muddy slime:

'The old battlefield was one vast tormented bog, seamed by narrow lines of corduroy or duck-board tracks which, marked down by the enemy's artillery, were swept with high explosive and shrapnel by day and night . . . Our own artillery lived and fought in conditions of constant physical distress. Guns sank in the mud till they became useless and ultimately disappeared beneath the surface; till our battery positions were dotted with little red flags marking the positions where guns had sunk from view.'[48]

This hideous picture has come to represent the whole battle, even, indeed, the whole of the wearing-out struggle and the artillery war. That is, of course, quite incorrect; the true tragedy lies in how close success sometimes seemed, and how it was so often snatched away by evil chance. The story of these hard years is the story of constant trial and error, constant evolution of new tactics, making possible brilliant occasions like Vimy, Messines, Hill 70, Menin Road, Polygon Wood, and Broodseinde. These are the true pointers to the new proficiency of British battle practice, as was the deafening roar of over 1,000 unsuspected guns at Cambrai on 20 November, proclaiming that the Royal Artillery had at last procured the vital advantages of surprise and precision, the combination of which would prove to be the most powerful ingredient of victory in 1918.

NOTES

1 Haig: *Despatches*, p. 320.
2 Ibid.
3 Falkenhayn: *General Headquarters and its Critical Decisions*, p. 217.
4 Ibid.
5 Ibid., p. 268.
6 Falls: *The First World War*, p. 156.
7 Jacques d'Arnoux: *Paroles d'un Revenant*, quoted *L'Atmosphère du Champ de Bataille*, ed. Lt-Col. J. Armengaud, pp. 118–19; Charles-Lavauzelle, 1940.
8 P. J. Campbell: *In the Cannon's Mouth*, p. 80; Hamish Hamilton, 1979.
9 Frederick Manning: *The Middle Parts of Fortune*, p. 222; Peter Davies, 1977.
10 E. Norman Gladden: *Ypres 1917: A Personal Account*, p. 178; William Kimber, 1967.
11 Gilbert Frankau: *The City of Fear and other Poems*, p. 46; Chatto & Windus, 1917.
12 Colonel Repington: *The First World War 1914–1918*, i p. 160; Constable, 1920.
13 Ibid., pp. 159–60.
14 Slang for French infantry: 'the bearded ones'. A journalistic contribution; they generally referred to each other as 'les bonhommes': 'the lads' is probably the British equivalent.
15 Mangin: *Lettres de Guerre*, pp. 154–5.
16 As usual, there are considerable variations in the totals presented; Churchill's would amount to nearly 850,000. The figure given here is generally accepted by reputable authorities.
17 Mangin, op. cit. p. 112.
18 Alexander Werth: *Russia at War 1941–1945*, p. 259, quoting Russian and German sources; Barrie & Rockliff, 1964.
19 Joffre: *Memoirs*, ii p. 461.
20 Ibid., p. 464.
21 *O.H. 1916*, ii p. 27.
22 From the Haig Papers.
23 See Terraine, *The Smoke and the Fire*, pp. 119–25.
24 *O.H. 1916*, ii p. 356.
25 Ibid., p. 444.

26 Hindenburg: *Out of my Life*, p. 245.
27 Ludendorff: *War Memories*, i p. 304.
28 Mangin, op. cit. pp. 168–9.
29 Esher to Haig, 9 November 1916; author's papers.
30 Terraine, op. cit. p. 101.
31 C. E. Carrington: *Soldier from the Wars Returning*, p. 120; Hutchinson, 1965.
32 See Terraine, *The Road to Passchendaele*, Leo Cooper, 1977, for a documentation of the origins and course of the British Flanders offensive.
33 Colonel G. W. L. Nicholson: *Canadian Expeditionary Force 1914–1919*, p. 249; Queen's Printer, Ottawa, 1962.
34 Ibid., p. 251.
35 Lancelot Dykes Spicer: *Letters from France*, pp. xvii–xviii; Robert York, 1979.
36 Lieutenant-Colonel J. H. Boraston: *Sir Douglas Haig's Command* (ed. Boraston & G. A. B. Dewar), p. 263; Constable, 1922.
37 Shelford Bidwell: *Gunners at War*, p. 34; Arms and Armour Press, 1970.
38 *O.H. 1917*, i p. 541.
39 Author's papers: note by Lieut-Gen. Sir Noel Birch on British Artillery in France 1916–1918, 1927.
40 *O.H. 1917*, ii p. 138.
41 General von Kuhl, quoted in *The Road to Passchendaele*, p. 211.
42 Haig, op. cit. pp. 322–3.
43 Lieutenant-Colonel J. H. Boraston: *The Eighth Division in War, 1914–1918*, p. 137; Medici Society, 1926.
44 German monograph, *Flandern 1917* quoted in *The Road to Passchendaele*, p. 281.
45 Ibid.
46 Dr. C. E. W. Bean: *The Official History of Australia in the War of 1914–1918*, iv p. 875; Angus & Robertson.
47 *The War Letters of General Monash*; Angus & Robertson, 1925.
48 Boraston, op. cit. p. 162.

The Wearing-Out Fight:
Southern Version

WE HAVE NOTED (p. 209) the entry of Italy into the war in May 1915. This meant, for the allies, an accession of strength of some 875,000 men, or 36 infantry divisions (facing about 100,000 Austrians). The Italian Army, however, was not to be measured by its numbers; war against Turkey in 1911–12 had proved a harder matter than the outward strength of the belligerents suggested, and it had left Italy's treasury and arsenals both gravely depleted. Her weakness in artillery (especially heavy guns) persisted throughout the war. Nor was her strategic position at all satisfactory, ringed to the north and north-east by the great Alpine barrier, with its heights in enemy hands, and the Trentino district thrusting down into northern Italy, threatening vital communications.

In these circumstances, it is scarcely surprising that no great dramatic stroke was seen on the Italian Front for a long time—not, indeed, until

'. . . geography permitted few options.' These Austrian troops are in a quiet sector of the Dolomites; the photograph shows the type of landscape in which the Italians suffered some of the highest rates of loss of the whole war.

attrition had done its work. And attrition began that work at once. For the Italian Chief of Staff, General Count Luigi Cadorna, politics and geography permitted few options. He had, in fact only two fronts available for fighting: the Trentino, a steeply mountainous region leading to the even steeper Tyrol, and in the east the area across the River Isonzo, also mountainous, with high pleateaux, chief of them the Carso, which has been described as 'a howling wilderness of stones sharp as knives.'[1] Here lay the much-valued prizes of Trieste and Fiume, and here Cadorna chose to fight. No fewer than eleven Battles of the Isonzo bear witness to his determination, and indicate why he has been called the 'arch-attritionist'.[2] Indeed, attrition on an astonishing scale is the only notable feature of the Italian Front fighting.

In 1915 four Battles of the Isonzo (on the Western Front they would only have rated as two) caused Italy 177,000 casualties out of a total for the seven operative months of the year of 250,000. In 1916 there were five more battles on the Isonzo front, and in addition an Austrian offensive in the Trentino which took 45,000 Italian prisoners and 300 guns. In May 1917 Cadorna launched his Tenth Battle of the Isonzo, which cost him 157,000 casualties in 17 days, and in August the Eleventh Battle, costing 166,000 in 11 days (one of the highest rates of loss of the whole war, and including, significantly, 18,000 prisoners). In the period May–September 1917, the Italians lost 346,000 men—and all this, this 3-year blood-letting, won only trifling gains of ground in that unfriendly region. This was attrition indeed, but it was the Italian attackers who paid the price.

What is remarkable is the attraction which this front, with all its difficulties of geography and logistics, exercised for certain Allied politicians—chief among them the British Prime Minister, Mr. Lloyd George. All through 1917 he and some like-minded supporters, argued that this was where the main Allied effort of the year should be made: an all-out attempt to knock Austria out of the war, in pursuance of their strategy of 'knocking away the props'—a strategy which refused to contemplate the possibility that it might be German strength that propped her weak allies, rather than the other way about. And in arguing that Austria was the weaker, and therefore more easily destructible, enemy, it also failed to take into account the fact that Italy was the enemy against which all the various races of the Austro-Hungarian Empire were prepared to combine with enthusiasm, so that by 1917 it could even be said that fighting the Italians was the cement which held the battered Empire together. But it was not careful strategic assessment which inspired Lloyd George and his associates, simply emotional revulsion against the conditions and cost of the Western Front, and lack of imagination enough to see that going to the Carso would merely (like Gallipoli; see pp. 176–7) transfer both conditions and cost to a more inconvenient place.

All such notions were swept away when the Austrians, with the aid of seven German divisions, themselves took the offensive on the Isonzo in October 1917. The key force was the German *Fourteenth Army*, commanded by General Otto von Below. To bring Austrian forces across from the now quiescent Russian front, to assemble the 1,550 guns and 420 heavy and medium mortars required, with their vast stocks of ammunition, was the work of 2,400 trains and a truck tonnage amounting to 6,000. Below's Army faced the little town of Caporetto, which gave its name to the battle which opened on 25 October—although by the end of it the front was some 70 miles away to the south-west. The Italian collapse began on the very first day; a German division penetrated some 14 miles, and Italian prisoners began to stream in by tens of thousands, as they did in the Western Desert in 1940–41. It was, in fact, a rout; by the time it ended (due chiefly to the exhaustion of the pursuing Austro-Germans, who had practically no cavalry or armoured cars to help them) the Italians had lost some 275,000 prisoners—but significantly again, only 10,000 killed and 30,000 wounded—and 2,500 guns. The Germans had shown their usual battle skills, and the Austrian mountain troops greatly distinguished themselves, but it was not tactics or techniques which really shattered the Italians—it was the demoralization brought about by their own attrition warfare in 11 hard-fought battles without success. It showed what might happen when a 'wearing-out fight' had done its work.

Five British and six French divisions were sent to help the Italian Army to rally. For the British, coming at the end of the Ypres battle, this was a serious diversion of strength which was severely felt at Cambrai at the end of November. And by the time the Anglo-French forces arrived the Italian retreat had, in fact, ended along the line of the River Piave. Under a new Chief of Staff, General Armando Diaz, their Army began a slow recovery. The British and French divisions did little fighting, though their presence no doubt brought encouragement to their allies. When the great German attacks began on the Western Front in March 1918 most of them had to return post-haste. The remainder stayed on to play a part in stopping the last Austrian offensive of the war in June, and then join effectively in General Diaz's own final offensive—the Battle of Vittorio Veneto, which brought Austria at last to her knees—in October. The last word on Austria-Hungary must be one of wonder at how that so-called 'ramshackle' Empire had stood up for so long to some of the most staggering attrition of the whole war—never more devastating than in 1916, when Imperial Russia made her last throw, as we shall now see.

NOTES

1 British Official History, quoted in Falls, *The First World War*, p. 123.
2 Cyril Falls: *Caporetto 1917*, p. 14; Weidenfeld & Nicolson, 1966.

The Wearing-Out Fight:
Eastern Version

A S WE HAVE SEEN (p. 189), by the end of 1915 'it was distressingly plain that no such thing as an effective coordinated Allied strategy for war on two fronts existed.' On 6–8 December of that year General Joffre presided over an inter-Allied conference at his headquarters at Chantilly which, he says, 'marks a vital date in the history of the conduct of the war'.[1] He gives his reason:

'For the first time since the war began, the Allies succeeded in establishing a general plan of action . . . What was still better than devising a plan, they put it into execution . . . all the Allies, in full accord, during the summer of 1916 engaged in a general attack whose plan had been drawn up in the month of December, 1915, at the Chantilly Conference.'[2]

In the sense that 1916 did, indeed, see all the Allies on the offensive (and, for a brief space, simultaneously) Joffre is correct; but he himself admits that there were 'formidable diversions'—Verdun above all, but also Conrad's offensive in the Trentino, referred to above, which opened with spectacular success on 15 May. This brought a series of appeals for help, 'each more peremptory in tone than the last',[3] addressed to the only ally capable of affording it: Russia—since France was locked in an intense phase of fighting at Verdun, and Britain was still in the process of assembling her army. The response was remarkable—the greatest Russian victory of the war, even greater than Lemberg in 1914.

Russia, after all that she had endured, was again performing a miracle of recovery. A cloud of myth surrounds the subject of the Russian war-economy—much of it deliberately manufactured for political purposes. The truth, as Dr. Stone points out, is that a 'gigantic industrial effort' was set on foot in 1915 which by 1916 was bearing fruit. (In 1917, he adds, it would bring 'its own social consequences'[4]—but that is another matter.) A great expansion of the engineering and chemical industries procured phenomenal increases in munitions production by the end of the year: shell production rose by 2,000 per cent, gun production by 1,000 per cent, rifle production by 1,100 per cent. It is widely believed that the improvement was largely due to foreign imports, but this is incorrect. Out of some 25,600 field guns supplied during the war, Russia herself produced 20,000; by the beginning of 1917 her total gun production amounted to 900 per month. Shell production, which had been 358,000 in the month of January 1915, rose to 1,512,000 in November, and 2,900,000 in September 1916. It is true that Russia imported 1,200,000 foreign rifles, but her own production rose to 100,000 a month. Out of a front-line strength of 1,693,000 in January 1916, 1,243,000 had rifles; 'a few weeks later, the Russian front-line strength became two million,

'". . . a general incontinent walk forward of all the Russian forces . . ."': this advance is through entanglements which are unimpressive by Western standards, and appear to have been well cut.

virtually all of them with rifles.'[5] It was a similar story with other vital munitions: aircraft, wireless sets, telephones (10,000 in 1914, 50,000 in 1916), gas-masks, barbed wire, bandages. Dr Stone comments:

'Legend has a picture of countless millions of peasant soldiers being thrust into battle, armed with long-handled axes, against overpowering German artillery and machine guns. It is a legend that owes almost nothing to reality; indeed, reality was the very reverse of legend. The army, by the beginning of the 1916 campaign, was not suffering from material shortages of any significance . . .'[6]

This was, in truth, an army in process of transformation; what had been in 1914, as we have seen (p. 115), an army 'unfit to undertake modern war', was about to prove, in one sector at least, that it had come a long way since then. The new commander of the Russian southern group of armies, General Alexei Brusilov, epitomized the change: here, at last, was a true professional in high command. He brought a new style to Russian warfare: a compact, unostentatious headquarters, crisp, clear orders, careful staff-work. On Brusilov's front, air reconnaissance and photography (virtually unknown elsewhere) were used to identify the opposing batteries, and a model of the Austrian positions was built and studied in the manner of the Western Front. Large dug-outs were constructed to contain and conceal the Russian reserves (the Germans had also done this at Verdun, but it is unlikely that the Allies were yet aware of the fact; Brusilov and his staff must be credited with original thinking). Saps were pushed out to, in places, some 50 yards from the enemy line along a front of about 200 miles. Close co-operation between artillery and infantry (also virtually unknown in other sectors) was a rule. In other words, this Army Group at least was going to wage war by modern methods.

To the surprise of colleagues and enemies alike (but the latter above all) when the Italian appeals came Brusilov promptly agreed to bring forward his offensive preparations, timed for commencement in the last week of June, to the first week. He launched his attack on 4 June: a one-day bombardment of selected targets (another innovation) by nearly 2,000 guns with—at last—ample ammunition. The next day the Russian infantry advanced; their numerical superiority in the entire sector was about 100,000, which was not at all excessive for that period of the war. Emerging from their forward saps (and in places from tunnels driven under their own wire, to the amazement of the Austrians) they rapidly over-ran the enemy front- and support-lines, their success being greatest on the two flanks. It was, said Churchill, 'a general incontinent walk forward of all the Russian forces along a line of nearly 200 miles.'[7]

What now followed was a débâcle, exceeding even Caporetto in the following year. On 12 June Brusilov reported the capture of 2,992 officers, 190,000 other ranks, 216 guns, 196 mortars, and 645 machine-guns; total Austro-Hungarian casualties were over a quarter of a million—in nine days. On his southern flank, he had advanced nearly 30 miles, on the northern, 50.

Then he was forced to pause, while Evert's Army Group to the north of him took up the fight, but without success against predominantly German forces. Brusilov attacked again at the end of July and again in August; by the 12th of that month, he reported, he had taken 7,757 officers, 350,845 other ranks, 405 guns, and 1,326 machine-guns. By the end of the month, the Austro-Hungarians had lost 614,000 men and the Germans 150,000. Brusilov's final effort was made in September, in support of Rumania, which had entered the war on the Allied side on 27 August. It was this September battle which saw the only true simultaneous action of all the Allies in the whole war: Russian and Rumanian attacks in Transylvania beginning on 12 September, the Italians launching the Seventh Battle of the Isonzo on 15 September, the French attacking on the Somme on the 12th, and the British joining in on the 15th. It was a bad moment for the Central Powers—but they survived. It was also the last spurt of action on Brusilov's front. His men were now exhausted, their communications seriously extended by an advance of as much as 70 miles at its furthest, Russia's casualties for the year now reaching a million. But Brusilov had taken over 400,000 prisoners and more than 500 guns.

These phenomenal captures clearly reveal a collapse of Austro-Hungarian morale, and are generally attributed to wholesale desertions by the Slav forces of the Empire. This factor must certainly account for a considerable number; the Bohemian and Ruthenian regiments in particular would seem to have shown little determination in holding the Russian attacks. But other factors have to be considered. Conrad himself was responsible for gravely weakening his Eastern front, especially in artillery, for the benefit of his Trentino adventure, which also occupied some of the best of the Austrian generals. Dr. Stone points to a remarkable degree of complacency and over-confidence in the Austrian Eastern armies, no doubt prompted by Russian failures earlier in the year. The sheer length of the front attacked (200 miles) astonished and bewildered them, making correct deployment of reserves unusually difficult. Above all, however, in accounting for a failure of morale, one has to remember that dreadful early loss of peace-trained officers referred to above (p. 94). About 75 per cent of these, and a similar proportion of warrant and senior non-commissioned officers had been German-speaking Austrians; as Churchill says,

'*It was this permanent Teutonic staff and structure that held the whole army together. These courageous, resolute professionals had exposed themselves with ardour. Their losses had been out of all proportion to those of the rank and file. More than half had perished. They were irreplaceable . . . The need of employing very large numbers of new officers of Czech, Romanian or Croat nationality offered positions of authority to many who hated the Teutonic race and cared nothing for the House of Habsburg.*'[8]

Brusilov's offensive was a nail in the coffin of the Habsburg Empire; it might have been the last nail, but instead it was Russia which now succumbed to the wearing-out fight. Her casualties, by the end of 1916, were in the region of 5 million. A huge stretch of her territory was occupied by the enemy. The pall of the 'Russian disease' (p. 115) hung over all her enterprises; Brusilov's success only threw into sharper relief the general incompetence and mediocrity of the men who ruled under a mediocre tyrant. Six months after the end of Brusilov's wonderful victory, the disheartened, embittered nation flared into revolution, and to all intents and purposes fell out of the war. Austria-Hungary was reprieved.

NOTES
1　Joffre: *Memoirs*, ii p. 390.
2　Ibid., p. 407.
3　Stone: *The Eastern Front*, p. 246.
4　Ibid., p. 211.
5　Ibid., p. 212.
6　Ibid.
7　Churchill: *The Eastern Front*, p. 336.
8　Ibid., p. 220.

CHAPTER VIII

Variants of the Offensive:
Underground

'VARIANTS OF THE OFFENSIVE' was the title that Churchill gave to a memorandum which he drew up on 3 December 1915 for the Committee of Imperial Defence, in which he made certain proposals for improving offensive tactics, most notably the use of armoured mechanical 'caterpillars'—a subject to which we shall shortly return. But the truth is that both sides were unceasingly seeking and experimenting with 'variants of the offensive' throughout the war. In the BEF an Inventions Committee was set up at GHQ in June 1915; this was soon replaced by the less cumbersome 'Experimental Section, Royal Engineers'. The Official History suggests that as the Citizen Army developed, the Royal Engineers became its 'probably most efficient arm'[1] because their proficiency in an increasingly mechanical and 'engineering war' depended less than others on military experience and more on their normal peacetime skills. The growth of the Corps was significant: 513 officers and 13,127 other ranks in August 1914, 11,830 officers and 225,540 other ranks in August 1918.

The Experimental Section conducted trials and experiments with hand and rifle-grenades, trench mortars, flares, land-mines, delay-action fuses, catapults, smoke producers and projectors, body armour, armour-piercing bullets (to penetrate armoured loopholes), wire-destroying apparatus, aeroplane height-finders and optical instruments—and much else besides. It had to inspect and assess (often at considerable risk) all manner of amazing devices put forward by their inventors as certain war-winners: a giant hose which would wash away the German trenches, a kite to drop explosives, a grapnel to pull away the enemy's wire, a bow to shoot high-explosive arrows at machine-gun emplacements, a boomerang hand-grenade to kill Germans behind traverses, a thing like a barrel-organ which would project a stream of disc grenades when the handle was turned, igniting each one by friction as it flew out, even (one is tempted to say 'inevitably') a 'death ray'. The idea of the First World War as a period of almost total intellectual and imaginative stagnation is the reverse of the truth; experiment was going on all the time in all armies. Never had the art of war undergone such intense change.

The underground war, to which we have alluded above (p. 144), everywhere directed by the Engineers, profited by the war's static nature to develop great sophistication. We have noted how the Germans massed and concealed their reserves in huge underground dug-outs (*stollen*) at Verdun, and how the Russians independently arrived at the same technique a few months later. The French, having down-graded their fortresses, realized during the course of the Battle of Verdun that they had overdone this; the deep underground chambers and galleries of Fort Douaumont, Fort de Vaux and the rest, even if the forts could not engage the enemy in battle as intended, offered, under their thick layers of concrete, protection for command posts, reserves, field hospitals, communications, and supplies. To lose a place like Douaumont, as the French did virtually by carelessness on 25 February, was not only to forfeit prestige but also to be deprived of a valuable adjunct to the defense. Recapturing Fort Douaumont thus became an important objective, costing many lives.

The Germans, too, applied themselves to field fortifications, and produced the most elaborate and famous of them all. Its very existence confirms the extent of their defeat on the Somme; hitherto the German doctrine had always been 'one line and a strong one', and we have seen (p. 210) how bitterly the German Army fought to hold their line. But when the new High Command took over at the end of August 1916, they found a position so critical—indeed, Germany was now facing manpower bankruptcy—that a complete abandonment of this policy had to be envisaged. Some way to avoid any repetition of this 'Somme fighting' had to be found; accordingly, as Ludendorff tells us, 'the construction had been begun as early as September of powerful rear positions in the West . . . Whether we should retire on them, and how the positions would be used, was not of course decided in September, 1916; the important thing then was to get them built.'[2]

These 'powerful rear positions', a novelty forced upon the High Command, were divided into sections, called '*stellung*' ('position'), each with its own name. The first to be constructed, in the vital Cambrai-St. Quentin sector, was the '*Siegfried Stellung*', prolonged to the north by the '*Wotan Stellung*' and to the south by the '*Alberich Stellung*'; further to the south (and later) came the '*Brunhild Stellung*' in Champagne, and the '*Kriemhilde Stellung*' in the Argonne. The personae of the Ring Saga supplied these names for German use; the British more crudely called the whole thing 'the Hindenburg Line'. The '*Siegfried*' position was the strongest and most elaborate. It was protected in places by as many as eight or nine thick belts of barbed wire, systematically arranged to be swept by hidden machine-guns in concrete posts, and consisted of a complex of trenches, gun-positions and shelters about ten miles deep. Work went forward on this and '*Alberich*' so urgently that the Germans were able to retire to them in February and March 1917, the retirement to '*Alberich*' greatly compromising General Nivelle's famous plan.

This was the supreme expression of the defensive aspect of the underground war; it was the British who supplied the supreme expressions of it offensively. For the Battle of Arras in April, the British Engineers utilized and improved upon a unique local feature: the outskirts of the town lay only about a mile from the front line at its nearest point, and a short distance inside the old fortifications were the *Grande* and *Petite Places*. Under both of these were large cellars, used in time of siege as refuges, and later for the storage of all kinds of goods. Cleared of these, the cellars could accommodate 13,000 men in safety. Following the course of the old ramparts and ditch was a great sewer, 8 feet high and 6 feet wide; tunnels were now driven from the

'The actual process of mining was difficult enough.' These British tunnellers are working in chalk (Somme area) and presumably at a distance from the enemy, otherwise picks would make too much noise.

cellars to the sewer. Outside the town, leading to the front line, two series of caves, some of them of vast size, had been discovered; these were levelled and cleared of loose chalk, and could accommodate another 11,500 men (the largest cave of all held 4,000). Two long tunnels were constructed to connect the sewer and these caves, so that over 24,000 men (the infantry of two divisions) could be sheltered up to the last moment as they approached the line. But even this feat of engineering would shortly be surpassed.

What is known as the Messines-Wytschaete Ridge (though its northern end is at St. Eloi, only about 1½ miles south of Ypres) had been captured by the Germans in November 1914, in the course of the 1st Battle of Ypres. Their possession of this feature locked in the south side of the Salient; rising to 150 feet at its highest point (Wytschaete), it gave excellent observation both westward and eastward, but whereas on the eastern side it falls away gently to the plain, on the westward a 1 in 10 slope gives it a sharp escarpment. It very obviously lent itself to mining operations, and it was here that 'the most dramatic mining exploit of the war' (see p. 144) took place in June 1917.

It is of the very nature of mining that it requires time; of the 19 mines exploded under the ridge, some had been begun as early as August 1915, others in December of that year, in expectation of action in 1916. Postponement, of course, greatly increased the risk of discovery, which was the great hazard of all mine warfare. And the actual process of mining itself was difficult enough: in this sector the topsoils consisted of sand or sandy loam, resting on a layer of semi-liquid 'slurry' or silt, with a deep seam of blue clay below that. Early mining equipment confined the tunnellers to the top layers, but by 1916 they were able to do better. Using mechanical diggers such as were used for driving the Tube railways through London clay, they began to penetrate the clay seam, which was obviously more suitable for galleries, as well as these being more difficult for the enemy to detect (because of the depth). The mechanical diggers were a disappointment—hand labour was quicker; but in other respects technology was more helpful, providing noiseless air and water pumps, better survey and listening instruments, better rescue apparatus and steel tubing for sinking shafts through the wet 'slurry'. The final hazard was disposal of the blue clay—any sudden appearance of dumps of this tell-tale substance on the surface would have told the Germans all they needed to know. Every shovelful of it had to be removed a long way away and hidden, or re-buried under sandbag parapets. How successfully this was done is proved by the absolute surprise of the Germans on the day of battle.

The mine galleries began as vertical shafts, sunk some 300–400 yards behind the British front-line; in view of the perfect observation enjoyed by the Germans, this alone presented formidable problems. Once down into the clay, the horizontal penetrations began; the furthest of these was the Kruisstraat No. 3 mine, with a gallery 2,160 feet long, and a charge of 30,000 lb. of ammonal; the Petit Bois No. 1 Right mine gallery was 2,070 feet long, with a charge of 21,000 lb. of ammonal and 9,000 lb. of blasting gelatine ('blastine'); seven more galleries were over 1,000 feet long (Spanbroekmolen, 1,710; Maedelstede, 1,610). The total charge of the 19 mines prepared along this front was just under one million pounds of high explosive.

All this careful preparation was carried out on the front of the Second Army (General Sir Herbert Plumer) under the direction of the Chief Engineer, Major-General F. M. Glubb and the O.C. Mines, Lieutenant-Colonel A. G. Stevenson. A well-authenticated story reveals much about General Plumer, the qualities of command, and the problems of the underground war. At the northern extremity of the front of attack was Hill 60, a locality notorious for the savage fighting that took place there. It was an artificial mound, formed by the spoil of the Ypres–Comines railway cutting; it was called 'Hill 60' by the British Army because of the ring contour which marked it on large-scale maps (60 metres). On the south side of the railway, a long, irregularly-shaped spoil-mound was called 'The Caterpillar'. Both these features had been lost to the Germans in May 1915; both were scenes of intense mining activity. Indeed, the Official History tells us:

'The underground battle for Hill 60 was of a severity unsurpassed of its kind on the British front throughout the war.'[3]

Deep mining towards Hill 60 and The Caterpillar was begun in August 1915. The Hill 60 gallery was completed in July 1916, 1,110 feet long, 90 feet below ground, and charged with 53,500 lb. of explosive. The Caterpillar gallery, 1,380 feet long, was completed in October 1916, and charged with 70,000 lb. of explosive. This work was carried out by the 3rd Canadian Tunnelling Company, which was relieved in November by the 1st Australian Tunnelling Company, and the galleries were maintained by the Australians throughout the winter. It may be imagined with what emotion General Plumer's Chief of Staff, the brilliant Major-General C. H. Harington, learned from Colonel Stevenson one night in February 1917 that the Germans were counter-mining only a few feet away from these two workings. They would have to be blown at once, said Stevenson—and the only person who could authorize that was the Army Commander. But (like other great commanders) Plumer made it a rule to go to bed at 9.30pm, and not to be disturbed. Harington decided to break the rule (he only did this twice in all his time as Plumer's Chief of Staff). He woke Plumer and told him:

'"Mines" says we must blow the Hill 60 mines tonight.'

Plumer replied immediately:

'I won't have them blown. Good night.'[4]

And he went straight back to sleep. His decision was correct; the Germans were not as close as they seemed. Careful listening indicated that they would just fall short of the British galleries at the date of attack—and so it turned out.

The date in question was 7 June, 3.10am. At that moment, according to a British soldier:

'The ground began to rock. My body was carried up and down as though by the waves of the sea. In front the earth opened and a large black mass mounted on pillars of fire to the sky, where it seemed to remain suspended for some seconds while the awful red glow lit up the surrounding desolation.'[5]

To a German observer the spectacle appeared as

'nineteen gigantic roses with carmine petals, or as enormous mushrooms, which rose up slowly and majestically out of the ground and then split into pieces with a mighty roar, sending multi-coloured columns of flame mixed with a mass of earth and splinters high into the sky.'[6]

The noise of this unparalleled explosion was distinctly heard in London—yet, by a trick of acoustics, it passed right over the British soldier quoted above, making the sensation that much more eerie. The craters torn by the upward thrust of these convulsions were enormous: at The Caterpillar,

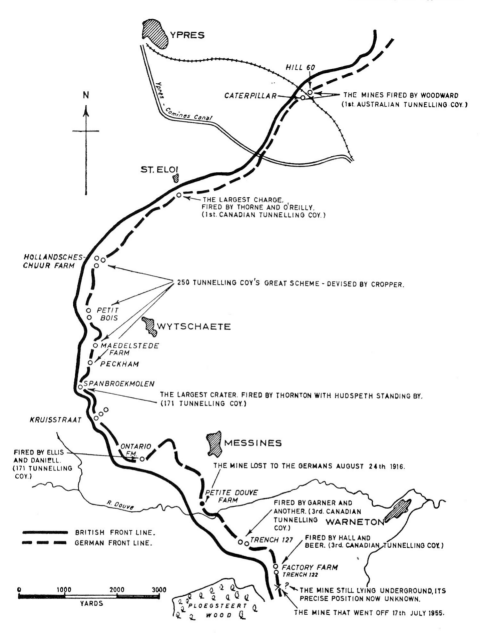

YPRES

HILL 60

CATERPILLAR — THE MINES FIRED BY WOODWARD
(1st. AUSTRALIAN TUNNELLING COY.)

Ypres - Comines Canal

N

ST. ELOI

— THE LARGEST CHARGE.
FIRED BY THORNE AND O'REILLY.
(1st. CANADIAN TUNNELLING COY.)

HOLLANDSCHES-
CHUUR FARM

250 TUNNELLING COY'S GREAT SCHEME - DEVISED BY CROPPER.

*PETIT
BOIS*

WYTSCHAETE

*MAEDELSTEDE
FARM*
PECKHAM

SPANBROEKMOLEN

THE LARGEST CRATER. FIRED BY THORNTON WITH HUDSPETH STANDING BY.
(171 TUNNELLING COY.)

KRUISSTRAAT

*ONTARIO
FM.*

MESSINES

FIRED BY ELLIS
AND DANIELL.
(171 TUNNELLING
COY.)

THE MINE LOST TO THE GERMANS AUGUST 24th 1916.

*PETITE DOUVE
FARM*

R. Douve

FIRED BY GARNER AND
ANOTHER. (3rd. CANADIAN
TUNNELLING WARNETON
COY.)

—— BRITISH FRONT LINE.
– – – GERMAN FRONT LINE.

TRENCH 127 FIRED BY HALL AND
BEER. (3rd. CANADIAN TUNNELLING COY.)

FACTORY FARM
TRENCH 122

0 1000 2000 3000
YARDS

*PLOEGSTEERT
WOOD*

? THE MINE STILL LYING UNDERGROUND, ITS
PRECISE POSITION NOW UNKNOWN.

THE MINE THAT WENT OFF 17th JULY 1955.

'. . . 19 mines exploded under the ridge . . .': the diagram shows the distribution of the
Messines mines, June 1917, 'the most dramatic mining exploit of the war'.

Name of Mine	Date of Completion of Charging	Depth of Charge in feet	Charge in Lbs.	Crater Dimensions in Feet			Length of Gallery in Feet	Diagram of Mines
				Diameter at Ground Level	Width of Rim	Diameter of Complete Obliteration		
HILL 60								
A LEFT	1.8.16	90	{ 45,700 Am. 7,800 Gc. 53,500	191	47	285	Branch 240	
B CATERPILLAR	18.10.16	100	Ammonal 70,000	260	77	380	1,380	
ST. ELOI	28.5.17	125	Ammonal 95,600	176	77	330	1,340 300	
HOLLANDSCHESCHOUR								
No. 1	20.6.16	60	{ 30,000 Am. 4,200 Blas. 34,200	183	80	343	825	
No. 2	11.7.16	55	{ 12,500 Am. 2,400 Bla. 14,900	105	55	215	Branch 45	
No. 3	20.8.16	55	{ 15,000 Am. 2,500 Bla. 17,500	141	30	201	Branch 395	
PETIT BOIS								
No. 2 LEFT	15.8.16	57	{ 21,000 Am. 3,000 Bla. 30,000	217	100	417	Branch 210	
No. 1 RIGHT	30.7.16	70	{ 21,000 Am. 9,000 Bla. 30,000	175	100	375	2,070	
MAEDELSTEDE FM.	2.6.17	100	{ 90,000 Am. 4,000 Gc. 94,000	205	90	385	1,610	
PECKHAM	19.7.16	70	{ 65,000 Am. 15,000 Blas. 7,000 Gc, Dyn. 87,000	240	45	330	1,145	
SPANBROEKMOLEN	28.6.16 (Recovered 6.6.17)	88	Ammonal 91,000	250	90	430	1,710	
KRUISSTRAAT								
Nos. 1 AND 4	{ 5.7.16 { 11.4.17	57 57	{ Ammonal 30,000 { 18,500 Am. 1,000 Gc. 19,500	235	80	395	—	
No. 2	12.7.16	62	Ammonal 30,000	217	75	367	Branch 170	
No. 3	23.8.16	50	Ammonal 30,000	202	65	332	2,160	
ONTARIO FM.	6.6.17	104	Ammonal 60,000	200	10	220	1,290	
TRENCH 127								
No. 7 LEFT	20.4.16	75	Ammonal 36,000	182	25	232	Branch 250	
No. 8 RIGHT	9.5.16	76	Ammonal 50,000	210	65	342	1,355	
TRENCH 122								
No. 5 LEFT	14.5.16	60	Ammonal 20,000	195	64	323	Branch 440	
No. 6 RIGHT	11.6.16	75	Ammonal 40,000	228	64	356	970	

The Messines mines—particulars in brief.

'The total charge was just under one million pounds of high explosive.' The mine charges and effects.

260 feet wide at ground level, with a circle of complete obliteration 380 feet across, at Spanbroekmolen, a 250-foot crater, and the diameter of obliteration 430 feet, Kruisstraat Nos. 1 and 4 (a single mine), 235-foot crater, diameter of obliteration 395 feet, Trench 122 No. 6 Right, 228-foot crater, diameter of obliteration 356 feet, etc., etc. Some of the German trench garrisons disappeared utterly; others were horribly maimed. General Harington, inspecting the ridge next day, entered a concrete dug-out and found four German officers sitting at a table—'all dead—killed by shock. They might have been playing bridge. It was an uncanny sight—not a mark on any of them.'[7]

Simultaneously with the mine explosions came the deafening crash of the British barrage: 2,266 guns and howitzers suddenly bursting into fire, backed by the 'rasping rattle'[8] of 454 machine-guns. In addition, 428 heavy and medium trench mortars, firing 'torpedo-mines' which made craters 6 feet deep and 5 feet across, engaged the forward German machine-gun posts. The time taken by mine-débris to settle had been calculated, and also the time that infantry would take to cross various conditions of ground in various lights—hence the 3.10 zero hour. Behind the screen of the barrage, some 80,000 infantry advanced to the attack; within a few minutes they held the whole German front-line, by mid-afternoon they had taken all their objectives, and the entire ridge was in British hands. 7,354 prisoners and 48 guns were captured; British casualties in the assault amounted to about 10 per cent of the number anticipated (though they increased through errors in the subsequent fighting, which continued for a week). Ludendorff wrote:

'The 7th of June cost us dear, and owing to the success of the enemy attack the drain on our reserves was very heavy . . . it was many days before the front was again secure.'[9]

The underground variant of the offensive had been an unqualified and awesome success.

NOTES
1 *O.H. 1917*, i p. 546.
2 Ludendorff: *My War Memories*, i pp. 307–8.
3 *O.H. 1917*, ii p. 60 f.n.2.
4 General Sir Charles Harington: *Tim Harington Looks Back*, p. 60; John Murray, 1940.
5 Norman Gladden: *Ypres 1917*, p. 61.
6 German Official Account, xii p. 453, quoted in *O.H. 1917*, ii p. 54 f.n.
7 General Sir Charles Harington: *Plumer of Messines*, p. 104; John Murray, 1935.
8 Gladden, op. cit.
9 Ludendorff, op. cit. ii p. 429.

Variants of the Offensive: *Mechanical*

THE STORY OF THE DEVELOPMENT of Churchill's armoured mechanical 'caterpillars' (christened 'Tanks' for security), the rôles therein of Lord Hankey, Major-General Sir Ernest Swinton, and Churchill himself, and the strange outcome that this important new weapon of land warfare was first developed by the Admiralty, has been told often enough. Unfortunately, in the telling, a whole mythology about the capabilities and the handling of 1914–18 tanks has grown up, which I have tried to demolish elsewhere.[1] Here it is necessary only to dwell upon certain fundamental matters.

First, we must be quite clear what the purpose of tanks was; they were, in the words of General Swinton, to be bullet-proof machines

'capable of destroying machine guns, of crossing country and trenches, of breaking through entanglements, and of climbing earthworks.'[2]

In other words, they were trench-warfare weapons, intended to break the machine-gun/barbed wire combination which lay at the very heart of the deadlock, as described on p. 105. They bore about as much relation to the tanks of the Second World War as George Stephenson's 'Rocket' to the London & North-Eastern Railway's record-breaking 'Mallard' of 1938, or a 1908 Model 'T' Ford to a Jaguar. Any notion of a *'blitzkrieg'* being possible between 1914 and 1918 is completely off the mark.

Secondly—and this really is fundamental—in all consideration of First World War tanks, one has to bear time-scales constantly in mind. One has to reflect that the internal combustion engine itself was still in its infancy, that automobile output was, by modern standards, still pitifully small, and that what was now required for tank development was, in effect, an entirely new branch of technology. Against that background, the time factors are more intelligible:

1915	
26 March	Churchill's instruction, 'Proceed as proposed and with all despatch', authorizes commencement of design.
3 December	Churchill circulates 'Variants of the Offensive'.
25 December	Haig notes on above, 'Is anything known about the Caterpillar referred to in para 4, page 32?'
1916	
2 February	First trials of prototype 'Mother'.
11 February	GHQ (France) orders 40 tanks; Swinton increases order to 100.
12 February	Ministry of Munitions authorizes commencement of manufacture.
March	Swinton circulates 'Notes on the Employment of Tanks'

May	'Tank Detachment' rechristened 'Heavy Section, Machine-Gun Corps'.
13 August	First batch (6) leaves England.
15 September	49 tanks available for battle.

So we see that it had taken 18 months to produce 49 tanks at the front in France. Haig, who had been hoping for 150, was naturally disappointed, but there was no question of his not using what he had. This September battle was, as we have seen (p. 228) 'the only true simultaneous action of all the Allies in the whole war'; its object was, in fact, to end the war. For that purpose every available weapon was evidently required, and there could be no excuse for holding anything back. But these were Mark I tanks ('Big Willie'):

Length (with steering tail)	32 feet 6 inches
Width	13 ,, 9 ,,
Height	7 ,, 4½ ,,
Weight	28 tons
Engine	6-cyl. 105 h.p. Daimler
Armament (male)	2 6-pdr. guns, 4 Hotchkiss machine-guns
(female)	5 Vickers and 1 Hotchkiss machine-guns
Crew	1 officer, 7 other ranks.

'The tank début was equivocal.' A Mark I tank at Thiepval, 1916; the 6-pdr. gun in the sponson distinguishes it as a 'male'; the two-wheeled 'hydraulic stabiliser' is for steering, and it carries a wire-netting anti-grenade cover.

Their maximum speed was 3.7 m.p.h., but a trial on 6 September on ground cratered by confluent shell-holes (characteristic of most of the Somme battlefield) showed them capable of only 15 yards a minute, or half a mile per hour. A tank historian wrote:

'. . . the whole steering arrangement of the Mark I was extraordinarily clumsy and laborious. She would not turn sharply at all on rough ground, and had to be coaxed to any change of direction. Her engine and tracks also needed constant adjustment, the rollers being an everlasting source of trouble . . .'[3]

Of the 49 tanks which were present for action on 15 September, only 32 even reached their starting-points. Of the 32, nine advanced ahead of the infantry, and caused considerable losses to the Germans, nine others could not keep up with the infantry, but were useful in the important rôle of 'mopping-up', five were ditched, and nine broke down with mechanical troubles. Of these last two categories, many were knocked out by direct hits by German artillery while immobile.

The tank début was clearly equivocal. The tank men themselves were probably the least pleased:

'Half choked with the engine fumes, boxed up for many hours without respite in the intolerable clamour and shaking of their machines, or, worse, having wrestled for hours under heavy shelling with a broken-down Tank, they were inclined to see the exasperations of the battle rather than its successes.'[4]

With so few tanks actually participating, most of the infantry present were unaware of their existence; not many of the senior officers who did know about them were very favourably impressed. Haig, who had been 'looking forward to obtaining decisive results' from them a month before they went into action,[5] was an exception. On 19 September he sent his Deputy Chief of Staff, Major-General R. H. K. Butler, to convey a request for 1,000 tanks to the War Office.

He never possessed that number, for any battle. Once more the time-scales of the new field of technology came into play. For the Battle of Arras, nearly seven months after the Somme début, only 60 tanks were available, mostly 1916 machines which had been repaired. By 31 July, the opening of the Third Battle of Ypres, there were still only 136—less than the number Haig had requested in April 1916. Planned production for the first 9 months of 1917 was 1,460 tanks, of which 1,000 were to be the new, supposedly bullet-proof Mark IVs (Marks II and III never went into large-scale production). There were even to be a number of the even better Mark Vs. None of these actually appeared until March 1918, and of the promised Mark IVs only 378 were available for the Battle of Cambrai on 20 November 1917. As Churchill, who became Minister of Munitions in July, admitted:

'Broadly speaking, I consider a year has been lost in tank development.'[6]

That was, indeed, the crux of the matter. The Allied High Commands (chiefly the British, since they were first in the field with the new weapon) have been endlessly criticized for 'throwing away' their tanks in 'penny packets'. Thus Churchill complains that 'they were plunged in fours and fives as a mere minor adjunct of the infantry into the quagmires and crater-fields of Passchendaele.'[7] The truth is that it was on those very crater-fields that the tanks achieved their absolute vindication at a time when many doubted them: the action at St. Julien on 19 August. On that day 12 tanks of the 1st Brigade went into action against a difficult group of German pill-boxes; one tank was ditched on its approach, but the remaining 11, assisted by a dense smoke-bombardment by the artillery, triumphantly took all their objectives. Delightedly, Haig recorded:

'a satisfactory attack this morning—advances made with 11 Tanks on one mile of front. All objectives taken, 12 infantry casualties, and 14 men of Tanks hit. Without Tanks we would have lost 600!'[8]

The historian of the Tank Corps (formed on 27 July 1917) goes so far as to say:

'. . . it was in some measure to the Tanks which won the little Battle of St. Julien that the Tank Corps owed the opportunity of winning the Battle of Cambrai.'[9]

As long as only 'penny packets' were available, obviously, that was how the tanks would have to be used, if any infantry lives were to be saved, whether generals or 'experts' liked it or not. It is futile for Lloyd George to say:

'Sir Douglas Haig insisted on throwing a few specimen machines into the fight without waiting until a sufficient number had been manufactured to enable him to hurl a resistless mass of them against the enemy lines.'[10]

He would have had to wait until about 1943.

Meanwhile, obviously, there was a war to be attended to, and as soon as something larger than a 'penny packet' existed—i.e. as soon as anything at all resembling a 'mass' of tanks was available—it was duly used. The occasion was Cambrai (20 November 1917), for which, in addition to the 378 Mark IV 'fighting tanks' General Byng's Third Army also used supply tanks, gun-carriers, grapnel-tanks for destroying wire, bridging tanks, tanks carrying wireless equipment (they only carried this; they could not use it while in motion because of noise and vibration), and one telephone cable tank. This was a good deal more sophisticated than 1916 fashion—but then, 14 months had gone by since the début, 2 years and 8 months since Churchill had authorized design to begin! And it rapidly became evident that the long-awaited new Mark IV was not all that much in advance of the Mark I. It had better means of entrance and exit, better and safer means of observation and fire control (but still not good enough), detachable spuds on the tracks to give grip on wet ground, it could steer without tail-wheels, it had improved transmission, a silencer (of sorts) for the engine, unditching gear (very clumsy), and carried a considerably larger petrol supply. On the other hand, its new bullet-proof armour turned out to be no such thing against the German armour-piercing bullets; its main characteristics were virtually identical with the Mark I; it had the same engine, the same armament, the same crew, the same speed, it was unhandy to drive and control, and interior temperatures often rose to 120°. It was, in other words, no war-winner.

Nevertheless, at Cambrai it was a large factor in one of the great surprises of the war. It was in order to give the tanks their chance of achieving surprise that General Byng had refused to allow his artillery to register (see p. 217) and so pulled off the double *coup* of a sudden predicted bombardment and the simultaneous onset of a large number of tanks. Success naturally varied in degree according to local conditions, and according to the extent of co-operation between tanks and infantry—a matter regulated by the temperament and vision of corps and divisional commanders. No such action as this had ever been tried before; there was no tested drill; there were bound to be some mistakes. If understandable panic took hold of some German infantry units as the steel monsters rolled towards them through the murk of a misty November dawn, their machine gunners and their artillery displayed all their customary steadfastness. As the light improved, field guns picked off the tanks as they crossed sky-lines; at Flesquières 16 were hit one after another, it is generally believed by a single German gun served by one devoted officer who was at last killed at his gun.[11] Yet the overall picture, as the battle rolled forward over this 'clean', uncratered ground, was one of unmistakable triumph; the Official History sums up:

'The day was one of memorable achievement. On a front of over six miles an advance had been made varying from three miles to four. The two strong trench systems, covered by an outpost zone, which formed the Hindenburg Position had been carried in not much more than four hours, a rate of progress which was without precedent on the Western Front . . . It was a triumph for the new tactics which, combined with the secret and meticulous preparation made possible by admirable staff work and the whole-hearted cooperation of all ranks of all arms and services, had produced a surprise of a character well-nigh irresistible. The unregistered bombardment of the artillery had done all that was claimed for it. The tanks had enabled the assault to burst without warning through un-cut wire, to over-run trenches, and to crush well-sited strongpoints which linked up the whole powerful system of defence.'[12]

It is small wonder if some at the time, and many ever since, believed that a new era had dawned on 20 November.[13] Indeed, it had; but a long time would elapse between dawn and full sunrise—a matter of over 20 years. What the tanks had decisively done at Cambrai was to show their effectiveness for breaking *into* even a very elaborate and strong trench position. Breaking *through* was another matter. Breaking through would take more

'. . . effectiveness for breaking into a very strong position . . .': these tanks are passing captured German guns on their way to attack Bourlon Wood on the third day of the Battle of Cambrai.

than one day in any circumstances, so what basically counts in this and later tank actions is Day 2; 'fighting' tank losses on 20 November were 179 (65 by direct hits, 71 by mechanical troubles, 43 by ditching or other causes) while many more required repairs and adjustments. By 23 November, only 92 were available for action. German anti-tank tactics were improving all the time, and on this day 'B' Battalion lost 10 tanks out of 13 engaged, while 'C' Battalion lost 6 out of 11. On 27 November the Tank Corps was withdrawn from the battle.

It was not before it was time; the effectiveness of the new arm depended not merely on the numbers of machines available for battle, but on the condition of the crews, and after a week's fighting the crews were dead tired. Too many accounts of First World War tank actions fail to take into consideration the appalling strain on the men inside the machines. Referring to the 1916 début, one officer wrote:

'Of my company, one officer went mad and shot his engine to make it go faster; another shot himself because he thought he had failed to do as well as he ought; two others had what I suppose could be called a nervous breakdown.'[14]

Such effects were normal throughout the war. It is unlikely that the Cambrai Mark IVs actually heated to 120° in November, but in the following year conditions in improved models operating under the August sun were such that

'The crews of one battalion after some hard fighting became absolutely exhausted and most of them physically ill. The pulses of one crew were taken immediately they got out of their tank; the beats averaged 130 to the minute or just twice as fast as they should have been. Two men of one crew lost their reason and had to be restrained by force, and one tank commander became delirious. In some cases where infantry were carried in the tank, they fainted within three-quarters of an hour of the start.'[15]

No tanks of the First World War were war-winners in themselves. It is not generally recognized in Britain that France actually produced more tanks than the British. In 1916 the French High Command boldly ordered 400 heavy Schneider tanks straight off the drawing-board, and (rashly) followed that with another order for 400 Saint Chamond models, also heavies. In the fighting on the Aisne in April and May 1917 these both proved to be failures; their engines were under-powered, giving a maximum *road* speed of only 5 m.p.h.; they were very hot inside, ventilation was poor, as was observation; their tracks were too narrow for soft going; their vertical armour did not keep bullets out; they caught fire easily. The British Official History refers to a 'veritable holocaust among the tanks'[16] in the first attack on 16 April. General Spears describes their attempts to advance, 'turning this way and that in a moving fence of explosions.' One group, attempting to deploy in a morass of mud, was caught by German guns:

'Machine after machine, festooned with reserve petrol cans, caught fire, and in a few seconds they were red glowing masses of metal, incinerators of their roasted crews. The exits were too small in most instances for them to escape . . . Out of forty-eight machines engaged, thirty-two were destroyed.'[17]

Not surprisingly, the French changed their production policy after this experience, switching to the 7-ton, 2-man Renault M-17. Still under-

'The French changed their production policy.' These Canadian infantry are resting beside a French 7-ton Renault tank near Arras in 1918.

powered, this had a road speed of only 6 m.p.h., and it was also under-gunned. Far better was the British Medium A ('Whippet'), with its road speed of 8.3 m.p.h., its 4 Hotchkiss machine-guns and its crew of 3; designed for exploitation, it had few opportunities to display itself, yet it ended with some notable feats to its credit. However, only 200 of these were built, compared with a total of some 4,000 of the Renaults. Total British production of all types during the war was 2,818,[18] and if this compares poorly with the French figures, it certainly surpasses the German: 15 A7Vs and 1 A7V-U. Despite powerful engines and thick armour, the German tanks were a complete failure. On the other hand, their progress with anti-tank weapons and tactics was impressive. America produced 17 tanks, none used in battle.

It cannot be disputed that the most effective tank contribution to the war was British, and it is fitting that the last word here should come from the 'Weekly Tank Notes' produced at Tank Corps headquarters. The success of the initial tank onslaught at Cambrai (despite subsequent disappointments and losses in the German counter-offensive) made a great impression every-where, but at Tank Corps HQ its special significance was readily seen:

'*Cambrai had become the Valmy of a new epoch in warfare, the epoch of the mechanical engineer.*'[19]

With the submarine and the aeroplane, the tank perfectly illustrates the strides of technology during the war.

NOTES
1 See Terraine, *The Smoke and the Fire*, pp. 148–60; *To Win a War*, pp. 109–111, 115–17.
2 Major-General Sir Ernest Swinton: *Eyewitness*, p. 79; Hodder & Stoughton, 1932.
3 Major Clough Williams-Ellis, MC & A. Williams-Ellis: *The Tank Corps*, pp. 18–19; *Country Life*, 1919.
4 Ibid., p. 31.
5 Haig Diary, 11 August 1916; author's papers.
6 Quoted in *The Smoke and the Fire*, p. 152.
7 Churchill: *The World Crisis*, i p. 525.
8 Haig Diary, 19 August 1917; author's papers.
9 Williams-Ellis, op. cit. p. 93.
10 Lloyd George: *War Memoirs*, ii p, 1334; Odhams, 1936.
11 In his Cambrai Despatch (20 February 1918) Haig wrote: 'Many of the hits upon our tanks at Flesquières were obtained by a German artillery officer who, remaining alone at his battery, served a field gun single-handed until killed at his gun. The great bravery of this officer aroused the admiration of all ranks.'
[The Official History (compiled by Captain Wilfrid Miles, published 1948; p. 59, f.n.2) says that Haig's Despatch 'gave rise to the legend', and adds: 'It seems certain . . . that the losses suffered could never have been inflicted by one gun or even by one battery.' It quotes, however, a German account which refers to an under-officer named Kruger who 'served one gun single-handed, hitting a number of tanks in succession as they crossed his line of fire.' On the other hand, C. R. M. F. Cruttwell, in his *History of the Great War* (pp. 472–3) says 'Lieut. Muller of the *108th Regiment*, single-handed, scored several final hits.' To make the historian's cup run over, Mr. Robert Woollcombe, in a letter to the Royal United Services Institute Journal in December 1971, says that *Unter-Offizier* Kruger was not at Flesquières on 20 November; that according to German accounts the last gun of the *3rd Battery, 108th Regiment* (Field Artillery) was served by *Unter-Offiziers* Klofe and Greising and *Grefreiter* (Lance-Corporal) Ludwigs; and that a British sniper claimed to have found Greising's body under the breech-block of the gun.]
12 *O.H. 1917*, iii p. 88.
13 Such was the excitement in London that church bells were rung in jubilation on 21 November.
14 Quoted in *The Smoke and the Fire*, p. 149.
15 Quoted in *To Win a War*, p. 117.
16 *O.H. 1917*, i p. 495.
17 Spears: *Prelude to Victory*, p. 497.
18 This may be compared with the Second World War production figures, e.g.:

Matildas 3,000; Valentines 8,275; Churchills 5,640; Covenanters 1,771; Crusaders 5,300.

Of that great Allied 'work-horse' tank, the Sherman (M4), no fewer than 49,234 were produced.

19 Quoted in Williams-Ellis, op. cit. p. 117.

Variants of the Offensive: *Naval*

THE BATTLE OF JUTLAND is yet another of the episodes of the First World War which have attracted much controversy and many chroniclers. It is not surprising; 13 May 1916 saw the one and only clash of the great dreadnought fleets in history. For that reason alone, the occasion was remarkable: 259 iron-clad warships, carrying about 100,000 men,[1] approaching each other at closing speeds of over 35 knots in a spread of sea of over 400 square miles at the moment of contact. The destructive power implicit in this array was stupendous; even light cruisers were, by the standards of land warfare, formidable batteries; the dreadnoughts were reckoned as each equivalent to an army division. It was, as Churchill said,

'The supreme moment on which all the thought and efforts of the British and German Admiralties had been for many years concentrated . . .'[2]

And yet, in the event, it was an enormous anti-climax—as though in a Test Match full of star batsmen, none of them make many runs. The spectators go away feeling cheated, but in cricket consoling themselves with the thought that the next encounter may tell a different story. But after Jutland there was no 'next encounter'—nothing like it was ever seen again.

Once more, we do not need to follow the hourly progress of the battle. The 'matters arising', however, are not without interest; they admirably illustrate the perplexing stage of technologies which had made such immense progress in so short a time—but still not quite enough. The first casualty was Fisher's dream, the battle-cruisers: Jutland was their searching test, and proved their weakness. Out of nine British battle-cruisers present, no less than three were lost, all by terrible instantaneous explosions which destroyed them utterly in great pillars of smoke and flame. The first to go was *Indefatigable*, launched in 1909; she was hit simultaneously by three 11 inch shells from *Von der Tann* and blew up at once, with the loss of 57 officers and 960 petty officers and ratings. Just over 20 minutes later the same fate befell the faster, more powerful *Queen Mary* (launched 1912), the crack gunnery ship of Sir David Beatty's Battle-Cruiser Fleet; she disappeared in a column of smoke 800 feet high, marking the resting-place of 57 officers and 1,209 men. Some two hours later, *Invincible*, the first of the line (1907) and of Falkland Islands fame, now the flagship of Rear-Admiral Hon H. L. A. Hood (3rd Battle-Cruiser Squadron) went the same way; only 2 officers, 1 petty officer and 3 ratings survived of her whole ship's company. In tragic fashion Fisher's

'Were they fit to "stand the line of battle?"' The fate of the battle-cruiser *Queen Mary* at the Battle of Jutland, 31 May 1916.

brain-children answered the question, were they fit to 'stand the line of battle?' It is scarcely believable that 25 years later yet another battle-cruiser would come to the same end: HMS *Hood* in May 1941.

So one field of technology was found wanting; the dreadnoughts themselves, however, lived up to expectation. Both British and German battleships showed themselves capable of withstanding and dealing out tremendous punishment. Their weakness lay in their very quality: each was such a powerful and costly instrument of war that commanders-in-chief did not seem to dare to delegate responsibility for them. In both fleets, with the exception of the battle-cruiser forces (called Scouting Forces by the Germans) under Beatty and Vice-Admiral Franz von Hipper, initiative lay exclusively with the C-in-C. In the Royal Navy, according to Churchill, 'all initiative except in avoiding torpedo attack was denied to the leaders of squadrons and divisions'.[3] Correlli Barnett goes even further:

'*The British sea officer was an automaton who only came to life at the impulse of a superior.*'[4]

In the action on 31 May there seems to have been little to choose in this matter between the two sides; constantly it is Admiral Sir John Jellicoe who orders the movements of the Grand Fleet as though it were one enormous

'. . . the haunting spectacle of *Invincible* at Jutland.' Rear-Admiral Hood's flagship, the third British battle-cruiser to be sunk, with only 6 survivors clinging to the raft in middle distance.

squadron, and his opponent, Admiral Reinhard Scheer, who does the same with the High Seas Fleet. Certainly there is something awe-inspiring about the image of the 24 dreadnoughts of the Grand Fleet forming and manoeuvring as a continuous line of battle under Jellicoe's direction, or the 22 German capital ships going about together at Scheer's signal, with all their attendant light craft conforming. Yet in truth these fleets were, as Churchill says, too large 'to be minutely directed by the finger of a single man.'[5] With that said, one can only admire the firm, professional handling of their huge forces by the two commanding admirals.

Since the Battle of Jutland stands isolated in history, its very scale ruling out antecedents and the progress of technology equally ruling out successors, its contribution to the art of warfare is not to be found in tactics. These were, in any case, dominated by two factors: time and space. It has to be remembered that the first contact between the two fleets was not until afternoon (2.20pm), that action between the leading units (battle-cruisers) only began at 3.45, and action between the main fleets not until 6.30pm. Even on a May evening, close to Midsummer's Day, this meant that only very few daylight hours remained in which to complete defeat or victory. 31 May had started clear and bright, but as the afternoon wore on increasing mist reduced visibility; funnel smoke and gun smoke reduced it still further, and by 9 o'clock summer night was bringing its own darkness. All this profoundly

'The Imperial Navy degenerated in its harbours . . .': a panoramic view of the High Seas Fleet at its moorings in the Kiel Canal. After Jutland it never fought again.

affected the space factor. The first action between the battle-cruisers opened at 16,500 yards; the 5th Battle Squadron (four ships of the *Queen Elizabeth* class, with 15 inch guns) came into action at 4pm at 18,000 yards, and at 5.30 was engaging at ranges of 19,000–20,000 yards (over 11 miles). Evidently, at such distances, good visibility is of the highest importance, and plenty of daylight very desirable; neither was on offer. Tactics accordingly were bound to be somewhat 'hit or miss'.

They were, furthermore, deeply affected by technology. The speed and precision with which the German gun-crews engaged their targets aroused wonder and admiration; excellent optical equipment had much to do with this. Clearly, there was a fundamental design defect in the British battle-cruisers; their German counterparts endured very heavy punishment without blowing up (though their flagship, *Lützow*, sank on the way home). The quality of the ammunition of the British 13.5 inch guns, of which much had been expected, gave great concern. British ships were less heavily armoured than their German equivalents, which was also a design error, but, worse still, their plate steel was less resistant; similarly, the Germans were able to obtain better results with lower-calibre guns because their steel was superior and their method of manufacture more modern. When night fell, Admiral Jellicoe broke off the main fleet action; he had little option, since his fleet had no star-shell and its searchlights were inferior. As Correlli Barnett says:

'*It was thus mainly the Admiralty's research and development organisation, and the British steel, chemical and armaments industries that robbed Jellicoe of sunk German ships during his total of forty minutes' bombardment at Jutland, and therefore of the only trophies that world opinion recognized as proving victory.*'[6]

There was one respect, however, in which the British and German experience was similar, and equally disconcerting to both. In both navies the peril of the torpedo was taken as axiomatic; Jellicoe was haunted by the dread that this weapon might wipe out his numerical superiority in battleships in a few minutes, before they could fire a shot; Scheer, a leading expert on torpedoes, was very anxious that this should indeed occur. Sixteen U-boats had been sent out ahead of the High Seas Fleet, to ambush the Grand Fleet as it concentrated; in addition, in action, he hoped to benefit from the torpedo

tubes of his 9 light cruisers and his 63 destroyers. Similarly, the 23 light cruisers and 81 destroyers under Jellicoe and Beatty were expected to do significant damage. In the event, they all disappointed. The Grand Fleet passed the U-boats unharmed. The German destroyers failed to push home any attack, and though they fired many torpedoes they did not hit a single major British unit—their only victims were British destroyers. The British did push home, on several occasions, and suffered losses accordingly (eight destroyers sunk), but though they, too, fired off torpedoes in shoals, the damage they did was very small. At Jutland the torpedo, which had so dominated naval tactical thinking, was seen to be seriously over-rated.

Above all, however, what Jutland presents is a failure of communication, which itself displays technology at one of those moments when it dispenses blows and favours with equal hand. Perhaps the most interesting thing about Jutland occurred before the battle even began, thanks to the radio surveillance referred to on p. 129. The manner of it was this: acutely conscious of the need for the Imperial Navy to justify itself in the eyes of a nation bearing an ever-increasing burden of land warfare, and being naturally of an aggressive disposition, Admiral Scheer was determined to strike a damaging blow at the Royal Navy in May. As early as the 15th he had sent out his U-boats to their intercepting positions to cover a decoy raid on Sunderland; now he only awaited favourable weather for the squadron of five Zeppelins on which he intended to rely for protective reconnaissance. Day after day this was denied him, and the moment came closer when his submarines would have to return to base; he therefore fell back on an alternative manoeuvre, up the Norwegian coast, and on 30 May he gave orders for High Seas Fleet to sail. Modern science and technology made it possible for the British Admiralty to follow virtually all of this: the U-boat movement was immediately detected; by 22 May it was known that certainly eight and probably more were out—though their purpose was not clear. 30 May brought clarifications: during the morning British Naval Intelligence became aware that the High Seas Fleet was moving into sailing positions in the Jade roads. At noon Jellicoe was warned that the Germans might sail next morning, and he was told that 16 U-boats were out (the exact number). At 5pm the Admiralty became aware that an important signal had gone out to all sections of the High Seas Fleet. Without waiting for deciphering, the Admiralty ordered the Grand Fleet, based at distant Scapa Flow and Invergordon, and the Battle-Cruiser Fleet, based at Rosyth, to concentrate off the Aberdeen coast and be ready for eventualities. By 10.30 that night, all these forces were at sea. The Germans themselves did not sail until 2am the next morning.

So wireless telegraphy dealt out a significant advantage to the British—in wonderful contrast with the dearth of information which took Nelson from Toulon to Alexandria and then to Barbados in search of the French in 1805. Well might Churchill say:

'Without the cryptographers' department there would have been no Battle of Jutland.' [7]

But no sooner had the new technology presented this gift than it snatched away the benefits. The Official History tells us:

'On the eve of sailing, Admiral Scheer, in accordance with the usual practice, had transferred the call sign of his flagship to the naval centre at Wilhelmshaven, so that, although it was thought he had sailed that morning, our directional wireless up till noon could only indicate that the battle fleet was still in the Jade. Thus, Admiral Jellicoe, who was informed of this by the Admiralty, had no special reason to expect the chance of an action.' [8]

The emphasis is mine; it reveals a matter of deep significance—that in Intelligence work it is not enough to receive information; there must also be a thought-out system of using it. David Kahn, in his majestic work *'The Codebreakers'*,[9] confirms that the Admiralty's famous and highly-secret Room 40 (the deciphering centre) was familiar with Scheer's procedure, but he then says that Room 40, asked where Scheer's call sign DK was, 'simply replied, "In the Jade River", without mentioning the transfer.' In other words, Intelligence had been asked the wrong question. What the Operations Room and the Grand Fleet needed to know was not where the call sign was, but where the High Seas Fleet was. Raw information about the call sign, though correct, was useless without a gloss—and a reliable 'glossing system' had not yet been evolved (indeed, such a system did not come into existence until the Second World War, to deal with ULTRA material).

The result, on 31 May, was of course lamentable: at 12.35 the Admiralty informed Jellicoe that the Germans were still in the Jade. Naturally, when three hours later the two fleets made contact in the middle of the North Sea, 'This rather shook Jellicoe's faith in Admiralty intelligence.'[10] And this was not all. Somewhat later still, Jellicoe's flagship *Iron Duke* plotted the position of the German light cruiser *Regensburg*, as given by Admiralty reports; it proved to be practically the very same position as that of *Iron Duke* herself! Once again Jellicoe was severely jolted; what neither he nor the Admiralty could know was that that imp of malice, human error, had been at work:

'. . . that the Regensburg navigator had made an error of ten miles in his

reckoning and that the fault for the absurd result lay with the German officer and not with the cryptanalysts of Room 40.'[11]

All through the battle Jellicoe was plagued by lack of information; the very tight radio discipline of the Grand Fleet itself was partly responsible for this. Also responsible was the lack of initiative of British officers mentioned above—with one splendid exception, Commodore W. E. Goodenough, of the 2nd Light Cruiser Squadron, who made the passing of swift information to the C-in-C his main duty in the battle. A seaplane from the carrier *Engadine* made one report—but it was misleading. When night fell, however, Jellicoe could no longer depend primarily on his own fleet for information. With 'unbelievable alacrity' Room 40 penetrated Scheer's intentions to race home across Jellicoe's rear, and by 10.41 a summary of intercepts was received aboard *Iron Duke*. Unfortunately, this Admiralty Intelligence contradicted such reports as Jellicoe already had from the fleet, and it omitted a call for air reconnaissance off the Jutland coast which would have made Scheer's intended movements obvious; Jellicoe, his faith in the new methods of Admiralty Intelligence by now very weak, ignored this message—and Scheer duly made his escape.

Escape it was. The tally of ships sunk[12] and casualties on 31 May favoured the Germans, but strategically there was no doubt about the result of this battle. The Grand Fleet was ready for action again by 2 June, the High Seas Fleet not until mid-August. The sinkings, in other words, were only part of the picture; stronger construction and better armour saved some German vessels from otherwise certain doom—but this did not save them from extensive damage. On 19 August the High Seas Fleet made another sortie—and ran for home as soon as Zeppelins reported (erroneously) the presence of the Grand Fleet. Its next and last sortie was in April 1918, and equally abortive. Thereafter the Imperial Navy degenerated in its harbours until the whole misconceived creation collapsed in mutiny in November.

So Jutland stands in the history of the war as a thing apart—indeed, it has been said that 'Its value as a battle was in every sense negligible'.[13] Its long-term significance was quite otherwise; for Britain, says Correlli Barnett, there was

'nothing accidental, nothing of bad luck, nothing of blame on individual officers in what happened at Jutland . . . It was part of a vast process of dissolution that began about 1870, when the British forgot that life is a continued response . . . that nothing is permanent but what is dead . . . In distant retrospect, Jutland was one of the critical battles of history; it marked the opening of that final phase of British world power and maritime supremacy that was to end in 1945 . . .'[14]

Not quite the opening; the opening was Gallipoli (see p. 177)—but Jutland certainly underlined the message.

NOTES

1   John Costello and Terry Hughes: *Jutland 1916*, p. 224 (Weidenfeld & Nicolson, 1976) say that the Grand Fleet totalled 60,000; calculations give the High Seas Fleet 40–45,000.
2   Churchill: *The World Crisis*, ii p. 1033.
3   Ibid., p. 1034.
4   Correlli Barnett: *The Swordbearers*, p. 184; Eyre & Spottiswoode, 1963.
5   Churchill, op. cit. p. 1035.
6   Barnett, op. cit. p. 189.
7   Churchill, op. cit. p. 1020.
8   *O.H. (Naval Operations)*, iii p. 326.
9   Weidenfeld & Nicolson, 1974; pp. 272–3.
10 Kahn, op. cit.
11 Ibid.

12

TYPE	BRITISH	GERMAN
Battleship	—	*Pommern* (pre-dreadnought)
Battle-cruiser	*Indefatigable* *Invincible* *Queen Mary*	—
Cruisers	*Black Prince* *Defence* *Warrior*	none present
Light cruisers	—	*Elbing* *Frauenlob* *Rostock* *Wiesbaden*
Destroyers	*Ardent* *Fortune* *Nestor* *Nomad* *Shark* *Sparrowhawk* *Tipperary* *Turbulent*	*S-35* *V-4* *V-27* *V-29* *V-48*

In the Grand Fleet, 6,097 officers and men were killed, 510 wounded, and 177 taken prisoner from the water; in the High Seas Fleet, 2,551 were killed and 507 wounded.

13 Liddell Hart: *History of the First World War*, p. 378.
14 Barnett, op. cit. pp. 193–4.

Variants of the Offensive: *Underwater*

TWO WEAPONS FAILED SCHEER COMPLETELY on 31 May: the Zeppelins, which in theory should have been able to discover both Beatty's force and the Grand Fleet and the wide gap between them, but in practice played no part at all; and the U-boats, which never even fired a shot at the Grand Fleet. Zeppelins were, indeed, a fading force by mid-1916, but U-boats were about to come into their own.

The signs of what was to come were soon apparent; in the month of September, gross sinkings of Allied shipping took a dramatic leap from some 205,000 tons (August) to about 315,000 tons; British losses alone rose from 43,354 tons in August to 104,572 in September.[1] In the last four months of the year, a global figure of some 1,120,000 tons was destroyed by U-boat action (632,000 tons British)—and this was still 'restricted' warfare, conducted under constraints which the U-boat enthusiasts found intolerable. Hitherto, they had been restrained chiefly by two considerations: first, that Germany counted on the Army to win the war, and therefore accorded it all priorities, and secondly, fear of making America an active enemy. The new High Command, appointed in August, took, as we have seen (p. 231), a gloomy view of the 1916 situation, and its sense of impending defeat is nowhere more evident that in its acceptance of the leading rôle of another Service than the Army in Germany's effort for 1917. Hindenburg and Ludendorff listened with more than sympathy to the complaints and claims of the U-boat lobby. The cautious Chancellor, Bethmann-Hollweg, himself swung towards an all-out submarine campaign. At a conference at Supreme Headquarters on 9 January 1917, Bethmann-Hollweg said:

'. . . *The decision to embark on the unrestricted U-boat campaign is . . . dependent upon the results we expect from it. Admiral von Holtzendorff*[2] *offers us the prospect that we shall have England at our mercy by the next harvest. The experiences of the U-boats in recent months, the increased number of boats, the bad economic situation of England, certainly form a reinforcement for luck. Taking it all round the prospects of the unrestricted submarine campaign are very favourable . . . if the military authorities regard the U-boat campaign as necessary I am not in a position to oppose them.'*[3]

Field-Marshal von Hindenburg at once insisted:

'*We need the most energetic and ruthless action possible. Therefore the U-boat war must begin not later than February 1, 1917.*'

Ludendorff stated that the U-boat war would 'improve the situation even of our armies . . . We must spare the troops a second Somme battle.' The Kaiser supported the High Command, and Bethmann-Hollweg himself pronounced:

'*Yes, we must act if victory beckons.*'[4]

The Kaiser signed the formal order on 31 January, and the campaign began officially on 1 February.

The pith and essence of the new campaign is expressed in a phrase of the German manifesto:

'. . . *sea traffic will be stopped with every available weapon and without further notice . . .*'[5]

Germany was at once denounced in forthright terms not only in Britain, but in the neutral countries whose seaborne trade was now threatened with extinction. The vehemence was born of deep alarm. Already, on 29 October, before the unrestricted campaign even began, Admiral Jellicoe, shortly to be appointed First Sea Lord, minuted:

'*There appears to be serious danger that our losses in merchant ships . . . may by the early summer of 1917 have such a serious effect . . . as to force us into accepting peace terms . . .*'[6]

The First Lord, Mr. A. J. Balfour, told Colonel Repington: 'The submarine influenced everything.'[7] And it was into this already highly dangerous situation that the unrestricted campaign was now launched, by a fleet of 111 U-boats whose captains were told that its object was:

'*to force England to make peace and thereby to decide the whole war.* Energetic *action is required, but above all* rapidity *of action . . . the sole aim is that each boat should fire her entire outfit of ammunition as often as possible . . . Short cruises, short visits to the dockyard, considerable curtailment of (routine) practices . . . During periods of overhaul only what is absolutely necessary to be done.*'[8]

The results were dramatic and terrifying; the statistics of sinkings in the months February to June tell the story with all necessary eloquence:

February	464,599 gross tons		
March	507,001 ,,	,,	(total: 971,600)
April	834,549 ,,	,,	
May	549,987 ,,	,,	
June	631,895 ,,	,,	(total: 2,988,031)[9]

As early as 11 February, Lord Derby (Secretary of State for War) quoted to Haig Repington's acid question 'whether our armies could win the war before our navies lost it', adding that the naval authorities were 'really at their wits' end as to how to deal with these submarines'.[10] On 18 April he went further:

'. . . *we have lost command of the sea.*'[11]

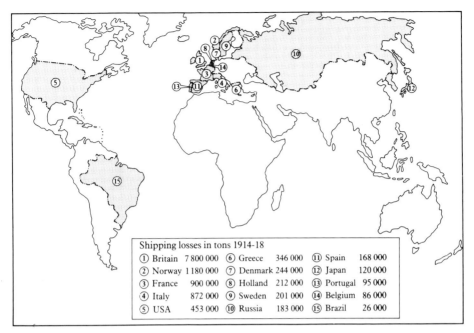

Shipping losses in tons 1914-18

① Britain	7 800 000	⑥ Greece	346 000	⑪ Spain	168 000
② Norway	1 180 000	⑦ Denmark	244 000	⑫ Japan	120 000
③ France	900 000	⑧ Holland	212 000	⑬ Portugal	95 000
④ Italy	872 000	⑨ Sweden	201 000	⑭ Belgium	86 000
⑤ USA	453 000	⑩ Russia	183 000	⑮ Brazil	26 000

'"The submarine influenced everything"': cumulative sinkings in both U-boat campaigns.

This was just about the truth, and to those who knew—the public, of course, was carefully kept in ignorance—the shock was profound. In the Second World War even more terrible losses were sustained,[12] but nothing is ever so frightening as the first experience of disaster. Furthermore, in the Second World War there was a store of knowledge and experience of anti-submarine measures on which to draw immediately—the knowledge hard-won in 1915 and 1917. For Government, Admiralty, and the sailors, both Navy and Merchant Marine, 1917 was a desperate year; merchant captains could hardly fail to know, when they set sail, that one in every four ships would not reach port. Nor, for a long time, did it seem that the Navy, for all its efforts, could do much to improve this situation.

Much nonsense has been talked about the anti-U-boat campaign of 1917, a great deal of it connected with the question of convoys. As the dreadful figures of sinkings rose to their April peak, there were many whose minds turned to the standard practice of Nelson's day, when British prosperity depended so much on the arrival of the East and West Indies convoys, and their safety was regarded as a prime objective of the Royal Navy. Now it was a question, not of the nation's prosperity, but of its very survival. Neutral traffic in British ports had dropped by 75 per cent; only six weeks' supply of corn remained in the country. Jellicoe told the American Admiral W. S. Sims on 9 April that unless the rate of sinking dropped Germany would win the war:

'"Is there no solution for the problem?" I asked.

"Absolutely none that we can see now," Jellicoe announced.'[13]

Yet Admiralty opinion remained firmly opposed to the convoy system. So serious was the situation that the Prime Minister, Mr. Lloyd George, told his colleagues that he intended to go to the Admiralty in person and insist on convoys; Lord Beaverbrook tells us:

'On 30th April, with the submarine peril at its height, the Prime Minister descended upon the Admiralty and seated himself in the First Lord's chair. This was possibly an unprecedented action . . . The meeting was a minor triumph for the Prime Minister . . . Lloyd George had staged a deliberate encounter with the Naval High Command, and had emerged triumphant.'[14]

It was not quite like that. Jellicoe, immediately after his appointment as First Sea Lord (29 November 1916), had appointed Rear-Admiral A. L. Duff Director of a new Anti-Submarine Division of the Naval Staff. Together they had pressed forward several important measures, and Duff was investigating the practicability of convoys. The arguments against these were strong. Naval officers doubted the ability of merchant ships (especially neutrals) to keep stations in convoy, above all at night—a reasonable doubt in both world wars; they pointed out that the speed of a convoy would be that of its slowest ship, which would make the convoy vulnerable and delay arrival of essential supplies; they believed that collecting a large number of ships together would provide the U-boats with perfect targets; they feared congestion in the ports with the arrival of numbers of ships all at once; above all, they believed that it was quite simply impossible to provide escorts for the number of ships that would require them. This last belief was based on two fallacies: first, that the escort should be twice as numerous as the convoy—which was absurd; secondly, a sad case of becoming the victim of one's own propaganda. Lloyd George tells us:

'For some time past the Admiralty had by order of the Government been in the habit of publishing week by week the number of vessels lost by submarine attacks. And in order to make this dismal news sound as helpful as possible, they had issued with it a return supplied by the Customs Authorities of the number of vessels that had entered and left British ports during the week. To swell this number, every entry and exit was counted, including the numerous going and comings of coastwise small craft of the smallest dimensions, passing from harbour to harbour on the coast, so that it reached a figure of about 2,500 weekly entrances and as many clearances.'[15]

No wonder the Admiralty was discouraged! Fortunately, a junior officer,

---

'. . . more vulnerable to air observation . . .': a naval airship escorting an inshore convoy. By 1918 the Navy had 103 airships in use.

Commander R. G. Henderson, decided to analyse the weekly return, and discovered that the number of ocean-going ships (i.e. ships vital for survival) included in it was no more than between 120 to 140 per week. This demolished the most powerful anti-convoy argument.

Meanwhile, there were other movements. Admiral Duff noted the startling contrast between the losses of general shipping and those of the coal trade with France, which operated by what were called 'controlled sailings'—actually, convoy with an escort of armed trawlers. Of 1,200 ships thus convoyed in March, only three were lost. The April performance was equally encouraging. By the 26th, Duff had been won over; he minuted to the First Sea Lord:

'It is to me evident that the time has arrived when we must be ready to introduce a comprehensive scheme of convoy at any moment.'[16]

Jellicoe concurred, and gave his approval next day—three days before Lloyd George's 'descent' upon the Admiralty. Small wonder that Lord Hankey describes his 'triumphant encounter' in somewhat quieter terms:

'This morning Lloyd George and I went to the Admiralty and spent the whole day there very pleasantly, lunching with Jellicoe and his wife and four little girls—Lloyd George having a great flirtation with a little girl of three.'[17]

So convoys were introduced belatedly, and sinking figures never again reached the dreadful height of April 1917. There is a tendency to write about the remainder of the U-boat war as though a magic wand had been waved (and by whom better than the 'Welsh Wizard', Lloyd George?). Even so normally shrewd and penetrating a historian as Cyril Falls says 'the introduction of convoy acted like a spell'.[18] Statistics do not bear out such beliefs. Thanks to the very heavy losses of April and May, the second quarter of 1917 was the worst: 2,016,431 tons. The third quarter was much lower: 1,298,033 tons, and the fourth lower still: 1,041,751. But the first quarter of 1918 showed a rise again: 1,143,336. It was not, in fact, until April 1918 that merchant ship construction exceeded the lost tonnage, and not until May (when 14 U-boats were sunk, and the heavy toll of loss in the Mediterranean was halved) that the Allies could really say the situation was under control.

The factors contributing to this were definitely plural. Convoys were clearly most important, but it is necessary to understand why. Most of the doubts expressed about them were justified, but the problems were overcome by patience, experience, and good organization. One, however, was not justified: the fear of the extra vulnerability of a large group of ships. As Churchill says:

'The size of the sea is so vast that the difference in size of a convoy and the size of a single ship shrinks in comparison almost to insignificance. There was in fact very nearly as good a chance of a convoy of forty ships in close order slipping unper-

'. . . never enough, nor enough projectors . . .': depth charges claimed 31 of the 175 U-boats sunk by the Royal Navy in the course of the war.

ceived between the patrolling U-boats as there was for a single ship; and each time this happened, forty ships escaped instead of one. Here then was the key to the success of the convoy system against U-boats.'[19]

Unable to locate their targets in the expanses of the ocean, the U-boats increasingly worked inshore. Here, though the convoys had less room for manoeuvre, the U-boats were more vulnerable to air observation and a higher density of patrol craft. Not all captains cared to press home attacks in these conditions.

From beginning to end the Admiralty had advocated an offensive response to the U-boat threat, and this it maintained even when the defensive expedient of convoy was adopted. By the end of the war, Germany had employed 372 U-boats, of which 192 were lost; 515 officers and 4,894 ratings were killed—more than 50 per cent of the total who served. The Royal Navy (including the RNAS) accounted for 175 of the losses, and it is possible to break down the methods by which it achieved its 'kills'.[20] Mines were responsible for destroying 42 U-boats; British mines were for a long time notoriously ineffective, and it was not until 1917 that this defect of naval technology was corrected. Mine nets sank another seven, but these were not a success; even the new explosive nets, fitted with electrically or contact-fired mines, did not seriously deter the Germans. Depth charges (originally thought of as 'dropping mines') did better, with 31 victims; an effective type only appeared in June 1916, 1,000 were ordered in August, and general distribution to the anti-submarine forces began in November. There were never enough, nor were there enough projectors; against the strong hulls of the U-boats, only very near detonations were effective. Gunfire accounted for 30 U-boats—merchant ships were armed in 1915, but naval gunfire was chiefly responsible for this total. In it note should be taken of the 11 kills attributed to the 'Q-ships'—merchantmen with concealed guns and torpedo tubes, manned by naval personnel, and acting as decoys. 19 U-boats were rammed; 17 were torpedoed—possibly all by British submarines, whose score was precisely 17. The idea that 'submarine does not fight submarine' was soon disproved. But British torpedoes, like mines, were a constant disappointment often not running true, often failing to explode—another fault of technology. Aircraft are credited with seven kills, but it is not always clear how they achieved these results. However, their use as spotters was of steadily increasing value, and they were sufficiently feared by the U-boat captains for air-search periscopes to be installed.

By 1918 there were 2,949 flying boats, seaplanes, and aeroplanes and 103 airships in naval use. Patrol vessels and escorts were (slowly) equipped with hydrophones, but these were at first non-directional, and could only be used by a ship which was not moving. The improved 'fish' hydrophones, which could be used in motion, did not appear until the summer of 1917. With simultaneous constant new developments taking place in surface and air warfare, it will be seen that naval technology was fully stretched.

The unrestricted U-boat campaign failed—in that it did not bring Britain to her knees, as intended. Why did it fail? Clearly, there was no single cause, but a combination: convoys, plus British offensive anti-submarine methods, weariness and deterioration of quality in the U-boat crews as the campaign lengthened and losses mounted—and a certain weakening of resolve in Germany. It was a serious error on the part of the Germans to set a date for the success of the campaign, generally taken to be six months, which should have meant definite signs of British collapse by July. When this failed to occur, there was disillusionment. A German historian, himself an old U-boat commander, later wrote that the declaration of unrestricted warfare 'carried with it a time bomb'—a bomb which was effective because it did *not* explode.[21] By mid-1917 German home morale was at a very low ebb,[22] and though the U-boat crews were entirely loyal there were symptoms of mutiny in the High Seas Fleet. Loyalty—and undoubted courage—were not enough, however; by this time over 150 U-boats had been lost, generally with their entire crews, and the new crews were not of the same quality. Above all, as Admiral von Tirpitz said, 'a mere work of destruction (wolves amongst a flock of sheep) had become a war operation involving great danger and loss.'[23]

'The U-boats had very nearly won the war.' Altogether, Germany produced 344; here we see part of a flotilla in harbour, photographed in 1912.

Despite its failure, however, the U-boat campaign was a terrible portent. The U-boats had, indeed, very nearly won the war. The 344 built during the war were mostly modifications and improvements upon the *U-30* class ordered in 1912 and coming into production in 1914, but ominous advances had been made by 1918. Chief of these was the class of U-cruisers, with some 2,000 tons surface displacement, comfortable crew quarters for long cruises, two 150 mm. guns, 4 torpedo tubes, and a surface speed of 18 knots. In these we perceive the clear harbingers of the Battle of the Atlantic in 1940–45; an attempt at 'wolf-pack' tactics in 1918 failed, lacking the necessary communications equipment, but pointed the same way. On the British side the R-boats designed in 1917, of which three were completed late in 1918, with a high underwater speed specifically for the purpose of attacking U-boats, 'were forebears of the hunter-killer atomic-powered submarines of today'.[24] On the debit side of the new weapon, it is a remarkable fact that not a single dreadnought was sunk by a submarine—yet dreadnought tactics, as we have seen, were deeply influenced by them. It is difficult indeed to dispute the verdict of the American Ambassador in London, Walter Page in July 1917:

'The submarine is the most formidable thing the war has produced.'[25]

NOTES

1 British figures are from a table in Lloyd George, *War Memoirs*, i p. 709; gross figures are from a chart in Churchill, *The World Crisis*, ii pp. 1246–7.
2 Chief of the Naval Staff.
3 The verbatim record of this meeting is quoted in Churchill, op. cit. pp. 1116–7.
4 Ibid.
5 Quoted in Lloyd George, op. cit. p. 683.
6 Quoted in Jameson, *The Most Formidable Thing*, p. 202.
7 Repington: *The First World War*, i p. 395.
8 Jameson, op. cit. p. 223.
9 Figures are from Jameson, op. cit.
10 Quoted in Terraine, *The Road to Passchendaele*, p. 38.
11 Derby to Haig, author's papers.
12 For 1942 sinkings see Churchill: *The Second World War*, iv p. 860.
13 The United States declared war on Germany on 6 April; the unrestricted U-boat campaign undoubtedly precipitated this event. Admiral Sims subsequently commanded the American naval forces in European waters.
14 Lord Beaverbrook: *Men and Power 1917–1918*, pp. 155–6; Hutchinson, 1956.
15 Lloyd George, op. cit. p. 682.
16 Jameson, op. cit. p. 219.
17 Hankey: *The Supreme Command 1914–1918*, ii p. 650.
18 Falls: *The First World War*, p. 273.
19 Churchill, op. cit. p. 1234.
20 See Churchill, *The World Crisis*, ii p. 1232 for a table showing the principal weapons of destruction, totalling 180 U-boats. According to Churchill, 199 were destroyed, but Jameson with later authority says 192. The 12 unaccounted for must be presumed lost by causes other than those listed by Churchill.
21 Jameson, op. cit. p. 228.
22 See Terraine, *The Road to Passchendaele*, pp. 190–2.
23 Jameson, op. cit. p. 233.
24 Ibid., p. 260.
25 Ibid., p. 227.

Variants of the Offensive: *Air*

1917 WAS A GRIM YEAR for all combatants; for the British, certainly, it was the year in which they really became acquainted with total war. While they were still digesting the heavy casualties of the Somme, the costly Arras battles began; the U-boats were striking at their very lifelines; and soon a new terror came to afflict them. In the late afternoon of 25 May, a Friday, with housewives crowding the shopping areas in preparation for the Whitsun weekend, 21 large German bombing aeroplanes appeared over Folkestone; they dropped most of their bombs on Tontine Street, crowded with shoppers, and in the space of some ten minutes killed 95 people and injured 195. It was the first of the 'Gotha raids' which, during the next twelve months, brought yet another new dimension to war: 'strategic bombing' had arrived.

'The Gotha was not a pretty aircraft.' Here we see the disproportionately long fuselage well displayed. Yet it was '"the most successful German bomber of the war"'.

Needless to say, this novelty, too, was the result of a further stride in technology: the development of the 'G-type' aircraft known as 'Gothas', after the name of their parent-company, *Gothaer-Wagonfabrik*, whose peace-time product was principally railway carriages. The first flights of 'G-types' took place in 1915, but the early models were undistinguished in performance; it was the G-IV which brought death and destruction to Folkestone in May 1917, and (with the G-V) great alarm to London, Essex, and south-eastern England for the next year. The Gotha IV was not a pretty aircraft; the length of its fuselage seems disproportionate—40 feet $6\frac{1}{4}$ inches; the span of its upper wing, 77 feet $9\frac{1}{4}$ inches, was remarkable for its time and actually exceeded that of any German aircraft sent against England in the Second World War. Powered by two 260 h.p. Mercedes engines, its speed, only 87 m.p.h., seems to us ludicrously low; but its three machine-guns, one firing through a tunnel in the fuselage towards the notorious 'blind spot' under the tail, made it an awkward enemy to attack. Its real menace, however, lay in its 500 kilogramme (1,102 lb.) bomb-load and its 3-foot long Goerz bomb-sight; it was this that made it 'the most successful German bomber of the war.'[1]

Delivery of the Gotha IVs began in March, and they were organized in a new squadron, *Kampfgeschwader* (*Kagohl*) *3*, known as the 'England Squadron'. Administratively part of the German *Fourth Army* in Flanders *Kagohl 3* took its orders direct from the High Command (*OHL*). It consisted (eventually) of six flights of six aircraft, using five airfields around Ghent—a total of some 40 Gothas, a strategic weapon whose effects were out of all proportion to its size. Between 25 May (Folkestone) and 25 September the Gothas attacked England twelve times, of which five were raids on London. Of the 21 Folkestone raiders, one was lost in the Channel, possibly due to damage inflicted by the RNAS squadron at Dunkirk, and another crashed inland for no apparent reason—it was suggested that the pilot may have had a heart attack. The next raid was carried out by 22 Gothas against Sheerness and Shoeburyness on 5 June; casualties were few, 13 killed, 34 injured—and this time one Gotha was definitely brought down by the defences, in this case anti-aircraft gunfire. But the raid that followed a week later, on London and Margate on 13 June, shattered British complacency.

Twenty Gothas took off that morning, but three had to turn back with engine trouble. Three more lost the formation before it reached London, but at half past eleven 14 aircraft were seen in diamond formation coming up the Thames towards Tower Bridge and St. Paul's Cathedral. A few bombs were dropped in the dock area, but *Kagohl 3*'s target was central London, and as it approached people gazed in astonishment. A *New York Times* correspondent wrote:

'It was amazing because it was so beautiful. It was not easy to believe that those little silver specks far up in the heaven had the power to bring death and destruction and unendurable suffering . . . I saw no quick searching for shelter, no taking cover. If it had been an exhibition of flying at Hendon, the attitude of the people would not have been very different, except in the immediately affected streets . . .'[2]

Bombs began to fall at 11.40, 72 of them within a mile of Liverpool Street Station; the raiders then split into two groups, and one of these, passing over Poplar, dropped a bomb on a school, killing 16 children and injuring 30 in an infant class. This was, in fact, from the point of view of casualties, the worst raid of the war: 162 killed and 432 injured. And not a single Gotha was lost by any cause; a defending Bristol Fighter was forced down with its observer-gunner dead in the rear cockpit.

London's first aeroplane raid showed what might be in store. There was great consternation; an alarmed Government demanded that two squadrons of modern fighters should be sent back from France to strengthen Air Defence, and Major-General Trenchard, commanding the RFC, was consulted on countermeasures. He said that the most effective step of all would be to capture the Belgian coast (linked to the great, but misplaced, alarm caused by the Flanders U-boat flotillas, this idea had baleful effects on the land campaign later in the year); he urged attacks on the German aerodromes—an obviously promising move, and pregnantly concluded:

'Reprisals on open towns are repugnant to British ideas but we may be forced to adopt them. It would be worse than useless to do so, however, unless we are determined that once adopted they will be carried through to the end . . .'

And he warned:

*'At present we are not prepared to carry out reprisals effectively, being unprovided
with suitable machines.'* [3]

The Gothas did not return to England until 4 July, when 18 attacked the East
Coast, killing 17 and injuring 30 without loss to themselves. Three days later
they made their second attack on London. Twenty-two raiders reached the
capital, and succeeded in doing over £200,000 worth of material damage.
Casualties, however, were far fewer than on the previous occasion—57
killed, 193 injured. One Gotha was shot down on 7 July, but more
significantly (though the British could not know this) four crashed on
landing. This raid, in other words, had cost the Germans nearly 25 per cent
of the attacking force, and inflicted less than 50 per cent of the casualties of 13
June. Yet the outcry in London on this occasion was deafening. The Press
dwelt on the humiliation of the raiders' apparent impunity—their slow speed
made it look as though they were gloatingly standing still above their target.
The failure of both air and ground defence (2 British fighters were shot
down) infuriated people and politicians alike; angry crowds marched
through the streets, smashing and looting 'German' property—and the
demand for reprisals naturally swelled. The historian F. S. Oliver pertinently wrote to *The Times* pointing out that attempts at reprisals across some
200 miles of German-held territory (as opposed to flights across the open sea
which brought the Germans within 40 miles of London) would probably
cause a heavy loss of pilots and machines which could only help Germany.
Privately, he admitted however,

*'there is no getting away from the fact that we ought to defend London better than
we are doing, for the moral reason that attacks upon the capital city are in the
nature of humiliations which must affect public opinion at home and abroad; also
for the practical reason that London is in a sense our base, not so much in a material
sense but because all the threads of organization are concentrated here. Still, it
seemed to me that the important thing for the moment was to stop the squealing.'* [4]

The squealing was not easily stopped; on 9 July the Chief of Imperial General
Staff told Haig, 'one would have thought the world was coming to an end.' [5]
The Prime Minister was so concerned that he set up a 'Committee on Air
Organization and Home Defence' under the South African, General Jan
Smuts. This step was to have far-reaching results:

*'More than any other single event, it led to the creation of the Royal Air Force in
1918.'* [6]

As so often, this dark hour did, in fact, mark one of the stages of the
campaign, if not a turning-point, at least a partial defeat for the Germans. A
raid on 22 July by 21 Gothas on the East Coast caused little damage and only

39 casualties; one Gotha crashed on landing. A raid on Southend, Shoebury-ness, and Margate on 12 August caused 68 casualties, but cost one Gotha shot down and four crashed on landing out of 11 which actually reached England. Then came a major disaster, on 18 August, when 28 Gothas—the largest number so far—took off; almost at once they ran into strong winds which blew them off course; none reached England, and about 10 were lost. Four days later 15 set out, 10 arrived over East Kent; they inflicted 39 casualties and three were shot down. It was the last of the daylight raids.

History is full of drama, and it would be dramatically satisfactory to record that the change in German policy was due to a defeat as clear as that which they suffered in 1940. However, that would not be tenable; rather the change has to be attributed to a sense of mounting resistance beyond the strength of *Kagohl 3*, and a desire to avoid the consequences of this. In the whole period, May–August, German losses in raids on Britain were only 6 Gothas shot down, and 11 crashed. However, British defences, virtually inert at first, had certainly been galvanised into mounting efficiency. A new command struc-ture was brought into being with the setting up of the London Air Defence Area under a single commander, Brigadier-General E. B. Ashmore, an officer with considerable flying experience. Under him the activities of fighters and anti-aircraft gunners were coordinated to produce at least dis-ruptive and at best deterrent effects. A serious problem for Ashmore was that, under the pressure of the U-boat campaign and the need to arm more merchant ships, guns were in very short supply. Nor, of course, were they anything like as effective as the AA guns of the Second World War. Aircraft, on the other hand, became actually plentiful in relation to the number of Gothas: on 12 August the British had 133 planes in the air, to deal with 11 Gothas over England, and on 22 August there were 120 British aircraft over London awaiting attack by no more than 10 Gothas.

Descriptions of scrambling techniques at the fighter airfields when the approach of raiders was signalled read very much like 1940 Battle of Britain narratives. But there were profound differences: first, there was no radar by which the course of the Gothas could be plotted; secondly, the fighters of 1917 took much longer to reach effective operational heights; thirdly, and perhaps most important of all, once airborne the pilots had no aids in finding the enemy. Air to air and ground to air radio communication still awaited a further advance in communications technology. The fighter pilot and his observer thus found themselves alone and facing a problem not unlike that of the U-boat captain trying to find a convoy in the Atlantic distances—except that looking for something so minute as aeroplanes in the immeasurable cubic space of the sky was even more daunting. However, the defenders persevered, and their increasing numbers at least must have been disturbing for the German aircrews. Better sound-locating equipment helped the gun-ners, and on 22 August we read of a 'devastating barrage over the Isle of Thanet'[7]—devastating not in terms of absolute destruction but of filling an air-space with explosions and flying fragments. This now became standard procedure. When the night raids began, a new technique of cooperation

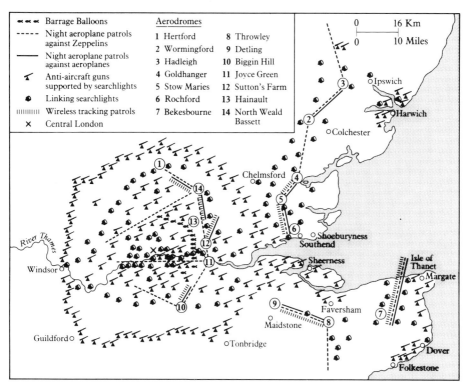

	Aerodromes	
◄ ◄ ◄ Barrage Balloons		
- - - - Night aeroplane patrols against Zeppelins	1 Hertford	8 Throwley
——— Night aeroplane patrols against aeroplanes	2 Wormingford	9 Detling
↗ Anti-aircraft guns supported by searchlights	3 Hadleigh	10 Biggin Hill
	4 Goldhanger	11 Joyce Green
◗ Linking searchlights	5 Stow Maries	12 Sutton's Farm
ⅢⅢⅢⅢ Wireless tracking patrols	6 Rochford	13 Hainault
× Central London	7 Bekesbourne	14 North Weald Bassett

'British defences . . . galvanised into mounting efficiency': the Air Defence of London in 1918.

between guns and searchlights was devised, with 'aprons' of heavy cables strung between static balloons to force the bombers up to altitudes at which gunners and night-fighters could find them more easily. Air defence, as the Second World War proved, is an ever-developing art; in the First World War it was also an absolutely new one. By April 1918, the London Air Defence Area disposed of 266 anti-aircraft guns, 353 searchlights, 159 day fighters, and 123 night fighters.[8]

On the German side also there were innovations. The G-V, an improved, more streamlined, and therefore slightly faster version of the G-IV, with fuel tanks in the fuselage instead of under the engines (thus reducing the chances of fire in a crash) made its appearance for the night offensive. Even more startling and futuristic, however, were the R (*Riesen*)—type 'Giants'. These were frankly inspired by Igor Sikorski's '*Ilya Mourometz*' (see p. 31); built by *Siemens-Schuckert*, the first models were of very little military significance, but as the Zeppelins faded into the background in 1916, OHL ordered more large aeroplanes, and two squadrons were formed on the Eastern Front. In 1917 *No. 501 Squadron* was ordered to the Western Front, and on the way it was re-equipped with the improved R-VI model produced by the *Schutte-Lanz Zeppelin-Werke* at Staaken (hence its designation *Staaken R-VI*). It was, indeed, a remarkable aircraft.

At 138 feet 5½ inches, its wing span was only 3 feet less than that of the B-29 Superfortress of the Second World War. Like the Superfortress, it was powered by four engines (either 245 h.p. Maybach or 260 h.p. Mercedes), but their curious feature was that they were mounted in pairs—one pusher and one tractor facing fore and aft in each of the two nacelles. The basic crew was seven, but it might be increased to nine if extra machine-guns were required; the R-VI could carry as many as six guns, though its normal complement was three, the favoured gun being the British Lewis (see p. 196). The aircraft's range was almost 300 miles, its ceiling was about 12,500 feet, its speed just over 80 m.p.h., and its bomb-load about 4,000 lb. Interesting elements of its equipment were the gyro-compass for navigation, which was also assisted by directional wireless; the bomber could send out a signal which was plotted by two ground stations, which then transmitted its exact position back to the aircraft. The wireless operator was a regular member of the crew, and sat in the control cabin. In one of the machines (actually an R-V) a pneumatic tube carried messages from one part of the aircraft to another, a light warning the receiver that a message was in the tube. Six 'Giants' operated against England; two crash-landed on return in March 1918—this was always a hazard, and a massive undercarriage consisting of no fewer than sixteen large wheels was devised to combat it. No 'Giant' was brought down by the Air Defence.

Between 3 September 1917 and 20 May 1918, 19 night raids were carried out against England; 434 people were killed, and 989 injured. German losses (including the two 'Giants') were 18 shot down or missing, and 27 crashed. Their most costly raid was on 28 September 1917, when they had three Gothas shot down, and six crashed on landing—it says much for their spirit that seven Gothas and three 'Giants' nevertheless took off to attack London the next night, and 11 Gothas took off again on September 30. The biggest raid was also the last: 19/20 May 1918, when 38 Gothas and three 'Giants' took off, of which 28 Gothas and all three 'Giants' reached their targets, London, Faversham, and Dover. As the Second World War would re-emphasize, night raids are exceedingly difficult to counter. Yet by September 1918, thanks to yet more strides of technology, new systems of Air Defence were in existence which are decidedly reminiscent of the Second World War. Above all, the advance of two-way radio made possible a London Air Defence Area headquarters linked through sub-controls to gun batteries, searchlights, balloons, aerodromes, and observer posts. In the absence of the Germans, the Royal Air Force mounted a dummy raid, and General Ashmore delightedly related:

'I sat overlooking the map from a raised gallery. In effect I could follow the course of all aircraft flying over the country as the counters crept across the map. The system worked very rapidly. From the time an observer at one of the stations in the country saw a machine over him, to the time when the counter representing it appeared on my map, was not, as a rule, more than half a minute. In front of me a row of switches enabled me to cut into the plotters' lines, and talk to any

subordinate commanders at the sub-controls.' [9]

The picture is not unfamiliar.

The casualty statistics which I have quoted do not give the full measure of success of the first strategic air offensive by heavier-than-air machines. That has to be sought in the moral effect of the raids; as Cyril Falls says,

'In a populace which had faced the burdens, losses, and privations of war so stoutly an astonishing weakness appeared.' [10]

Their new sense of vulnerability deeply shocked the British people, and was reflected in the production figures. A survey at Woolwich Arsenal in September 1917 showed that only one-third of the night shift was actually working, that production on one night was down to under 20 per cent of normal, and that even daytime production was less than 75 per cent of normal. Every night, raid or no raid, some 300,000 Londoners took shelter in the underground railway system. The Germans, of course, were not able to measure this result of their activities, but they soon had the opportunity to appreciate what it might be. Frightened, angry, and vindictive, British popular opinion called for reprisals with a voice so strident that it could not be denied. It was out of these sentiments, rather than with a view to any substantial material results, that the first British strategic air offensive was born.

Despite the understandable reluctance of the Army and Flying Corps High Command, fully stretched by the Flanders offensive, and aware of the almost total lack of suitable machines for bombing Germany (there were only four bomber squadrons—about 80 aircraft—in the whole BEF), the Government insisted on reprisal action. This could, in view of current level of performance, only be done from eastern France; Trenchard had already selected a suitable airfield, Ochey, near Nancy. Here, in October, he assembled No. 41 Wing, with specific instructions to bomb 'targets of military importance in Germany.' The first raid was carried out, against the *Burbach* iron-works near Saarbrucken, in daylight on 17 October, and one week later the same target was attacked by night. The British strategic air offensive had begun.

Unfortunately, it lacked (as the High Command had feared) the aircraft to do the job—with one superb exception. The 41st Wing, as at first composed, consisted of one squadron (No. 55) of DH-4 day bombers, and one squadron (No. 100) of FE-2b night bombers. The single-engined DH-4 was the first British aircraft to be designed strictly for bombing; it first went into squadron use in 1917, and proved at once successful. Its excellent design lent itself to considerable future modification for various purposes; 1,449 DH-4s were built in Britain, and nearly 5,000 in America, where it remained in Army service until 1932. Its speed of 136 m.p.h. and range of 420 miles were far in advance of the Gothas, but its bomb-load of only 460 lb. meant that it had severe limitations in its new rôle. The FE-2b suffered even more serious

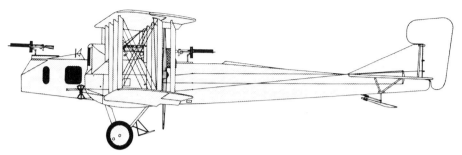

ABOVE: The G-IV; together with the G-V the mainstay of *Kagohl 3*.

drawbacks—indeed, by late 1917 it had a distinctly archaic look. It was designed as a fighter in 1913, but did not go into production until 1915, by which time its pusher propeller was already becoming obsolescent. As a night bomber its speed of 81 m.p.h. compared satisfactorily with the Gotha, but for the purposes of the strategic offensive its range of only 180 miles and its bomb-load of 336 lb. were quite inadequate. In due course the DH-4s were supplemented by the newer DH-9s, but this was an aircraft which never overcame the dubious circumstances of its birth. The same panicky frame of mind in October 1917 that had insisted on a reprisal programme ordered a doubling of the size of the RFC in France, most of the new squadrons to be

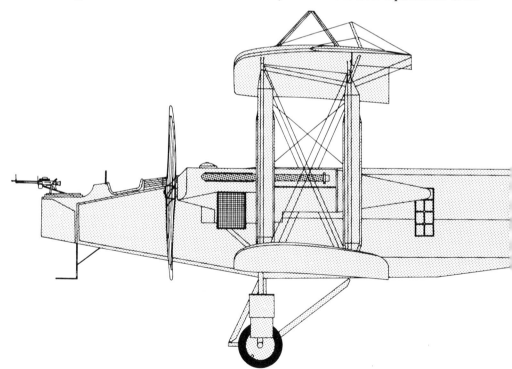

ABOVE: The Handley Page 0/100 heavy bomber—a true strategic weapon.

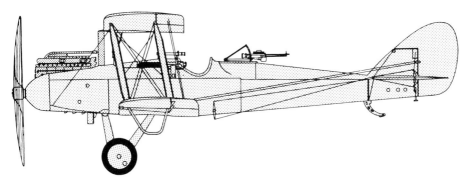

ABOVE: The DH-9, born of the panic created by the Gotha raids.

day bombers. The DH-9 was rushed through its design for mass production (3,204 were built, and 885 of the far better 9a model) with sad results:

'. . . *bombing formations of D.H.9s were apt to be very much reduced in strength before the lines were crossed, for the simple reason that the engines would not develop enough power to enable pilots to keep their station. Nor when flying at its best can it be said that the D.H.9 . . . was good enough for really effective long-distance attacks by daylight, more particularly because its "ceiling" was comparatively low.'*[11]

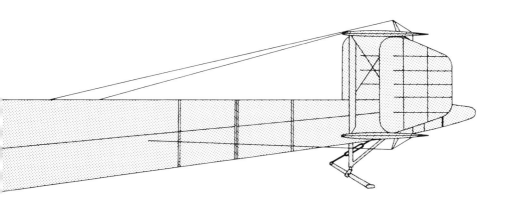

In one 1918 raid (31 July) three out of 12 DH-9s turned back with engine trouble before crossing the line; four were shot down before reaching the target; three more on the way home.

The 'one superb exception' was the Handley Page 0/100 and its successors. And once again it was the Royal Navy that took the lead in a sphere not properly its own. The Admiralty ordered a large bombing aircraft from the Handley Page Company in December 1914, Winston Churchill being First Lord, and thus playing the same rôle of godfather to the heavy bomber that he did to the tank. Powered by two 250 h.p. Rolls Royce engines (speed 76 m.p.h.) the 0/100 came into production in 1916; it could carry its bomb-load of 2,000 lb. to a range of 450 miles. Very shortly it was followed by the 0/400, powered usually by two 360 h.p. Rolls Royce engines, or alternatively two 350 h.p. American 'Liberty' engines, or other; its range, with full bomb-load, was 650 miles, and its maximum speed 97 m.p.h. In May 1918 came the V/1500, 62 feet long, with a wing-span of 126 feet; this massive aeroplane was powered by four 375 h.p. Rolls Royce engines, and was capable of carrying two 3,300 lb. bombs a distance of 1,200 miles—a true strategic weapon. It was designed to attack Berlin, but it arrived just too late: three V/1500s were actually standing by, bombed-up, when the Armistice was signed. Eight Naval Handley Pages formed part of the 41st Wing in October 1917.

In February 1918 the 41st Wing became the VIII Brigade, Royal Flying Corps, and in June, with the addition of a third Wing, the Independent Force, Royal Air Force, under Major-General Sir Hugh Trenchard. 'Independent of what?' asked a sarcastic French officer. 'Of God?'[12] The question had a point: operations of war are not susceptible to hard and fast divisions—war is generally conducted successfully by the judicious combination of all arms. The Germans, by tying down no less than 16 squadrons of badly needed aircraft for the defence of Britain, had shown how a strategic offensive could affect operations in other theatres. Trenchard's idea was to carry home an attack on the German Army in the field by crippling its sources of supply and breaking the will of its Government. He concluded that the best way to do this, with the forces available, was 'to attack as many of the large industrial centres as it was possible to reach.' His reasoning was clear: there was, as he saw it, no question of trying to destroy completely any single German industrial centre—for that the war would have had to last another four or five years! On the other hand,

'*By attacking as many centres as could be reached, the moral effect was first of all very much greater, as no town felt safe, and it necessitated continued and thorough defence measures on the part of the enemy to protect the many different localities over which my force was operating.*'[13]

So, for the remaining six months of the war, Trenchard pushed home his strategic offensive on these lines, despite generally unfavourable weather conditions which frequently ruled out long-distance raids, and in the face of increasing opposition. September was the peak month, when the Independent Air Force carried out 62 raids, although strong winds, low clouds, and rain made raiding impossible on 19 days and 18 nights. All told, between 6 June and 11 November, the IAF carried out 242 raids and dropped 543 tons of bombs on German targets (220 tons on aerodromes). The precise number of casualties inflicted is not known; the German total for the war was 746 killed and 1,843 injured, and the damage done amounted to some 24 million marks-worth (about £1,200,000 at contemporary exchange rates). For this the IAF paid a price of 109 aircraft missing and 243 wrecked; its casualties were stated as 29 killed, 64 wounded, and 235 missing (of whom a number must have been killed). But as with the German offensive against England, these statistics are only part of the story; a German authority wrote in 1928:

'The direct destructive effect of the enemy air raids did not correspond with the resources expended for this purpose. On the other hand, the indirect effect, namely, falling off of production of war industries, and also the breaking down of the moral resistance of the nation, cannot be too seriously estimated.'[14]

Trenchard's policy and the perception behind it spelt out a lasting and ominous lesson for this new style of war:

'. . . the moral effect of bombing stands to the material effect in a proportion of 20 to 1, and therefore it was necessary to create the greatest moral effect possible.'[15]

NOTES

1   Major Raymond H. Fredette: *The First Battle of Britain 1917–1918 & The Birth of the Royal Air Force*, p. 36; Cassell, 1966.
2   Ibid., pp. 55–6.
3   Andrew Boyle: *Trenchard*, p. 222; Collins, 1962.
4   Oliver: *Anvil of War*, p. 201.
5   Falls: *First World War*, pp. 347–8.
6   Fredette, op. cit. p. 84.
7   Ibid., p. 108
8   *RUSI Journal*, June 1976 pp. 68–9: Dr. Malcolm Smith: The RAF and Counter-force Strategy before World War II.
9   Fredette, op. cit. p. 212.
10   Falls, op. cit. p. 347.
11   *O.H.* (*The War in the Air*), vi p. 142.
12   Boyle, op. cit. p. 293.
13   *O.H.* op. cit. pp. 135–6.
14   Major Grosskreutz in *Die Luftwacht*, October 1928, quoted in *O.H.* op. cit. pp. 152–3.
15   *O.H.* op. cit. pp. 135–6.

Main Events 1918

3 March	Treaty of Brest Litovsk
21 (–5 April)	German offensive in Picardy
26	General (later Marshal) Foch appointed Allied C-in-C
27	Germans renew hostilities on Eastern Front
9 (–30) April	Battle of the Lys
25	First tank versus tank action at Villers-Bretonneux
1 May	Germans enter Sebastopol
7	Treaty of Bucharest
27 (–6 June)	Third Battle of the Aisne
9 (–14) June	Battle of the Matz
15 (–24)	Italy: Austrian offensive on the Piave
4 July	Battle of Le Hamel
15	Last German offensive on the Marne
18	Beginning of Allied Final Offensive (see p. 301 for detail)
18 (–26) September	Macedonia: Battle of Monastir-Doiran and pursuit
19 (–30 October)	Palestine: Battle of Megiddo and pursuit
30	Armistice signed with Bulgaria
24 October (–4 November)	Italy: Battle of Vittorio-Veneto and pursuit
26	General Gröner succeeds General Ludendorff as First Quartermaster-General
30	Armistice signed with Turkey
4 November	Armistice signed with Austria-Hungary
11	Armistice signed with Germany

CHAPTER IX

The Decisive Blow

IN 1918 THE FOURTH phase of war, as predicted by Field-Marshal Haig (p. 92) was seen: 'the eventual decisive blow'. There were, in fact, many blows; they fell into two clearly-defined groups—German, which failed, and Allied, which succeeded (in large part due to the efforts of Haig's armies). The conditions for the German blows were created by a number of factors which require to be briefly reviewed.

First, there was the final collapse of Russia. The March Revolution of 1917 (see p. 229) caused the overthrow of the Tsarist régime and the setting up of a Provisional Government of assorted 'progressives'. The new Government proclaimed its intention of continuing the war, and was widely acclaimed by its western allies who expected it to do so with increased efficiency. The extreme (Bolshevik) revolutionaries, however, led by Lev Davidovich Bronstein ('Trotsky') and Vladimir Ilyich Ulyanov ('Lenin'; his return to Russia from Swiss exile in April was facilitated by the German High Command—a misjudged essay in psychological warfare) fostered the anti-war spirit by all possible means. Under Alexander Kerensky as War Minister and later Prime Minister (July), Russia made one last attempt to take the offensive; this swiftly collapsed in disorder, lending added fuel to the Bolshevik propaganda. In October the Bolsheviks seized power by a coup d'état with the slogan 'Bread and Peace'; peace negotiations with the Central Powers began in December, and on 3 March 1918 the Bolshevik Government signed the draconian Treaty of Brest-Litovsk.[1] This collapse of their Eastern enemy freed a large number of German troops for other enterprises, but fortunately, owing to Ludendorff's grandiose political ambitions in the Baltic and the Ukraine, nothing like so many as there should have been.[2]

The eyes of the German High Command were focussed upon the West, where matters looked hopeful for them. The breakdown of French morale in the aftermath of the Nivelle offensive, referred to on p. 212, reached the pitch of outright and widespread mutiny on the Champagne front in May and June 1917. This was caused chiefly by the sickening disappointment of the high hopes raised by Nivelle's injudicious promises. Contributory causes were resentment at lack of leave, bad food, and inadequate medical services, and hatred of the *embusqués* (shirkers and profiteers in the rear areas and at home). The fact that the peak of the mutinies (16 May–10 June) coincides with a peak of heavy fighting at the front shows that they were not (as in Russia) fundamentally anti-war in content, though political agitators naturally sought to exploit them. Under Pétain the French Army made a considerable recovery. A well-conducted attack at Verdun on 20 August 1917 brought in over 10,000 prisoners, and indicated to Ludendorff that 'the

French Army was once more capable of the offensive'.[3] A second attack, on the Aisne in October, took 11,157 prisoners and 180 guns and raised French spirits again. Yet as the New Year of 1918 came in French losses totalled 3,831,000; manpower reserves were low, and sharp-eyed observers, not least of them General Pétain himself, doubted whether the recovery was really complete; this was an army which still needed to be 'nursed'.

There was no moral failure in the British Army, though the Third Battle of Ypres had been an exhausting and harrowing experience, and the German counter-attack at Cambrai on 30 November had produced an unpleasant shock. The British problem was sheer lack of numbers. Owing to misconceptions of the strategic situation and dissatisfaction with the military leadership's record in 1917 on the part of the Prime Minister, the BEF was dangerously below strength and at the same time holding an extended front. Furthermore, in February and March 1918 it underwent (except for the 10 Dominion divisions) a radical reorganization, whereby each infantry brigade was reduced from four battalions to three. No fewer than 141 battalions were disbanded in order to bring the remainder up to strength--a grim portent for the coming life-and-death struggle.

There was also, for the Allies, the puzzling and disappointing fact that although the United States had been in the war since April 1917, by December there were only four American divisions (about 140,000 men) in France, of which only one was actually in the line, on a quiet front. The heavy fighting of 1917 had found 'the American Army always a conspicuous absentee from the battlefield'.[4] The Germans, for their part, were lulled into complacency about American potential; to their eyes it seemed plain that the next six months held a glittering opportunity of crushing Allied resistance in the West before American manpower reserves could become effective. The period of the German offensives thus took on the aspect of a race with time.

Finally, there was another factor which impelled the German High Command towards an all-out offensive solution: two gruelling years of the wearing-out fight had had their effect. In Ludendorff's words:

'The Army had come victoriously through 1917; but it had become apparent that the holding of the Western Front purely by a defensive could no longer be counted on, in view of the enormous quantities of material of all kinds which the Entente now had at their disposal . . . Against the weight of the enemy's material the troops no longer displayed their old stubbornness; they thought with horror of fresh defensive battles and longed for the war of movement . . . In the West the Army pined for the offensive, and after Russia's collapse expected it with the most intense relief.' [5]

NOTES

1 Terraine: *To Win a War*, p. 36.
2 Ibid., pp. 36–7.
3 Ludendorff: *My War Memories*, ii p. 479.
4 Terraine, op. cit. p. 18.
5 Ludendorff, op. cit. pp. 541–2.

The Decisive Blow: *Failure 1.*

NEITHER THE TRUE SIGNIFICANCE of the bloody wearing-out battles on the Western Front during the middle period of the war, nor their outcome in the war of movement which returned in 1918, are to be understood without taking into account this condition of the German Army, the 'motor of the war' (pp. 44, 91). What had happened, by 1918, was a levelling-down of quality of the magnificent instrument with which Germany had waged war in 1914–16, accompanied by a hard, painful levelling-up of the spirited but amateur Army raised by Britain in 1915 and grimly blooded in 1916 and 1917, until in the last year of the war the British achieved a slender but decisive superiority. Ever since the using up of the old Regulars in 1914 and 1915, the British Army had been, in effect, a militia. Now the Germans were the same. By the end of 1917, says Ludendorff,

'our infantry approximated more nearly in character to a militia, and discipline declined . . .'[1]

A post-war opinion gives more detail:

'The best of the old German Army lay dead on the battlefields of Verdun and the Somme. What had later appeared bore an ever-increasing militia-like character. As time passed, the picture gradually changed for the worse, in proportion as the number of old peace-time officers in a unit grew smaller and as they were replaced by young fellows of the very best will, but without sufficient knowledge. At the same time, the old corps of N.C.O.s rapidly disappeared, so that finally the difference between N.C.O. and private vanished, very much to the detriment of discipline.'[2]

It was these factors, says the author, plus bad rations, depression at deteriorating conditions in the Fatherland, and socialist propaganda, that caused Germany's most powerful offensive of the war to peter out in less than two weeks. The British Official Historian casts some doubt on this analysis, pointing to the wonderful response made by the German Army in 1918 to the demands upon it. Contemporary accounts from both sides suggest, however, that the undoubted tactical successes gained by the Germans in their offensive were bought by an expedient which itself confirms the general deterioration to which Ludendorff and others refer.

It was the decline of overall quality (attested by a serious increase of desertion—Ludendorff speaks of 'tens of thousands' who escaped to neutral countries and 'a far greater number' who 'lived happily at home'[3]) added to increasing material weakness[4] that forced the German High Command into an unwelcome step. Divisions intended for offensive purposes were taken out of the line in January and February in order 'to devote themselves entirely to training and equipment'.[5] These formations enjoyed priority in the distribution both of *matériel* and horses—the latter now in universal short supply. The remainder had to accept lower establishments, less artillery, fewer mortars, less transport, and even less forage. OHL, says Ludendorff,

'regretted that the distinction between "attack" and "trench" divisions became established in the Army. We tried to eradicate it, without being able to alter the situation which gave rise to it.'[6]

There is no doubt that the German 'attack divisions', when they appeared in battle, were formidable. Their prowess, and their dramatic initial success on 21 March, have led to a legend that 'Storm Troops' were a brilliant German tactical innovation of 1918. This is far from the truth. It was, in fact, a French officer, Captain André Laffargue, who first advocated a system of 'infiltration' by carefully trained *'groupes de tirailleurs'* armed with automatic rifles, hand grenades, and gas bombs, in a pamphlet written in the autumn of 1915 and published in May 1916. The British Official history says that Laffargue's pamphlet 'had no influence on either the French or the British training manuals at the time'—which is curious in the light of Major-General Sir Edward Spears's description of the French infantry attack on the Somme on 1 July 1916:

'The French had already adopted the self-contained platoon as a unit. Tiny groups, taking every advantage of cover, swarmed forward, intangible as will o' the wisps, illusive (sic) *as quicksilver. The German artillery was baffled and their defences overrun by these handfuls of men who were everywhere at once. In a few minutes they had disappeared over the skyline. The attack had been successful.'*[7]

According to the Official History, a copy of Laffargue's pamphlet was found in a captured trench shortly after its publication, 'and was at once translated and issued as a German manual for tactical training at the new assault-troop (*Sturmtruppen*) schools, Laffargue's idea being made a form of battle-drill.'[8] It would seem probable that German interest was inspired rather by practical experience of the new French method than just by the printed word.

However, for whatever reason, the interest was undoubtedly there; in late 1916 assault-troop detachments (*Sturmkompagnie*) were forming part of divisional establishments, and in due course each Army had a battalion (*Sturmbataillon*) formed of four such companies and used for special operations and raids. They were, in fact, the equivalent of the Commandos of the Second World War; the 1918 innovation was to train whole divisions on these lines—yet as that year's campaigns and Second World War experience showed, this was still not the right way to go about the matter. Field-Marshal Slim tells us:

'Armies do not win wars by means of a few bodies of super-soldiers but by the average quality of their standard units . . . Any well-trained infantry battalion

'The German counter-attack at Cambrai marks their real début . . .': 'storm troops' with flame-throwers practising anti-tank tactics.

should be able to do what a commando can do; in the Fourteenth Army they could and did.'[9]

This is clearly correct, and we shall see that in due course in 1918 a profound effect was exercised on the war by an army which may be said to have been entirely composed of 'Storm Troops'.

While the German Army was on the defensive, naturally, few opportunities occurred for the use of the *Sturmtruppen*, though their presence was noted in the later stages of fighting at Verdun in 1916. The German counter-attack at Cambrai on 30 November 1917 marks their real début, together with their version of the infiltration tactic which the French had used since 1916 and the British had developed in 1917, particularly for attacking 'pill-boxes'. At Cambrai the Germans first pushed out patrols, followed by 'small columns bearing many light machine guns and, in some cases, flame-throwers . . . few posts appear to have been attacked from the front, the assault sweeping in between to envelop them from flanks and rear.'[10] Clever use of valleys in order to penetrate the defence was noted by British observers, and also the excellent liaison between infantry and artillery by means of light signals. 1918 added little to this already sophisticated technique except enormous numbers and extra emphasis on the need to 'push on, keep inside the divisional areas, do not trouble about what happens right or left.'[11] The method achieved striking success on 21 March, but one British divisional historian comments that it was 'well known' to the Regular Army of 1914 and emphasized in the Infantry Training manual; he adds:

'An army of the same experience as that of "The Contemptibles" (1914) would have had no difficulty in coping with Ludendorff's Sturm truppen, but the New Armies of Britain through sheer lack of opportunity for training were much below that standard.'[12]

What was undoubtedly a *tour de force* on the part of the Germans—though not entirely surprising in an army so dominated by staff officers—was the quality of the staff work in the preparation for their great attack on the Cambrai–St. Quentin front in March. Three armies were assembled, totalling 74 divisions, or about one million men, with 6,473 guns and howitzers and 3,532 trench mortars (light and heavy). This constituted a hitherto unparalleled concentration of fire-power. To feed it, enormous quantities of ammunition had to be assembled. And in addition, of course, there were the mountains of supplies of all descriptions which constituted the apparatus of war for such a vast force. To assemble all this in precisely considered detail constitutes, says the British Official History,

'one of the most remarkable pieces of staff work that has ever been accomplished, and it appears to have been carried out without any mishap, in spite of Allied aeroplane action and long-range fire.'[13]

Good staff work was not only to be seen on the German side. As far back as 7 December 1917 British GHQ Intelligence had predicted a German attack 'in great strength not later than March.'[14] On 18 January 1918 British Intelligence stated that the Germans were likely to attack near the junction of the British and French armies, while 'another vital blow might be made between the La Bassée Canal and the sea'.[15] These were, in fact, the precise areas attacked. In February it began reporting the German build-up as divisions came over from the Eastern Front to the West:

6 February	174 divisions in the West	
21 February	179	,, ,, ,, ,,
25 February	180	,, ,, ,, ,,
3 March	182	,, ,, ,, ,,
10 March	184	,, ,, ,, ,,
11 March	185	,, ,, ,, ,,
18 March	187	,, ,, ,, ,,
22 March	190	,, ,, ,, ,,

Generally speaking, British Intelligence was able to identify and locate a newly-arrived German division within 48 hours of its appearance in the West. On 3 March it stated categorically that a German offensive 'on a big

'. . . a 5-hour hurricane bombardment . . .': this battery of 210 mm. (8 inch howitzers) well conveys the destructive power of the massed German artillery in March 1918.

scale will take place during the present month', and that this would be 'in the Somme area'.[16] On 19 March a British staff officer wrote:

'It is certain that the attack will be launched either tomorrow or the day after.'[17]

Unfortunately, however, German feints and demonstrations were entirely successful in persuading General Pétain that the preparations on the British front were deceptions, and the real attack was to be delivered in Champagne. This belief persisted even after the attack was launched, and was largely responsible for the absence of French reserves on which the British counted near the junction of the two armies.

The German attack began with a 5-hour hurricane bombardment (with lavish use of gas-shell) at 4.40am on 21 March on the fronts of the British Fifth and Third Armies. The Fifth Army front was 42 miles long, held by eleven divisions in line, with one in reserve; the Cavalry Corps of three divisions was also present in this sector, but it has to be remembered that in dismounted action a cavalry division was only equivalent to an infantry brigade, and lacked all heavy weapons. The Third Army front, further north, was 28 miles long, held by 10 divisions in line with four in reserve. Two divisions were held in GHQ reserve behind each Army. When the crushing bombardment lifted (the field howitzers fired 800 rounds per battery at the British defences in the 5 hours; the 150 mm. howitzers fired between 300 and 600 according to pattern, and the super-heavies 325) the *Sturmtruppen* came over, followed by the bulk of the infantry. Fifty German divisions were identified in action on that day.

These statistics alone are sufficient to account for a severe defeat, certainly on the Fifth Army front (General Sir Hubert Gough). Severe strictures have been uttered upon the British defensive system, and an apparent failure to counter German infiltration by defence in depth. These would seem to have been only marginally deserved. It is quite obvious that, after three years of virtually constant attack, the British Army lacked experience of defensive fighting, and it lacked also the training opportunities to correct this fault; the German attack at Cambrai in November had shown how easily it could be caught off balance, and how clumsily it could respond. Defence in depth was warmly advocated by GHQ, but at an Army Commanders' conference on 17 February it was admitted:

'The expression "defence in depth" is not generally understood by the troops.'[18]

Not only was the concept not understood; it was actively disliked. Theorists who urge its manifest advantages often lose sight of its practical drawback, clearly expressed by the historian of one of the London regiments in the Third Army:

'The fact that the line was held in depth decreased individual confidence, though no doubt it increased the general feeling of security. To have fourteen healthy specimens of flesh and blood beside one is far more comfortable psychologically than to know that one is covered by a potential barrage of fourteen machine guns.'[19]

This was not a purely British fault. No army liked defence in depth.

The truth, certainly on the long Fifth Army front, is that the defences lacked depth because they lacked the manpower to construct them in depth (on the eve of the German offensive the Army could muster no more than 8,830 labourers for this work) and also to defend them in that manner. It is of the essence of defence in depth that when the attacker's impetus is absorbed there shall be a resolute counter-attack; General Gough's reserves were totally inadequate for such a purpose. So it came about that the pulverizing weight of the heaviest bombardment yet seen fell upon an Army hard put to it to man even its 'Forward Zone'—with the consequence that many units were overwhelmed (frequently annihilated) in their front positions. And to fill the cup, on the morning of 21 March the Somme area was shrouded in thick fog, which meant that when the German infantry came over, such defenders as had survived the storm of fire—and above all the defending machine-guns—were blinded. The first they knew of the attack was the presence of the Germans either on top of them or, too often, behind them. Much unreal argument has taken place about the effect of this fog—whether it favoured the Germans more than the British, the attack rather than the defence. The latest historian of 21 March, after a careful analysis of the factors involved, concludes:

'It is my opinion that if there had been no fog the German infantry casualties on 21 March 1918 would have greatly exceeded the 40,000 men actually killed and wounded in the fog and that the German advance could have been halted in most places in front of the Battle Zone, as intended by the British defensive planners. The second phase of the battle would then have started under conditions much more favourable to the British. The presence of thick fog on the battlefield on 21 March 1918 completely distorted the outcome of fighting and led to many false conclusions being drawn about it.'[20]

The last word must surely be that when the British themselves were attacking later in the year, they benefited greatly from fog on several important occasions, and when Nature failed to supply it they went to considerable trouble to manufacture it in the form of smoke.

For a combination of reasons, then, 21 March was a disaster for the British—above all on the Fifth Army front, though the right and centre of the Third Army were also heavily smitten. It is difficult to be precise about casualties on such an occasion; Mr. Middlebrook, after much careful work, offers an estimate of 38,512 British casualties (German, 39,929) which he breaks down as follows:

Killed:	7,512
Wounded	10,000
Prisoners	21,000

Only on one other day in the war (1 July 1916) did British losses exceed this figure. The loss of guns was never exceeded, on any day: 382 by the Fifth Army, 150 reported lost by the Third Army. This represents about one fifth of the number present with the two Armies. On a front of some 50 miles there was the spectacle of universal retreat—at its furthest point, to a depth of nearly 10 miles. Without doubt, this was one of the most dramatic days of the whole war. Yet though the Germans had struck a smashing blow, and given the British (and their allies) a great shock, this was not another Gorlice-Tarnow (pp. 180–83) as the following days would show. Even 21 March itself spoke with equivocal voices; as Mr. Middlebrook says,

'The Germans had achieved their full hopes on only a little over one quarter of the front that they had attacked . . . moreover, what German successes had been achieved were at the cost of casualties that could not be replaced.'[21]

The most serious defect of the German performance, however, lay not in its cost or in its failure to do what had been hoped for it; it lay in the mind of the presiding genius of the battle—Ludendorff. Despite all his careful preparations, despite the massive build-up of force on the selected front, despite the undoubted skill of Colonel Georg Bruchmüller, the brilliant artillerist who had 'orchestrated' the opening bombardment, the fact remains that he had set the German Army an impossible task. This was the result of an endemic fault, a frame of mind which recurs in German military leadership: as the

British Official History expresses it:

'German strategy, both in peace and war, has always been opportunist, and concerned with looking for weak places rather than with formal objectives.'[22]

In Ludendorff's own words:

'Tactics had to be considered before purely strategical objects which it is futile to pursue unless tactical success is possible.'[23]

It does not, however, require an advanced thinker to perceive that unless an overall objective is held in mind (a strategy) it is impossible to measure the force required (and the nature of that force) for a military operation. Yet, when an Army Group commander, Crown Prince Rupprecht of Bavaria, enquired of him during the battle what his strategic objective was, Ludendorff replied:

'I forbid myself to use the word "strategy". We chop a hole. The rest follows. We did it that way in Russia.'[24]

As I have said elsewhere,[25] this was not the way to win the war. In March 1918, it had two effects: first, because tactical success shone most brilliantly at the southern extremity of the German line, Ludendorff followed this misleading beacon into an advance which ultimately penetrated some 40 miles—but led nowhere. Secondly, because he had failed to decide the nature of the force that he might require, this deep thrust was made, not only in the wrong direction, but also without benefit of any arm of exploitation. As I have indicated above, tanks of First World War vintage were not the arms of exploitation that they had become by 1939; yet it cannot be doubted that the German success on 21 March would have been greater if tanks had participated to any real extent—perhaps sufficiently greater for the axis of advance not to be pulled off course. But only nine tanks were used—five of them captured British Mark IVs and four of their own A7Vs. These were huge machines, weighing 33 tons, with a crew of 18, armed with a 57 mm. cannon and 6 machine-guns. On a smooth surface they could work up to 8 m.p.h., but their weight and awkward shape made them very slow cross-country performers. Only 15 were ever built, and they had no effect whatever on the March battle. Armoured cars and motorized machine-guns would seem to have been completely absent. The German cavalry was in Russia. As the year would show, the days of cavalry as an arm of exploitation on a modern battlefield were over; yet, feeble as it was, the cavalry was the only exploiting arm that existed. To launch an offensive intended to win the war with none at all was not just foolish: it was criminal.

To the British, the days following 21 March became known as 'The March Retreat'—taking its place, for a nation which weirdly revels in such defeats, alongside the Retreat to Corunna and the Retreat from Mons (and easing the

pain of the subsequent Retreat to Dunkirk)—but it was a retreat without
pursuit, or rather with a pursuit at the speed that the German infantryman's
legs could carry him—no more. The German divisions were sucked into
battle at a rate which tells its own tale of disappointment: 50 on the first day,
76 on the seventh day, 78 on the day after that, and 83 by the end of the
month. Never have British generals and British soldiers had to encounter
that degree of force on any other battlefield. Losses mounted, more guns
were lost, huge quantities of stores were captured, but both the Fifth Army
and the Third Army continued to fight. The Storm Troops were expended
against a resistance which never collapsed in the way that the Russians
collapsed at Gorlice-Tarnow or the Italians at Caporetto. As their best men
became casualties, German tactics became clumsier, until they resembled
the shoulder-to-shoulder onslaughts of 1914; a British officer describes an
undoubted German defeat on the First Army front on 28 March:

'*Quite suddenly the smoke cleared; and there, barely 200 yards in front, were the
enemy in full view bearing down on us in a compact and huddled mass . . . I have
never been able to estimate the numbers . . . I counted five lines, each, I calculated, five deep, so deep, in fact, that I had to rub my eyes to make sure that they
were not new belts of wire grown up in the night. . . . In an instant the rattle of
rapid fire, a fire sustained almost continuously for an hour till rifles were red hot and
bolts jammed, broke out from every fire bay . . . Rapid fire, intense, concentrated,
sustained, never before had I realised so vividly its terrific potentialities!*'[26]

The British Official History remarks of this particular battle in front of Arras
that 'there is little to record except the severe casualties inflicted on the
enemy.'[27]

By this date, in fact, the great offensive was clearly fading; even two days
earlier General Byng had told Haig:

'*In the south, near the Somme, the enemy is very tired and there is no real fighting
taking place there. Friend and foe are, it seems, dead beat and seem to stagger up
against each other.*'[28]

On the 28th clear signs of demoralization were visible in the German ranks,
partly due to their losses and dismay at the tough resistance that they were
encountering, partly to fatigue, and partly to the amazement with which they
beheld the huge stocks of war supplies behind the British front. Wholesale
looting became commonplace, and operations were suspended while this was
happening. Captain Rudolf Binding describes amazing scenes on that day in
Albert; he met soldiers going to the rear with every kind of booty from a cow
on a line to a drawing-room curtain or a top hat. Some were staggering; some
could hardly walk—for obvious reasons:

'*When I got into the town the streets were running with wine. Out of a cellar came a
lieutenant of the Second Marine Division, helpless and in despair. I asked him,*

"What is going to happen?" It was essential for them to get forward immediately. He replied, solemnly and emphatically, "I cannot get my men out of this cellar without bloodshed." When I insisted . . . he invited me to try my hand, but it was no business of mine, and I saw, too, that I could have done no more than he. I drove back to Divisional H.Q. with a fearful impression of the situation.' [29]

An authoritative German account of that day says:

'. . . there was a feeling that the Army, owing to its vanishing offensive powers, had come to a standstill.' [30]

The emphasis is mine.

German offensive power was indeed vanishing; on 4 April a fresh attempt was made to capture the one strategic prize which had come into view —Amiens, with its rail junctions, only some 10 miles behind the front line. The attack was an absolute failure, and the following day the 'March Offensive' was formally stopped. In Hindenburg's words: 'our strength was exhausted'. Ludendorff admitted:

'The enemy's resistance was beyond our powers.' [31]

Never having had a strategic objective, not surprisingly Ludendorff had failed to gain one; for all its flashy opening, and striking advances in the southern sector, the great offensive which, by the end, had absorbed 90 German divisions, was strategically insignificant. Indeed, one German authority says:

'The conclusion of the fighting left our troops, especially on the Avre (south of Amiens), in very unfavourable positions, which led to extraordinary wastage.' [32]

A second blow against the British front, in the area of the River Lys in Flanders, although it drew from the normally undemonstrative Haig his famous 'Backs to the Wall' Order, was even more unsuccessful. Repeated attacks between 9 April and 30 April, though they stretched the weakened British forces to their very limits, and produced crises only matched by the First Battle of Ypres in 1914, again failed to obtain any strategic prize, only leaving the Germans once more in unfavourable positions, difficult and costly to hold. The close of the Battle of the Lys on 30 April marked the final admission of failure against the British front.

One thing the German offensive had done, however: it had restored open warfare. That is not to say that suddenly the armies abandoned their trenches; it simply means that from now on the trenches were what they awaited action in; once it began, it resumed the characteristics familiar in 1914, and general throughout on the Eastern Front. What had turned the key in the deadlock? Clearly, it was not tanks, or any anticipation of the *blitzkriegs* of 1939–41. The answer, in March 1918, was distressingly simple:

brute force—the brute force of 90 German divisions, and the brute force of Bruchmüller's 10,000 guns and mortars. Infiltration, as we have seen, was an expedient born of declining human quality and material shortages. It would be wrong, however, to brush aside the skilful use made by the Germans of machine-guns. Their ubiquitousness was noted time after time; in the forward, infiltrating groups, this would commonly be due to the Bergmann light machine-gun, distributed to the German infantry in March 1917 in answer to the British Lewis. It was better than the Lewis for the simple reason that it was designed somewhat later, specifically as an Army, not an Air Force, weapon. Weighing 43lb. with its bipod, it could be carried (by a sling) and operated by one man; unlike the Lewis (and the more reliable) it was belt-fed, the belts containing either 100 or 250 rounds. In 1918 the German Army possessed 37,000 of these useful weapons.

For the defence, there was one striking and significant innovation. When the weight of the German impact had set the battle rolling, and the fog had cleared away, huge numbers of men, with all their diverse war-machinery, were visible above ground. To airmen, they presented targets the like of which they had never seen. British and French flyers seized their opportunities; German regimental records pay rueful tribute to their work on 21 March itself. On 25 March the Royal Flying Corps squadrons' orders were 'to bomb and shoot up everything they can see on the enemy's side of the line . . . Very low flying is essential. All risks to be taken.'[33] The pilots flew a 'shuttle service', using up their bombs and ammunition quickly on the

'. . . the German offensive had restored open warfare . . .': waves of German infantry practising an advance in the manner which they displayed repeatedly in Picardy and Champagne in 1918.

plentiful targets presented, then returning for more to repeat the process. The Official History says:

'Their determined efforts did much to discourage and hold back the enemy advance by impeding the movement of his reserves.'[34]

The next day, no fewer than 27 out of 34 squadrons on the Third Army front were successfully employed in this manner. This, certainly, was a firm step towards the 'interdiction' strategy attempted with such feeble means in 1915 (see pp. 195–6). What is strange is that, with equally splendid targets presented by the retreating British, the Germans appear to have made little effort to turn retreat into rout in this disturbing manner, though aircraft strongly assisted their more deliberate attacks.

A curiosity of the defence was the valuable rôle of the British cavalry. At Cambrai in 1917, their performance in attack had been unimpressive; later in 1918 they would again disappoint. But in the crisis of March the cavalry proved useful by virtue of its mobility, and its dismounted brigades, though weak (3 'battalions' of 550 per brigade) gave great help in puttying gaps and supporting counter-attacks. They thus won great credit in the capacity that cavalry had always affected to despise—mounted infantry, as at Ypres in 1914.

The Tank Corps, caught in the midst of re-equipping (with Mark Vs and 'Whippets') and expansion (five new battalions were added at the end of 1917) played little part in the great defensive battles. Indeed, its defensive rôle had not been properly analysed and expounded; one proposal—and there were far worse—was to station individual tanks in large dug-outs along the front, from which they would emerge at suitable moments to disconcert the enemy. This tactic was known as 'Savage Rabbits'. In general the tanks were used in very small numbers at a time, despite the protests of the Corps, with the result that 120 were lost (many through lack of petrol) by 27 March for no result worth noticing (though many crews did good service as Lewis gun detachments). Yet before the German offensives ended a landmark in armoured warfare was passed. At Villers Bretonneux, near Amiens, on 24 April, the Germans made a successful attack featuring 13 A7Vs; 'wherever tanks appeared the British line was broken.'[35] At 9.30am three tanks of the British 1st Battalion, one 'male' and two 'females' (see p. 239), arrived to take part in the defence of the village of Cachy. An A7V came on the scene, and at once knocked out the two 'female' tanks; the 'male', although damaged by artillery fire, scored a hit on the A7V, whose crew then abandoned it. Two more German tanks appeared, and the 'male' engaged them; one was hit and again abandoned by its crew, the other veered away, but was later subjected to concentrated fire by six guns of the 58th Machine-Gun Battalion which caused so much 'splash' of molten lead inside the tank that the crew surrendered. So the first action of tanks against tanks in history ended, as one might expect, with advantage to the side which had possessed them longest and had most experience of them.

Only one more point needs to be noticed, and as usual its significance is technological. During 1916 and 1917 something approaching a revolution in industrial production techniques had taken place. In July 1917 Winston Churchill became Minister of Munitions (a post which suited him very well indeed), and it fell to him to preside over the final period of staggering achievement. We have noted that British losses in guns during the German offensives were very large; Churchill informs us:

'Before the end of (March) I was able to assure the War Cabinet and General Headquarters that nearly two thousand new guns of every nature, with their complete equipments, could be supplied by April 6 as fast as they could be handled by the receiving department of the Army. In fact, however, twelve hundred met the need.' [36]

It could be said that Germany's approaching defeat was spelt out in this statement of industrial power as certainly as it was on the battlefield where her armies had been halted.

It remains only to count the cost of this offensive. In the two battles, Picardy and the Lys, between 21 March and 30 April, British casualties amounted to 236,300, divided between Picardy and Flanders in the proportion of roughly two to one. Precise breakdowns of the nature of these casualties are virtually impossible to arrive at; in both battles the number of 'missing' is high—in Picardy the gross (uncorrected) total is 81,149, and in Flanders 31,881. But these figures have to be adjusted in relation to the number (approximately 10 per cent in March, 7 per cent in April) who would later return to the ranks, and also to the number (about 10 per cent) who were either dead or dying when last seen, or died before the Germans took them in. For March the British Official History estimates (on the strength of officer prisoners' reports to a Court of Enquiry) that 30 per cent of British prisoners taken by the Germans were wounded and another 10 per cent gassed; unwounded prisoners in the first battle therefore amount to some 42,000. The category of 'killed' amounts, in Picardy, to almost 12 per cent of the total, in Flanders to just over 10 per cent. It is noticeable, in all the 1918 fighting, that the proportion of dead in a casualty total is much lower than, often less that half, that of 1916. The *gross* total of killed for the two battles (41 days) is 22,741, which may be compared with 19,240 on 1 July 1916 alone. On the other hand, the full British total for the 6 weeks of defensive fighting, 236,300, may be compared with the total for the $15\frac{1}{2}$ weeks of the Third Ypres ('Passchendaele') offensive: 244,897. The comparison supplies its own commentary on the widespread belief that in the warfare of the First World War the defensive was always less costly than the attack.

As might be expected in such critical times, the strain on the alliance was very great, and it was a constant British complaint that the French were never there when they were needed, and that when they did arrive they did not do much fighting. Their casualties of 92,004 suggest that they must have been doing *something*. The Allied total is thus 328,304. For once, German returns are reasonably exact: a total of 348,300 for the whole period. Not only did this constitute a fearful and damaging loss for Germany; for the three great European powers it meant a total of nearly 700,000—a rate of loss of about 17,000 a day. And this was just the beginning of the year.

<hr>

NOTES

1 Ludendorff: *My War Memories*, ii pp. 541–2.
2 *Wissen und Wehr*, September 1924; quoted in *O.H. 1918*, ii pp. 462–3.
3 Ludendorff, op. cit. p. 585.
4 John Williams (*The Home Fronts*, p. 273; Constable, 1972) says that Germany's 1918 New Year prospects 'were dark indeed. Month by month the material weaknesses that were threatening to paralyse her war industries and her whole economic life—breakdowns on the railways, lack of coal, absence of oils and lubricants—were operating with an increasingly destructive chain-effect.'
5 Ludendorff, op. cit. p. 583.
6 Ibid.
7 Spears: *Liaison 1914*, p. 109.
8 *O.H. 1917*, p. 62 f.n.1.
9 Field-Marshal Sir William Slim: *Defeat into Victory*, p. 547; Cassell, 1956.
10 *O.H. 1917*, iii p. 177.
11 *O.H. 1918*, i p. 157.
12 John Ewing: *The History of the 9th (Scottish) Division 1914–1918*, pp. 251–2; John Murray, 1921.
13 *O.H. 1918*, ii p. 461.
14 Charteris: *At GHQ*, p. 273.
15 GHQ Paper, 'Note On The Present Situation', 18 January; author's papers.
16 Robert Blake: *The Private Papers of Douglas Haig 1914–1918*, p. 291; Eyre & Spottiswoode, 1952.
17 Charteris, op. cit. p. 290.
18 Conference record, author's papers.
19 J. Q. Henriques: *The War History of the 1st Battalion Queen's Westminster Rifles 1914–1918*, p. 212; Medici Society, 1923.
20 Martin Middlebrook: *The Kaiser's Battle*, pp. 331–2; Allen Lane, 1978.
21 Ibid., pp. 240–1.
22 *O.H. 1918*, ii p. 464.
23 Ludendorff, op. cit. p. 590.
24 *O.H. 1918*, ii p. 464.
25 Terraine: *Impacts of War 1914 & 1918*, p. 163; Hutchinson, 1970.
26 Henriques, op. cit. p. 222.
27 *O.H. 1918*, ii p. 53.
28 Haig Diary, author's papers.
29 Binding: *A Fatalist at War*, pp. 209–10.
30 *O.H. 1918*, ii p. 76.
31 Hindenburg: *Out of my Life*, p. 350; Ludendorff, op. cit. p. 600.
32 *O.H. 1918*, ii p. 137.
33 *O.H. 1918*, i p. 472.
34 Ibid.
35 *O.H. 1918*, ii p. 389.
36 Churchill: *The World Crisis*, ii p. 1296.

The Decisive Blow: *Failure 2.*

LUDENDORFF NEVER WAVERED in his conviction that the British front was the decisive sector, in particular Flanders, where the front line ran close to the sea and perilously close to vital rail communications, notably the Hazebrouck junction. By the end of April, however, he was aware that the French were giving the British strong support; there were, in fact, 20 French infantry and three cavalry divisions either in line on the British front, or in reserve behind it, or close to it. Until these French forces could be pulled away from the British area there could be no question of another attack there. Clearly, there would have to be a diversion on a considerable scale against the French, and then, if it succeeded, it would be time to seek a decision again in Flanders. This was German strategy in May.

On the Allied side, the crises of March had produced a valuable result: at Haig's instigation General (later Marshal) Ferdinand Foch had been appointed Commander-in-Chief of the Allied forces on the Western Front. Inasmuch as the existence of a single strategic authority (as opposed to separate national C-in-Cs, or the Supreme War Council, a glorified international committee set up in November 1917) was an obvious step forward, this appointment served the Allies well for the remainder of the war. It was a long way, however, from the institution of Supreme Allied Commander, as evolved in the Second World War.[1] Foch had neither the staff with which to exercise actual command, nor the power to do so if a foreign C-in-C (Haig, or the American General John J. Pershing, or the King of the Belgians) fundamentally disagreed with him. But by persuasion, calling for a great exercise of tact, he was, as he said, able to 'stimulate or restrain . . . decide upon the policy to follow, and thus bring about those concerted actions which result in victory.'[2] His position, as General Pétain acutely observed somewhat later, depended on his being successful; in May 1918 it was almost fatally undermined.

The area selected by Ludendorff for his diversion was Champagne, the sector between Soissons and Reims which includes the famous *Chemin des Dames* ridge where the Germans had halted their retreat from the Marne in 1914, the scene of the bitter Champagne battles of 1915, General Nivelle's unfortunate offensive in April 1917, and hard fighting in the early summer of that year culminating in General Pétain's little triumph in October. For France this was sacred soil, like Verdun two years before. The concept of 'sacred soil', unfortunately, is frequently an impediment to sound tactics, and so it proved now.

In May 1918 the *Chemin des Dames* was considered a 'quiet sector' so much so that a corps of five weak British divisions which had already suffered heavy losses was sent there to recuperate and free French divisions for a strategic reserve. It was also considered to be a showpiece of a really well fortified front. Yet there was no agreement among the French generals concerned as to how it should be defended—a circumstance which itself illustrates the limitations of Foch's position. Foch himself had laid down that while on the northern part of the Allied front there must be a 'foot by foot' defence of every position, along the eastern portion, including Champagne, 'it was possible, without serious inconvenience, to abandon a certain amount of ground in the face of a violent enemy onslaught.'[3] The French C-in-C, General Pétain, who still took a very pessimistic view of the condition of the French Army, and did not conceal his opinion that it had to avoid losses by all means until the Americans were present in great strength, was prepared to retreat 'whenever and wherever the enemy attacked, without the discrimination laid down by General Foch'.[4] The commander of the Northern Army Group, General Franchet d'Espérey, contemplated defence in depth with a limited retirement from what the British called the 'Forward Zone' to the 'Battle Zone'. The Army commander on the spot, however, General Duchêne (Sixth Army) flatly refused to permit any withdrawal whatever, on the grounds that this sector directly covered Paris, that it was very strong, and that the morale of both the Army and the nation would be seriously affected if the *Chemin des Dames* was abandoned. These differing points of view were never properly resolved; Pétain and Franchet d'Espérey gave way to Duchêne, considering that defence in depth had not been sufficiently tried out to justify their over-ruling him. Foch did not intervene. The protests of

'. . . tanks . . . could not keep up with the rapidly moving infantry . . .': these are the heavy German A7Vs, but in Champagne they usually preferred to use captured British machines.

the British Corps commander, Lieutenant-General Sir A. H. Gordon, based on his experience of the April battle, were brushed aside by Duchêne with the words: '*J'ai dit.*'

Clearly, the makings of a disaster were present in Champagne from the first; to make it more certain, French Intelligence, which had been seriously deceived by the Germans in March, predicting an attack which never came, was now once more deceived into a totally false sense of security. This was fortified by complacency in the Sixth Army, but it has chiefly to be attributed to another masterpiece of German staff work. Characteristic German attention to detail was applied to the build-up of appropriate force on the selected front of attack, secrecy being cultivated and maintained by the most rigorous supervision of all movement and assembly. The extent of this was too great and the methods employed too numerous to be listed here;[5] suffice to say that they worked like magic—30 additional divisions were brought into the battle area with all their impedimenta without arousing any suspicion until the afternoon of the day before the attack (26 May).

The new battle (designated the Third Battle of the Aisne) began at 1am on 27 May; it opened with another Bruchmüller bombardment, as carefully planned as that of 21 March, but far heavier. The number of guns used was smaller (about 4,000) but the density of fire much greater: 1,706 German batteries on a 64-mile front on 21 March gave an average of 26.6 per mile; 1,036 batteries on a 35-mile front on 27 May averaged 29.6. But in the centre, where one French and one British division held $11\frac{1}{2}$ miles of front, an assembly of 466 batteries produced an average of 40–41 per mile. The zone of fire extended as far as 12 miles behind the front line:

'*Every battery position, village, farm, and railway station, every bridge and road-junction was systematically shelled.*'[6]

For the first ten minutes all the German guns and mortars were using gas in order, as a German account says, 'to create at the very start irremediable confusion and moral effect among the enemy.'[7] Everyone, right back to divisional headquarters, was forced to wear gas-masks, a severe handicap in the dark. Then with gas and high-explosive shell mixed, the German artillery engaged the Allied batteries, while the trench mortars pounded the front defences and destroyed the wire. This treatment continued until 3.35am, when a creeping barrage was formed; five minutes later the German infantry rose for the assault. By that time the effect of Bruchmüller's 'orchestra' had been devastating:

'*All headquarters had been under fire, and most communications had been cut. The Front Zone had nearly everywhere been rendered untenable, the strongpoints obliterated. Casualties in the infantry had been very heavy, and most of the machine guns and artillery were out of action. For the second time in the War, the first having been at Messines in June 1917, what had been so often attempted in vain had been accomplished: so thorough had been the preliminary destruction that all resistance was crushed and the infantry had only to advance to take possession of the front position.'*[8]

27 May 1918 was the apotheosis of the artillery war; the German guns, in $2\frac{1}{2}$ hours, had done everything that artillerists claimed they could do. The extent of the damage was, of course, much enlarged by General Duchêne's massing of troops in the confined space north of the Aisne. There was also, once again, a morning fog, thickened by gas and smoke, to help the attack; in the British 8th Division, which had already on two occasions in that year had to try to beat off attacks in fog, 'men and officers began firmly to believe that the enemy had discovered means to put down a mist whenever it was wanted.'[9] No doubt the fog did help to reduce German losses, but the defence was already largely smashed before the infantry advanced; an officer at a British brigade headquarters records the amazement with which the message was received:

'Can see enemy balloons rising from our front line.'[10]

He continues:

'Before a word had come that our front had been assaulted, the enemy had turned both flanks . . . Our position was no longer a stronghold but a death-trap. There was nothing left but to obey orders and fall back across the Aisne—a decision no sooner taken than acted upon.'[11]

Unfortunately, in the general confusion and breakdown of communications, many of the Aisne bridges were not blown up when the retreating Allied troops crossed them; thus, while large numbers of men and a great many guns were trapped and captured on the north bank, the Germans themselves had little difficulty in pressing their advance across the river. Indeed, on 27 May they crossed three rivers—the Ailette, running between the original front lines, the Aisne (with its accompanying canal) and in places the Vesle, twelve miles behind the front. They had thrust a salient that deep on a 9-mile front into the Allied line, the base of the salient being 25 miles wide. Four front-line divisions—two French and two British—had ceased to exist as organized bodies; four more had been very seriously weakened. 'No such day's work had been done in France since trench warfare began.'[12]

The Germans themselves were startled by the extent of their victory on 27 May; they found themselves pulled forward by their own momentum, and it was certainly not in the nature of a fundamentally opportunist High Command to hold back after such an opening. By the end of the next day their salient was 15 miles deep and 40 wide at the base. By 3 June they had advanced 30 miles, and stood again on the River Marne, as they had done in 1914. Infiltration (against disorganized and frequently raw troops) was chiefly responsible for this deep penetration, coupled with a dangerous shortage of Allied artillery until losses could be replaced. The Germans used some tanks, mostly captured machines (which they preferred to their own), but they found that these could not keep up with rapidly moving infantry; used by themselves and in very small numbers, they were ineffective and suffered heavy losses. By the official end of the Battle of the Aisne, 6 June, the Germans claimed 45,000 Allied prisoners and a very large number of guns taken (the British 50th Division lost its entire artillery, the 8th was reduced to seven 18-pdrs on 28 May; the French suffered likewise). Once again the Germans had struck a spectacular blow; yet their situation had disagreeable features. The High Command noted that it was the central thrust, on a relatively narrow front, that had made the progress, while the wings hung back, creating serious logistical problems. And that was not all: a captured British officer who was kept near the battlefield for some days registered the course of the German advance by watching the semi-circular bulge of the line of their observation balloons:

'That great sweeping semi-circle in the sky marked out the German position and suggested its dangers in an extraordinarily clear and graphic manner. The possibilities of a counter-offensive, thrusting at either angle of the bulge, was inevitably brought to his mind.'[13]

This was the strategic debit to be reckoned against a brilliant tactical success. The British Official History goes so far as to say that for the Germans the glitter of 27 May marked, in fact, 'the beginning of the end.'[14]

One thing was perfectly clear to OHL: since the whole purpose of this battle was a diversion, there would have to be an early return to the defensive in Champagne, and a front line shaped like this would not do. Something more would have to be done to eliminate the obvious dangers of counter-attack. The 'diversion', in other words, was becoming a drain. Accordingly, on 9 June, the Germans launched a fresh attack on a 21-mile front on the western side of their bulging salient; this is known as the Battle of the Matz. Once more there was a substantial success on the first day: an advance of some 6 miles in the centre, with 8,000 prisoners. But there the resemblance to 27 May ended. The French were not taken by surprise—indeed, their counter-bombardment opened ten minutes before the German; they still had too many troops in forward positions (as a result of which 3 divisions were almost destroyed) but their reserves were stronger; above all, there was no rout. On 10 June the Germans attacked again, but made much less progress. On the 11th there was a portent: General Charles Mangin, a very aggressive, offensive-minded officer, who had been disgraced in 1917 in the aftermath of the Nivelle fiasco, launched a counter-attack against the German right. It did not achieve very much in concrete terms, but its mere occurrence emphasized a shift in the balance of forces. On 13 June the Battle of the Matz ended, with the German situation as awkward as it had been before.

The sombre fact remained, however, that between 27 May and 13 June the Germans had taken 60,000 prisoners and 850 guns and carried their advance as far as Château Thierry, less than 50 miles from Paris. Foch's Supreme

'. . . a significant accretion of new strength . . .': machine-gunners of the American 3rd Division played a useful part in the defence of Château Thierry on 3 June.

Command was not making a very brilliant beginning; the removal of Pétain was seriously considered; General Franchet d'Espérey was sent to Salonika in semi-disgrace (from which he redeemed himself by a successful campaign later in the year), General Duchêne was dismissed, and two corps commanders went with him. Yet there were hopeful signs for the Allies, even in these dark moments. There remained Germany's unfavourable strategic position, and the strong hint that Mangin had given of what might be done about it; there was the price that she had paid for her success—not less than 130,000 officers and men, who now could not be replaced. And there were the first signs of a significant accretion of new strength for the Allies: the first American attack of the war, at Cantigny on 28 May; there followed a defensive action by the American 3rd Division at Château Thierry on 3 June; and a counter-attack by the 2nd Division at Belleau Wood on 6 June—the beginning of a hard fight which continued until the American Marines cleared the wood on 25 June. Above all, there was the arrangement by which 250,000 American soldiers were brought to France in June and the same number again in July. They came without any weapons heavier than machine guns; they were not organized or equipped for battle—in fact, they were not an army. But they were coming, they could actually be seen arriving in their multitudes—a potent source of encouragement for the Allies and of increasing dismay for the Germans. The sands were running out.

Three months of massive exertion were now followed by a few weeks' lull in major activity on the Western Front. Reluctantly Ludendorff concluded that the business in Champagne was still uncompleted, and until it showed clearer signs of completion Flanders would still have to wait. Once more Bruchmüller's talents were called upon, to prepare the way for an attack on both sides of Reims; more than 5,000 guns and 43 divisions were assembled for what was hoped would be the final blow in this area: a Second Battle of the Marne. Final it was indeed, but not in the manner the Germans had intended. Once more the French were warned, and this time their artillery counter-preparation anticipated the German by half an hour, with serious consequences for the massing German infantry. But even more significant was the fact that in one French Army at least, General Gouraud's Fourth, on the eastern side of Reims, the lesson of defence in depth had at last been learned. The German bombardment opened with customary intensity at 12.10am on 15 July, and lasted for 3 hours and 40 minutes; the infantry then began what should have been their forward rush deep into the French position—but next day a German officer gloomily wrote:

'I have lived through the most disheartening day of the whole War, though it was by no means the most dangerous. This wilderness of chalk is not very big, but it seems endless when one gets held up in it, and we are held up . . . Into this the French deliberately lured us. They put up no resistance in front; they had neither infantry nor artillery in this forward battle-zone, the full use and value of which they had learned from Ludendorff. Our guns bombarded empty trenches; our gas-shells gassed empty artillery positions; only in little folds of the ground, sparsely distributed, lay machine gun posts, like lice in the seams and folds of a garment, to give the attacking force a warm reception . . . After uninterrupted fighting from five o'clock in the morning until the night, smothered all the time with carefully directed fire, we only succeeded in advancing about three kilometres . . .'[15]

West of Reims, against a defence still too crowded in the forward zone, the Germans did better, but by the end of 16 July it was clear that the great attack had failed. On the 17th spasmodic French counter-attacks showed which way the wind was blowing; that night the German High Command was forced to order the evacuation of its bridgehead over the Marne. Heavy artillery, mortars, and aircraft were already on their way to Flanders to attack the British, and Ludendorff himself was in Mons, conferring with Crown Prince Rupprecht. The question now was, not whether Champagne might pave the way for a Flanders victory, but whether Flanders might save something from the ruin in Champagne. The answer came with shattering abruptness.

NOTES
1 For more on this, see Terraine, *The Smoke and the Fire*, pp. 77–8.
2 Foch: *Memoirs*, pp. 210–1.
3 Foch, memorandum of 19 April, quoted in *O.H. 1918*, iii p. 39.
4 Ibid., f.n.2.
5 A full analysis in very interesting detail may be found in *O.H. 1918*, iii pp. 69–71.
6 *O.H. 1918*, iii p. 47.
7 Ibid., p. 48.
8 Ibid., p. 49.
9 Boraston and Bax: *The Eighth Division in War 1914–1918*, p. 223.
10 Sidney Rogerson: *The Last of the Ebb*, p. 31; Arthur Barker, 1937.
11 Ibid.
12 Falls: *The First World War*, p. 327.
13 Boraston and Bax, op. cit. p. 239.
14 *O.H. 1918*, iii p. 24.
15 Binding: *A Fatalist at War*, p. 234.

The Decisive Blow: *Success 1.*

THE GERMANS BEGAN the Second Battle of the Marne; it was the Allies who ended it. Offensive ideas were never far distant from the mind of General Foch, and his preparations were well advanced before the Germans even struck. No sooner was their attack seen to be halted, than Foch launched his own blow. Spearheaded by two American divisions in General Mangin's Tenth Army, and including British and Italian divisions as well as French, the counterstroke took place on 18 June. In two days Mangin alone took 15,000 prisoners and 400 guns; by the time the battle ended, on 7 August, the tally of prisoners had risen to over 29,000, and 793 guns had been taken. The Germans were back on the Vesle, a retreat of some 20 miles. But more important was the strategic reality which Foch expressed in the words:

'. . . *since July 18th, the control of events had passed into our hands.*'[1]

The Allies, in other words, had at last regained the strategic initiative which they had lost in August 1914 (see p. 91).

'Position warfare', said Foch, 'comes to an end when a position has been taken; the war of movement then resumes all its rights and all its exigencies.'[2] It was one of his prime objects, after 18 July, to make sure that the war of movement continued without check. And indeed, the history of the remainder of the war is the history of a continuous series of battles, a continuous forward pressure on all fronts, but above all in the West, which has no parallel. I have attempted to do belated justice to the Western campaign in my book '*To Win A War: 1918, The Year of Victory*'; here it is only possible (and appropriate) to extract some indications of style from the events described there. For an indication of their continuity and the scale of the whole endeavour, as well as of where the main effort lay, the chart opposite, which represents a lot of military history, is probably the most convenient means of expression.

THE ALLIED FINAL OFFENSIVE IN 1918

	FRENCH	BRITISH	AMERICAN	BELGIAN
15 July	Second Battle of the Marne			
18	Battle of the Soissonais & the Ourcq (–28)			
19	Battle of the Tardenois (–7 August)			
8 August	Battle of Montdidier (–11)	Battle of Amiens (–11)		
20	Battle of Noyon (–29)			
21		Battle of Albert (–29)		
26		Battle of the Scarpe (–30)		
30		Battle of Bapaume (–3 September)		
2 September		Battle of Drocourt-Quéant (–3)		
12		Battle of Havrincourt	Battle of St. Mihiel (–13)	
18		Battle of Epéhy		
26	Battle of Champagne-Argonne (–15 October)		Battle of the Argonne (–3 October)	
27		Battle of the Canal du Nord (–7 October)		
28	Battle of Ypres (–2 October)	Battle of Ypres (–2 October)		Battle of Ypres (– 2 October)
29		**Battle of St. Quentin Canal (–2 October)**		
3 October	Battle of Courtrai	Battle of Beaurevoir Line (–5)		
8		Battle of Cambrai		
14		Battle of Courtrai (–19)		Battle of Courtrai (–19)
17		Battle of the Selle (–24)		
1 November	Battle of Meuse-Argonne (–11)	Battle of Valenciennes (–3)	Battle of Meuse-Argonne (–11)	
4		Battle of the Sambre (–11)		

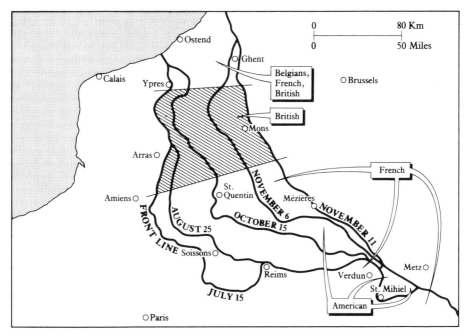

'. . . the main offensive was made at the wrong place . . .': this map shows the advances on the British sector which drew in the bulk of the German forces, and also illustrates the contracting front.

It is a remarkable fact about this final Allied offensive that at no time were the Allies seriously held up by German action; no counter-attack threw them back from any significant gain. The progress of victory was completely continuous. What were its ingredients?

First, though this should not be exaggerated, there was the factor of combination. It was Foch's object to reproduce on the Western Front as a whole, and on the grand scale, that inter-Allied cooperation which had been a feature of the Marne battle. Only once was he able to achieve this satisfactorily (and this was only the second time in the war) but he never ceased to work for it, and the spectre of it was always present in German thoughts. It was not a complicated idea; on the contrary, it had the simplicity of most first principles. As Haig, who was very much in tune with Foch's general intentions, expressed it:

'Foch's strategy is a simple, straightforward advance by all troops on the western front and to keep the enemy on the move.'[3]

Foch's own words were simpler still: *'Tout le monde à la bataille!'*[4] It was a stirring call, but the British Official History notes that what it turned out to mean was that:

'Strategically the main offensive was made at the wrong place, because the Army

most fighting-fit happened to be holding that front.' [5]

The chart indicates clearly which Army that was; its commander, Haig, unhesitatingly accepted the arduous but brilliant rôle for which his Army had been cast, and Foch paid handsome tribute to the way commander and Army played their part.

More potent and rewarding than inter-Allied co-operation, which sometimes happened and sometimes did not, was the co-operation of all arms in battle which was the outstanding characteristic of the remainder of the war. Indeed, it may be said that this was the true elixir of Allied success. There have, naturally, been special champions of various arms, and because armoured warfare became a developing theme in the post-war years and a very important element in the Second World War, tanks have been singled out as the decisive weapon of 1918. This is mythology, as I have said above (pp. 243–4) and elsewhere.[6] In the tank actions of the First World War it is not Day 1 that counts, no matter how spectacular its achievements, but Day 2; tanks scored a great success at Cambrai on 20 November 1917, but they lost 179 machines out of 378, and their rôle on 21 November was accordingly much reduced. It was the same in 1918: for the counterstroke on the Marne on 18 July, General Mangin's Tenth Army had 346 tanks, of which 225 got into action; 102 became casualties, so that on 19 July there were 195 available, of which 50 were hit. These losses, with breakdowns and exhaustion, meant that only 32 were available on Day 3. The Battle of Amiens, 8 August, saw the largest deployment of tanks in any British engagement of the war: 534, of which 414 were fighting tanks (Mark Vs and Whippets). On Day 2 (9 August) the number available had dropped to 145, on 10 August it was 85, and on 11 August it had dropped to 38. The battle formally ended on that day, which was just as well, because on 12 August only 6 tanks were fit to fight; as I said in '*To Win a War*', 'The German empire was not going to be overthrown by six tanks.'

This pattern was normal. Never again was the British Army able to field over 500 tanks on one day; 150 was a high total, and on 29 September, the day of the Army's most spectacular achievement, only 141 went into action, of which 75 became casualties. By 4 November, for the last set-piece attack of the war, only 36 tanks were available. And meanwhile German anti-tank methods were becoming more sophisticated and effective; 'tank forts', highly reminiscent of all-round defences in the Second World War, were distributed along their front,

'*each fort containing at least one or two field guns, several heavy and light machine guns, anti-tank rifles, and an infantry escort. The infantry were also supported by attached sections of field batteries and by "close fighting batteries" (Nahkampf-batterien)—methods in which the Germans were far more practised and skilful than most British or Dominion forces and to which they resorted more than ever after the "tank battle" of August 8th.'* [7]

As the war neared its end, tanks were used as much as possible in half-light to avoid anti-tank fire, though this naturally hampered their already restricted vision. Indeed, they fought at an increasing disadvantage, yet there is no doubt whatever that they did help the infantry. The Official History sums up:

'Their effect was largely moral . . . (they) did good service in crushing machine gun posts and in village fighting. The infantry liked to see them, and as the enemy in his regimental histories has invariably exaggerated the numbers employed, and has often reported their presence when none were there, he evidently stood in fear of them.'[8]

The Allied airmen, having already found new rôles in the defensive battles, now sought to extend them in the final offensive. By 1918, air warfare had undergone a transformation; the production lines in the Allied factories were multiplying aeroplanes in a manner amazing to the lonely veterans of 1914 and 1915. In large actions the sky swarmed with aircraft: for the Battle of the Matz, in June, General Fayolle's Army Group had the support of over 1,000 machines. These consisted of its own *'groupement'* of about 200, the IX Brigade of the Royal Air Force (9 squadrons = about 140) and the *'Division Aérienne'*, a new formation which acted as a mobile Air Reserve for the purpose of ensuring air supremacy over a front of attack; it consisted of four *'groupements'*. On 18 July Mangin's Tenth Army disposed of 581 aircraft, and General Degoutte's Sixth Army had 562; IX Brigade, RAF, was also present. At Amiens on 8 August, General Rawlinson's Fourth Army called on no fewer than 800 aircraft (376 of them fighters), while the French First Army on its right deployed 1,104 (including the *'Division Aérienne'*), making the Allied total 1,904 over that single battlefield. The masses were taking to the air.

In the German retreat from the Marne, Allied aircraft played an important part in bombing the numerous foot-bridges over the river; in the counterstroke they effectively attacked ground targets, the Germans conceding them a 'great success'.[9] This, however, was not always the case; on 22 July the Germans established temporary local supremacy (it was virtually impossible to prevent this happening when one side or the other rushed powerful reinforcements to a scene) and their machines seemed to be over the French lines at all hours of the day.[10] By night they bombed Allied road communications. Night bombing was now their basic tactic, sometimes inflicting heavy casualties on camps and crowded rest areas, sometimes doing severe damage by blowing up ammunition dumps and wrecking railway stations and junctions, and always being a serious nuisance by causing alarm, and depriving weary soldiers of rest and other amenities. At the Battle of Amiens, when the RAF attempted to destroy the Somme bridges behind the German front in daylight, the German Air Force made a magnificent response. Some pilots were in the air for as much as ten hours on 8 August, 'taking part in combat

'. . . aircraft played an important part . . .': a direct hit by a British aircraft on a railway line and train near Maubeuge.

after combat'.[11] A day remembered as 'the black day of the German Army in the history of the war',[12] was also a black day for the RAF: 45 aircraft shot down and 52 more so badly damaged that they had to be written off—13 per cent of the total force engaged, 23 per cent of the bombers.

It was unfortunate for eager airmen, wanting to show what the new arm could do, that as the Germans were forced into increasingly difficult retreat, autumn conditions of north-western Europe made air intervention increasingly impossible. Elsewhere, however, the possibilities of air pursuit of a beaten enemy were dramatically demonstrated. General Sir Edmund Allenby's final offensive against the Turks in Palestine opened on 19 September, and was immediately successful; an important ingredient in this was RAF bombing of enemy headquarters, 'which paralysed his nerve centres and spread death and destruction behind his front'.[13] Lines of retreat and lateral communications were heavily attacked and blocked by smashed vehicles and dead horses. Two days later the RAF's performance was even more spectacular: as Turkish forces retiring from Nablus crowded into the precipitous gorge of the Wadi Fara, Bristol fighters and SE-5s fell upon them with bombs and machine-gun fire; the ensuing damage completely blocked the road. According to one British report:

'Over 100 guns, 55 trucks, and 92 country carts were found in complete confusion.

Ammunition, stores, and food were spilled all over the place . . . What had happened in one case was that truck drivers had jumped out, leaving their engines running; the trucks had then run into the tail of artillery in front; the guns in their turn had been carried into transport wagons; and finally an accumulation of dead horses and smashed material had brought the avalanche to a halt.[14]

It was noted that the actual bomb damage was very small; there was hardly any sign of a direct hit, and there were very few dead men. This was not, after all, surprising; few targets are so difficult for air bombing as a narrow road twisting along the side of a gorge. But it was clear that the moral effect of the air attack had been devastating; panic had achieved more than high explosive. The results were particularly impressive in relation to the small force employed—Allenby's whole air component was only seven squadrons and one single Handley Page bomber. Conditions, however, could otherwise hardly have been more favourable; on the Western Front there were no gorges, all too often no visibility, and plenty of opposition at all times.

If Bruchmüller provided the apotheosis of the artillery war (p. 296) it was the Allies, in their final offensive, who brought it to fruition. Time after time, it was artillery which decided the issue of the day, crushed German resistance, kept the front fluid and the war mobile. Artillery, in fact, in all the Allied armies, was the sanction by which other arms did their work and gained their successes. In the British Army, the achievement of the Royal Artillery in 1918 was the more remarkable inasmuch as its guns were outranged in all calibres; the 18-pdr. field gun, for example, had a range of 6,200 yards,[15] compared with the German improved 77 mm.'s 11,000—a very serious disadvantage. The German 380 mm. naval gun could reach at least 35,000 yards; the specially designed 210 mm. '*Pariskanone*' (usually referred to erroneously as 'Big Bertha'; the Germans called it 'Long Max' on account of its 130-foot barrel) had an extreme range of 82 miles, and actually bombarded Paris from a distance of 79 miles on 23 March. It fired 203 shells all told, most of which hit the city; 256 people were killed and 620 were injured, but the normal functioning of the French capital was unaffected. The life of this super-gun's barrel was considered to be 60 rounds, and 60 numbered shells were provided for each successive barrel; each shell was a little larger in calibre than the one before, the first of each batch having the prescribed calibre of 210 mm., the sixtieth being enlarged to 222 mm. The Artillery Adviser at British GHQ, Lieutenant-General Sir Noel Birch, considered that it was chiefly improvements in the design (stream-lining) of German shells that gave their artillery its advantage.

Because the British Army was the pacemaker of the Allied advance from August to November, the rôle of the British artillery was crucial. Never at any time did it possess the numbers of guns deployed by the Germans or the French; at the Armistice its total was 6,406 (compared with 15,598 German and 11,647 French). Yet the artillery accounted for between 30 per cent and

40 per cent of the total strength of the BEF. What mattered far more than its numbers was its performance; despite being outranged and despite a relative weakness in numbers, according to the Official History:

'The British artillery throughout had the upper hand of the German batteries, whose fire, if not quickly subdued, was gradually lessened directly they disclosed their positions by fire.'[16]

This is confirmed by General Birch, who wrote:

'In the summer of 1918 Ludendorff complained bitterly in a German Army Order that the British artillery had destroyed no less than 13% per month of the German artillery opposing it . . .'[17]

The Battle of Amiens set the tone of all that followed. On 8 August General Rawlinson had 1,386 field guns and 684 heavies for a front of 11 miles; the French First Army, which was also under Haig's command (its battle is officially called 'Montdidier') extended the front another 5 miles, on which it deployed more heavy (826) than field guns (780)—definitely a sign of the times. Zero hour was at 4.20am, and punctually at that moment, says the Fourth Army's history, 'the storm broke'. It continues:

'For some days previously the sound-ranging sections and flash-spotting observation posts (see p. 217), sited well forward, had been engaged in locating the enemy's battery areas in conjunction with the Royal Air Force. Consequently, the moment the assault began the enemy's batteries . . . were deluged by a hurricane bombardment and neutralised to such an extent that the hostile artillery retaliation was almost negligible.'[18]

General Birch confirms and adds a significant detail:

'Hostile artillery fire was insignificant and several enemy batteries were captured with the muzzle covers still on the guns, showing that the detachments had failed to reach their positions.'[19]

Numbers of dead horses lying in or around the German battery positions also showed how effective the British guns had been.

In action after action the British artillery achieved this supremacy and paved the way for the advance of the infantry, sometimes accompanied by tanks, sometimes not. What was the secret of this new competence of the gunners? There were three; they may be summarized as: SURPRISE, PRECISION, PROTECTION. Predicted shooting (see p. 216) restored at last that vital element of tactical surprise which the long bombardments of the wearing-out fight had made impossible. Now, battle could flare up at any point of the front without warning—and this indeed became the rule. Calibration enabled the guns, when they opened fire, to shoot with precision—that is to say, they could engage precise targets with a reasonable expectation of scoring direct hits or damaging near misses, instead of, in effect, blazing away at a landscape. General Birch remarks that on one corps front, when subsequent advance made investigation possible, it was found that 70 per cent of the German gun positions had been hit. Finally, protection— protection of the attacking infantry, indeed, sometimes also protection of tanks; this was achieved by increasing use of smoke-shell. Smoke helped the infantry to locate and follow a barrage; smoke hid them from the German machine-gunners and artillerymen. In combination with fog or heavy mist, it provided a sure formula for success. On the other hand, it was one more reason why the infantry leaned ever more heavily on the artillery for support, and why generally 'the extreme range of the barrage formed the limit of the infantry advance.'[20] But the fact remains that the revival of these three fundamental elements of war in 1918 transformed its nature; this was what made the war of movement possible.

By September, the Allies had captured over 2,000 guns since their counter-offensive began on 18 July, and with them, of course, vast quantities of ammunition. Replacement of such losses was now a matter of increasing difficulty for the Germans. The entry of America into the war had redoubled the effectiveness of the Allied blockade, and Germany was now in the grip of strangling shortages; the worst was of food, affecting both the home popula-tion and the Army, but munitions manufacturers acutely felt the lack of brass and copper. Harsh requisitions in the occupied territories, down to copper pans and brass door-knobs,[21] could not make up for lost imports. Strikes in the munitions industries made matters even worse; as autumn came, the power of the once-devastating German artillery was diminishing fast—an accurate reflection of Germany's declining capacity to continue the war.

On the Allied side, the picture was very different; there, no such impedi-ment detracted from the power of the artillery war. The French 75 mm. field guns, whose fast rate of fire ate up ammunition, called for a diet of 280,000 rounds per day—and received it. Between 8 August and 6 September the British 18-pdrs. fired 5,372,000 rounds, their 4.5 in. field howitzers fired 1,443,400, and the 'sturdy work-horse' of the medium artillery, the 6 in. howitzers (firing a 100 lb. shell) 1,566,800. The maximum ammunition expenditure on one day by the British Army was attained in the 24 hours, noon 28 September to noon 29 September, attacking the 'Hindenburg Line': 943,947 rounds. These unimaginable statistics did, of course, spell problems of their own, to which we shall return. But this was the hammer that was smashing up the German Army.

It was still, in 1918 as ever, the infantry which had to carry out the advances and bear the brunt of loss. Better supported they certainly were, less naïve in exposing themselves than their predecessors, better tutored in survival techniques by the survivors of the bloody years; yet for each individual infantry soldier there remained the ultimate lonely test of zero hour.

'The Americans were now pouring in.' Scene at the U.S. base at St. Nazaire; note the light 'trench' engines in the foreground, invaluable for hauling supplies across devastated areas.

The French, on 18 July, 'fought like men possessed'; a British officer who saw them 'was amazed at their fanatical ardour'.[22] Their losses in the Second Battle of the Marne were 95,165; Pétain reported to Foch that on 30 July the shortage of infantry in the French Army was 120,000, with nothing like that number in the depôts. The French continued to fight hard, but never again with quite the dash of 18 July; their victory at Noyon on 20 August (once again under Mangin) was referred to by Ludendorff as 'another black day' on which the Germans suffered 'heavy and irreplaceable losses'.[23] But the French were suffering too: between 1 July and 15 September their losses were 7,000 officers and 272,000 men. Victory beckoned, but as it did so prudence urged war-weary men not to take unnecessary risks. The nation which had borne the brunt of the Allied war for the first two dreadful years now looked to its Allies, especially the teeming Americans, to do most of the hard work. This naturally caused some acid comment, which ignored the fact that in 1918 France's casualty total amounted to no less than 1,095,000.[24]

The Americans were now pouring in: by mid-September there were 1,450,000 of them in France (by the Armistice there were 1,876,000). Most of them, of course, were very raw soldiers, with only the most basic training; they suffered from an absolute dearth of experienced commanders and staff officers (as the British had done in the early years). General Pershing's determination nevertheless to build up a separate American Army delayed their participation in the decisive events taking place around them; his desire to bring his units up to West Point standards had the same effect, and sometimes, indeed, lowered their effectiveness in battle.[25] In the American Army the infantry was regarded as the arm of decision; they gave it high regard, and used it in battle more freely than any other Allied Army. Colonel Repington paints a vivid picture of this formidable force that was building up on the Allied side:

'*The battalion of 1,000 bayonets is kept up . . . and all accessories for the infantry divisions are found from sources outside the battalion strength. Thus though the division is only twelve battalions . . . the bayonet strength in the field is twice or three times that of Boche, British or French, and the American division has 28,000 fighting troops. The Americans, while keeping their eyes and ears open and accepting our own and French instructors, are set on having their own code of tactics . . . and as they are different the Americans fight better by themselves. Everything has to be, and so is, American. The pride of race is very strong. The Americans are earnest, serious people, even the private soldiers, who have nothing of the devil-may-care light-heartedness of our men. They have come here to do or die and are as keen as mustard, but still very serious and quiet about it all. They are in truth Crusaders.*'[26]

The belief in a special American tactic was not justified; General Pershing was a strong advocate of open warfare, which he believed that Americans understood and their Allies, trench-bound for three years, did not. Long regular lines of American dead on the Marne battlefield showed that this was sadly far from the truth. On 30 August Pershing formed the American First Army, and on 12 September it fought the first American battle of the war at St. Mihiel. The Americans used 3,010 guns, not one of them of American manufacture; the French provided most of the 1,400 aircraft and also lent 267 light tanks. The attacking infantry was American; catching the Germans in the act of withdrawal, it scored a great success: 15,000 prisoners and 450 guns at a cost of some 7,000 casualties. But visiting the scene the next day Colonel Repington noted an ominous sign:

'. . . *we found the country roads much blocked with troops and transport of all kinds. The Staff work has failed here, and for miles transport congested all the approaches. One enterprising Boche air squadron, flying low, could have played the deuce on these roads, but not one came.*'[27]

Such scenes would be witnessed again.

A long way away from the American sector, another Allied army returned to the fray in late 1918: the Belgians, who had done very little fighting since 1914. Thanks to their King's policy, the Belgian Army had conserved its strength for this hour of national liberation. Now it was able to put 12 strong divisions into the battle, their ranks filled with young men of military age and good physique. A British division fighting beside them recorded that it 'never desired on its flanks better troops than the Belgians proved to be.'[28] From a strategic point of view, however, the thrust of the Flanders Group (Belgians, six French infantry divisions and three cavalry, British Second Army, 10 divisions) was eccentric; it drove up towards Bruges and the Dutch frontier, forcing the Germans to abandon the Belgian coast and scurry out of the net that was enfolding them, but it lent little to the main effort of the Allied armies. It did, however, provide another glimpse of the future techniques of war. On 4 July, at the Battle of Le Hamel on the Somme, the RAF had dropped 100,000 rounds of ammunition to forward Australian machine-gunners—the first air-supply of munitions to a battle in progress in history. Now, on 2 October, as the leading French and Belgian units outran their food supplies in a sector once more reverting to swamp in the autumn rain, Allied aircraft (including two RAF squadrons) dropped 15,000 rations to them. As I have said in *'To Win A War'*:

'The total amount dropped was thirteen tons, a ludicrously small quantity by the standards of, say, the Fourteenth Army's air supply during the monsoon advance to the Chindwin in 1944—but everything has to have a beginning.'[29]

By 1916 the great voluntary recruiting impulse which created the British New Armies had died away; the Army of 1918 was a very different article from the strapping but unskilled enthusiasts of earlier years. Increasingly, the ranks were filling with young conscripts of $18\frac{1}{2}$, men of the older age groups (35 and upwards), and wounded returning to duty (in some cases for the second or third time—a cruel consequence of Government manpower policies). Not surprisingly, there are conflicting views of the value of the new drafts. One divisional history calls the young soldiers 'most excellent material', but adds:

'Owing to age and physique some of these immature boys were quite incapable of carrying the weight and doing the work required of an infantry soldier in the line: their presence in the ranks rendered them a danger to their units. To use them at the time was only a waste of those who might later on, with proper training and physical development, have become valuable reinforcements for the Army.'[30]

And the same source continues:

'The scarcity of men of the best fighting ages between 21 and 28 was most noticeable in every unit. The older men, largely combed out from administrative employment and past the best fighting age proved the fallacy of the theory that it is possible to make a fighting soldier of the man of 35 equal to the continental soldier of the same age, who has performed military service in his youth.'

The 'boy-soldiers' of 1918 have attracted much sympathy, not always well-placed. There is much evidence that the older conscripts deserved more; a survivor told the author:

'Their days and nights were an endless round of misery, bewilderment and discomfort . . . They did not get enough to eat. Their teeth (natural or artificial) were quite incapable of dealing with the hard-tack biscuits that were the staple diet for the front line. We youngsters ate the biscuits—dry. We gave the jam to the old chaps to eat by the spoonful; it made some nourishment for them.'[31]

Of the young conscripts the Official History says:

'Their discipline was good . . . They were keen and physically fit, and, however tired, a night's rest was certain to restore them.'[32]

These considerations aside, there were two hard facts about the British infantry which makes its performance the more remarkable. First, its weakness in numbers; by the Adjutant-General's reckoning, the infantry was 123,000 below establishment in May (and this was with divisions reduced to nine battalions). In June he reported that 'bayonet strength' (i.e. infantry) was 210,000 below that of a year earlier. Battalions now considered themselves fortunate to go into action with as many as 300 men; in the later stages companies of 50 were normal. In mid-September the 1/Queen's Westminster Rifles found 'considerable difficulty' in manning its front with companies of that strength, while 'platoons could barely raise a single section to man a Lewis gun.'[33] And in addition to this numerical weakness there was the consideration that, in the hard words of the Official History, as a result of long years of trench warfare, this was 'an army which was prepared to stand enormous losses uncomplainingly, but was practically devoid of real tactical sense.'[34]

In open warfare this was a grave defect. Through lack of practice, junior officers had difficulty in map-reading, and their reports were often unreliable. Communications, which in trench warfare relied on a dense complex of telephone wires and exchanges, now presented almost insuperable difficulties. In the mobile advance, telephones rarely extended further forward than brigade headquarters, which meant that the leading units had to revert to little-understood earlier systems. The Official History notes that 'little use was made of visual signalling'—no doubt because of a well-planted dislike of exposing oneself. With forward communication so difficult, it is not to be wondered at that 'lateral communication . . . was seldom attempted'—yet the lack of it would clearly be painfully felt. Wireless was generally avoided for fear of it being heard by the enemy; in the later stages this caution would seem to have been misplaced, since there was very little the Germans could have done even if they had overheard conversations and orders. Radio communication was not yet a habit carried over from civil life, as it was in the next war. So motor-cycle despatch riders, officers in motor-cars, mounted orderlies, and runners were the mainstay of communication in the advance.

'Communications . . . presented almost insuperable difficulties.' This American signaller is learning his trade at a Corps School, but the telephone was at a handicap during the advance.

One divisional commander remarked to Colonel Repington that 'it was a great change for him to command on horseback and use gallopers.'[35] Nothing, perhaps, illustrates the change in the war more vividly than this simple sentence. Certainly the Official History does not exaggerate when it says:

'The remarkable feature of the operations was their success in spite of the weakness of the battalions and their almost total lack of training in open warfare.'[36]

The success was remarkable indeed: in August and September, the period which includes the battles officially known as 'Amiens', 'Albert', 'The Scarpe', 'Bapaume', and 'The Drocourt-Quéant Line', the three British Armies concerned took 2,730 German officers prisoner, and 108,876 other ranks:

First Army	17,206
Third Army	42,436
Fourth Army	51,964

And to this total of over 111,000 prisoners they added nearly 1,000 guns. But the best was yet to come. These battles brought the British Armies to the outposts of the 'Hindenburg Line'; the next stage carried them through that forbidding obstacle. The assault on the Hindenburg Line was in fact the British contribution to that solitary occasion when Marshal Foch was able to bring off a concerted action by all the Allied Armies together (see p. 302):

26 September	Franco-American attack in the Argonne;
27 September	preliminary attack by British First and Third Armies;
28 September	Flanders Group attack;
29 September	main attack by British Fourth Army.

The British actions, according to Haig's Despatches, led to the capture of 35,000 prisoners and 380 guns between 27 September and 5 October. Within that total lies one of the finest feats of the British Army in its whole history: the crossing of the St. Quentin Canal, whose steep sides made it a perfect anti-tank obstacle, by the 46th (North Midland Territorial) Division. The canal was an integral part of the Hindenburg defences, an immensely strong position. Aided once more by fog, and by meticulous preparation,[37] the 46th Division broke clean through in about $2\frac{1}{2}$ hours on 29 September. It took 4,200 prisoners and 70 guns—at a cost of less than 800 casualties. The Staffordshire battalions of the 137th Brigade led the way in one of the best days' work ever done by British infantry.

In all these British advances, beginning with its own private triumph at Le Hamel on 4 July, the Australian Army Corps had been a spearhead. It now (see p. 137) had its own Australian-born commander, Lieutenant-General Sir John Monash, a most careful planner of battle. Monash's belief in planning and detailed preparation was absolute:

'A perfected modern battle plan is like nothing so much as a score for an orchestral composition, where the various arms and units are the instruments, and the tasks they perform are their respective musical phrases. Every individual unit must make its entry precisely at the proper moment, and play its phrase in the general harmony.'[38]

The Battle of Le Hamel was a case in point; it was, said Monash, 'free from any kind of hitch. It was all over in 93 minutes.'[39]

The Australian battles in 1918 were not all like that; war is generally full of hitches, mostly caused by the presence of the enemy. However, the Australian Army Corps did certainly produce an effect, as I have suggested on p. 281, of a kind which one would be tempted to associate with a *corps d'élite*, call it 'storm troops', 'shock troops', 'Guards', or what you will. The point was, however, that in this case the whole force was of the same quality;

'. . . one of the best days' work ever done by British infantry.' Men of the 46th Division on the banks of the St. Quentin Canal, where they broke through the Hindenburg Line on 29 September. Note the ubiquitous Lewis gunners in the foreground.

the five Australian divisions were interchangeable. They were all élite. And in their own fashion they had evolved a tactic which closely resembled the 'infiltration' of the text-books, but not being text-book soldiers, and being Australian, they gave it a different name: 'peaceful penetration'. From the German point of view, it appeared like this:

'The enemy, who has grown up in the Australian bush,[40] *wriggles to our posts with great dexterity from flank and rear in the high crops in order to overwhelm them. It has often happened that complete pickets have disappeared from the forward line without trace . . .'*[41]

The British Official History remarks that in the index of its Australian counterpart the reference to such incidents is over 6 inches long; it notes:

'The cumulative effect of them on the Germans was tremendous.'[42]

The Australians entered the 1918 fighting during the German offensives, on 27 March; they were withdrawn, weak, tired, but utterly victorious, on 5 October. By that time, says General Monash,

'the total captures made by them were:

Prisoners	*29,144*
Guns	*338*

. . . During the advance, from August 8 to October 5, the Australian Corps recaptured and released no less than 116 towns and villages. Every one of these was defended more or less stoutly . . .

The total number of separate enemy divisions engaged was 39. Of these, 20 were engaged twice, 6 three times, and one 4 times . . .

Up to the time of the Armistice we definitely ascertained that at least 6 of these 39 enemy divisions had been entirely disbanded as the result of the battering which they had received . . .

I doubt whether there is any parallel for such a performance in the whole range of military history.'[43]

The cost of this amazing achievement, between 8 August and 5 October was:

Killed	3,566
Died of wounds	1,432
Wounded	16,166
Missing	79
Total	21,243

These figures also vividly display the change that had taken place in the style of warfare.

'. . . a misleadingly encouraging performance . . .': New Zealanders of the Desert Mounted Corps in the Palestine advance under General Allenby.

For one branch, however, there was no change. The Western Front remained an impossible theatre for cavalry to the end. For the Battle of Amiens, the whole British Cavalry Corps of three divisions was assembled, and there were high hopes of what it might accomplish in conjunction with Whippet tanks or armoured cars . As at Cambrai in 1917, they came to nothing; across country the cavalry could move much faster than any 1918 tank—until it met the German machine-guns. Then it could not move at all; as an American officer tersely remarked, 'You can't have a cavalry charge until you have captured the enemy's last machine gun.' The cavalry did its best, and chalked up some cheering successes during the last stages; yet the final verdict of the Official History is that it

'had done nothing that the infantry, with artillery support and cyclists, could not have done for itself at less cost; and the supply of the large force of horses with water and forage had gravely interfered with the sending up of ammunition and rations for the other arms, and with the allotment of the limited water facilities.'[44]

The French retained seven cavalry divisions (three in Flanders); there is no indication that their performance was any different from that of the British. Armoured cars were few in number; they had one glorious hour on 8 August, but at the end of the day only three out of 12 remained in action. Yet they had shown what they might achieve on better surfaces than the battlefields of the Western Front.

On other fields the mounted arm managed a misleadingly encouraging performance; in Palestine the Desert Mounted Corps (two cavalry divisions, two 'mounted' divisions) led General Allenby's forces in their victorious final campaign in the traditional manner, offering, according to Lord Wavell, 'the most striking example of the power of the cavalry arm in the whole history of war'.[45] Against a weak and largely demoralized enemy, they were often able to charge home, an Australian Light Horse brigade on one occasion wielding bayonets instead of swords. Their feats were held by some to have vindicated the cavalry in modern war, but as Wavell said,

'the true lesson is not so much the value of the horseman as the value and power of mobility, however achieved.'[46]

It would take some time for that to sink in.

NOTES

1 *The Two Battles of the Marne*, by Marshal Joffre, the Ex-Crown Prince of Germany, Marshal Foch, Marshal (*sic*) Ludendorff, p. 194; Thornton Butterworth, 1927.
2 *O.H. 1918*, iii p. 355.
3 Haig, diary, 22 August, quoted in Duff Cooper, *Haig*, ii p. 354.
4 Falls: *The First World War*, p. 387.
5 *O.H. 1918*, iv p. 510.
6 *The Smoke and the Fire*, pp. 148–60.
7 Australian Official Account vi pp. 986–7; the *Nahkampf-Batterien* and *Infanterie-Geschütz-Batterien* ('Infantry guns') consisted of captured Russian 76.2 mm. guns, shortened, re-sighted, and mounted on low-wheel carriages, or German 77 mm. guns on low wheels, employing special anti-tank shells with hardened steel points and delay-action fuses to burst inside the tank.
8 *O.H. 1918*, v p. 377.
9 Falls: *The First World War*, p. 351.
10 *O.H. 1918*, iii p. 259.
11 *O.H.* (*The War in the Air*), vi p. 443.
12 Ludendorff: *My War Memories*, ii p. 679.
13 Cyril Falls: *Armageddon 1918*, p. 75; Weidenfeld & Nicolson, 1964.
14 Ibid., p. 80.
15 The defects of the Mark I 18-pdr. were perceived in 1916, and experiments were made to improve upon it the following year. They bore fruit in the Mark IV version, with a maximum range of 9,300 yards; unfortunately, production of this gun only became effective towards the end of 1918, and only very few reached France before the Armistice.
16 *O.H. 1918*, v p. 574.

17 General Sir Noel Birch: 'Note on the British Artillery in France 1916–1918', 29 September 1927; author's papers.

18 Major-General Sir Archibald Montgomery: *The Story of the Fourth Army in the Battles of the Hundred Days, August 8th to November 11th, 1918*, pp. 31–2; Hodder & Stoughton, 1919.

19 Birch, op. cit.

20 *O.H. 1918*, iv p. 184.

21 The author has a clear memory of the unpleasant look and feel of iron door handles, and the prevalence of iron cooking utensils, in Belgium in the 1920s.

22 Cruttwell: *The Great War*, pp. 545–6.

23 Ludendorff, op. cit. p. 694.

24 Paul-Marie de la Gorce: *The French Army*, p. 103; Weidenfeld & Nicolson, 1963.

25 I have pointed out in *To Win a War* (p. 167), that the American 106th Regiment, of 3 battalions, numbering some 2,000 men, endeavouring to clear the outposts of the Hindenburg Line on 27 September, took only 18 officers into action. The bulk of the remainder were improving their military knowledge at various 'schools'. The 106th Regiment, rendered virtually leaderless, failed in its task with heavy loss.

26 Repington: *The First World War*, pp. 393–4.

27 Ibid., p. 394.

28 Ewing: *History of the 9th Division*, p. 363.

29 *To Win a War*, p. 161.

30 Lieutenant-Colonel M. Kincaid-Smith: *The 25th Division in France and Flanders*; Harrison & Sons, 1919 (?).

31 Letter to author, 11 November 1964, from Mr. W. C. Glazebrook, DCM (corporal, East Surrey Regiment).

32 *O.H. 1918*, iv p. 184.

33 Henriques: *War History of the 1/Queen's Westminster Rifles*, p. 264.

34 *O.H. 1918*, v p. 375.

35 Repington, op. cit. p. 405.

36 *O.H. 1918*, v pp. 183–4.

37 For a fuller account of the care and ingenuity which went into this magnificent feat of arms, see Terraine, *To Win a War*, pp. 162–74, and *Breaking the Hindenburg Line: The Story of the 46th (North Midland) Division*, by Major R. E. Priestley: T. Fisher Unwin, 1919.

38 Lieutenant-General Sir John Monash: *The Australian Victories in France in 1918*; Angus & Robertson, 1936.

39 Ibid.

40 Then as now, the majority of Australians were, of course, city-dwellers—as were the Japanese who fought so skilfully in the jungles of Burma and New Guinea in the Second World War. They, and the Australians in the same war and the First World War, and the British conscripts in Malaya (1948–60), all show what sound training and high morale can do.

41 Commander of the German *41st Division*, quoted in *The Times*, 19 August 1918.

42 *O.H. 1918*, v p. 178, f.n.2.

43 Monash, op. cit.

44 *O.H. 1918*, v p. 235.

45 Colonel A. P. Wavell: *The Palestine Campaigns*, p. 235; Constable, 1928.

46 Ibid., p. 234.

The Decisive Blow: *Success 2.*

G ENERAL MONASH REMARKED that after the war it became 'an article of faith' that the final offensive of the Allies had been conducted by minute organization and precise timing on the part of the Supreme Command and other General Headquarters. He comments:

'All who played any part in these great events well know that it was nothing of the kind . . . All commanders, and the most exalted of them in a higher degree even than those wielding lesser forces, became opportunists, and bent their energies . . . (to) the problem of hitting whenever and wherever an opportunity offered, and the means were ready to hand.'[1]

We have noted (p. 293) the limitations on Foch's position as Supreme Commander, and (p. 302) the simplicity of the strategy he adopted for practical reasons. He would not have disagreed with Monash's assessment. Monash himself, however, is a proof that the war of movement called for high qualities of generalship, and also of staff-work. At the highest command levels, it is hard not to conclude that, with two exceptions, the French generals found it hard to grasp the extent of the German collapse; their battles were well planned and well conducted, but they tended to lack thrust. It was as though these veterans of so many epic struggles— Pétain, the Group Commanders, Fayolle, Maistre, de Castelnau, and their Army commanders—feared falling into the Nivelle trap, of scenting a victory that was not there. The exceptions, of course, were Foch himself, always an optimist, and Mangin, whom Churchill called 'the fiercest warrior-figure of France'.[2]

General Pershing remained to the end preoccupied with the building up of a great American Army which could function virtually independently of the other Allies. In July Haig noted that the Americans were planning an army of 100 divisions by July 1919. In October the formation of a Second American Army gave Pershing the status of a group commander. His soldiers were fighting an arduous battle in the Argonne, difficult country where progress was slow; but Pershing grudged every unit lent to other fronts where they might have had more effect. The American II Corps, which had done good service in the British Fourth Army, was withdrawn for needed rest on 21 October, and not replaced. In the north, the Belgians were also fighting their own war; they gave higher priority to the liberation of Western Flanders than to carrying forward the Allied advance. Both Pershing's motives and King Albert's are understandable; the results, however, delayed rather than aided the common victory.

One commander shared Foch's vision—with advantage: Haig. Even in the dark hour of the German breakthrough on the *Chemin des Dames* (30 May), though Foch remained undaunted, a British staff Officer noted:

'Foch apparently does not think the war can be finished this year. D.H. (Haig)

thinks it can and should.' [3]

On 21 August Haig received a visit from Churchill, who talked about munitions requirements:

'He is most anxious to help us in every way . . . His schemes are all timed for "completion in next June"! I told him we ought to do our utmost to get a decision this autumn.' [4]

The next day he told his Army commanders:

'Risks which a month ago would have been criminal to incur, ought now to be incurred as a duty.' [5]

It was with this anticipation of early victory and peace that Haig made all his plans and framed all his orders from now on. He received conspicuous support from Generals Sir Henry Rawlinson (Fourth Army) and Sir Julian Byng (Third Army). The Fourth Army began the British offensive (Le Hamel on 4 July being the 'overture') and remained at the forefront of it to the end; between 8 August and 11 November, 24 divisions (12 British, five Australian, four Canadian and three American) served in it, and defeated 67

'. . . brigade staffs were usually exempted' from the universal loathing of staff officers in the British Army (and others). This is the Headquarters of the 21st Infantry Brigade, seen under unusual circumstances in 1915.

separately identified German divisions. The Fourth Army took 79,743 prisoners and 1,108 guns; its casualties were 122,427 killed, wounded, and missing.[6] In the same period, the Third Army had 119,094 casualties, indicating that its rôle was little less significant than the Fourth's. On 1 October the two Army commanders, fresh from the Hindenburg Line triumph, told Haig

'that no further orders from me were necessary, and both would be able to carry on without difficulty.'[7]

They were as good as their word. Yet this was the same Rawlinson whose Army had suffered the terrible casualties for almost no result of 1 July 1916, and the same Byng who had been badly surprised and defeated on 30 November 1917 at Cambrai. Their 1918 successes show how much the war itself was an educator.[8]

It was not only generals who had learnt their trade: their execrated staff officers had done the same. In the middle period of the war, the BEF was possessed at all front-line levels from private to colonel with 'distrust, indeed loathing . . . for the staff'[9] — despite the fact that the majority of staff officers were, as one critical front-line officer admitted, 'formerly gallant and capable regimental officers.'[10] Generally this universal condemnation tended to break down under pressure: brigade staffs were usually exempted, as were divisional staffs—but for those upward of that there were few kind words. The exception was the Second Army, under General Sir Herbert Plumer and his brilliant Chief of Staff, Sir Charles Harington. A distinguished divisional historian wrote:

'The sympathy and understanding which existed between the Staff of the Second Army and the man in the fighting line created a moral tone of incalculable value to the Army's efficiency as a striking force.'[11]

The same authority adds, speaking of that dismal year, 1917:

'The system of liaison was practised in the Second Army as in no other. General Harington's car stopped at every door, and the cheerful young staff officers, who knew every communication trench on the Army front, who drank with company commanders in their front-line dug-outs before coming back to tea with a Brigadier, or with General Nugent (Divisional commander) at his headquarters, formed a very real link between the Higher Command and the troops.'[12]

Others were less admired; it is evident that the Fourth Army staff, in 1916, gravely lacked experience (though the preparation for the entirely successful dawn attack on 14 July shows that it was improving fast). The Third Army staff prepared a brilliant opening for the Battles of Arras in April 1917—but was entirely at a loss when it came to exploiting the success. The Fifth Army staff attracted fierce odium during the Third Battle of Ypres—despite the friendly quality of the Army commander, General Gough, and the indefatigable dedication of his Chief of Staff, Major-General Neill Malcolm. Major-General Vaughan, Chief of Staff of the Third Army, was a most knowledgeable and clear-headed soldier, as his orders show; yet that Army's staff was definitely caught out on 30 November at Cambrai.

At Amiens, however, the brilliant staff-work of the Fourth Army virtually assured success before the battle even opened. Everything that the Germans had done in the way of meticulous preparation in Champagne was equalled or surpassed by the Fourth Army in Picardy. Never had secrecy been so cultivated; never was camouflage used to better effect (including the concealment of over 500 tanks and the entire Cavalry Corps on the empty Somme uplands); there was even another technological 'first' – the first use of a wireless deception plan to disguise the movement of the Canadian Corps from Flanders to the Somme. We glimpse here the origin of the elaborate ploy which so thoroughly deceived the Germans in 1944.[13] In the attack on the Hindenburg Line, the preparations of the Fourth Army, IX Corps (Lieutenant-General Sir Walter Braithwaite) and the 46th Division (Major-General G. Boyd) were again worked out to the last detail, with corresponding results. It was as though a new race of staff officers had arrived. They were not new; they were the same men—older, more experienced, a good deal wiser.

What they could not overcome, with the technological resources of 1918, was the insuperable logistical problem of trying to maintain the impetus of an advance across the wilderness of the earlier battlefields, along cratered, booby-trapped roads, wrecked railways, over blown bridges, under the drenching autumn rains. In the Argonne, the American attacks foundered despite all the heroic fury of the soldiers; here the local conditions and the absolute inexperience of the staffs caused a virtually total breakdown on the lines of communication. 'There was even talk of men starving to death in the front line.'[14] In Flanders a halt had to be called for almost a fortnight for similar reasons, although German resistance had practically ceased. But all along the front the going was hard; a good advance was 4 to 5 miles in a day; 8 to 10 miles was very good. German demolitions, attentively carried out all along the line, were partly responsible for this, but chiefly the brake on progress was the enormous amount of ammunition which had to be constantly brought forward for the purposes of the artillery war, the food and forage needed by the mass armies, and, in the later stages, food for liberated populations which would otherwise have starved. The Supply Services were strained to their limits; Sir Frederick Maurice relates, from personal experience:

At the time of the Armistice the motor lorries were working in double and treble shifts, and the strain upon them caused by the bad roads and the incessant work was such that in the Fourth Army on November 11 more than half the lorries at the service of the Army had broken down. The troops were receiving no more than bare necessities, and at one time had with them nothing more than the day's food carried by the men.'[15]

He concludes:

'The plain fact is that on, or very soon after, November 11 it would, had hostilities been continued, have been necessary to call a halt of the Allied armies between the Dutch frontier and the Meuse until the roads and railways behind them had been repaired and the services of supply were again able to work normally.'[16]

Then, as always, supply was an inexorable 'discipline of the wars'. Only in 1918 the scale was beyond any previous reckoning: at the Armistice, the Allies had just under 6½ million men on the Western Front, and the Germans just over 3½ million. Even the full array of Industrial Revolution technology was strained by such numbers as these.

It is appropriate to end where we began—with the 'motor of the war', the German Army. By November, the motor had almost totally run down. Between 21 March and 1 October, its losses were no less than 1,222,299 Ludendorff resigned on 26 October, unlamented; his successor, General Wilhelm Gröner, took over an army 'incapable of accepting or refusing battle'.[17] At the front, the deterioration was most clearly perceptible in the infantry; the consequences of creaming off the best men into 'Storm Troops' and 'attack divisions' became apparent in the demoralization of the remainder when these became casualties. This appeared very early: reserves arriving to plug the gap at Amiens on 10 August were greeted by drunken Bavarians who shouted:

'What do you war-prolongers want? If the enemy were only on the Rhine—the war would then be over!'

Others were told:

'We thought that we had set the thing going—now you asses are corking up the hole again!'[18]

Dismounted cavalry divisions, still containing a number of peace-trained men of good physique, were universally known as 'war-prolongers'. At the depôts there were complaints about the quality and spirit of the 1919 class of conscripts; even louder were the criticisms of the returned prisoners of war from Russia—their re-enrolment says Ludendorff, caused 'a decided deterioration in the army's *moral* . . . They introduced a spirit of general insubordination, showing itself particularly in definite refusal to return to the front . . .'[19] Divisions and drafts from the East showed similar symptoms:

'According to the explanations of General Hoffmann, the temptations to which the men were exposed from the corruption of Jew traders in the East and from

Bolshevik propaganda, as, indeed, from propaganda from home, had broken their fighting spirit.'[20]

Conscripts from Alsace and Lorraine, normally only used on the Eastern Front, had to be brought to the West, where they lost no opportunity to desert. The poor spirit of the once redoubtable Bavarians was especially noted; they had come 'to regard the war as a purely Prussian affair'.[21] Yet in truth war-weariness in some degree or other had taken hold of the whole Army. Two factors were perceptible throughout; in the words of General Fuller:

'Wedged between his starving family and a hopeless future' (the German soldier's) 'morale was shattered by the realization that the succession of offensives since March 21 had been in vain, and that their result was a defensive which could see no offensive dawn.'[22]

Yet even amidst this almost universal gloom, there were bright lights. The German machine-gunners established themselves as the hard core of the defence, a trouble and impediment to all the Allies to the very end. They could be dealt with, certainly, by the sophisticated techniques of 1918—the British Army alone captured 29,000 machine-guns—but wherever they were encountered in numbers there would be delay. Equally resolute was the German artillery, although outmatched now by the Allied guns, lacking replacements, lacking ammunition, and frequently lacking even horses to pull it. Against all these factors commanders and staffs struggled as best they could; a British officer wrote:

'. . . never did the work of their divisional and regimental commanders shine more brightly than in those days.'[23]

Haig himself remarked as late as 31 October that 'the enemy is fighting a very good rear-guard action'[24]—but the end was clearly in sight. Conditions behind the German front—all too plain to their leaders—made it a matter of only days, even hours, before they had to send a delegation across the lines with a white flag:

'Every road was littered with broken-down motor trucks, guns, machine guns and trench mortars. Great stacks of supplies and of military stores of all kinds were abandoned. Every railway line was blocked with loaded trucks which the Germans had been unable to remove . . . It is beyond dispute that on November 11 the lines of communication immediately behind the German armies had been thrown into complete disorder by the streams of traffic converging on the Meuse bridges, disorder greatly intensified by the attacks of the Allied airmen. The German armies, unable to resist on the fighting front, could no longer retreat in good order, partly because of the congestion on the roads and railways behind them, which not only hampered the movements of the troops, but prevented the systematic supply to

'The German Armistice delegation crossed the lines on 7 November; the end came at 11am on 11 November.'

them of food and ammunition, partly owing to the fact that there were not horses left to draw the transport of the fighting troops.' [25]

In other words, catastrophe.

The German Armistice delegation crossed the lines on 7 November; the end came at 11am on 11 November. The manner of it was unmistakeable; in the course of their final offensive, from 18 July, the Allies had taken nearly 400,000 prisoners and 6,615 guns. As Lloyd George said:

'The conclusion is inescapable that Germany and her allies were defeated in the field.' [26]

The part played in this consummation by the British armies under Haig is also inescapable:

	PRISONERS	GUNS
British	188,700	2,840
French	139,000	1,880
Americans	43,000	1,421
Belgians	14,500	474

For the first, *and only*, time in its entire history, the British Army had engaged and defeated the main body of the main enemy in a continental war.

NOTES

1 Monash: *The Australian Victories in France in 1918.*
2 *The World Crisis*, ii p. 1108.
3 Charteris: *At GHQ*, p. 311.
4 Blake: *Private Papers of Douglas Haig*, p. 324.
5 O.A.D. 911; author's papers.
6 Montgomery: *The Story of the Fourth Army*, p. 262. The table on page 275 (28 March–November) shows that the proportion of 'wounded' to 'killed' during that period was 5.8:1. There were, in addition, nearly 13,000 'missing', the majority, no doubt, prisoners, but a certain number actually killed; this would not, however, seriously affect the proportion.
7 Blake, op. cit. p. 329.
8 Some light on education itself is thrown by Colonel Repington's diary entry of 17 May 1919: 'Byng says that he himself was the stupidest boy at Eton till Rawly (General Rawlinson) arrived, when the latter was in a class by himself . . . We agreed that the best men matured late and practically never at school.'
9 Colonel R. S. Stafford, letter to the author, 26 September 1964.
10 *General Jack's Diary* (ed. Terraine), p. 177 (23 October 1916); Eyre & Spottiswoode, 1964.
11 Falls: *History of the 36th Division*, p. 87.
12 Ibid., p. 122.
13 For more detail see *To Win a War*, p. 107.
14 Ibid., p. 157.
15 Maurice: *The Last Four Months*, p. 231; Cassell, 1919.
16 Ibid., p. 233.
17 Sir John Wheeler-Bennett: *Hindenburg: The Wooden Titan*, p. 186; Macmillan, 1967.
18 Quoted in *O.H. 1918*, iv p. 139.
19 Ludendorff: *War Memories*, ii p. 642.
20 Ibid., p. 749. There is irony in this; the Bolshevik 'October Revolution' owed much to Ludendorff himself; it was the German High Command which made possible the return to Russia of Lenin 'in a sealed truck like a plague bacillus', in Churchill's words (see p. 277).
21 Ibid., p. 643.
22 Fuller: *Decisive Battles of the Western World*, iii p. 296.
23 Falls, op. cit. p. 289.
24 Haig diary, author's papers.
25 Maurice, op. cit. pp. 224–5.
26 *War Memoirs*, ii p. 1946.

POSTSCRIPT

S O ENDED THE GREAT WAR of the First Industrial Revolution—unquestionably the 'great' war, because the Second World War, although it carried many aspects of technology a long way forward and produced some striking new advances (radar, penicillin, and nuclear fission spring immediately to mind as major war innovations) never faintly matched its predecessor as regards the 'white heat' of change. Indeed, it was not merely war that changed between 1914–18; it was the world that made the war, and 1939–45 simply completed many of the processes and pushed others onward.

For military men, the inter-war decades saw significant triumphs over the technological obstacles that had afflicted them in the First World War. Nowhere were these more striking than in the field of communications; electronics was a new science in 1914, but by 1939 it had developed sufficiently for radar to provide an entirely new information source, and computers an entirely new way of processing it (e.g. the 'Colossus' which operated on ULTRA information at Bletchley Park[1]). But for the generals who actually conducted battles, and the front-line soldiers who fought them,

'The Allies had taken nearly 400,000 prisoners and 6,615 guns.' The ones below were taken on the Somme, where the Australian and Canadian Army Corps spear-headed the Allied advance.

nothing was more important than the two-way portable radio sets ('Walkie-Talkies') which restored voice control to war.

Mobility, as Wavell foresaw (see p. 318), was also restored when horse-power replaced horses. For that the First World War paved the way, but the improved performances of later generations of armoured vehicles in the 1930s and 1940s were required to bring the process to fruition. The same applied to aircraft. The First World War had thrust design forward at a furious rate; only towards the end of the 1930s did markedly new types again come into view, but once the demands of war were heard again, fresh progress was made at an even more astonishing rate, culminating in the missiles which fore-shadowed the space race.

It would be tempting to say that the heavy loss of life which was such a marked feature of the First World War, and which continues to be associated with it and give it a name of dread to this day, was due to the technological hiatus, the gap between promise and fulfilment. Certainly, on specific occasions, it is clear that technology could have saved lives if only it had been a little further advanced. The British Army would not have had 57,000 casualties on 1 July 1916 if it had had, say, 150 'Walkie-Talkies'. But then, Julius Caesar would have found it very difficult to conquer Britain if the Britons had produced even the rudimentary cannon of the fourteenth century. These are not profitable speculations. Hard fact, however, reminds us that the advance of the technology of killing between the wars, as one might suppose, led to some four times as many people losing their lives in the Second World War as in the First World War[2]. Progress will not be denied.

NOTES
1 See Lewin: *Ultra Goes to War*, pp. 129–33.
2 See *The Smoke and the Fire*, pp. 37–8.

APPENDIX I
German and Austro-Hungarian Army Formations in 1914

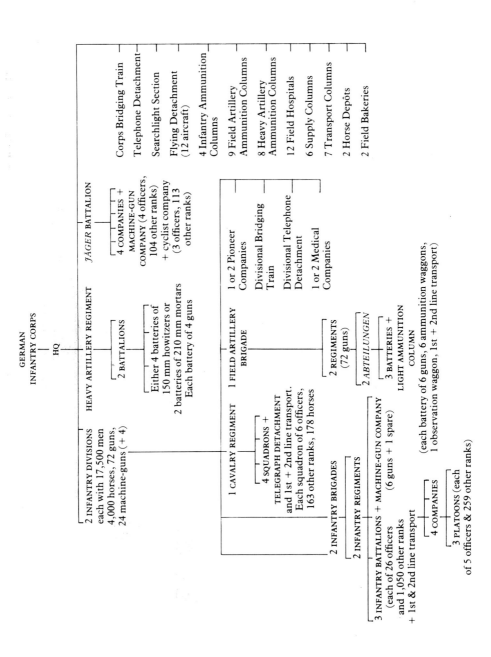

GERMAN
INFANTRY CORPS
HQ

2 INFANTRY DIVISIONS
each with 17,500 men
4,000 horses, 72 guns,
24 machine-guns (+ 4)

HEAVY ARTILLERY REGIMENT

2 BATTALIONS

Either 4 batteries of
150 mm howitzers or
2 batteries of 210 mm mortars
Each battery of 4 guns

JÄGER BATTALION

4 COMPANIES +
MACHINE-GUN
COMPANY (4 officers,
104 other ranks)
+ cyclist company
(3 officers, 113
other ranks)

Corps Bridging Train
Telephone Detachment
Searchlight Section
Flying Detachment
(12 aircraft)
4 Infantry Ammunition
Columns
9 Field Artillery
Ammunition Columns
8 Heavy Artillery
Ammunition Columns
12 Field Hospitals
6 Supply Columns
7 Transport Columns
2 Horse Depôts
2 Field Bakeries

1 CAVALRY REGIMENT

4 SQUADRONS +
TELEGRAPH DETACHMENT
and 1st + 2nd line transport.
Each squadron of 6 officers,
163 other ranks, 178 horses

1 FIELD ARTILLERY
BRIGADE

2 REGIMENTS
(72 guns)

2 *ABTEILUNGEN*

3 BATTERIES +
LIGHT AMMUNITION
COLUMN
(each battery of 6 guns, 6 ammunition waggons,
1 observation waggon, 1st + 2nd line transport)

1 or 2 Pioneer
Companies
Divisional Bridging
Train
Divisional Telephone
Detachment
1 or 2 Medical
Companies

2 INFANTRY BRIGADES

2 INFANTRY REGIMENTS

3 INFANTRY BATTALIONS + MACHINE-GUN COMPANY
(each of 26 officers   (6 guns + 1 spare)
and 1,050 other ranks
+ 1st & 2nd line transport

4 COMPANIES

3 PLATOONS (each
of 5 officers & 259 other ranks)

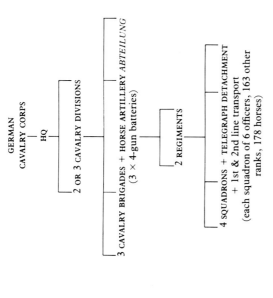

GERMAN
CAVALRY CORPS

HQ

2 OR 3 CAVALRY DIVISIONS

3 CAVALRY BRIGADES + HORSE ARTILLERY *ABTEILUNG*
(3 × 4-gun batteries)

2 REGIMENTS

4 SQUADRONS + TELEGRAPH DETACHMENT
+ 1st & 2nd line transport
(each squadron of 6 officers, 163 other
ranks, 178 horses)

OTHER FORMATIONS

Reserve Division: Active division, but with 6 Field Artillery batteries instead of 12
Reserve Corps: Active corps, but with 12 Field batteries instead of 24, no heavy guns, no aeroplanes and correspondingly
fewer ammunition columns
Landwehr **Brigade:** 2 Regiments of 3 battalions
1 Cavalry squadron
1 Field Artillery battery

Note: These are 1914 peacetime establishments; needless to say, they changed greatly in the course of the war. The *German Army Handbook, April 1918*, compiled by the British General Staff, describes the changes in great detail, as well as the developments in technical equipment. This invaluable work of reference was republished by the Arms and Armour Press in 1977.

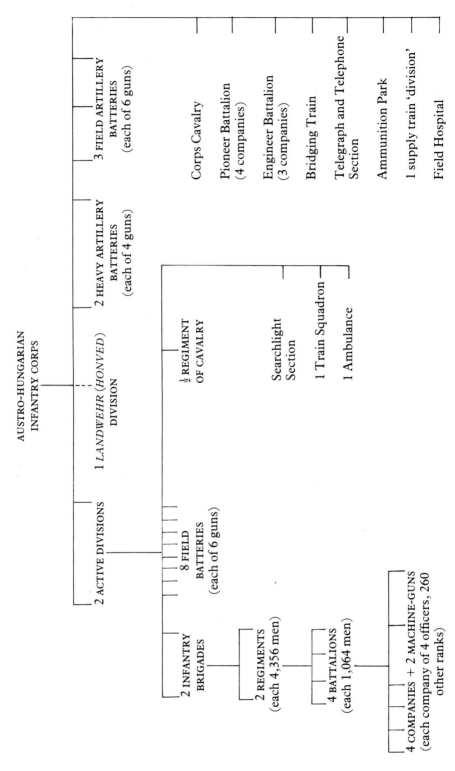

AUSTRO-HUNGARIAN INFANTRY CORPS

2 ACTIVE DIVISIONS

1 *LANDWEHR* (*HONVED*) DIVISION

2 HEAVY ARTILLERY BATTERIES (each of 4 guns)

3 FIELD ARTILLERY BATTERIES (each of 6 guns)

2 INFANTRY BRIGADES

8 FIELD BATTERIES (each of 6 guns)

½ REGIMENT OF CAVALRY

Searchlight Section

1 Train Squadron

1 Ambulance

2 REGIMENTS (each 4,356 men)

4 BATTALIONS (each 1,064 men)

4 COMPANIES + 2 MACHINE-GUNS (each company of 4 officers, 260 other ranks)

Corps Cavalry

Pioneer Battalion (4 companies)

Engineer Battalion (3 companies)

Bridging Train

Telegraph and Telephone Section

Ammunition Park

1 supply train 'division'

Field Hospital

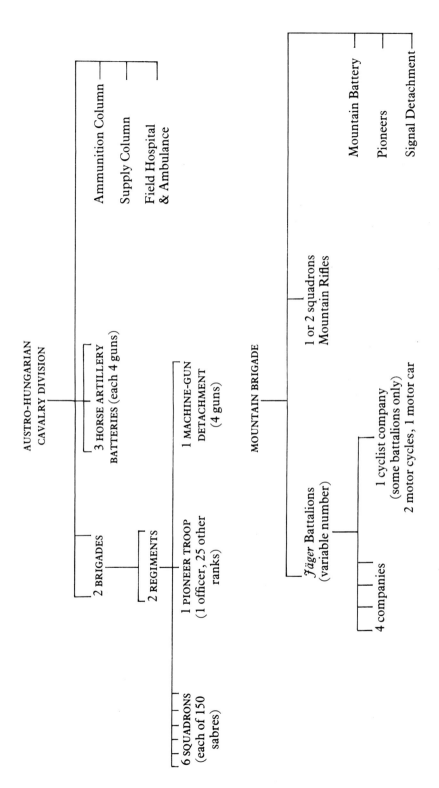

AUSTRO-HUNGARIAN CAVALRY DIVISION

2 BRIGADES
- 2 REGIMENTS
  - 6 SQUADRONS (each of 150 sabres)
- 1 PIONEER TROOP (1 officer, 25 other ranks)

3 HORSE ARTILLERY BATTERIES (each 4 guns)

1 MACHINE-GUN DETACHMENT (4 guns)

Ammunition Column

Supply Column

Field Hospital & Ambulance

MOUNTAIN BRIGADE

Jäger Battalions (variable number)
- 4 companies
- 1 cyclist company (some battalions only) 2 motor cycles, 1 motor car

1 or 2 squadrons Mountain Rifles

Mountain Battery

Pioneers

Signal Detachment

NB: No statement about the higher formations of the Austro-Hungarian Army can be taken as absolute. The establishments indicated above were in some cases notional rather than actual, intentions rather than realities.

APPENDIX II
Russian, French, Belgian, and British Army Formations in 1914

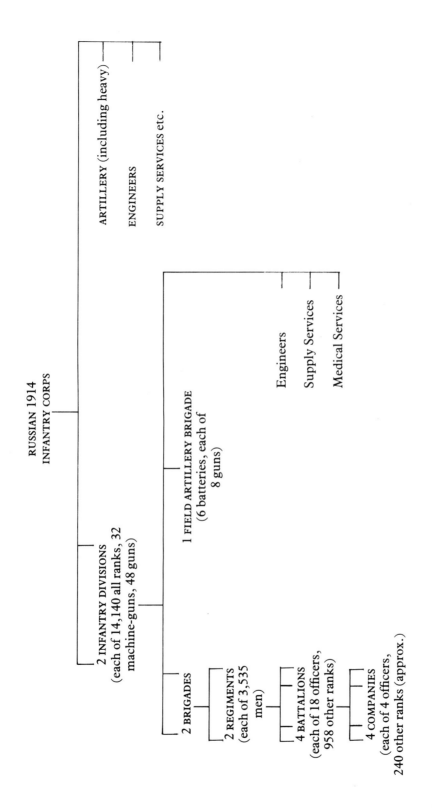

RUSSIAN 1914
INFANTRY CORPS

2 INFANTRY DIVISIONS
(each of 14,140 all ranks, 32
machine-guns, 48 guns)

ARTILLERY (including heavy)

ENGINEERS

SUPPLY SERVICES etc.

1 FIELD ARTILLERY BRIGADE
(6 batteries, each of
8 guns)

Engineers

Supply Services

Medical Services

2 BRIGADES

2 REGIMENTS
(each of 3,535
men)

4 BATTALIONS
(each of 18 officers,
958 other ranks)

4 COMPANIES
(each of 4 officers,
240 other ranks (approx.))

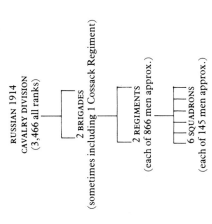

RUSSIAN 1914
CAVALRY DIVISION
(3,466 all ranks)

2 BRIGADES
(sometimes including 1 Cossack Regiment)

2 REGIMENTS
(each of 866 men approx.)

6 SQUADRONS
(each of 145 men approx.)

OTHER FORMATIONS

Cossacks   Cossack men were liable to military service for life, in return for certain privileges. Their full effective strength was about 500,000, organized in 12 'armies' (*Voiskos*). These were mostly cavalry, consisting of a varying number of squadrons (*Sotnias*), but there were also Cossack Horse Artillery batteries and the Kuban Cossack Infantry Brigade of 6 battalions. Two *Sotnias* of Cossacks formed part of the Imperial Guard.

Note: As with so much else in Imperial Russia, a certain mystery surrounds the organization of the Army. This was partly deliberate – a sensible recognition that too much symmetry makes the hostile Intelligence Officer's task unnecessarily easy. These tables are therefore fragmentary, and suggestive rather than exact.

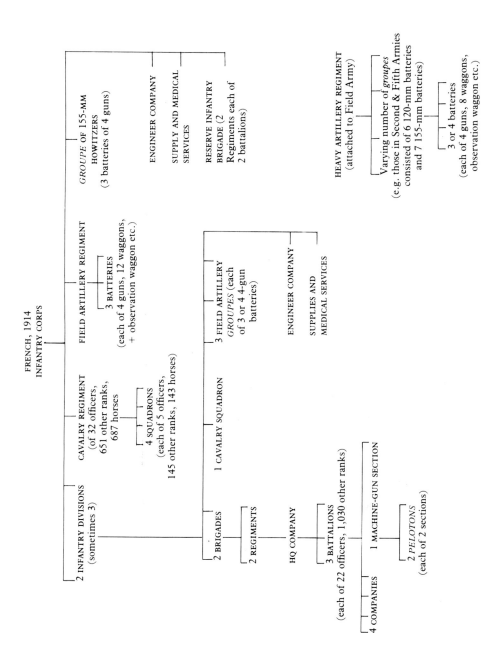

FRENCH, 1914
INFANTRY CORPS

2 INFANTRY DIVISIONS
(sometimes 3)

CAVALRY REGIMENT
(of 32 officers,
651 other ranks,
687 horses

4 SQUADRONS
(each of 5 officers,
145 other ranks, 143 horses)

FIELD ARTILLERY REGIMENT

3 BATTERIES
(each of 4 guns, 12 waggons,
+ observation waggon etc.)

GROUPE OF 155-MM
HOWITZERS
(3 batteries of 4 guns)

ENGINEER COMPANY

SUPPLY AND MEDICAL
SERVICES

RESERVE INFANTRY
BRIGADE (2
Regiments each of
2 battalions)

2 BRIGADES

2 REGIMENTS

HQ COMPANY

3 BATTALIONS
(each of 22 officers, 1,030 other ranks)

4 COMPANIES

1 MACHINE-GUN SECTION

2 *PELOTONS*
(each of 2 sections)

1 CAVALRY SQUADRON

3 FIELD ARTILLERY
GROUPES (each
of 3 or 4 4-gun
batteries)

ENGINEER COMPANY

SUPPLIES AND
MEDICAL SERVICES

HEAVY ARTILLERY REGIMENT
(attached to Field Army)

Varying number of groupes
(e.g. those in Second & Fifth Armies
consisted of 6 120-mm batteries
and 7 155-mm batteries)

3 or 4 batteries
(each of 4 guns, 8 waggons,
observation waggon etc.)

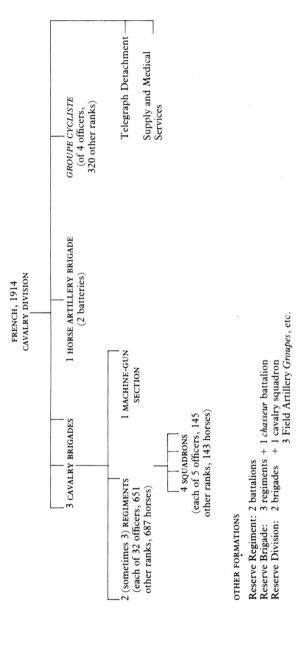

FRENCH, 1914
CAVALRY DIVISION

3 CAVALRY BRIGADES

1 MACHINE-GUN SECTION

2 (sometimes 3) REGIMENTS
(each of 32 officers, 651
other ranks, 687 horses)

4 SQUADRONS
(each of 5 officers, 145
other ranks, 143 horses)

1 HORSE ARTILLERY BRIGADE
(2 batteries)

GROUPE CYCLISTE
(of 4 officers,
320 other ranks)

Telegraph Detachment

Supply and Medical
Services

OTHER FORMATIONS

Reserve Regiment: 2 battalions
Reserve Brigade: 3 regiments + 1 *chasseur* battalion
Reserve Division: 2 brigades + 1 cavalry squadron
                   3 Field Artillery *Groupes*, etc.

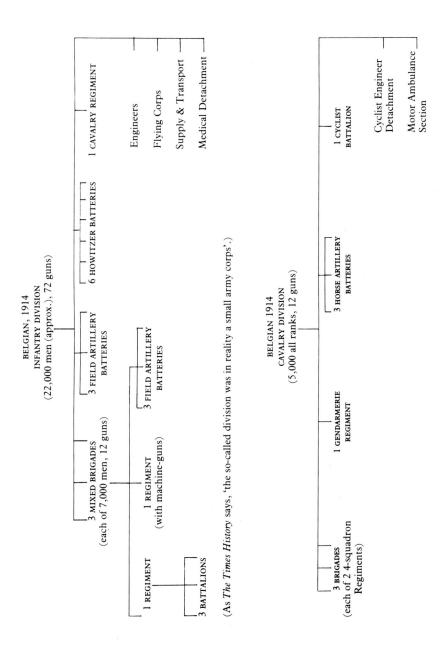

BELGIAN, 1914
INFANTRY DIVISION
(22,000 men (approx.), 72 guns)

3 MIXED BRIGADES
(each of 7,000 men, 12 guns)

1 REGIMENT
(with machine-guns)

1 REGIMENT

3 BATTALIONS

3 FIELD ARTILLERY BATTERIES

3 FIELD ARTILLERY BATTERIES

6 HOWITZER BATTERIES

1 CAVALRY REGIMENT

Engineers

Flying Corps

Supply & Transport

Medical Detachment

(As *The Times History* says, 'the so-called division was in reality a small army corps'.)

BELGIAN 1914
CAVALRY DIVISION
(5,000 all ranks, 12 guns)

3 BRIGADES
(each of 2 4-squadron Regiments)

1 GENDARMERIE REGIMENT

3 HORSE ARTILLERY BATTERIES

1 CYCLIST BATTALION

Cyclist Engineer Detachment

Motor Ambulance Section

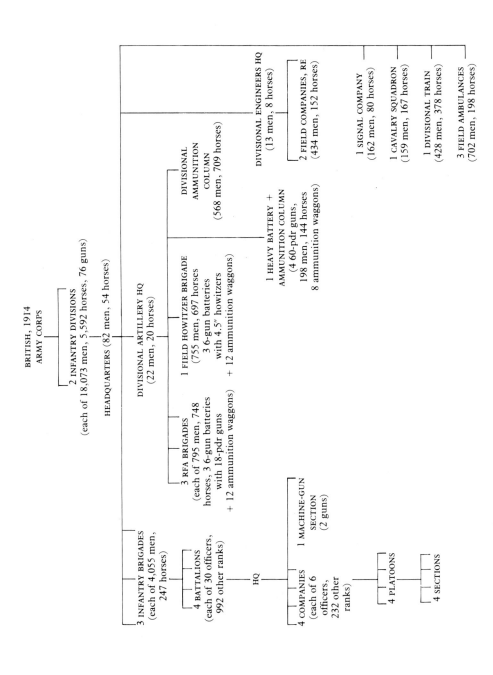

BRITISH, 1914
ARMY CORPS

2 INFANTRY DIVISIONS
(each of 18,073 men, 5,592 horses, 76 guns)

HEADQUARTERS (82 men, 54 horses)

DIVISIONAL ARTILLERY HQ
(22 men, 20 horses)

3 RFA BRIGADES
(each of 795 men, 748
horses, 3 6-gun batteries
with 18-pdr guns
+ 12 ammunition waggons)

1 FIELD HOWITZER BRIGADE
(755 men, 697 horses
3 6-gun batteries
with 4.5" howitzers
+ 12 ammunition waggons)

1 HEAVY BATTERY +
AMMUNITION COLUMN
(4 60-pdr guns,
198 men, 144 horses
8 ammunition waggons)

DIVISIONAL
AMMUNITION
COLUMN
(568 men, 709 horses)

DIVISIONAL ENGINEERS HQ
(13 men, 8 horses)

2 FIELD COMPANIES, RE
(434 men, 152 horses)

1 SIGNAL COMPANY
(162 men, 80 horses)

1 CAVALRY SQUADRON
(159 men, 167 horses)

1 DIVISIONAL TRAIN
(428 men, 378 horses)

3 FIELD AMBULANCES
(702 men, 198 horses)

3 INFANTRY BRIGADES
(each of 4,055 men,
247 horses)

4 BATTALIONS
(each of 30 officers,
992 other ranks)

HQ

1 MACHINE-GUN
SECTION
(2 guns)

4 COMPANIES
(each of 6
officers,
232 other
ranks)

4 PLATOONS

4 SECTIONS

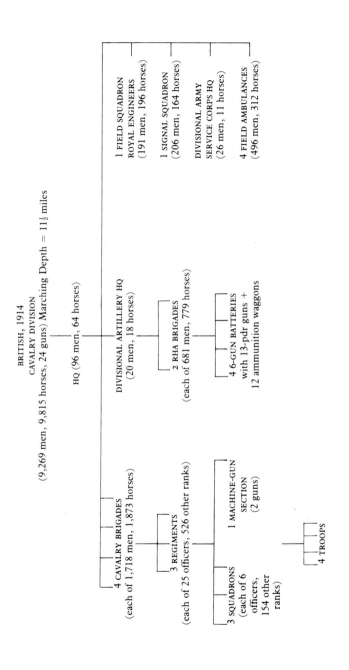

BRITISH, 1914
CAVALRY DIVISION
(9,269 men, 9,815 horses, 24 guns) Marching Depth = 11½ miles

HQ (96 men, 64 horses)

DIVISIONAL ARTILLERY HQ
(20 men, 18 horses)

2 RHA BRIGADES
(each of 681 men, 779 horses)

4 6-GUN BATTERIES
with 13-pdr guns +
12 ammunition waggons

1 FIELD SQUADRON
ROYAL ENGINEERS
(191 men, 196 horses)

1 SIGNAL SQUADRON
(206 men, 164 horses)

DIVISIONAL ARMY
SERVICE CORPS HQ
(26 men, 11 horses)

4 FIELD AMBULANCES
(496 men, 312 horses)

4 CAVALRY BRIGADES
(each of 1,718 men, 1,873 horses)

3 REGIMENTS
(each of 25 officers, 526 other ranks)

1 MACHINE-GUN
SECTION
(2 guns)

3 SQUADRONS
(each of 6
officers,
154 other
ranks)

4 TROOPS

Acknowledgments

The Publishers wish to thank the following for their kind permission to use their illustrations:

BBC Hulton Picture Library: p. 67

Bundesarchiv: pp. 89, 104, 115, 117, 118, 143, 153, 157, 208, 263, 265, 283, 289, 294.

E. C. P. Armées: pp. 145, 159, 205, 326, 328.

Robert Hunt Library: pp. 97, 163, 172, 181, 223, 317.

Imperial War Museum: pp. 24, 52, 54, 58, 73, 78, 80, 95, 107, 124, 136, 137, 149, 150, 175, 176, 183, 186, 187, 191, 195, 198, 213, 216, 218, 232, 239, 243, 245, 249, 281, 305, 309, 313, 315, 321.

MARS: pp. 12, 32, 34, 259.

MARS/Foto Drüppel, Wilhelmshaven: p. 127.

MARS/Imperial War Museum: pp. 37, 131, 194, 248.

MARS/Luftschiffbau Zeppelin GmbH, West Germany: p. 28.

MARS/Marconi photo: p. 40.

MARS/National Army Museum, London: p. 9.

MARS/U.S Navy official photo, Washington D.C.: p. 261.

MARS/U.S. Signal Corps Collection in U.S. National Archives: p. 298.

J. G. Moore: p. 167.

Novosti Press Agency: p. 226.

Smithsonian Institution: p. 15.

Ullstein Bilderdienst: p. 64.

Artwork by Blitz Publications Ltd.

Map artwork by M. L. Gilkes

Diagram on p. 235 and chart on p. 236 from *War Underground* (Frederick Muller Ltd., London, 1962) by permission of the author, Alexander Barrie.

The poem on p. 206–07 by permission of Mrs Susan Frankau.

Index